ESSENTIALS OF
RESEARCH METHODS
IN PSYCHOLOGY

For co

To My Mother, Jean N. Sumi
and to the Memory of My Father,
Harold W. Sumi
(J.S.Z.)

To My Father and My Sister Kathie
(E.B.Z.)

To Paula
(J.J.S.)

ESSENTIALS OF RESEARCH METHODS IN PSYCHOLOGY

Jeanne S. Zechmeister

Loyola University of Chicago

Eugene B. Zechmeister

Loyola University of Chicago

John J. Shaughnessy

Hope College

Boston   Burr Ridge, IL   Dubuque, IA   Madison, WI   New York   San Francisco   St. Louis
Bangkok   Bogotá   Caracas   Lisbon   London   Madrid
Mexico City   Milan   New Delhi   Seoul   Singapore   Sydney   Taipei   Toronto

McGraw-Hill Higher Education

A Division of The **McGraw-Hill** Companies

ESSENTIALS OF RESEARCH METHODS IN PSYCHOLOGY

Published by McGraw-Hill, an imprint of The McGraw-Hill Companies, Inc., 1221 Avenue of the Americas, New York, NY 10020. Copyright © 2001 by The McGraw-Hill Companies, Inc. All rights reserved. No part of this publication may be reproduced or distributed in any form or by any means, or stored in a database or retrieval system, without the prior written consent of The McGraw-Hill Companies, Inc., including, but not limited to, in any network or other electronic storage or transmission, or broadcast for distance learning.

Some ancillaries, including electronic and print components, may not be available to customers outside the United States.

This book is printed on acid-free paper.

6 7 8 9 0 QPF/QPF 0 9 8 7 6 5 4

ISBN 0–07–238815–3

Vice president and editor-in-chief: *Thalia Dorwick*
Editorial director: *Jane E. Vaicunas*
Senior sponsoring editor: *Melissa Mashburn*
Editorial coordinator: *Barbara Santoro*
Marketing manager: *Chris Hall*
Project manager: *Sheila M. Frank*
Media technology senior producer: *Sean Crowley*
Production supervisor: *Enboge Chong*
Design manager: *Stuart D. Paterson*
Cover/interior designer: *Rebecca Lloyd Lemna*
Cover image: *The Stock Illustration Source, Inc.*
Senior photo research coordinator: *Carrie K. Burger*
Photo research: *LouAnn K. Wilson*
Supplement coordinator: *Sandra M. Schnee*
Compositor: *GAC—Indianapolis*
Typeface: *10/12 Palatino*
Printer: *Quebecor Printing Book Group/Fairfield, PA*

The credits section for this book begins on page C1 and is considered an extension of the copyright page.

Library of Congress Cataloging-in-Publication Data

Zechmeister, Jeanne S.
    Essentials of research methods in psychology / Jeanne S. Zechmeister, Eugene B. Zechmeister, John J. Shaughnessy. — 1st ed.
        p.   cm.
    Based on: Research methods in psychology.
    Includes bibliographical references and index.
        ISBN 0–07–238815–3
    1. Psychology—Research—Methodology.   2. Psychology, Experimental.   I. Zechmeister, Eugene B., 1944–.   II. Shaughnessy, John J., 1947–.   III. Title.

BF76.5 .Z42   2001
150'.7'2—dc21   00–058729
                                                            CIP

www.mhhe.com

BRIEF CONTENTS

CONTENTS

ABOUT THE AUTHORS

JEANNE S. ZECHMEISTER is associate professor of psychology at Loyola University of Chicago, where she has taught undergraduate and graduate courses in research methodology since 1990. Professor Zechmeister completed her B.A. at University of Wisconsin–Madison (1983) and her M.S. (1988) and Ph.D. (1990) in clinical psychology at Northwestern University. Her current research interests are in the area of psychology of religion, and she is conducting research on forgiveness. Her effectiveness as a teacher is evidenced by her many years of high teacher ratings and by her being identified consistently by graduating seniors as one of their best teachers at Loyola. She also authored, with J. J. Shaughnessy and E. B. Zechmeister, *Research Methods in Psychology* (5th edition; McGraw-Hill, 2000).

EUGENE B. ZECHMEISTER is professor of psychology at Loyola University of Chicago, where he has taught both undergraduate and graduate courses since 1970. Professor Zechmeister completed his B.A. in 1966 at the University of New Mexico. He later received both his M.S. (1968) and his Ph.D. (1970) from Northwestern University. A specialist in the field of human cognition, Professor Zechmeister authored, with S. E. Nyberg, *Human Memory: An Introduction to Research and Theory* (Brooks/Cole, 1982) and, with J. E. Johnson, *Critical Thinking: A Functional Approach* (Brooks/Cole, 1992). He is a Fellow of both the American Psychological Association (Divisions 1, 2, and 3) and the American Psychological Society. He was awarded the Loyola University Sujack Award for Teaching Excellence in the College of Arts and Sciences. Professor Zechmeister currently is the undergraduate program director for the Loyola University of Chicago Psychology Department.

JOHN J. SHAUGHNESSY is professor of psychology at Hope College, a relatively small, select, undergraduate liberal arts college in Holland, Michigan. After completing the B.S. degree at Loyola University of Chicago in 1969, he received his Ph.D. in 1972 from Northwestern University. He is a Fellow of the American Psychological Society, and his recent research has focused on practical aspects of memory. He is coauthor, with Benton J. Underwood, of *Experimentation in Psychology* (Wiley, 1975). He was selected by students as the Hope Outstanding Professor Educator; he serves as a mentor in Hope College's faculty development program for younger faculty; and he was chairperson of the Hope College Psychology Department (1997–2000).

PREFACE

To use a well-worn cliché, we have written a research methods book that brings you up close and personal to the research process. Psychological research is, of course, often about people, how they behave and think, but we sometimes forget it is also *by* people. Undergraduate and graduate students, perhaps like you, as well as professional psychologists and scientists, are behind the research process. Have you ever wondered, Where does psychological research start? Who comes up with the ideas for the many psychological studies we see published in scientific journals? What problems did the researchers have while doing their research? How did they deal with ethical issues? Were they surprised by their findings? What would they have done differently?

Our emphasis in this book is on introducing you to psychological research through the eyes of the researchers who do the investigations. You will meet researchers who investigate storytelling in children, the ways in which writing about emotional and upsetting events in your life can make you healthier (both psychologically and physically), the long-term consequences of eating disorders, treatment of individuals with obsessive compulsive disorders, and other topics. Not only will you learn much about psychological research as you explore the topics in this book, but we think you will learn a lot about the process of research as it comes to life in the laboratories and field settings in which researchers work. In this way, we hope to capture for you some of the excitement researchers feel about doing psychological research.

Throughout the book we use case illustrations to introduce you to the various research methods available to psychologists. For each of the major methods discussed in this book, we contacted authors of current studies and asked them to put in their own words some of their thoughts about their research. We first describe their study for you and then ask the researchers themselves to elaborate on what they did and found. You may be surprised at what they say—we were! When we asked one prominent researcher, for example, what he thought about a research finding, his comment was, "It blew me away!" Even the "big names" in the field still get excited about their research. But perhaps that is why they are still engaged in this process. It *is* exciting. Beneath all the procedures, techniques, statistical terms, and concepts is the joy of discovery. We want students to experience that, too.

This book is based on our McGraw-Hill textbook, *Research Methods in Psychology* (5/e, 2000). Nevertheless, *Essentials* is a very different textbook. First, it is intended for instructors who seek a briefer research methods textbook than *RMIP* (5e)—hence the title *Essentials*. We have distilled the larger methods book to provide coverage of the basic methods and ideas of doing psychological research. We have not, however, given up on our attempt to provide broad coverage of research methods and an emphasis on a multimethod approach to doing psychological research. *Essentials* covers the various research methods used by psychologists, including observational methods, correlational/survey methods, experimental designs, and applied research designs (e.g., single-case and quasi-experimental designs). *Essentials* also addresses data analysis for each design, highlighting appropriate statistical procedures and helping you learn how to interpret the analyses in the context of the research design and hypotheses.

Essentials in particular emphasizes the *process* of conducting research (e.g., developing research ideas, forming hypotheses, choosing a design, etc.). A guide for the research process is presented in the second chapter, and these guidelines are reinforced as each method is introduced in subsequent chapters by illustrating how an actual research study in psychology was conducted. *Essentials* uses a "case approach" by highlighting *one* study in each chapter. This allows us to illustrate the important concepts in the book. We prefer presenting "real" research rather than offering countless hypothetical examples to illustrate our concepts. Real research, as it is conducted every day, demonstrates the challenge of conducting sound research, and it informs us of the questions that psychologists are currently addressing. Information obtained from the authors of the research example (including pictures of the authors) is interspersed throughout the chapter. By discussing at length an interesting psychological study and including "The Researchers' Point of View," we attempt to take you behind the scenes as we track the process of research from the beginning research idea to the published article.

Our goal in this book is to help you think critically about research methods. Each research methods chapter includes a section entitled, "Thinking Critically About Research." Using information from the text, from the case illustration, and from the authors' comments, we address key issues associated with the research method that is the main topic of the chapter. At the end of each chapter, we have also included bullet points for you to review, and "Applying Your Knowledge" problems and exercises to permit you to apply what you have learned to a new research question or situation. These exercises are particularly important for this book because we spend considerable time in each chapter discussing one major research study. The application problems at the end of each chapter challenge you to use your newly minted skills in a slightly different way. Authors, like researchers, want their work to generalize.

There are several pedagogical features that are unique to this book. In addition to the Research Examples and many tables and figures designed to illustrate and summarize important concepts, you will find review tests for Chapters 1–9 at the end of the book. Although these problems and exercises are also found on the website accompanying this book, they appear as hard copy in the book itself. Thus, no matter where you may find yourself when studying, you can quickly and efficiently check your knowledge of the text material. Of course, if you find it easier to use a computer, you can access these tests and additional exercises to practice your skills on the book's website at www.mhhe.com/zechmeister. In Chapter 1, we direct you to the web pages of the American Psychological

Association Science Directorate and American Psychological Society. The website for this book also contains links to other important psychology-related sites.

Words of Thanks

One goal of this book was to make the research process personal and engaging. We think we have succeeded in large part because of the thoughtful, informative, and lively responses offered by the researchers whose work is highlighted in this book. We are indebted to: Catherine Haden (*Loyola University Chicago*), Saul M. Kassin (*Williams College*), K. Lee Kiechel (*George Mason University*), Daniel J. Simons (*Harvard University*), Daniel T. Levin (*Kent State University*), Todd F. Heatherton (*Dartmouth College*), James W. Pennebaker (*University of Texas–Austin*), Doris G. Bazzini (*Appalachian State University*), David R. Shaffer (*University of Georgia*), Tamara L. Hartl (*University of Connecticut*), Randy O. Frost (*Smith College*), and Thomas K. Greenfield (*Alcohol Research Group*).

In addition, many knowledgable and discerning reviewers helped strengthen the book through their critiques, suggestions, and words of encouragement. Thanks for pushing us to make this a readable and thorough presentation of research methods *Essentials*. We are grateful to these reviewers and several who wish to remain anonymous: Annette Taylor (*University of San Diego*), Steven Turner (*East Central University*), Tom Mitchell (*University of Baltimore*), Garrett Berman (*Roger Williams University*), Susan K. Marell (*St. Thomas Aquinas*), Pamela Ludemann (*Framington State University*), David Conner (*Truman State University*), Bernard C. Beins (*Ithaca College*), O. Joseph Harm (*University of South Carolina*), Lynn Shelley (*Westfield State University*), Jerome Siegel (*The City College of New York*), Martha Shalitta (*Eastern College*), and Jeffrey S. Berman (*University of Memphis*).

Finally, we would like to acknowledge the several people at McGraw-Hill who helped get this book to you. Jane Vaicunas, as editorial director, has been with us for several editions of the "big book" and fully supported this *Essentials* edition. Joe Terry was the senior sponsoring editor who brought things together, with a lot of help from his editorial assistant, Barbara Santoro. Barbara's encouraging e-mails kept us going. Christine Hall was responsible for development and marketing from the beginning of our ideas for this book. Our project manager, Sheila Frank, and production supervisor, Enboge Chong, got us through copy editing and page proofs, and then got the book out the door. Lou Ann Wilson found us photos for the book, and Deb DeBord worked hard to polish our writing. Our cover designer, Rebecca Lemna, made our book look like something we'd want to pick up. Finally, the supplement coordinator, Sandy Schnee, helped us develop the instructor's manual. Our thanks for a great team effort!

Please let us know what you like about our approach—what we hope is a unique and stimulating approach to research methods in psychology. And tell us what you don't like, too, so we can improve our book in the next edition. Our e-mail addresses follow:

Jeanne S. Zechmeister, jzechme@luc.edu
Eugene B. Zechmeister, ezechme@luc.edu
John J. Shaughnessy,
    shaughnessy@hope.edu

Chapter One

INTRODUCTION: THE SCIENCE OF PSYCHOLOGY

INTRODUCTION

Let's begin our introduction to research methods in psychology with a test. Don't worry; it isn't about methodology, but about how people think and behave. And there's no grade. Please take a moment to respond "true" or "false" to the following:

1. Most individuals will notice if a person they are talking to is replaced by another person. T or F
2. Mothers talk to their younger children differently than they talk to their older children. T or F
3. Few students will confess to ruining a computer program if they didn't do it. T or F
4. Students who have eating-disordered attitudes in college maintain these attitudes through their twenties. T or F
5. Writing about adjusting to college improves students' grades. T or F

Before revealing the correct answers, we want to explain the rationale for beginning this book with such a test. One point we wish to make is that deciding what people will do or how they think is not always easy. Even if you should answer all these statements correctly, we feel confident that you wavered on some of them. We can make this prediction because we wavered, and we have been research psychologists for quite a few years. Sometimes we just don't know what people will do until we do research to find out. We made up these statements based on recent psychological research findings. Of course, that is a major point, too. Psychological research gives us important information about the way people think and behave. And that is what this book is about.

Another characteristic you may have noticed about the true/false items is the diversity of topics. The statements are about what psychologists call "change blindness" (the inability to notice how things change), mothers' language style, false confessions, eating-disordered attitudes, and adjustment and student grades. Psychology is a broad field, encompassing many topics. Nevertheless, one thing unites the research behind these articles: the use of the *scientific method* for learning about behavior and mental processes. As we'll describe in this chapter, the scientific method is a way of gaining knowledge. The use of the scientific method makes psychology a scientific discipline similar to other scientific disciplines such as biology, chemistry, and sociology. What differs among these scientific disciplines is the *content* of researchers' investigations. Psychologists study the working of the mind and behavior, whereas biologists study cells, chemists study molecules, and sociologists study societies.

Throughout this book, you will find examples of actual research that illustrate various methods and concepts. As you read each chapter's research example you will learn the psychologists' research question, hypotheses, procedures for answering the question, results, and conclusions. Additionally, you will find excerpts from interviews with the researchers as they talk about their work. Some of these researchers were students when they conducted their research. In fact, each of the previous true/false statements was derived from a research study that we will discuss in some detail in later chapters. This will give you a chance to compare your thinking about the answers to the statements with the researchers' findings and with their thoughts about these psychological processes. By the way, all the statements except the last one are false.

We hope we captured your interest in finding out more about these research topics and about how psychologists carry out their research. If you are like us, you are very curious about the mind and behavior. You like to think about people's (and animals') behavior. You wonder about people—why they act the way they do, how they became the people they are. And you may wonder about your own behavior and how your mind works. These thoughts and reflections set you apart from other people—not everyone is curious about the mind and not everyone considers the reasons for behavior. But if you are curious, if you do wonder about why people and animals behave the way they do, you have already taken the first step in the intriguing, exciting journey into research methods in psychology.

In this chapter we will describe the scientific method and the goals of psychological research. We will distinguish between basic research in psychology and applied psychological research. Finally, we will present an overview of the textbook to prepare you for what's to come.

LEARNING OBJECTIVES

By the end of this chapter, you will
- *know how the scientific method differs from "everyday ways" of gaining knowledge;*
- *learn the four goals for psychological research: description, prediction, understanding, and creating change; and*
- *know the difference between basic and applied research.*

PSYCHOLOGY AS A SCIENCE

No one has records of who first observed behavior carefully and systematically, who conducted the first public opinion survey, or who performed the first psychology experiment. No one really even knows exactly when psychology first became an independent discipline. Psychology emerged gradually, with roots in the thinking of Aristotle, in the writings of later philosophers such as Descartes and Locke, and later in the work of early nineteenth-century physiologists and physicists. The official beginning of psychology is often marked as occurring in 1879, when Wilhelm Wundt established a formal psychology laboratory in Leipzig, Germany, to study sensory and perceptual experiences.

As you have seen, psychologists today are interested in many different topics in addition to sensory and perceptual processes. Researchers study topics in clinical, social, industrial, counseling, physiological, cognitive, educational, and developmental psychology.

Two large psychology associations promote the science of psychology: the American Psychological Association (APA) and the American Psychological

Society (APS). Psychologists attend annual conventions of these organizations to learn about recent developments in their fields. Each organization also publishes scientific journals which communicate the latest research findings, and both organizations encourage student affiliation. Undergraduate and graduate psychology students who join these organizations gain educational and research opportunities. Information about APA and APS can be obtained at their World Wide Web pages on the Internet at

(APA) http://www.apa.org
(APS) http://www.psychologicalscience.org

The APA and APS websites provide news about important recent psychological research findings, information about psychology publications, and links to many psychology organizations. Take a look.

THE SCIENTIFIC METHOD

There is one way in which psychology has not changed in its 100+ years: Psychologists still emphasize the **scientific method** as the basis for investigation. What exactly is the scientific method? As you will see, it does not require a particular type of equipment, nor is it associated with a particular procedure or technique. The scientific method is something abstract. It is an approach to gaining knowledge that distinguishes it from approaches followed by philosophy, theology, literature, art, and other disciplines that rely on different means for obtaining knowledge about humans and animals. It can also be distinguished from an "everyday" approach to knowledge.

Several major differences between a scientific and a nonscientific, or everyday, approach to knowledge are outlined in Table 1.1. The characteristics listed under "Scientific" define the scientific method.

Table 1.1   Characteristics of Scientific and Nonscientific (Everyday) Approaches to Gaining Knowledge

	Nonscientific (Everyday)	Scientific
General approach	Intuitive	Empirical
Observation	Casual, uncontrolled	Systematic, controlled
Reporting	Biased, subjective	Unbiased, objective
Concepts	Ambiguous	Clear definitions
Instruments	Inaccurate, imprecise	Accurate, precise
Measurement	Not valid or reliable	Valid, reliable
Hypotheses	Untestable	Testable
Attitude	Uncritical, accepting	Critical, skeptical

Based in part on distinctions suggested by Marx (1963).

Characteristics of the Scientific Method

General Approach.   We make many of our everyday judgments using intuition. This usually means that we act based on what "feels right" or what "seems reasonable." Although intuition can be valuable when we have little other information, intuition is not always correct. For example, intuition tells us that when many people witness an emergency, there's a greater likelihood someone will help the victim. However, psychological research shows that just the opposite is true: A bystander is more likely to help when alone than when a group of people is present (Latané & Darley, 1970). When we rely on intuition to make judgments we often fail to recognize that our perceptions may be distorted or that we may not have considered all available evidence.

The scientific approach to knowledge is empirical rather than intuitive. An **empirical approach** emphasizes *direct observation* and *experimentation* to answer questions. This doesn't mean that intuition has no role in science. The beginning of a research program is often guided by scientists' intuition. Eventually, however, scientists are guided by direct observation and experimentation.

Observation.   We can learn a great deal about behavior simply by observing the actions of others. However, everyday observations are not always made carefully or systematically. Most people do not attempt to control or eliminate factors that might influence the events they are observing. As a result, they often make incorrect conclusions based on their casual observations.

Consider the case of the horse named Clever Hans. Hans' owner believed his horse had amazing talents. Hans could count, do simple addition and subtraction (even involving fractions), read German, answer simple questions (such as "What is the lady holding in her hands?"), give the date, and tell time (Watson, 1914/1967). Hans answered questions by tapping his forefoot or by pointing his nose at various alternatives shown to him. His owner considered Hans to be truly intelligent and denied using any tricks to guide his horse's behavior. And, in fact, Clever Hans was clever even when the questioner was someone other than his owner. Hundreds of people went to view this amazing horse.

In 1904 a scientific commission was established to discover the basis for Hans' abilities. Much to his owner's dismay, the scientists observed that Hans was not clever in two situations. First, Hans did not know answers if the questioner also did not know the answers. Second, Hans was not very clever if he could not see his questioner. What did the scientists observe? They discovered that Hans responded to the questioner's subtle movements. A slight bending forward by the questioner would start Hans tapping, and any movement upward or backward would cause Hans to stop tapping. The commission demonstrated that questioners were unintentionally cueing Hans as he tapped his forefoot or pointed. Thus, it seems Hans was a better observer than many of the people who observed him!

This famous account of Clever Hans illustrates the fact that scientific observation (unlike casual observation) is systematic and controlled. Indeed, some

Figure 1.1   (a) Clever Hans performing before onlookers. (b) Hans being tested under more controlled conditions when Hans could not see the questioner.

(a)

(b)

say that **control** is the essential ingredient of science (Boring, 1954; Marx, 1963). In the case of Clever Hans, investigators exercised control by manipulating, *one at a time,* conditions such as whether the questioner knew the answers to the questions and whether Hans could see the questioner. By using control—

investigating the effect of various factors one at a time—scientists gain a clearer picture of the factors that produce a phenomenon. Each chapter of this book will emphasize how researchers use control techniques to study behavior and the mind.

Reporting.   Suppose you ask someone to tell you about a class you missed. You probably want an accurate report of what happened in class. Or perhaps you missed a party in which two of your friends had a heated argument, and you want to hear from someone what happened. As you might imagine, personal biases and subjective impressions often enter into our everyday reports. When we ask anyone to describe an event we receive details (not always correct) of the event and personal impressions.

When scientists report their findings, they seek to separate what they have observed from what they conclude, or infer, on the basis of these observations. For example, an objective report of your friends' argument would describe what was said and what happened, but would leave out personal interpretations as to who caused the argument or why they were arguing. Scientific reporting is unbiased and objective. One way to determine if a report is unbiased is to determine whether it can be verified by an independent observer. This is called interobserver agreement (see Chapter 4).

Concepts.   We use the term *concepts* to refer to *things* (both living and inanimate), *events* (things in action), and *relationships* among things or events (Marx, 1963). "Dog" is a concept, as are "barking," and "obedience." Concepts are the symbols we use for communication. Clear, unambiguous communication of ideas requires that we clearly define our concepts.

In everyday conversation we get by without worrying too much about how we define a concept. Many words, for instance, are commonly used and apparently understood even though speakers and listeners don't know *exactly* what the words mean. People frequently communicate with one another without really knowing what they are talking about! This may sound ridiculous, but to illustrate this point, try the following.

Ask a few people whether they believe intelligence is mostly inherited (genetic) or mostly acquired (learned). You might try arguing a point of view opposite to theirs just for the fun of it. After discussing the roots of intelligence, ask them what they mean by "intelligence." You will probably find that most people have a difficult time defining this concept, even after debating its origins. And different people will provide different definitions. "Intelligence" means one thing to one person and something else to another. However, it is critical that scientists clearly define their concepts. We'll discuss how they do that in Chapter 2.

Instruments.   You depend on instruments to measure events more than you probably realize. For example, you probably regularly rely on the speedometer in your car and the clock in your bedroom. And you can appreciate the problems that arise if these instruments are inaccurate. *Accuracy* is the difference between what an instrument says is true and what is actually true. A clock that is consistently 5 minutes slow is not very accurate. Inaccurate clocks can make us late, and inaccurate speedometers can earn us traffic tickets.

Measurements can be made at varying levels of *precision*. A measure of time in tenths of a second is not as precise as one that is in hundredths of a second. One instrument that yields imprecise measures is the gas gauge in most cars. Although reasonably accurate, gas gauges do not give very precise readings. Most of us have wished at one time or another that the gas gauge would permit us to determine whether we had that extra half gallon of gas that would get us to the next service station.

We also need instruments to measure behavior, and many types of instruments are used in contemporary psychology. Researchers who conduct psychophysiology experiments (e.g., assessing a person's arousal level), for instance, require instruments that give accurate measures of heart rate and blood pressure. With increased technology, the precision and accuracy of

Instruments differ in their precision.

THE FAR SIDE by Gary Larson

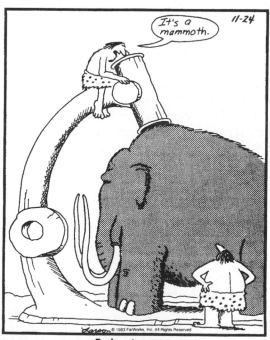

Early microscope

psychologists' instruments have improved significantly since psychology's early days. Other behavioral instruments are of the paper-and-pencil variety. Questionnaires and tests are popular instruments used by psychologists to measure behavior. So, too, are the rating scales used by human observers. Behavioral scientists use instruments that are as accurate and as precise as possible.

Measurement.   Scientists use two types of measurement. The first type, *physical measurement*, involves dimensions for which there is an agreed-upon standard and an instrument for doing the measuring. For example, length is a dimension that can be scaled with physical measurement, and there are agreed-upon standards and instruments for units of length (e.g., inches, meters).

In most psychology research, however, the measurements do not involve physical dimensions. Rulers do not exist for measuring beauty, aggression, or intelligence. These dimensions require a second type of measurement: *psychological measurement*. Agreement among a number of observers provides the basis for psychological measurement. For example, if several independent observers agree that a certain action warrants a rating of 3 on a 7-point rating scale of aggression, that is a psychological measurement of the aggressiveness of the action.

Measurements must be valid and reliable. In general, **validity** is the "truthfulness" of a measure. A valid measure of a concept is one that measures what it claims to measure. Suppose a researcher defines intelligence according to how long a person can balance a ball on his or her nose. Is this a *valid* measure of intelligence? The validity of a measure is supported if people do as well on it as on other measures that presumably measure the same concept. For example, if time spent balancing a ball is a valid measure of intelligence, then a person who does well on the balancing task should also do well on other accepted measures of intelligence.

The **reliability** of a measurement is indicated by its consistency. Several kinds of reliability can be distinguished. When we speak of instrument reliability, we are discussing whether an instrument works consistently. A car that sometimes starts and sometimes doesn't is not very reliable. Observations made by two or more independent observers are said to be reliable if they show agreement—that is, if the observations are consistent from one observer to another. The psychologist's goal is to develop psychological measurements that are reliable as well as valid.

Hypotheses.   A hypothesis (plural: hypothe*ses*) is a tentative explanation for something. Hypotheses frequently attempt to answer the questions "How?" and "Why?" Nearly everyone has proposed hypotheses to explain some human behavior at one time or another. Why do people commit apparently senseless acts of violence? What causes people to start smoking cigarettes? Why are some students academically more successful than others? No doubt you have entertained some hypotheses or tentative explanations for why some things happen as they do. One characteristic that distinguishes casual, everyday hypotheses from scientific hypotheses is *testability*. If a hypothesis cannot be tested, it is not useful to science.

Hypotheses are not testable *if the concepts to which they refer are not adequately defined or measured*. To say that a would-be assassin shot a U.S. president because the assassin was mentally disturbed is not a testable hypothesis unless we can agree on a definition of "mentally disturbed." Unfortunately, psychologists and psychiatrists cannot always agree on what terms such as "mentally disturbed" mean. (This is another example of the problems associated with defining concepts.) You may have learned in a psychology class that many of Freud's hypotheses are not testable. This is because there are no clear ways to define and measure key concepts in Freud's theory, such as *id*, *ego*, and *superego*.

Hypotheses are also untestable if they are *circular*. A circular hypothesis occurs when an event itself becomes an explanation for the event. Circular hypotheses are readily apparent on talk shows and in our everyday conversations. Consider this example given by one prominent psychologist (Kimble, 1989, p. 495): "Your eight-year-old son is distractable in school . . . because he has an attention deficit disorder." By saying a boy is distractable *because* he has an attention deficit disorder doesn't explain his behavior. An attention deficit disorder is *defined by* the inability to pay attention, and being distractable is the same as not being able to pay attention. Thus, this statement simply says that he doesn't pay attention because he doesn't pay attention. This is a circular hypothesis.

A hypothesis also may be untestable if it *appeals to ideas or forces that are not recognized by science*. Science deals with the observable, the empirical. To suggest that people who commit horrendous acts of violence are controlled by the devil is not testable because this hypothesis invokes a principle (the devil) that is not in the province of science. Such hypotheses might be of value to philosophers or theologians, but not to the scientist.

Attitude.   More than anything else, scientists are skeptical. Behavioral scientists are skeptical because behavior is complex, and often many factors interact to cause a psychological phenomenon. Scientists recognize that discovering these factors is a very difficult task. Scientists also recognize that science is a human endeavor. People make mistakes. Human inference cannot always be trusted; therefore, scientists are often skeptical and cautious about "new discoveries" and extraordinary claims.

In our everyday lives we tend not to be very cautious about claims, and many of us easily accept explanations that are based on insufficient or inadequate evidence. This is illustrated by the widespread belief in the occult. Rather than approaching the claims about paranormal events cautiously, many people accept these claims uncritically. According to public opinion surveys, a large majority of Americans believe in ESP (extrasensory perception), horoscopes, and the idea that aliens from outer space have visited earth. People hold these beliefs despite the poor evidence for the validity—truthfulness—of these beliefs. This human tendency to ignore certain kinds of evidence is not new. When scientists successfully demonstrated why Clever Hans appeared to be so clever, many people continued to believe in his superior reasoning ability.

Obstacles to Scientific Thinking

Why do people resist scientific evidence? One explanation might be the media (Singer & Benassi, 1981). The public is constantly exposed to television shows, newspaper accounts, and other reports of events presumably caused by supernatural forces. (Consider the popularity of movies such as *The X Files* or *The Sixth Sense.*) Reports in the media are often presented with little critical evaluation, and scientific evidence is frequently ignored. The sheer *number* of media reports may lend credibility to them. Another reason for the widespread acceptance of the occult may be deficiencies in human reasoning. As mentioned earlier, everyday inferences are susceptible to many biases.

Singer and Benassi (1981) also fault science education. Too often, they suggest, science is taught as a set of facts rather than as a way to approach knowledge critically and systematically. People are often impatient with the scientific process and even confused when scientists appear to change their minds or when they attempt to clarify earlier findings. Singer and Benassi also find that the general public exhibits woefully little general scientific knowledge. For example, many people believe that islands float on the ocean surface and that the moon is fixed in the sky but only visible at night.

Scientists do not automatically assume that unusual interpretations of unexplained phenomena could not possibly be true. They simply insist on testing all claims and withholding judgment about claims that are inherently untestable. Scientific skepticism helps protect the public against frauds and phonies who wish to sell ineffective medicines and cures, impossible schemes to get rich, and paranormal explanations for natural phenomena.

We will return to many of these ideas throughout the book as we discuss the various research methods psychologists use to learn about behavior and mental processes. By learning the scientific method, you should be able to evaluate critically the many claims that are presented in advertisements and news reports. As you develop your critical thinking skills, you also will appreciate the complexity of human and animal behavior.

THE GOALS OF RESEARCH

Description, Prediction, Understanding Causes, Creating Change

Psychologists use the scientific method to meet four research goals: description, prediction, understanding, and creating change (see Table 1.2).

Description.   *Description* refers to the procedures researchers use to define, classify, catalogue, or categorize events and their relationships. Clinical research, for example, provides practitioners with criteria for describing and classifying mental disorders. Many of these are found in the American Psychiatric Association's *Diagnostic and Statistical Manual of Mental Disorders* (4th ed., 1994), also known as *DSM-IV.* Consider, for instance, "dissociative fugue." According to the *DSM-IV,* some of the defining characteristics of this mental disturbance are that it involves "sudden, unexpected travel away from home . . . with inability to recall one's

Table 1.2   Four Goals of Psychological Research

Goal	What Is Accomplished
Description	Researchers define, classify, catalogue, or categorize events and their relationships to describe mental processes and behavior. *Example:* Psychologists describe symptoms of helplessness in depression, such as failure to initiate activities and pessimism regarding the future.
Prediction	When researchers identify correlations (relationships) among variables they are able to predict mental processes and behavior. *Example:* As level of depression increases, individuals exhibit more symptoms of helplessness.
Understanding	Researchers understand a phenomenon when they can identify its cause(s). *Example:* Research participants exposed to unsolvable problems become more pessimistic and less willing to do new tasks (i.e., become helpless) than participants who are asked to do solvable problems.
Creating Change	Psychologists apply their knowledge and research methods to change people's lives for the better. *Example:* Treatment that encourages depressed individuals to attempt tasks that can be mastered or easily attained decreases depressives' helplessness and pessimism.

past" and includes "confusion about personal identity or assumption of a new identity (partial or complete)" (*DSM-IV*, 1994, p. 481). Researchers also seek to provide clinicians with descriptions of the prevalence of mental disorders, as well as the relationship between the presence of various symptoms and other variables such as gender and age.

Psychology (like science in general) develops descriptions of behaviors and events using the *nomothetic approach.* Using the nomothetic approach, psychologists try to establish broad generalizations and general laws that apply to a diverse population. This is why psychological studies most often involve large numbers of participants. Researchers seek to describe the "average" or typical performance of a group. This average behavior may or may not describe the performance of any one individual in the group. That is, researchers typically seek to describe what organisms are like *in general,* and they use information based on the average performance of a group to form their descriptions.

Some psychologists argue that the nomothetic approach is inadequate—unique individuals cannot be described by an average value. Researchers who use the *idiographic approach* study the individual rather than groups. These researchers believe that although individuals behave in ways that conform to general laws or principles, the uniqueness of individuals must also be described. A major form of idiographic research is the case study method, which you will find discussed in Chapter 8.

Depending on their research question, psychologists decide whether to describe groups of individuals or one individual's behavior. Researchers also must decide whether to do quantitative or qualitative research. *Quantitative research* involves studies in which research findings are presented in terms of statistical summaries and analysis. *Qualitative research* produces verbal summaries of research findings with no statistical summaries and analysis. Psychological research is more frequently nomothetic and quantitative. Although qualitative research is described in Chapter 4 and idiographic research in Chapter 8, the emphasis throughout this book is on nomothetic, quantitative research.

Prediction.   Once events and behaviors have been described, we can approach the second goal of the scientific method: **prediction.** Many important questions in psychology call for predictions—such as the following: Does the early loss of a parent make a child especially vulnerable to depression? Are overly aggressive children likely to have emotional problems as adults? Do stressful life events lead to increased physical illness? Research findings suggest that the answer to all of these questions is yes. This information not only adds valuable knowledge to psychology but also helps psychologists treat and prevent emotional disorders.

Successful prediction relies on knowing the relationship between variables. A *variable* is a dimension on which people differ, or vary. Childhood loss of a parent, symptoms of depression, aggressiveness, emotional problems, stressful life events, and physical illness are all examples of things that vary among people. They are all variables.

When scores on one variable can be used to predict scores on a second variable, the two variables are correlated. A **correlation** exists when two different measures of the same people, events, or things vary together or go together. When two variables are correlated, scores on one of the variables tend to be associated with particular scores on the other variable. When this occurs, the scores are said to "covary." For example, stress and illness are known to be correlated: The more stressful life events a person experiences (one variable), the more likely he or she is to experience physical illnesses (a second variable). We will discuss the topic of correlational research in Chapter 5. Correlational research, which seeks to identify predictive relationships among variables, is a major area of psychological research.

It is important to note that successful prediction doesn't depend on knowing *why* a relationship exists between two variables. For example, in some cultures people observe animal behavior to help them predict earthquakes. Certain animals apparently behave oddly just before an earthquake. A dog that barks and runs in circles and a snake seen fleeing its hole, therefore, may be reliable predictors of earthquakes. If so, observing such behavior can warn people of forthcoming disasters. To make this prediction we do not need to understand *why* certain animals behave strangely before an earthquake, or even why earthquakes occur.

Understanding.   Although description and prediction are important goals, they are only the first steps in understanding a phenomenon. *Understanding* is the third goal of the scientific method. We understand an event or a behavior when we can identify its cause(s). Understanding involves more than description and prediction. You may have already learned the phrase "*correlation does not imply causation.*" This means that simply knowing that two variables are correlated doesn't mean that we know what causes the relationship. Recall that observing a dog's odd behavior may be used to predict an earthquake. However, even though the dog's behavior may predict an earthquake, we wouldn't say that the dog's behavior *causes* the earthquake. Obviously, we need more information to understand what causes the relationship.

Psychologists conduct *experiments* to identify the causes of a phenomenon. Experimental research differs from descriptive and correlational research because of the high degree of control scientists seek in experiments. Recall that when researchers *control* a situation they manipulate factors one at a time to determine their effect on the phenomenon of interest. You probably already understand intuitively the principles of control. Here's an example: Suppose a friend tells you she tried to leave a message on your telephone answering machine but the machine didn't work. We can develop several hypotheses for why it didn't work. For example, there may be something wrong with the electrical outlet, or the phone line isn't working, or the message tape is worn and needs to be replaced (you probably can think of additional hypotheses).

How would we figure out the cause of the answering machine problem? One possibility—the nonexperimental approach—would be to plug the machine into a different electrical outlet *and* a different phone line *and* replace the message tape. Now your friend calls again and the machine works. What caused the problem in the first place? It's impossible to know because it could have been the electrical outlet, the phone line, *or* the message tape. We don't know the cause because we manipulated all three factors at the same time.

To understand the cause of the answering machine problem we would have to manipulate—control—each factor one at a time. Our first "experiment" could be to plug in a working clock or radio to determine whether the outlet is defective. However, if our first effort doesn't reveal the cause of the phenomenon, then we might conduct another experiment to test a different hypothesis. Continuing our answering machine example, if the electrical outlet works fine, another experiment might test the hypothesis that the phone line is out of order. We might move the answering machine to a different telephone line and ask our friend to call. The process of experimental research in psychology is much the same: We control, one at a time, each factor we believe may cause a particular event to occur. Because behavior and mental processes are complex, we often have to conduct many experiments to understand the causes of psychological phenomena.

By conducting controlled experiments psychologists infer what causes a phenomenon. A **causal inference** is a statement about the cause of an event or a behavior. When we discuss experimental research in greater detail in Chapters 6 and 7, we will address specific control techniques that allow researchers to understand the causes of phenomena.

Creating Change.   The fourth goal of research in psychology is to create change. Although psychologists are interested in describing, predicting, and understanding behavior and mental processes, this knowledge doesn't exist in a vacuum. Instead, this knowledge exists in a world in which people suffer from mental disorders, in which people are victims of violence and aggression, and in which stereotypes and prejudices affect how people live and function in society (to name but a few problems we face). The list of problems in our world at times may seem endless, but this shouldn't discourage us. The breadth of psychologists' research questions and findings provides many ways for researchers to help address these aspects of human life and create change in individuals' lives. Additionally, as psychologists in the twenty-first century focus on "positive psychology"—the ways we can maximize our growth and potential—we will discover new avenues for creating positive change (Seligman & Csikszentmihalyi, 2000).

Basic and Applied Research

Research on creating change is often called "applied research." In **applied research,** psychologists conduct research in order to change people's lives for the better. For people suffering from mental disorders, this change may occur through research on therapeutic techniques. However, applied psychologists are involved with many types of interventions, including those aimed at improving the lives of students in schools, employees at work, and individuals in the community. On the other hand, researchers who conduct **basic research** seek primarily to understand behavior and mental processes. People often describe basic research as "seeking knowledge for its own sake." Basic research is typically carried out in a laboratory setting with the goal of testing a *theory* about a phenomenon.

Theories are "ideas" about how nature works. Psychologists propose ideas about why behavior occurs the way it does (e.g., what causes schizophrenia), about the nature of cognition (e.g., how people solve problems), and so on. Researchers develop their scientific theories from a mixture of intuition, personal observation, and discovered knowledge (known facts and ideas). In Chapter 2 we'll talk more about the characteristics and goals of psychological theories.

THE ORGANIZATION OF THIS BOOK

This book introduces you to the ways in which psychologists use the scientific method. As you know, psychology is a discipline with many areas of study and many questions. No single research methodology can answer all the questions psychologists have about behavior and mental processes. Thus, the best approach to answering our questions is the **multimethod approach**—that is, searching for an answer using various research methodologies. The goal of this book is to help you to fill a "toolbox" with strategies for conducting research. These tools will then be available to you for answering psychology's questions.

The organization of the book follows loosely the goals for the scientific method. Following a discussion of the research process (Chapter 2) and ethical issues in research (Chapter 3), you will be introduced to *descriptive methods*. Observation, for instance, is an important tool of psychologists who want to describe behavior (see Chapter 4). Questionnaires are among the most commonly used instruments in psychology and frequently are the basis for making *predictions* about behavior. The nature of questionnaires and their use in survey research are discussed in Chapter 5. The third goal, *understanding causes,* is addressed using *experimental approaches* for studying behavior. In Chapters 6 and 7, we explore experiments done with groups of participants. Experimental approaches are aimed chiefly at discovering cause-and-effect relationships (i.e., causal inferences).

Finally, we examine *applied research* methods used to *create change* in people's lives. In Chapter 8, we discuss research conducted with small numbers of participants—in fact, with single individuals ($N = 1$). Chapter 9 deals with quasi-experimental designs and program evaluation, which are concerned with assessing the effects of "treatments" applied in natural settings. The book comes to a close with a discussion of how your knowledge of research methods can help you be a better consumer of psychological research findings (Chapter 10).

At the end of each chapter, questions and exercises will help you test your knowledge about research methods. One set of questions is called "Checking the Essentials" and provides questions for review of the major points in each chapter. Another set of exercises, called "Applying Your Knowledge," asks you to think critically about what you have learned and to apply your knowledge to new problems and situations. In addition, at the end of the book you will find self-tests for you to test your understanding of material in each chapter and to help you prepare for exams (see Appendix C).

KEY CONCEPTS

scientific method	correlation
empirical approach	causal inference
control	applied research
validity	basic research
reliability	multimethod approach
prediction	

KEY POINTS TO LEARN

Psychology as a Science

- The scope of scientific psychology has increased dramatically in the 100+ years since its inception.
- The American Psychological Association (APA) and the American Psychological Society (APS) promote the science of psychology.

The Scientific Method

- Psychologists use the scientific method to gain knowledge about human and animal behavior.

- The scientific method differs from nonscientific (everyday) approaches to gaining knowledge.
- The scientific method is empirical, and requires systematic, controlled observation.
- Scientific reporting is unbiased and objective and requires clear communication of concepts.
- Scientific instruments are accurate and precise; physical and psychological measurement should be valid and reliable.
- A hypothesis is a tentative explanation for a phenomenon; testable hypotheses have clearly defined concepts, are not circular, and refer to concepts that can be observed.
- Scientists adopt a skeptical attitude and are cautious about accepting explanations until sufficient empirical evidence is obtained.

The Goals of Research

- Psychologists seek to describe events and relationships between variables; most often, researchers use the nomothetic approach and quantitative analysis.
- Correlational relationships allow psychologists to predict behavior or events, but do not allow psychologists to infer what causes these relationships.
- Researchers conduct controlled experiments to make causal inferences.
- Psychologists who conduct basic research primarily seek to understand a phenomenon by testing theories in laboratory settings.
- Applied research is often conducted in the "real" world to change and improve people's circumstances.

The Organization of This Book

- The best approach to answering psychology's questions is the multimethod approach; that is, we search for answers using various research methodologies.

CHECKING THE ESSENTIALS

1. The scientific method uses an empirical approach to answer questions. What two sources of evidence are emphasized in an empirical approach?
2. What two characteristics distinguish scientific observation from more casual, everyday observations?
3. Identify two types of measurement used by psychologists and differentiate between the validity and reliability of a measurement.
4. What characteristic distinguishes scientific hypotheses from casual, everyday hypotheses?
5. Identify the four research goals that psychologists strive to meet by using the scientific method.
6. Distinguish between (a) nomothetic and idiographic approaches to psychological research and (b) qualitative and quantitative research.
7. Explain what is meant when psychologists say that "correlation does not imply causation."
8. Psychologists strive to achieve one primary goal of research when they conduct controlled experiments. Which goal is it?

9. Which type of research (basic research or applied research) is more directly involved with the goal of research in psychology to create change?

APPLYING YOUR KNOWLEDGE

1. One of your friends who is taking introductory psychology this semester tells you about something her professor covered in class that was a little distressing for her. The professor described a study dealing with how satisfied married people are in their marriages. The professor emphasized that the study was very well done. For example, a large sample was used from a well-defined population, and the measures of marital satisfaction were reliable and valid. The finding from the study that your friend found distressing was that, on average, 65% of the married people surveyed were less satisfied with their marriage than they had expected they would be. Your friend is now wondering whether this finding means that she will end up being less satisfied with her marriage someday.
    A. Identify whether the study described by your friend's professor represents the nomothetic or idiographic approach to research in psychology.
    B. Identify whether the study described in your friend's class represents qualitative or quantitative research.
    C. How would you respond to your friend's concern that these research results mean that she will end up being less satisfied with her marriage if she should someday get married?

2. Consider how you would respond if you read the following report in a newsletter:
    Is your child's behavior out of control? While considering this question, are you reaching for a cigarette to "calm" your nerves? Before you smoke it, consider this: Researchers investigated 2,356 children from ages 4 to 11 and found a direct link between parents who smoke and children with behavioral problems. Misbehavior increased with the number of cigarettes smoked by a parent. Smoking more than a pack a day increased behavioral problems 1.5 times; smoking less than a pack a day still increased problems 1.4 times. Researchers have several theories to explain this link, but the bottom line is this: TO IMPROVE YOUR CHILD'S BEHAVIOR, GIVE UP YOUR SMOKING HABIT.
    The last sentence (the underlined one) clearly implies a causal relationship between smoking and children's behavior. Explain why a causal relationship is not warranted on the basis of this study.

3. A faculty adviser at a small college worked diligently over the summer to prepare an attractive brochure to give to her advisees when she first met them on campus. The brochure described the various ways the adviser could be helpful to the students, and the adviser hoped that using the brochure would increase the number of students who came in to see her early in the semester. To try to maximize the effectiveness of the brochure, the adviser also worked hard at being especially upbeat and friendly during the first advising meeting with students. Seventy percent of the students who received the brochure came in to see her more than once, as compared with only 35% of the students who came in to see her the previous year (when no brochure was used). The adviser concluded that the brochure had had the desired effect.
    A. What problem with the way the adviser carried out her study would lead you to be hesitant to conclude that the brochure was effective?
    B. On the basis of the problem you have identified, would you be able to conclude that the brochure was not effective? Why or why not?

2

THE RESEARCH PROCESS

INTRODUCTION

As you might imagine, conducting a research project from start to finish involves a great deal of planning and effort. Like any big task, it is best accomplished by first identifying smaller parts of the task and tackling each part in turn. For some, the most difficult aspect of completing a large project is simply getting started. This seems to be especially true for students who are just becoming acquainted with research in psychology and are not sure what research questions to ask. And, although the whole process may seem daunting at this point, by taking small steps, one at a time, you will soon see how a psychological research project is accomplished.

One of the best ways to learn to do research is to follow the path taken by an experienced researcher. In this chapter, and in those that follow, you will go behind the scenes to look at psychological research from the researcher's point of view. We'll first discuss a published research project, and then you'll hear from the researchers themselves as they comment on their ideas, methods, results, and conclusions. These interviews with the researchers also provide insights into their research that did not make it into their published articles. By being "up close and personal," you will quickly learn to appreciate the steps in doing psychological research. Most important, by putting a "face" to the research process, you will recognize this process as something that you, too, can do.

In this chapter we consider how one researcher, Dr. Catherine Haden, conducts her research on mothers' styles of communicating with their children. As you learn about her research, Haden will explain how she developed her research interests and methods of studying mothers and their children. We will use Haden's research project and her comments about the research process to discuss the major steps of doing psychological research.

LEARNING OBJECTIVES

By the end of this chapter you will be familiar with the steps of the research process (see Table 2.1). You will

- *know ways to generate ideas for research, as well as develop hypotheses and operational definitions for your variables;*
- *understand the difference among observational/correlational, experimental, quasi-experimental, and single-case research designs; and*
- *be familiar with the steps involved in evaluating the ethics of a research project, collecting data, analyzing data, and reporting research results.*

INTRODUCTION TO THE RESEARCH EXAMPLE: HOW MOTHERS TALK WITH THEIR CHILDREN

 Imagine members of a family at the dinner table, recounting the day's events. How do they tell their stories? What information do they share? Do others in the family ask questions? Consider your family gatherings at holidays or special events such as weddings.

Table 2.1 Steps of the Research Process

Step	How?
1. Develop a research question.	• Be aware of cultural influences. • Gain personal experiences (e.g., research teams, attend colloquia). • Read psychological literature.
2. Generate a research hypothesis.	• Read psychological theories on your topic. • Consider personal experience, think of exceptions, notice inconsistencies in previous research.
3. Form operational definitions.	• Look to previous research to see how others have defined the same or similar concepts. • Identify the variables you will examine.
4. Choose a research design.	• Decide whether your research question seeks to describe, allow prediction, or identify causal relationships. • Choose observational and correlational designs for description and prediction. • Choose an experimental design for a causal research question. • Choose a quasi-experimental design for a causal research question in settings where experimental control is less feasible. • Choose a single-case design when seeking to understand and treat one individual.
5. Evaluate the ethics.	• Identify the potential risks and benefits of the research and the ways in which participants' welfare will be protected. • Submit a proposal to an ethics review committee.
6. Collect data.	• Identify a sample of participants. • Seek permission from those in authority.
7. Analyze data and form conclusions.	• Get to know the data. • Summarize the data. • Confirm what the data reveal.
8. Report research results.	• Present the findings at a psychology conference. • Submit a written report of the study to a psychology journal.

Perhaps you've spent time with your family retelling stories about shared experiences. As children hear stories from their parents, and share their own memories of special trips to amusement parks or vacations, families develop a shared family history—a special bond that joins family members together.

Dr. Catherine Haden, a developmental psychologist, is interested in how children learn to tell their stories. In particular, she wonders what children learn about family storytelling from their mothers. Mothers spend a great deal of time talking with their children, and it's reasonable to believe that children learn important conversational skills and clues about storytelling from their mothers. Thus, Haden (1998) designed a research study to observe how mothers and children talk about family experiences.

THE RESEARCHER'S POINT OF VIEW

Question to Dr. Haden: How did you become interested in studying how mothers reminisce with their children?

As adults, most of us have few memories for events from before about 3 to 4 years of age—a phenomenon that is referred to as infantile, or childhood, amnesia. And yet, anyone who has spent time with toddlers (and infants!) knows they can remember quite a bit about their experiences over extended periods of time. I became interested in children's memory development from infancy to middle and later childhood. Of course, an obvious difference is that by 3 or 4 years of age, children can access their memories in the same way they have stored them, through language. Because much of young children's memory talk occurs in conversations with their parents, I became interested in exploring how mother-child conversations influence children's abilities to talk about their past.

Dr. Catherine Haden and her daughter, Paige

DEVELOPING IDEAS FOR RESEARCH

Researchers make many decisions before conducting their research project. The first decision, of course, involves answering the question "What should I study?" Psychology provides a great variety of research possibilities to explore, as illustrated by the hundreds of scientific journals that publish the results of psychological research. In this section we will consider several *sources* of ideas for psychological research, including cultural influences, personal experiences in the field of psychology, and psychological literature.

The Cultural Context of Our Ideas

With only a little bit of reflection it's easy to see how our current ideas about behavior and mental processes are greatly different from the ideas held by people in the past. No one thinks anymore that "bumps on the head" reveal our personality, but phrenology did just that, and this idea persisted into the twentieth century. Mental patients are no longer given laxatives to help cure them, but this was a treatment in the nineteenth century. Technological advances have resulted in a wealth of new information about the workings of the brain, and every day we hear about more sophisticated measures of behavior and mental processes. Cognitive neuroscientists, for example, rely on PET (positron emission tomography) scans and MRI (magnetic resonance imaging) to "see" what is going on in the brain. In addition, theories (explanations) about behavior and mental processes are becoming increasingly complex as psychologists describe interactions among biological, social, and psychological factors.

Researchers seeking the causes of schizophrenia, for instance, now look for subtle genetic dispositions and environmental stress factors that might bring on this disease, when only a few decades ago theories suggested that "bad mothers" were the cause.

In addition to these temporal (time-related) characteristics of knowledge, we must also consider the cultural context of our ideas. Just as our ideas about behavior are determined by the era in which we live, our ideas are also determined by the culture in which we live. Indeed, an entire branch of psychology, *cross-cultural psychology,* compares people across cultures. But, we must ask, what is culture? A simple way to define *culture* would be to point to different nationalities. Thus, Spaniards may behave differently than Chinese, Germans, or Mexicans. This definition, however, is too simplistic.

Culture refers to the attitudes, values, beliefs, and behaviors that are shared by a group of people, and that are communicated from one generation to the next (Matsumoto, 1994). With this definition, it's easy to see that various cultures can exist within a nationality. For example, within any nationality are cultures based on gender and ethnic origin. A problem occurs when we attempt to understand the behavior of individuals in a *different* culture through the framework or views of our *own* culture. This potential source of bias is called **ethnocentrism.**

As an example of ethnocentrism, let's consider the controversy concerning theories of moral development. Kohlberg (1981, 1984) identified six stages of moral development that individuals go through as they learn to reason about what is right and wrong. Kohlberg's highest stage, postconventional morality, reflects individuals' self-defined ethical principles and their recognition of individual rights. Research evidence suggests that Kohlberg's theory seems to describe moral development for American and European educated, middle-class males—a culture that emphasizes *individualism*. In contrast, individuals who live in cultures that emphasize *collectivism,* such as communal societies in China or Papua New Guinea, do not show this type of reasoning (Myers, 1998). Collectivist cultures value the well-being of the community. It would be ethnocentric to declare that these individuals are less morally developed, according to Kohlberg's stages, because this would involve interpreting their behavior through an inappropriate cultural lens, or way of understanding moral development (individualism). A similar argument can be made for gender differences in moral reasoning. Gilligan (1982) theorized that women's moral reasoning reflects an "ethic of care" rather than individual rights. Women's focus on relationships can make their responses appear less morally developed when viewed through the lens of Kohlberg's stages of development.

A researcher's culture also can influence the questions he or she thinks are important to study. For example, American culture tends to value youth rather than age. As a result, many of the research questions addressed in gerontology (the study of aging processes) concern the *deficits* that occur with age, such as declining physical strength and memory impairment. Consider the possible research topics if age were *valued,* such as wisdom, self-sacrifice, and maturity. New and seldom-researched topics become available to researchers when they take off their cultural lenses (see Figure 2.1).

Figure 2.1   By removing our cultural lenses, we gain new ideas for research topics that investigate (a) strengths in aging, (b) abilities rather than disabilities, and (c) nurturing fathers and career mothers.

(a)

(b)

(c)
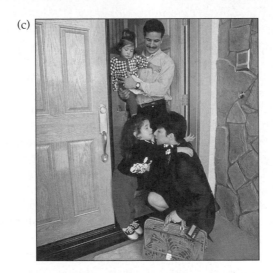

Personal Experiences in Psychology

By now you've probably learned about the breadth of topics considered by psychologists. A quick glance through an introductory psychology textbook will provide an overview of the many topics and research findings in psychology. Also, you've probably gained more specific information about psychology topics in classes offered by the psychology department of your college or university. Psychology topics also receive widespread coverage in the media. All of these sources are potentially fruitful orchards from which you can pick a research topic.

Perhaps one of the best sources for developing research ideas is right under your nose—in your own psychology department. Many students become involved in research through interactions with their psychology instructors. Many professors conduct research and are eager to involve students on research teams. You may need only to ask. Psychology departments also offer many other resources to help students develop research ideas. One opportunity is in the form of "colloquia." A colloquium (plural: colloquia) is a formal research presentation in which researchers, sometimes from other universities, present their theories and research findings to the faculty and students in the department. Watch for announcements of upcoming colloquia in your psychology department.

Searching the Psychological Literature

No matter how or where you begin to develop a research question, you will need to study published reports of psychological research. In fact, searching the psychology literature can provide a wealth of ideas for research. There are several reasons why you must search through the psychology literature before beginning to do research. One obvious reason is that the answer to your research question may already be there. Someone else may have studied the same question and provided an answer, or at least a partial one. It is very likely you will find research findings related to your research question. This should not discourage you; in fact, it should be a source of satisfaction. Learning that other people have done research on the same or a similar idea should let you know you are on the right track and will allow you to build the science of psychology.

Science is a cumulative endeavor: Current research builds on previous research. Having identified relevant studies, a careful reading may reveal inconsistencies or contradictions that provide a starting point for a research project. You may also find that previous research was limited in terms of the nature of the participants studied or the circumstances under which the research was done. On other occasions, you may find a psychological theory in need of testing. Once these discoveries in the literature are made, researchers have a solid research lead, a path to follow. (See McGuire, 1997, for more ideas on how to develop research ideas when reading psychological literature.)

Searching the psychology literature used to be pretty tedious. Now, with computer-aided literature searches, including use of the Internet, identifying related research is a relatively easy and exciting task. PsycLIT is the CD-ROM version of *Psychological Abstracts*. The American Psychological Association has published *Psychological Abstracts* since 1927. The abstracts (summaries) of research reports, taken from more than 1,000 national and international periodicals, are published monthly in the periodical *Psychological Abstracts*. PsycLIT includes *Psychological Abstracts* going back more than 25 years and is updated quarterly. PsycINFO is the online version of PsycLIT. Other online databases that permit electronic searching are *FirstSearch* and *InfoTrac 2000*. You should check with your local library staff to find out what online services are available to you and for help in using these services.

To illustrate the use of electronic databases to search the psychological literature, the following is a description of a computer-assisted search done by an undergraduate student. The student's research idea was to survey students on her campus to determine the incidence of rape and other sexual assault on dates (i.e., "date rape"). She came across a few references to this topic in her general reading in the area of women's studies, and then wanted to make a more systematic search of the psychological literature. A reference librarian helped her make a search of PsycLIT.

The student used a "keyword" search on PsycLIT (see Table 2.2). An electronic database makes it possible to scan the titles and abstracts of articles in the database and to identify all those that contain particular keywords. The most effective approach to this type of search is to have intersecting keywords, both of which must be present before the computer will "flag" an article. For example, the student used the keyword *RAPE* and the letter string *DAT* to guide her search. She chose the letter string *DAT* in order to catch such variants as *DATE*, *DATES*, and *DATING*. This intersection identified 75 references, 73 of which were written in English.

Of course, searching the literature is only the first step. Computerized literature searches will provide the title, authors' names, and journal or book name in which the article appears. It's up to you to retrieve and read the articles *(not just the abstracts)*. Some libraries offer computerized "full-text" databases in which students can retrieve the full article online. Often this is not possible for all journals. At this point, then, you need to go to the periodicals section of your library and read the articles identified in your literature search. As you read the article you will find other studies the author cites that will be relevant to your own research. In the "References" section at the end of the article you will find the

Table 2.2   Conducting a Literature Search

Electronic databases allow users to search using keywords and key phrases, subject words, authors' names, titles of articles or books, and year. The following are sample search terms for a literature search related to Haden's work on childhood memory.

1. Search journal articles by *subject* words using the terms *autobiographical memory and children* between the years 1995 and 1999:

    PsycINFO revealed 10 documents.

2. Search journal articles by *keywords* using the terms *mothers and children and conversations* between the years 1995 and 1999:

    PsycINFO revealed 13 documents (1 also was identified in the first search).

Thus, these two literature searches identified 22 journal articles related to children's memory and mothers' conversations with their children. Haden's reference section at the end of her article identified 49 journal articles, books, chapters, and presentations related to this topic.

---

titles and journals for these sources (so don't omit the "References" section when photocopying an article).

HOW MOTHERS TALK WITH THEIR CHILDREN: THE RESEARCH QUESTION

Haden's work with children began while she was a graduate student at Emory University in Atlanta, Georgia. She worked on a *research team* with her faculty mentor, Dr. Robyn Fivush. Haden read the published *research literature* on how mothers and children reminisce together about past events, but she found very few studies that examined whether mothers talk similarly or differently with their different children. Previous research examined how mothers reminisce with one child. This research showed differences among mothers in how they talk with children. Some mothers are "elaborative" because conversations with their children are long, richly embellished, and collaborative—they ask their children many questions and offer many details about events. In contrast, some mothers are "repetitive." Their conversations tend to be shorter and with few details. Although these mothers also ask questions, they tend to be questions that can be answered with a simple yes or no.

Haden's *research question* asked whether mothers are consistent in how they talk with their children. Thus, if a mother is elaborative with one child, will she also be elaborative with her second child? More generally, Haden asked, do mothers talk similarly with their different children about past family events?

THE RESEARCHER'S POINT OF VIEW

Questions to Dr. Haden: What are your basic research questions?

Much of my work has focused on three questions: (1) How do mothers structure early conversations about the past with their young children? In other words, how can we characterize mothers' reminiscing styles? (2) What impact do mother-child conversations about past events have on children's remembering? (3) How might mother-child conversational interactions as events unfold relate to children's subsequent event recall? Although adult-child discussions as events unfold have not been explored as thoroughly as conversations about past events, it seems likely that talk *during* an event can focus children's attention, increase understanding, and, in turn, influence remembering.

What are the key words you use when searching the psychological literature?

Autobiographical memory, memory development, children's memory, mother-child conversations

FORMING THEORIES, HYPOTHESES, AND OPERATIONAL DEFINITIONS

The next question in the research process is a bit harder: "How do I come up with a *research hypothesis*?" In Chapter 1 we defined a research hypothesis as a tentative explanation for a phenomenon. After researchers develop a research question, the next step is to come up with a potential explanation. Hypotheses are most often based on a *theory* of a phenomenon or behavior of interest, and they are stated in the form of a prediction about the outcome of a research investigation.

Theories

As previously mentioned, theories are ideas about how nature works. Psychologists propose ideas about the nature of behavior and mental processes, as well as about the reasons people (and animals) behave and think the way they do. A psychological theory can be developed using different levels of explanation (e.g., physiological or symbolic levels). For example, a theory of schizophrenia may propose biological causes (e.g., specific genetic carriers), psychological causes (e.g., patterns of emotional conflict, stress), or both.

Theories often differ in their *scope*—the range of the phenomena they seek to explain. Some theories attempt to explain *specific* behaviors or phenomena. For example, Brown and Kulik's (1977) theory attempted to explain "flashbulb memory," in which people remember very specific personal circumstances surrounding a surprising or an emotional event (such as where you were when you learned John Kennedy died) (see Figure 2.2). Other theories explain more *complex* phenomena such as love (Sternberg, 1986) or cognition (Anderson, 1990, 1993). In general, the greater the scope of a theory, the more complex it is likely to be.

Figure 2.2   Do you remember where you were when John Kennedy died?

Psychological theories are often complex because behavior and mental processes are so complex. However, complex theories are very difficult to test. As a result, most theories in contemporary psychology tend to be relatively modest in scope, attempting to explain only a limited range of phenomena.

Whatever its nature and scope, a theory includes certain assumptions and concepts that must be explained before the theory can be understood and tested (see Table 2.3). A theory of flashbulb memory, for instance, must state exactly what a flashbulb memory *is* and how flashbulb memory differs from a typical memory. A complete theory must also explain why in some cases a person's flashbulb memory is clearly wrong, even though the individual is very confident about the memory (Neisser & Harsch, 1992). To be complete, therefore, a **theory** must include definitions of various events or concepts, must contain information about relationships between these events, and must explain the causes of the events.

The major functions of a theory are to *guide* research and to *organize* empirical knowledge (Marx, 1963). A scientific theory guides research by suggesting testable hypotheses. A research **hypothesis,** like a theory, is an explanation for behavior; however, a hypothesis typically is simpler and more tentative than is a scientific theory (Marx, 1963). Researchers empirically test hypotheses to find support for a theory or to disconfirm a theory (Kimble, 1989). Successful tests of a hypothesis increase the acceptability of a theory; unsuccessful tests decrease the theory's acceptability.

How we evaluate and test scientific theories is one of the most difficult issues in psychology and philosophy (e.g., Meehl, 1978, 1990a, 1990b; Popper, 1959). Scientists often first evaluate a theory by considering whether it is logical—does the theory make sense, and are its propositions free of contradictions? Can predictions for behavior be logically deduced from the theory, and can these predictions be tested easily? Scientists also consider the nature of the predictions: Does the theory offer precise predictions about behavior, or are the predictions

Table 2.3 Characteristics of Theories

A theory is a logically organized set of statements that define events (concepts), describe relationships among these events, and explain the occurrence of these events.	
Scope	Theories differ in the breadth of events they seek to explain, from specific phenomena (e.g., flashbulb memory) to complex phenomena (e.g., love).
Functions	A theory organizes empirical knowledge from previous studies and guides future research by suggesting testable hypotheses.
Important features	Good theories are • *Logical.* They make sense and predictions can be logically deduced. • *Precise.* Predictions about behavior are specific rather than general. • *Parsimonious.* The simplest explanation for a phenomenon is best.

very general? For example, a theory that predicts children will typically demonstrate abstract reasoning by age 12 is more precise (and testable) in its predictions than a theory that predicts the development of abstract reasoning by ages 12–20. Finally, an important tool for evaluating theories is the *rule of parsimony* (Marx, 1963). The best theories are parsimonious because they offer the *simplest* explanations for phenomena.

Although theories can be challenging to work with, the process of constructing and evaluating scientific theories is at the core of research in psychology. As researchers continue to develop and refine psychological theories, they gain better understanding of behavior and mental processes.

Hypotheses

In order to test theories, researchers must develop testable hypotheses. In Chapter 1, we saw that testable hypotheses have clearly defined concepts, are not circular, and refer to concepts that can be observed.

One way to generate hypotheses is to consider personal experiences and how you or others may behave in a particular situation. McGuire (1997) suggests that we can develop hypotheses by imagining how we would behave when faced with a specific problem or task, or by making careful observations of individuals in a particular situation. We can extend these personal reflections to include imagining how people need to behave in a situation in order to perform well. Our hypotheses, then, may involve thinking of factors that could influence or improve people's performance in various situations. There are also many ways to "twist" conventional thinking about a phenomenon in order to generate research hypotheses (McGuire, 1997). For example, we can think about "exceptions to the rule" and try to develop explanations for these exceptions. Based on a literature search, we may also identify inconsistencies in previous results; hypotheses may attempt to explain and reconcile these conflicting outcomes.

It's important to recognize the cultural context in which hypotheses are developed. We've already noted that the ideas we have about behavior and mental processes are culture-dependent; that is, we tend to see behavior through the specific lens or filter of our own culture. We must also evaluate our hypotheses for evidence of ethnocentric bias. Our hypotheses may reflect biases if we expect people of different cultures (including different genders and ethnicities) to behave in ways that reflect our own culture. We can develop and test new hypotheses by considering how our thinking is shaped by the particular cultural context in which we live.

Operational Definitions

In order to test hypotheses, researchers must clearly define the concepts they are testing. For example, if we plan to test a hypothesis that "glink" increases during situations of "friss," we certainly would want to know exactly what we mean by "glink" and "friss." The same is true when we test hypotheses about our more usual psychological concepts. Thus, if we were to test a hypothesis about "anxiety" increasing during "stressful situations," we would first have to define exactly what we mean by "anxiety" and "stressful situations." When forming hypotheses, researchers define their concepts using operational definitions.

An **operational definition** defines a concept solely in terms of the "operations" (or methods) used to produce and measure it. We may operationally define "anxiety" more specifically by using a paper-and-pencil questionnaire that asks about symptoms such as worry and heart palpitations. Thus, our operational definition of "anxiety" would be participants' scores on the anxiety questionnaire. We might operationally define "stressful situation" as having to make a speech in front of a large audience. Some people may not like these operational definitions. For example, they may argue that our questionnaire about anxiety doesn't describe the full experience of anxiety because it omits some symptoms. Other may criticize our operational definition of a stressful situation because giving a speech is only one of many types of stressors. From a cross-cultural perspective, this operational definition of a stressful situation may apply to only a small segment of the population, and other stressors may be more relevant to individuals in other cultures. However, once the particular measure or definition is identified for a study, people cannot argue about what the concepts mean *according to this definition* for this study. In this way, operational definitions help researchers communicate about their concepts (see Table 2.4 for examples of operational definitions and hypotheses).

Table 2.4   Examples of Operational Definitions and Hypotheses

Concept	Operational Definition
Memory for details	Participants watch a videotape of a crime and are asked what number was on the boy's football jersey. Memory for details is operationally defined by whether participants correctly identify the number (a measured variable).
Emotionally shocking event	Participants watch either a violent videotape (a boy is shot in the face) or a nonviolent videotape (a boy is not shot). The presence of an emotionally shocking event is operationally defined by the violent and nonviolent conditions (a manipulated variable).

Hypothesis: Individuals who see an emotionally shocking event will have poorer memory for details than individuals who do not see the event (Loftus & Burns, 1982).

Concept	Operational Definition
Well-being	Staff members rate the happiness, alertness, level of activity, and sociability of nursing home residents on rating scales (measured variables).
Personal responsibility	Nursing home residents are assigned to one of two conditions: (1) they are made responsible for making decisions about their care and activities, or (2) they are told that staff members are responsible for making decisions. "Responsibility" is operationally defined by who makes personal decisions for nursing home residents (a manipulated variable).

Hypothesis: Well-being will be greater for nursing home residents who are responsible for personal decisions than for nursing home residents who are not responsible (Langer & Rodin, 1976).

As researchers develop operational definitions, they identify the **variables** they will investigate in their research. Variables are factors that *vary*. For example, people naturally vary in the amount of anxiety they experience. Similarly, some events are more stressful than others; that is, the amount of stress in different situations varies. Researchers work with variables in two ways: They *measure* variables and they *manipulate* (or control) variables (see Figure 2.3). Thus, by using an anxiety questionnaire as an operational definition for anxiety, the researcher *measures* the extent to which anxiety varies in a sample of participants. By *controlling* whether participants make a speech or do not make a speech, the researcher varies whether people experience a stressful situation.

HOW MOTHERS TALK WITH THEIR CHILDREN: THEORIES, HYPOTHESES, AND OPERATIONAL DEFINITIONS

As Haden (1998) developed her research question into a research study, she examined the research literature and theories about how children construct memories for their experiences. Several *theories* guided her work. Labov's (1982) theory of narratives helped her understand linguistic aspects of mothers' and children's stories. This theory emphasizes the interpersonal quality of narratives—people tell stories in ways that can be understood by others. To understand how children develop storytelling skills, Haden also learned Vygotsky's (1978) theory about the "zone of proximal development" and Rogoff's (1990) theory about "guided participation." Both theories emphasize that children develop skills through their social interactions with more skilled partners. These theories describe how adults structure children's performance as they learn the necessary skills to complete tasks such as storytelling. Over time, adults decrease the amount of structure they provide, and children take on more responsibility for completing tasks on their own. These theories provide a context for understanding how mothers use questions and elaborations to help structure their children's stories about past events.

Based on these theories and evidence from previous research, Haden (1998) developed her research *hypotheses*. Prior research indicated that mothers are consistent over

Figure 2.3   Researchers manipulate and measure variables.

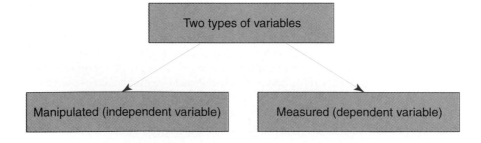

time in how they talk to their children; therefore, she predicted that mothers in her study also would be consistent over a four-week period. Haden also hypothesized that mothers may use different styles with their different children, and change their styles over time as the children get older. This hypothesis was based on the theory that younger children require different amounts of structure than older children.

In order to test her hypotheses, Haden next identified the variables she would study and her *operational definitions.* Although "mother" and "child" might seem pretty easy to define, Haden considered several factors *(variables)* concerning the families in her study, including the gender of the children, whether there were other children in the home, and the different ages of the siblings in her study. Each mother talked to two of her children about family events.

An important aspect of Haden's (1998) study was describing the mothers' styles and the children's responses in their conversations about family events. Haden had to operationally define what she meant by mothers' "elaborative style" and "repetitive style." She recorded all of the conversations and then "coded" all of the comments made by the mothers and children. Coding involved categorizing the mothers' comments into different categories of elaboration or repetition. For example, elaborative memory questions were questions that asked the child to provide a new piece of memory information about an event (e.g., "Who was there?" or "What did we do?"). In contrast, repetitive memory questions were questions that repeated the information provided in a previous question or statement (e.g., the mother asks, "Who was there?" and in her next conversational turn asks again, "Do you remember who was there?"). Haden then counted how frequently mothers used elaborative and repetitive statements and questions to operationally define their style. These counts (or "frequencies") were important *variables* she *measured* in her study.

THE RESEARCHER'S POINT OF VIEW

Questions to Dr. Haden: How did you develop your hypotheses?
My hypotheses were based on the previous literature on mother-child reminiscing and research on whether parents treat (and are perceived to treat) siblings similarly or differently.

Can you describe what the coding process was like?
I adapted a coding system that I had helped develop in my previous research (Reese, Haden, & Fivush, 1993). In this study I wanted to capture the ways in which mothers were elaborating—through different types of questions and statements. I came up with definitions for the different coding categories based on my reading of the transcribed memory conversations.

CHOOSING A RESEARCH DESIGN

A research design is a plan for answering a research question. Psychology researchers typically rely on four main types of research designs: observational and correlational, experimental, quasi-experimental, and single-case designs (see Table 2.5). In this section we will briefly examine these research designs. In

Chapters 4–9, we will examine more fully how researchers use these designs to test their hypotheses and answer their research questions.

Observational and Correlational Research Designs

As described in Chapter 1, two important goals of research in psychology are description and prediction. Researchers seek to describe and predict psychological phenomena when they ask questions such as "What are the primary symptoms of depression?" (descriptive) and "Are personality differences in traits such as introversion-extraversion related to the occurrence of depression?" (predictive). Table 2.6 has more examples of research questions that are descriptive and predictive.

In observational studies researchers attempt to describe fully all aspects of a behavior in a situation. Correlational studies take observations one step further by attempting to find predictive relationships (correlations) among variables that are measured. Observational and correlational studies are combined here because a key feature of these designs is that researchers typically do not attempt to control or manipulate characteristics of the participants or the setting. Thus, these designs are sometimes called *"passive observational studies"* (Kazdin, 1999, p. 14).

When researchers choose observational and correlational research designs they typically first select a sample of research participants and then *observe* and *measure* the variables of interest (as defined by operational definitions). Psychologists can make observations either directly by watching and recording in-

Table 2.5   Four Research Designs

Designs	Characteristics
Observational and correlational designs	Researchers measure variables through observation or surveys to describe and predict behavior.
Experimental designs	Researchers manipulate an independent variable to determine the effect on a measured dependent variable. The goal of experimental designs is to identify the causes of behavior.
Quasi-experimental designs	Researchers manipulate an independent variable and measure a dependent variable, but the setting of the research limits the researcher's control over potential confounding variables.
Single-case designs	Researchers describe, predict, and control variables in order to understand and treat the behavior of one individual.

dividuals' behavior, or indirectly (for example, by checking records of individuals' behavior). Another form of observation occurs when individuals are asked to complete questionnaires or interviews about their behavior; this is called survey research. Researchers "measure" individuals' behavior by assigning numerical values to the observations. For example, we may count the number of different depressive symptoms individuals experience (an operational definition of depression), and we may ask individuals to rate on a numerical scale whether they tend to be shy and withdrawn (introverted) or outgoing and sociable (extraverted). Our observations would allow us to describe the depressive symptoms of introverts and extraverts, and by assessing the relationship between depressive symptoms and introversion/extraversion, we can predict whether introverts or extraverts are more likely to experience depression.

In sum, if your research question seeks to describe and/or predict an aspect of behavior, you should use an observational or correlational research design.

Experimental Designs

Experimental designs are useful for answering research questions about the *causes* of psychological phenomena. To discover the causes of a phenomenon researchers need to maximize the *control* over the variable of interest. Experimental designs differ from passive observational or correlational studies because researchers exert control over variables in an experiment rather than simply measuring individuals' responses as they occur naturally. Table 2.7 has examples of research questions that seek to identify causes.

An example may help clarify what is meant by control. A researcher may ask whether students' perceptions of date rape are influenced by the presence of alcohol in a sexually coercive situation. After a review of previous research, the researcher may form the hypothesis that students are less likely to perceive sexually coercive situations as date rape when alcohol is involved. To test this hypothesis, the researcher could write two scenarios (or "vignettes") to describe a sexually coercive situation. The researcher could *control* the presence and absence of alcohol in the scenario. Thus, the two scenarios would be identical except for one key difference: One scenario would describe that the two individuals had been drinking, and the second would not mention alcohol. This

Table 2.6 Examples of Research Questions Addressed by Observational and Correlational Research Designs

Do mothers talk similarly with their different children about past family events? (Haden, 1998)

Do people notice significant changes in their environment? (Simons & Levin, 1998)

How have college students' values and goals changed over the past four decades? (Astin, Parrott, Korn, & Sax, 1997)

Do people in wealthy countries have a greater sense of well-being than those in poorer countries? (Myers & Diener, 1995)

Table 2.7   Examples of Research Questions Addressed by Experimental Research Designs

Do individuals who write about emotional experiences have better health outcomes than individuals who write about superficial events? (Pennebaker & Francis, 1996)

Do people's moods (e.g., depressed, happy), as manipulated by the experimenter, influence how they perceive other people? (Erber, 1991)

Do people evaluate Black and White candidates for a job differently? (Hass, Katz, Rizzo, Bailey, & Eisenstadt, 1991)

Are people who are physiologically aroused more likely to retaliate following a slight interpersonal harm than are individuals who are not aroused? (Garcia, Zechmeister, & Vas, 2000)

would be the operational definition of the presence of alcohol in the situation. The researcher could *measure* participants' perceptions of date rape by asking them to respond to a question such as "To what extent does this situation represent date rape?" Participants could rate their response on a 1–10 rating scale, with 1 indicating not at all and 10 indicating completely. This would be the operational definition of the concept "perception of date rape." The participants would read one of the two scenarios, and the researcher would measure the participants' responses to this question to determine whether the information about alcohol in the scenarios causes the students in the two groups to differ in their perception of date rape.

This hypothetical study involves two key ingredients of an experiment: an *independent variable* and a *dependent variable*. An independent variable is *controlled*, or manipulated, by the researcher. In this hypothetical experiment, the researcher controls whether alcohol is present or absent in the scenario. Thus, the presence or absence of alcohol varies in the scenario. Researchers *measure* dependent variables to determine the effect of the independent variable. In this experiment the dependent variable is students' perception of date rape. If the ratings for the date rape question differ for the two scenarios, then we can state that the presence or absence of alcohol in a sexually coercive situation causes individuals to perceive date rape differently. The hypothesis would be supported if students in the alcohol scenario were to perceive less date rape (i.e., lower ratings on the rating scale) than students in the no-alcohol scenario.

Experimental designs are the most powerful research designs for identifying cause-and-effect relationships (causal inferences) between variables. *Thus, if your research question seeks to identify the causes of a relationship between variables, you should use an experimental design.*

Quasi-experimental Designs

Sometimes researchers are not able to control all aspects of an experimental situation; this occurs most often when research is conducted in natural settings rather than laboratory settings. When researchers seek to control some aspects of a research study but are not able to control all important aspects, they may

Table 2.8 Examples of Research Questions Addressed by Quasi-experimental Research Designs

Do courses in research methods, compared with developmental psychology, improve students' critical thinking skills? (VanderStoep & Shaughnessy, 1997)

Do exprisoners who receive financial assistance have better employment outcomes than exprisoners who do not receive assistance? (Berk, Boruch, Chambers, Rossi, & Witte, 1987)

Does community service help prevent violence among adolescents? (O'Donnell et al., 1998)

Do warning labels on alcoholic beverages in the United States decrease problem drinking behaviors (relative to Ontario, Canada)? (Greenfield, Graves, & Kaskutas, 1999)

conduct a quasi-experiment. "Quasi" means almost; thus, quasi-experiments are "almost-experiments" because researchers lack the degree of control found in true experiments. Examples of research questions addressed using quasi-experiments are found in Table 2.8.

Suppose a researcher hypothesizes that students who are allowed to choose the type of assignments they complete in a course perform better than students who are not given such control. The independent variable in this experiment is whether students are allowed choice. The dependent variable could be their final grade for the course.

However, you may see that it wouldn't be fair to allow some students in a class to choose their assignments and give other students in the class no choice. Therefore, this researcher may manipulate the independent variable across two different sections of the course. That is, students in one section may be allowed to choose their assignments, and students in another section of the course would be told what assignments they must complete.

Although the researcher controls (manipulates) the independent variable of "choice" in this quasi-experiment, he or she has no control over key aspects of this study. First, the students in the two sections are likely to be different. You may see how this could be true if one section meets at 8:30 A.M. and the other section meets at 1:30 P.M. Students who enroll in the 8:30 section may differ from students who prefer the 1:30 time slot. Furthermore, the time of day may influence participants' performance. Additionally, during the academic term the class discussions may differ in the two sections. As a result, the instructor may cover different material across the two sections; this might also influence a student's final grade.

Quasi-experiments provide some information about variables, but the cause-and-effect relationship between assignment choice and subsequent performance may not be clear at the end of the research. Suppose, for example, that the students who chose their assignments earned better grades than the students who did not. Can we state with confidence that the independent variable, choice, caused this effect on the dependent variable? Researchers who conduct quasi-experiments often face difficult decisions about whether other variables, such as time of day or material covered in the class, could have caused the different outcomes. Despite these problems, however, quasi-experiments are often the best option when we can exert some, but not complete, control over important variables.

In sum, if in your research question you seek to examine the causal effect of an independent variable on a dependent variable but you cannot control other important variables in the research, you should use a quasi-experimental design.

Single-case Designs

In observational, correlational, experimental, and quasi-experimental designs, researchers focus on groups of participants; the goal is to identify "general laws," or how participants behave *on average*. As the name implies, single-case designs focus on the behavior of an individual. Single-case research designs are most often used in the context of clinical psychology, in which the psychologist wishes to describe, predict, understand, and treat the problems faced by a client. Although results may be obtained for only one individual, a successful intervention may suggest this treatment be used with other individuals. Examples of research questions addressed using single-case designs are found in Table 2.9.

Similar to quasi-experimental designs, single-case designs force researchers to deal with many factors that limit their control over key variables. For example, suppose a psychologist seeks to understand and treat the symptoms of a client who reports panic attacks when in crowds. The psychologist's research question might be whether a particular treatment improves the client's symptoms and behavior. The psychologist and client may first observe what the panic behavior is like *without* treatment; this is called *baseline* observation. That is, the psychologist observes behavior as it naturally occurs. Then the psychologist may treat the client with therapy designed to eliminate the panic attacks. Psychologists conclude a treatment is effective if the client's behavior and symptoms improve following treatment. Although it may seem easy to determine a treatment's effectiveness, many alternative explanations can frustrate psychologists' attempts to claim that a treatment has changed individuals' behavior. For example, it's likely that a client seeking treatment may attempt many methods to end the symptoms, such as reading self-help books and

Table 2.9   Examples of Research Questions Addressed by Single-case Research Designs

Does cognitive therapy help alleviate symptoms of guilt in Vietnam veterans? (Kubany, 1997)

Can cognitive-behavioral treatment decrease a woman's compulsive hoarding? (Hartl & Frost, 1999)

Does mild electric shock help autistic and schizophrenic children develop appropriate social responses? (Lovaas, 1993)

What do observations of a 46-year-old man with severe head trauma reveal about brain functioning? (Riddoch & Humphreys, 1992)

talking to friends or pastors. Any of these other "treatments," rather than the psychologist's treatment, may change the client's symptoms. Single-case research designs require that the psychologist control as many aspects of the treatment situation as possible in order to test the effectiveness of the treatment.

To summarize, if your research question seeks to describe, predict, understand, and treat the behavior and mental processes of one individual, you should choose a single-case research design.

HOW MOTHERS TALK WITH THEIR CHILDREN: THE RESEARCH DESIGN

Haden's (1998) study of mothers talking with their children about past events used an *observational design*. Recall that Haden's research question was "Do mothers talk similarly with their different children about past family events?" In order to answer this question, Haden needed to *describe* how mothers talk with their different children. She designed her study so that each mother would talk to two of her children about family events. She "observed" these conversations by tape recording them and then typing exactly what mothers and children said so that their responses could be easily coded. By categorizing mothers' questions and comments as elaborative or repetitive for each child, Haden was able to observe whether mothers talk similarly or differently with their children.

Haden's results indicated that mothers were very consistent in their use of elaborative or repetitive conversation styles with their children. That is, if a mother was elaborative with her older child, she was also elaborative with her younger child. Haden (1998) concluded that "different children growing up in the same family are receiving very similar messages about the forms and the values of sharing past experiences with others" (p. 112).

THE RESEARCHER'S POINT OF VIEW

Question to Dr. Haden: Were you surprised by your findings?
I was really surprised by the degree of consistency demonstrated by the mothers across conversations about past events with their two children. Although the results I found were consistent with previous research, it still seemed possible to me that maternal styles for talking about the past might be more "responsive" than "strategic" [that is, more responsive to the child's level of skills]. But, mothers who were highly elaborative with their older child were similarly elaborative with their younger child. This suggests to me that the differences we see among siblings in their memories for childhood are not likely the result of parents. It seems parents are communicating to their different children very similar values regarding the importance of sharing past experiences with others.

EVALUATING THE ETHICS OF A RESEARCH PROJECT

An evaluation of a study's risks and benefits is a very important step before collecting data; in fact, in most cases a research project cannot begin until the ethics of the project have been reviewed.

Special committees exist at most universities and hospitals for the sole purpose of considering ethical issues associated with each research project, such as
possible risks to research participants, the procedures for gaining participants'
consent, and the protection of participants' welfare. The review committee (and
participants) will want to know how participants' responses will be kept confidential, and how their privacy will be protected. A research project is approved
if the ethics committee decides that the benefits of the study outweigh any risks
to participants and society, and that participants' welfare is protected. Because
the ethical conduct of research is so important, Chapter 3 will be devoted to a
more detailed discussion of ethical issues in psychological research with human
and animal subjects.

How Mothers Talk with Their Children: Ethical Considerations

Before Haden (1998) could conduct her research she needed to submit a research proposal to an ethics committee at her university. This committee evaluated the potential
risks and benefits of the study, as well as whether adequate safeguards were in place to
protect participants from any risks. Although there seems to be little risk associated with
mothers and children talking about family events, the mothers may have been concerned
that their children might reveal potentially embarrassing information about the family.
To protect the participants against risk of embarrassment, Haden and her research assis-
tants ensured the confidentiality of their stories.

THE RESEARCHER'S POINT OF VIEW

*Question to Dr. Haden: Did your Institutional Review Board [ethics committee]
have any concerns about the study?*
One special concern in working with children is informed consent. Each
mother in our study received a verbal and written research description of
the research questions and task, and she gave written consent indicating
that she and her child agreed to participate in the study. In addition, with
children age 3 and older, researchers must obtain the child's consent as
well. In this study, the children gave their verbal assent to participate, with
the interviewer saying to each child, "Hi (child's name), I'm so glad for the
chance to see you today. My job is to visit with boys and girls your age and
their moms. Today I want to listen while you and your mom talk about
some things you have done together. Your mom has picked out several
things she wants to talk with you about while I am here. And she says that
it is okay with her if I listen while you talk. Is that okay with you, too?" At
all times the child's response was respected.

COLLECTING DATA

As you can see, researchers need to make many decisions before beginning to
collect data. After deciding on a hypothesis and choosing a research design,

"THEN, AS YOU CAN SEE, WE GIVE THEM SOME MULTIPLE CHOICE TESTS."

© 1989 by Sidney Harris-'Einstein Simplified'.
Rutgers University Press.

researchers are in a position to collect data. Before collecting data, however, there are a few more things to consider.

Suppose you have chosen a research question and hypothesis, have decided which research design to use, and have defined your variables using operational definitions. The next step is to identify the sample of participants who will provide data for your research. Here again, we can raise the issue of ethnocentrism, as many psychology studies are conducted with samples comprised of predominantly White American college students. As we make choices about who will participate in research, it is important to consider what cultures will be represented. However, caution is in order. Suppose a researcher *does* include members of different cultures (e.g., gender, ethnicity, age, sexual orientation) in the sample of participants. Can we assume that these research participants represent all members of their cultural groups? Probably not. It is very tempting to pat ourselves on the back because our sample includes participants of different cultures and to assert that these cultural groups are now represented in research. However, we must be careful when drawing conclusions about entire groups based on the attitudes, opinions, and behaviors of a few participants in a particular study.

A very common mistake students make is to claim that a sample of research participants has been selected *randomly*. Random selection means that everyone in the population has an equal chance of being included in the study. In fact, a random sample is quite rare, and many research samples are formed based on availability. That is, research participants are usually those who are available and willing to participate.

A great deal of psychological research is conducted with college student samples; this makes sense if you consider the statement about convenience. Many psychology researchers work in psychology departments at colleges and universities, and the individuals who are most conveniently available for research participation are students. Many psychology departments ask students in their introductory psychology courses to participate in research projects as a way to learn about psychology research and earn course credit. If you choose to recruit these college student participants, you must follow the guidelines developed by your psychology department.

Often, however, researchers recruit special samples of research participants to answer their research questions. This is especially true for applied research in natural settings. For example, researchers may wish to recruit children and their parents from local schools, employees at a nearby corporation, or patients at a hospital. Before asking individuals in these settings to participate, researchers usually must first gain permission to conduct their study in the particular institution or organization. In order to gain permission, researchers can expect to explain to authorities at the setting the study's rationale and procedures, as well as the ways in which the participants will be protected from any risks.

Finally, as researchers collect data, it is imperative that they treat research participants with utmost respect. In many cases, the participants are doing the researchers a favor by volunteering to participate. Researchers must behave professionally and ethically—they are representing the science of psychology.

How Mothers Talk with Their Children: Data Collection

Haden (1998) recruited participants through county birth records and newspaper advertisements. Her final sample included 24 mothers with 1 child approximately 5½ years old and 1 child approximately 3 years old. Participants in her sample "were White, middle-class, two-parent families in which the mothers were the primary caregivers" and highly educated (p. 101). Haden cautioned about using her findings to describe the storytelling within families of different cultural groups (p. 112). Research is needed that extends the understanding of family storytelling to other cultural groups.

Haden's (1998) data collection involved a great deal of effort. She and another researcher made four visits to the participants' homes. Each family was involved in the project for an average of six weeks. The mothers talked about past events with each of their two children separately, twice with each child. All of the conversations were audiotaped and then transcribed. That didn't end data collection, however. The final step in data collection was to code each of the mothers' and children's comments into the elaborative and repetitive categories. Haden had approximately 24 hours of tape-recorded conversations between mothers and their children. Each hour required approximately six hours to transcribe and code. As you can see, data collection for a study can involve a great deal of effort.

THE RESEARCHER'S POINT OF VIEW

Question to Dr. Haden: How did you obtain your sample of participants? Were there any particular challenges?

I placed an advertisement in an Atlanta newspaper to recruit my sample. I was looking for families who had on the one hand two *same-sex*, preschool-aged children, and on the other, had time to participate in research! So, although the response to the ad was good, I did struggle to "find" those last few families who met my sample criteria.

All of the visits were conducted in the families' homes, and although some of the families lived within a 10-mile radius of the university, as it turned out, over half of the families lived well outside "the Perimeter." There were many days I put over 100 miles on my car to do one visit with a family. And one family had to jump-start my car after a session! Driving issues aside, the opportunity to study children's everyday memory for personally experienced events in their "everyday" environment added to the external validity of the work.

ANALYZING DATA AND FORMING CONCLUSIONS

Imagine we have asked 200 individuals to complete a 50-item survey. What are we going to do with these *10,000* responses (called *data*)? The next step in a research project is *data analysis,* in which we summarize individuals' responses and determine whether the data support a claim about mental processes and behavior (Abelson, 1995). There are three distinct stages of data analysis:

1. *Get to know the data.* In the first stage we want to become familiar with the data. We inspect the data carefully, get a feel for it, and even, as some have said, "make friends" with it (Hoaglin, Mosteller, & Tukey, 1991, p. 42). Visual displays of the distribution of numbers provide a sense of what the responses are like. We also want to see if there are any errors in the data and whether the data make sense (Abelson, 1995). Only when we have become familiar with the general features of the data, have checked for errors, and have assured ourselves that the data make sense should we proceed to the second stage.

2. *Summarize the data.* In the second stage we summarize the data in a meaningful way. Descriptive statistics, such as measures of central tendency (e.g., mean) and variability (e.g., standard deviation) are important at this stage. Our summaries of the data tell us what happened in the study. We can see trends and patterns in the data. When the data are appropriately summarized, we are ready to move to the confirmation stage.

3. *Confirm what the data reveal.* In the third stage we decide what the data tell us about behavior, and we decide whether the data confirm our tentative claim (research hypothesis). At this stage we may use various statistical techniques to test whether our results are simply "due to chance."

Today, most researchers have access to computers and software to analyze data. In order to conduct statistical analyses using computer software, researchers need two types of knowledge. First, they must have a good knowledge of research design and statistics. Second, they must be familiar with the requirements and capabilities of the statistical software package. Although a computer will quickly and efficiently perform the computations necessary for obtaining statistical results, researchers must be able to interpret the output showing the results of the analysis.

In order to make a convincing argument for a claim about behavior we need to do more than simply analyze the data. A good argument requires a good story. A trial attorney, in order to win a case, not only points out the facts of the case to the jury, but also weaves those facts into a coherent and logical story. If the evidence points to the butler, then we want to know "why" the butler (and not the cook) might have done it. Consequently, after we complete our data analysis, the next step is to construct a coherent story that explains our findings and justifies our conclusions.

How Mothers Talk with Their Children: The Data Analysis

 In her research report, Haden (1998) described many data analyses. In addition to first checking her data, Haden conducted many types of statistical procedures using computer software in order to describe fully how mothers talk with their children about family events. These descriptive statistics provided information that allowed her to answer (tentatively) her research question "Do mothers talk similarly with their different children about past family events?" Haden's descriptive statistics revealed that mothers talk similarly with each child about events. Additional statistical procedures allowed her to confirm that these were reliable findings, and she was confident that her data provided a trustworthy answer to her research question.

REPORTING RESEARCH RESULTS

Many psychologists and psychology students belong to professional organizations such as the American Psychological Association (APA), American Psychological Society (APS), regional associations (e.g., Midwestern Psychological Association), and associations organized around special research interests (e.g., Society for Psychopathology Research, Psychonomic Society). These organizations sponsor annual conferences for their members and students. These meetings typically last a few days, and provide an opportunity for researchers to present their latest research findings and to talk to others about research ideas. Conferences are one of the best ways to learn about what's "hot" in psychology, and they represent psychology's way of networking. Attending conferences is an important way for students to become familiar with the investigators and ideas at the forefront of psychology. Across the country there also are many research conferences, specifically for undergraduates, sponsored by various colleges and universities. Watch for notices on your department bulletin board!

In addition to conference presentations, researchers communicate their research findings by publishing reports of their studies in scientific periodicals (journals). Publishing the results of a scientific investigation can be very challenging, especially if the researcher wishes to publish in one of the more prestigious scientific journals (see Table 2.10). Journals sponsored by the APA, such as the *Journal of Abnormal Psychology, Journal of Educational Psychology, Journal of Experimental Psychology: Learning, Memory, and Cognition,* and *Psychological Review,* can have rejection rates as high as 80 percent (American Psychological Association, 1998). This means that for every 10 research manuscripts submitted to a journal, only 2 will be selected for publication.

Table 2.10 Journals Published by the American Psychological Association

American Psychologist	Journal of Experimental Psychology: Human Perception and Performance
Behavioral Neuroscience	
Developmental Psychology	Journal of Experimental Psychology: Learning, Memory, and Cognition
Experimental and Clinical Psychopharmacology	
Health Psychology	Journal of Family Psychology
Journal of Abnormal Psychology	Journal of Personality and Social Psychology
Journal of Applied Psychology	Neuropsychology
Journal of Comparative Psychology	Professional Psychology: Research and Practice
Journal of Consulting and Clinical Psychology	Psychological Assessment
Journal of Counseling Psychology	Psychological Bulletin
Journal of Educational Psychology	Psychological Methods
Journal of Experimental Psychology: Animal Behavior Processes	Psychological Review
	Psychology and Aging
Journal of Experimental Psychology: Applied	Psychology, Public Policy and Law
Journal of Experimental Psychology: General	

In order to submit their research for publication, investigators must prepare written reports that follow specific guidelines (see Appendix B), and their research must be free of methodological flaws and appropriate for the particular journal to which the manuscript is submitted. Journal editors must decide whether the study makes a significant contribution to scientific progress in psychology. They usually make their decision based on comments made by experts in the field, a process known as *peer review*. Although the process of submission, review, and eventual publication of a research report usually takes many months (often years), the rewards are great. The most satisfying culmination of a research project is to communicate the findings in a peer-reviewed journal. In this way, researchers make a contribution to the ongoing science of psychology.

HOW MOTHERS TALK WITH THEIR CHILDREN: PUBLISHING THE RESULTS

Haden's study of mothers' conversations with their children was published in a prominent psychology *journal* published by the American Psychological Association, *Developmental Psychology*. The research project was her dissertation research at Emory University; thus, when she completed the project and her other program requirements she was awarded a doctorate (Ph.D.) in developmental psychology. Haden also presented portions of her research at professional *conferences* such as the annual meetings of the Society for Research in Child Development and the Society for Applied Research in Memory and Cognition.

Publishing a report of psychological research can take a long time. Haden first submitted her manuscript in May 1996. After several months, during which the editor and experts reviewed the paper, they asked her to revise and resubmit the manuscript. These revisions took time, and Haden resubmitted the manuscript in July 1997. These revisions satisfied the journal editor's requirements, and the paper was accepted for publication at that time. It takes additional time for the manuscript to be printed—Haden's article appeared in the January 1998 issue of *Developmental Psychology*, approximately 18 months after first submitting the research report, and more than 3 years since beginning her research project.

THE RESEARCHER'S POINT OF VIEW

Questions to Dr. Haden: You've also obtained a research grant to continue your research. Can you describe the grant and the research you are doing now?

I have recently received funding from the National Institutes of Health for a longitudinal study to track changes in children's memory from 18 to 72 months of age. During this period children move through three key transitions in their abilities to remember: (1) the early nonverbal expression of memory, as in a child's imitation of actions he or she has seen an adult perform some time earlier; (2) the shift in use of language to talk about past experiences; and (3) the development of strategies to deliberately memorize sets of materials in preparation for future tests of remembering. One reason this work is important is that most of the previous studies of children's memory are cross-sectional studies [these examine different age groups, but do not examine changes over time within a group of children]. Longitudinal research is needed to address research questions about the developmental course of memory within individual children. We are also doing a "training study" in which we instruct mothers to use an elaborative style and then look at the impact of this on children's remembering. This is an effort to make causal statements about the link between maternal style and children's memory performance.

Has your research influenced the conversations you have with your daughter?

My daughter Paige is 18 months old, so she is the same age as the youngest children in the longitudinal study I am preparing to start. Fortunately, she is a willing "pilot subject," as we work to develop several tasks to tap children's abilities to nonverbally imitate sequences of actions they had been previously shown. Also, as Paige gains skills for talking about people, objects, and actions, I find myself prompting her to "tell me more." I ask her a lot of questions intended to elicit her response ("What was that big brown animal you saw today? *Vs.* "Did we see a reindeer today at the tree farm?"), and I try to help her link things in the present environment to things she has experienced previously or knows well ("That reindeer has antlers on its head just like your friend Antlers [her bright green stuffed reindeer] at home"). I try to construct stories about her experiences, to create a context that makes things more memorable. I know that my behavior is guided by the work I have done with somewhat older children showing the important role that parents play in memory development.

READ MORE ABOUT IT

You can read more about Dr. Haden's research on children's memory development in the following two journal articles:

Haden, C. A. (1998). Reminiscing with different children: Relating maternal stylistic consistency and sibling similarity in talk about the past. *Developmental Psychology, 34,* 99–114.

Haden, C.A., Haine, R. A., & Fivush, R. (1997). Developing narrative structure in parent-child reminiscing across the preschool years. *Developmental Psychology, 33,* 295–307.

Consult these books to learn more about the theories Dr. Haden used to form her hypotheses:

Labov, I. (1982). Speech actions and reaction in personal narrative. In D. Tannen (Ed.), *Analyzing discourse: Text and talk* (pp. 219–247). Washington, DC: Georgetown University Press.

Rogoff, B. (1990). *Apprenticeship in thinking: Cognitive development in social context.* New York: Oxford University Press.

Vygotsky, L. S. (1978). *Mind in society: The development of higher psychological processes.* (M. Cole, V. John-Steiner, S. Scribner, & E. Souberman, Trans.). Cambridge, MA: Harvard University Press.

KEY CONCEPTS

ethnocentrism   **operational definition**
theory   **variables**
hypothesis

KEY POINTS TO LEARN

Developing Ideas for Research

- Psychological research occurs in a temporal and cultural context.
- Ethnocentrism occurs when people's views of another culture are biased by the framework or lens of their own culture.
- Ideas for research come from our culture, from our personal experiences, and through searches of the psychological literature.

Forming Theories, Hypotheses, and Operational Definitions

- Theories define events and concepts, describe relationships among events, and explain the occurrence of events.
- Theories guide research and organize empirical knowledge, and they suggest hypotheses for testing.
- Researchers generate hypotheses by using personal experiences and observations, by trying to explain exceptions or inconsistencies in previous research studies, and by applying methods and ways of thinking from other areas.
- An operational definition explains a concept solely in terms of the methods used to produce or measure it.
- Researchers work with variables in two ways: They measure variables and they manipulate variables.

Choosing a Research Design

- Researchers choose from four types of research designs: observational and correlational, experimental, quasi-experimental, and single-case designs.

- Observational and correlational designs are used when research questions seek to describe and/or predict an aspect of behavior.
- Researchers choose experimental research designs when they seek to identify the causes of a relationship between variables.
- Researchers use quasi-experimental designs when their research questions seek to examine causal relationships but they cannot control important variables in the research.
- Single-case research designs help psychologists describe, predict, understand, and treat the behavior and mental processes of an individual.

Evaluating the Ethics of a Research Project

- Research projects often cannot begin until ethical considerations have been evaluated.
- Special committees exist to evaluate the ethics of research projects, including the risks and benefits, individuals' consent to participate, and the ways in which participants' welfare will be protected.

Collecting Data

- Researchers typically identify a sample of individuals to participate in their research, but they must be cautious about using these individuals to represent the population.
- Research samples usually are formed based on convenience; that is, researchers choose people who are available and willing to participate.
- Researchers must follow the guidelines in the setting where they collect their data and must treat research participants with respect.

Analyzing Data and Forming Conclusions

- The three steps of data analysis are getting to know the data, summarizing the data, and confirming what the data reveal.
- Researchers "get to know the data" by checking for errors and making sure the data make sense.
- Descriptive statistics, such as estimates of central tendency (e.g., mean) and variability (e.g., standard deviation), help researchers summarize their data.
- Researchers use statistics to confirm what the data reveal about the research hypothesis; these procedures test whether the results are due to chance.

Reporting Research Results

- Researchers report their findings at psychological conferences and in journals.
- When researchers submit a research manuscript to a journal editor, the peer review process is used to judge the merit of the research.
- When researchers communicate their findings in a peer-reviewed journal they contribute to the science of psychology.

CHECKING THE ESSENTIALS

1. Briefly describe how ethnocentrism influenced the controversy concerning theories of moral development.

2. Identify at least two reasons why we must search the psychological literature before beginning to do research.
3. What are the two major functions of a theory in the research process?
4. Describe how personal experiences can be useful in generating testable hypotheses.
5. What research design should you use if your research question and hypothesis seek to describe or predict an aspect of behavior?
6. For what type of research question should an experimental design be used?
7. What research design should you use if you are seeking to examine a causal relationship between an independent and a dependent variable but you cannot control other important variables in your research?
8. Under what conditions will a special committee that evaluates the ethics of a research project approve that a research project can be done?
9. What two types of knowledge does a researcher need in order to carry out the data analysis of a research project using computer software?
10. Identify three common reasons why journal editors decide to reject a manuscript that has been submitted for possible publication in a psychology journal.

APPLYING YOUR KNOWLEDGE

1. Provide an operational definition for each of the following concepts: *anxiety, gapers' delay, memory, stress, xenophobia.*
2. The concepts in the following pairs have been shown to be related. Identify a testable hypothesis for *why* they might be related.
   stress/smoking behavior   anxiety/test performance
3. In each of the following descriptions of research studies, identify the operational definitions of the independent variable(s) and the dependent variable(s).
   A. A psychologist was interested in the effect of food deprivation on motor activity. She assigned each of 60 rats to one of four conditions differing in the length of time for which the animals were deprived of food: 0 hours, 8 hours, 16 hours, 24 hours. She then measured the amount of time the animals spent in the activity wheel in their cages.
   B. A developmental psychologist was interested in the amount of verbal behavior very young children displayed depending on who else was present. The study he did involved selecting children who were 4 years old. These children were observed in a laboratory setting for a 30-min period. Half of the children were assigned to a condition in which an adult was present with the child during the session. The other half of the children were assigned to a condition in which another young child was present during the session. The psychologist measured the number, duration, and complexity of the verbal utterances of each observed child.
4. For each of the following, identify the research design that best fits the study being described.
   A. A researcher was trying to modify a maladaptive behavior of a severely mentally impaired 8-year-old girl. The maladaptive behavior was spoon banging during mealtime. The researcher was able to show that a specific treatment was effective in eliminating the girl's spoon banging (Horton, 1987).
   B. A team of researchers studied gender differences in need for affiliation. Need for affiliation was measured by observing students entering the college cafeteria and recording whether each student was alone or with other students. Females were significantly more likely than males to be in the presence of another person when

entering the cafeteria. This finding is consistent with a description of females as having a greater need for affiliation (Latané & Bidwell, 1977).

C. A researcher studied the effectiveness of two different approaches that small groups use in making decisions. The researcher randomly assigned 20 groups of two participants to use a cooperative approach and 20 groups of two people to use a competitive approach. The researcher measured the degree of satisfaction with the final decision that each group member reported after the group had reached its final decision. The members of the groups who used the cooperative approach reported more satisfaction than did those who used the competitive approach.

ETHICAL ISSUES IN PSYCHOLOGICAL RESEARCH

INTRODUCTION

When a researcher asks individuals to participate in research or observes individuals without their awareness, a number of ethical issues arise. Will participants be harmed by the research? What are the benefits of the research? How will individuals' privacy be protected? Will information provided by participants be confidential? Consider further the ethical questions that arise when animals are used in research. Perhaps you've seen news reports describing conflicts between researchers and individuals seeking to protect animal rights. Should animals be used in research? What may be considered humane use of animals in research? These are important questions that researchers must address. Table 3.1 outlines major ethical issues in psychological research. However, before we address these issues, we introduce you to the research example for this chapter, a study of false confessions by Dr. Saul Kassin and K. Lee Kiechel.

LEARNING OBJECTIVES

After reading this chapter, you will be able to
- *identify important ethical issues in psychological research,*
- *describe how researchers attempt to behave ethically, and*
- *describe the steps involved in ethical decision making.*

INTRODUCTION TO THE RESEARCH EXAMPLE: FALSE CONFESSIONS

The strongest piece of evidence in a criminal trial is the defendant's confession of guilt (McCormick, 1972, as cited in Kassin, 1997). As you might expect, the likelihood of conviction increases greatly when a defendant confesses to committing the crime. But can we believe these confessions? Is there any reason that someone might *falsely* confess—that is, confess to a crime he or she did not commit?

In fact, there are many documented cases of false confession (see Kassin, 1997, for a review). Why do individuals confess to crimes they did not commit? Kassin suggests that police interrogations often include deception (including false evidence and false witnesses) and coercive techniques. Some individuals may be especially vulnerable to these tactics. For example, individuals who are young, naive, suggestible, anxious, stressed, or sleep deprived; those who lack intelligence; or those who are under the influence of alcohol or other drugs may be more likely to submit a false confession and even *believe* their confession (Kassin, 1997; Kassin & Kiechel, 1996).

Little empirical research has investigated the factors that may cause people to confess to crimes they did not commit. The purpose of Kassin and Kiechel's (1996) experiment was to examine two factors: false evidence and individual vulnerability. In this laboratory study, student participants were asked to complete a "reaction time" task with another student (a "confederate," who actually was working with the experimenter). Each participant was asked to type letters the confederate read aloud. They were told not to hit the "Alt" key on the keyboard because this would cause the program to crash and their data would be lost. The computer was rigged to crash after one minute of typing, and the very distressed experimenter accused the participant of hitting the "Alt" key. All participants correctly denied hitting the "Alt" key at this point.

Some of the participants were in a "vulnerable" condition. They were asked to type letters at a very fast pace (67 letters per minute), compared with participants who were

Table 3.1   Ethical Issues in Psychological Research

Ethical standards	Researchers follow the standards identified in the APA Ethics Code to protect the rights and welfare of research participants.
Institutional Review Boards (IRBs)	Before research can begin, an IRB reviews the ethics of a research project.
Risk/benefit ratio	Investigators may conduct a research project if the benefits are greater than the risks.
Minimal risk	Minimal risk means that the harm or discomfort in a research project is not greater than what may be experienced in everyday life.
Confidentiality	Participants' risk of social injury (e.g., personal information becoming public) is protected by making their responses anonymous or confidential (i.e., by using no identifying information).
Informed consent	Before agreeing to participate in research, individuals learn about the nature of the research task, any risks, and the ways in which their rights will be protected.
Privacy	Research participants have the right to decide how their personal information is communicated to others.
Deception	Some projects may require investigators to withhold information or misinform participants about aspects of the research.
Debriefing	After completing the study, researchers inform participants about the research, remove any harmful effects or misconceptions, and explain any deception.
Use of Animals	Researchers must treat animal subjects humanely and protect their welfare.
Publication credit	Individuals who have made significant contributions to a research project are identified as authors when the findings are communicated.
Plagiarism	Plagiarism occurs when individuals present substantial elements of another's work or ideas as their own.

asked to type at a slower pace (43 letters per minute). Because of the higher stress, Kassin and Kiechel believed these students would be more uncertain about hitting the "Alt" key, and more vulnerable to submitting a false confession.

Kassin and Kiechel also manipulated the presence of false evidence. After participants denied the charge of hitting the "Alt" key, the experimenter turned to the confederate. For half of the participants, the confederate "witnessed" that she had seen the participant hit the "Alt" key; for the remaining participants, she said she had not seen what happened.

Did participants confess to hitting the "Alt" key? Kassin and Kiechel stated that 69% of their 75 participants signed a written confession, 28% told a waiting participant in the reception area (actually, another confederate) that they had "ruined the program," and 9% made up specific details to explain how they could have hit the "Alt" key. The likelihood of confession was especially great for participants working at a fast pace and for whom the confederate had "witnessed" their "mistake": 100% of these participants signed a confession, 65% truly believed they had hit the "Alt" key, and 35% made up details to explain their behavior.

Thus, Kassin and Kiechel (1996) demonstrated that it's quite easy to get people to confess to things they did not do. Simply by presenting false evidence in a stressful situation, participants falsely confessed and most even came to believe in their own guilt. Kassin

and Kiechel note that false evidence and false witnesses are common during police interrogations and accepted in many courts (including the U.S. Supreme Court). Thus, their research challenges our criminal justice system and the ways in which police interrogations
are conducted.

As we discuss ethics in psychological research we will return to Kassin and Kiechel's
(1996) experiment. As you will see, a critical feature of their experiment is that participants were not aware of the true nature of the experiment. We will discuss the risks and
benefits of their experiment, and the procedures they used to minimize potential risks
faced by their participants.

THE RESEARCHERS' POINT OF VIEW

*Question to Dr. Kassin: How did you
become interested in studying false
confessions?*

For many years I had studied the psychology of jury decision making. I was interested primarily in some of the ways
that juries are influenced by their own
personal biases and by factors not in evidence—such as pretrial publicity. In doing this research, I kept noticing that
whenever a trial contained a confession,
even one that was possibly coerced, jurors
almost always voted for conviction. This
fact that confessions are so powerful led
me to become interested in how that evidence was obtained—which took me into
the interrogation room, so to speak.

Dr. Saul Kassin

*Question to Lee Kiechel: How did you
decide to do an honor's thesis under Dr.
Kassin's direction?*

As an undergraduate, I anticipated pur-
suing an advanced degree in psychology
and was well aware of the challenges of
applying to a Ph.D. program. I realized
that I needed to gain research experience
in order to be competitive. During my
junior year I enrolled in Dr. Kassin's Psy-

K. Lee Kiechel

chology and the Law course, and it wasn't long before I was fully en-
grossed in the subject matter. After a week or two of class I introduced
myself to Dr. Kassin and told him of my interest in conducting research.
That semester I worked as a research assistant, which enabled me to interact with study participants for the first time. Then, as part of a class assignment, I helped design and conduct a study regarding false
confessions. The results were unbelievable! Dr. Kassin suggested that I
base my honor's thesis on a more refined version of this study.

ETHICAL STANDARDS

The American Psychological Association (APA) developed its Ethics Code for individuals who conduct research, teach, conduct therapy, or serve as administrators (American Psychological Association, 1992).[1] The Ethics Code presents *standards* to guide ethical behavior. For example, Section 6.09 of the APA Ethics Code describes how researchers must seek approval before beginning their research:

> Psychologists obtain from host institutions or organizations appropriate approval prior to conducting research, and they provide accurate information about their research proposals. They conduct the research in accordance with the approved research protocol.

This standard, and 20 others, inform researchers how to conduct their research in an ethical manner. In addition to the standards for research procedures, the Ethics Code deals with issues such as sexual harassment, fees for psychological services, test construction, classroom teaching, and expert witnesses.

Psychologists are expected to act ethically and to encourage others to act ethically. Psychology students also need to make this commitment, and should become familiar with the Ethics Code and make every effort to live up to its ideals and standards of behavior.

The ethical standards in the APA's Ethics Code tend to be general, and specific situational factors help determine how the standards are applied. Often, more than one ethical standard can be applied to a research situation, and at times the ethical standards may even appear to contradict one another. For example, ethical research requires that human participants be protected from physical injury. However, even ethical research involving drugs or other treatments may potentially harm participants. The Ethics Code also states that the welfare of animal subjects should be protected; however, certain kinds of research involve inflicting pain or other suffering on an animal. Solving these ethical dilemmas is not easy. Thus, researchers must become familiar with the ethical standards and consult with others to solve ethical problems.

In some situations, it is a *legal* requirement that research plans be reviewed by a committee of persons not involved in the research *before the research can begin* (review Section 6.09 above). The 1974 National Research Act requires that institutions, such as colleges and hospitals, form committees to review research sponsored by those institutions. Such committees, referred to as *Institutional Review Boards* (IRBs), review psychological research in order to protect the rights and welfare of human participants (see Table 3.2). An IRB has the authority to approve, disapprove, or require modifications in a research study. Once IRB approval is obtained, the proposed research may begin.

Similarly, in 1985, the U.S. Department of Agriculture and the Public Health Service formulated new guidelines for the care of laboratory animals (Holden, 1987). Every institution doing research with animal subjects is required to have an

---

[1]A copy of the complete APA Ethics Code can be obtained from the APA Order Department, American Psychological Association, 750 First Street, N.E., Washington, DC 20002-4242.

Table 3.2   Institutional Review Boards (IRBs)

According to federal regulations, an Institutional Review Board must meet the following criteria:

   1. It must include at least five members with varying backgrounds and fields of expertise.

   2. It must have at least one member not affiliated with the institution (e.g., someone from the community).

   3. It must include both women and men.

Source: Kimmel (1996).

Institutional Animal Care and Use Committee (IACUC) to protect the welfare of animal subjects. In addition to reviewing research procedures, IACUCs review how researchers maintain appropriate animal living quarters and how researchers train personnel who work directly with the animals.

Nearly every college and university requires that all research conducted at the institution be reviewed by an independent committee. Violation of federal regulations regarding the review of research can stop all research at an institution, lead to the loss of federal funds, and result in large fines (Holden, 1987; Smith, 1977). *Therefore, any individual who wants to do research should consult with the proper authorities, prior to starting research, about the appropriate procedure for institutional review.*

FALSE CONFESSIONS: ETHICAL STANDARDS

 Before Kassin and Kiechel (1996) could conduct their experiment on false confessions they had to seek approval from their university's *Institutional Review Board*. IRB proposals include sections that describe the purpose of the investigation, procedures that will be used to recruit and compensate participants, procedures and tasks participants will complete during the study, risks participants may experience and ways in which individuals will be protected from risk, informed consent procedures, and an evaluation of the risk/benefit ratio. Additionally, when completing an IRB application for approval, investigators are asked to affirm that they are familiar with the ethical guidelines associated with their particular area of study.

THE RESEARCHERS' POINT OF VIEW

 Question to Dr. Kassin: As you indicated in your article, it's very difficult to study processes associated with false confessions using experimental methods. How did you come up with the idea for this study?

I had struggled for a couple of years to come up with an experimental paradigm to study false confessions. The problem was to create a method that was ethical. It would have been easy to stage a situation in which we offer participants money to do well on a test, provide an opportunity to cheat, and then try to get them to confess. But this procedure would mean inducing participants to do something they would later regret and find embarrassing. I was talking about the problem in my Psychology and Law class one day when Lee Kiechel, along with two other students, said they wanted to work on a project related to false confessions. That's when we came up with the idea of creating a situation in which we accuse participants of producing a negative outcome through an act of negligence—without casting them in a negative light.

THE RISK/BENEFIT RATIO

In addition to checking if ethical principles are being followed, an IRB considers the *risk/benefit ratio* for a study. When deciding to do a research study, researchers and members of an IRB rely on a *subjective* evaluation of the costs and benefits both to individual participants and to society. Society and individuals benefit from research when new knowledge is gained and particular treatments improve the human condition. There are also potential costs if research is *not* conducted: New knowledge is not gained and, ultimately, opportunities to improve the human condition are lost. Research can also be costly to individual participants. For example, research participants risk injury when exposed to potentially harmful circumstances. The principal investigator must, of course, be the first one to consider these potential risks and benefits. However, before research may be conducted, the IRB considers the risk/benefit ratio.

The **risk/benefit ratio** asks the question, *is it worth it?* There are no mathematical answers for the risk/benefit ratio. Instead, the IRB asks, *are the benefits greater than the risks?* If the benefits seem to be greater than the risks, the research is approved. However, if the risks outweigh the benefits, the research is not approved.

In determining the risk/benefit ratio, researchers also consider whether valid and interpretable results will be produced. Rosenthal (1994) argues that when research is done poorly and has little scientific value, researchers cannot justify participants' time spent in the study, money spent on the research, and the use of other valuable resources required for the study. *Thus, an investigator has an ethical obligation to do research that meets the highest standards of scientific excellence.*

When there is potential risk, a researcher must make sure there are no alternative, low-risk procedures that could be substituted. The researcher must also be sure that previous research has not already successfully addressed the research question being asked. Without careful prior review of the psychological literature, a researcher might carry out research that has already been done, thus exposing individuals to needless risk.

Determining Risk

Determining whether research participants are "at risk" illustrates the difficulties involved in ethical decision making. Life itself is risky. Commuting to work or school, crossing streets, and riding elevators have an element of risk. Simply showing up for a psychology experiment has some degree of risk. To say that human participants in psychological research can never face any risks would bring all research to a halt. Participants wouldn't even be able to use a car, travel in a bus, or take the elevator to get to the research lab! Decisions about what constitutes risk in research must consider risks that are part of everyday life.

We must also consider the characteristics of the participants. Certain activities might pose serious risk for some individuals but not for others. Running up a flight of stairs may increase the risk of heart attack in an elderly person, but the same task probably would not be risky for most young adults. Similarly, individuals who are exceptionally depressed or anxious might show more severe reactions to certain psychological tasks than would other people. Thus, when considering risk, researchers must consider the specific populations or individuals who are likely to participate in the study.

We often think of risk as the possibility of physical injury. Frequently, however, participants in social science research risk social or psychological injury. For example, if participants' personal information were revealed to others, a potential for social risk such as embarrassment exists. Personal information collected during psychological research may include facts about intelligence; personality traits; and political, social, or religious beliefs. A research participant probably does not want this information revealed to teachers, employers, or peers. Thus, failure to protect the *confidentiality* of a participant's responses may increase the possibility of social injury.

Some psychological studies may induce serious mental or emotional stress in participants. Imagine the stress a participant may experience when smoke enters a room where she is waiting. This smoke may be created by a social psychologist to simulate an emergency. Until the true nature of the smoke is revealed, participants may experience a substantial amount of emotional stress. In addition, simply participating in a psychology experiment is anxiety-provoking for some individuals. For example, after learning a list of nonsense syllables

Everyday life has risks and benefits.

(e.g., *HAP, BEK*), a student participant once said he was sure the researcher now knew a great deal about him! The student assumed the psychologist was interested in discovering his personality by examining the word associations he used when learning the list. In reality, it was a simple memory experiment designed to measure forgetting. Even here, the researcher is responsible for putting the participant's mind at ease and for making sure he left the experiment knowing the true nature of the experiment. *Thus, a researcher is obligated to protect participants from emotional or mental stress, including, when possible, stress that might arise due to participants' misconceptions about the psychological task.*

Minimal Risk

A distinction is sometimes made between a participant who is "at risk" and one who is "at *minimal* risk." **Minimal risk** means that the harm or discomfort participants may experience in the research *is not greater than* what they might experience in their daily lives or during routine physical or psychological tests. As an example of minimal risk, consider the fact that many psychology laboratory experiments involve lengthy paper-and-pencil tests intended to assess various mental abilities. Participants may be asked to complete the tests quickly, and they may receive specific feedback about their performance. Although there is likely to be stress in this situation, the risk of psychological injury is probably no greater than that of being a student. Completing paper-and-pencil tests and receiving feedback is a routine part of a student's life. Therefore, college students would be judged to experience only minimal risk in such experiments.

When the possibility of injury is judged to be more than minimal, individuals are considered to be at risk. When this occurs, more serious obligations fall on the researcher to protect the welfare of such participants.

Dealing with Risk

Even if the potential risk is small, researchers should try to minimize risk and protect participants. For instance, simply by stating at the beginning of a memory experiment that the tasks do not measure intelligence or personality reduces the stress that some participants experience. In order to protect research participants from social injury, data collection should keep participants' responses anonymous by asking individuals not to use their names or any identifying information. When this is not possible, researchers should keep participants' responses confidential by removing any identifying information from their responses during the research task. This situation arises when individuals participate in several sessions of an investigation or when individuals provide their name so they can receive course credit for participating. *Thus, a researcher should obtain information about participants in a manner that does not require individuals to be identified, or the researcher should remove any identifying information.*

Making sure participants' responses are anonymous or confidential can also benefit the researcher if this leads participants to be more honest and open when responding. Participants will be less likely to lie or withhold information if they do not worry about who will have access to their responses. Box 3.1 presents sample research situations. Do you think participants would be at risk in the studies?

Box 3.1

MINIMAL RISK: WHAT DO YOU THINK?

For each of the following research situations, do you think only "minimal risk" (i.e., risk not greater than that of everyday life) is present, or is more than minimal risk present? If more than minimal risk is present, then participants are judged to be at risk. In this case, you might think of safeguards researchers could use to reduce risk. As you do so, you will undoubtedly begin to anticipate some of the ethical issues yet to be discussed in this chapter.

1. College students complete an adjective checklist describing their current mood. The researcher seeks to identify depressed students so that they can be included in a study examining cognitive deficits associated with depression.
2. A psychologist administers a battery of achievement tests to elderly adults in the dayroom at their nursing home. The psychologist seeks to determine if there is a decline in mental functioning with advancing age.
3. Students in a psychology research methods class see another student enter their classroom in the middle of the class period, speak loudly and angrily with the instructor, and then leave. As part of a study of eyewitness behavior, the students are then asked to describe the intruder.
4. A researcher recruits students from introductory psychology classes to participate in a study of the effects of alcohol on cognitive functioning. The experiment requires that some students drink 2 ounces of alcohol (mixed with orange juice) before performing a computer game.

FALSE CONFESSIONS: THE RISK/BENEFIT RATIO

Were there any *risks* to participants and others in the Kassin and Kiechel (1996) study? What were the *benefits* of the study? These are the questions asked when considering the *risk/benefit ratio*.

One risk to some participants in their study was the stress they may have experienced in the fast-pace condition. This, however, may be an example of *minimal risk* because college students often need to complete tasks quickly and under pressure to do well (e.g., on exams). In contrast, all participants in their study were falsely accused and deceived about the true nature of the research. Many of the research participants believed they were guilty of ruining the experiment. This probably caused some participants to be anxious and upset. Was this deception necessary? To answer this question we need to consider also the benefits of the study. Kassin and Kiechel's (1996) study contributed to our understanding of factors that may influence false confessions. These findings have important implications for our criminal justice system. Their careful methods allowed them to make valid interpretations of their findings.

The subjective evaluation of the risk/benefit ratio is difficult. Participants faced risk because of the experimental procedures. Additionally, deceptive research practices can pose a risk to society as individuals learn to be suspicious of psychologists' activities. In contrast, the benefits to society include gaining knowledge about criminal justice practices that may lead to false confessions. Kassin and Kiechel also reported that their participants experienced satisfaction because once they learned the true nature of the research, they believed they contributed to an important study.

How did Kassin and Kiechel (1996) protect their participants from risk? First and most important, they fully *debriefed* participants about the true nature of the experiment and reassured them that they did not "ruin the experiment." Second, all participants' responses were *confidential;* no individual can be identified in the report of their findings. Thus, in considering the risk/benefit ratio and procedures to protect individuals from risk, the IRB at Kassin and Kiechel's university approved their research proposal.

THE RESEARCHERS' POINT OF VIEW

Question to Dr. Kassin: What were the risks in your study?

The risks we were concerned about were that participants would become stressed by the accusation and later be upset about being deceived. Our study was approved, however, because we were very careful to create a situation that did not make participants seem like bad people. We also built into the procedure a complete debriefing in which we told participants all about the study, assured them that they had not damaged the computer, and pointed out why the deception was necessary to study such a potentially important social problem.

INFORMED CONSENT

Successful psychological research depends on the willingness of students, patients, clients, and other members of the community to take part in scientific investigations. In some research, participants are given money or other compensation for their time and effort. Often, people simply volunteer to participate in research with no compensation. In either case, researcher and participant enter into a social contract. The contract may be informal—for example, a verbal agreement may be made. In other circumstances, the contract includes written statements signed by both researcher and participant, and possibly witnesses. As part of this research contract, *a researcher has an ethical responsibility to make clear to the participant what the research entails, including any possible risk to the participant, and to respect the dignity and rights of the individual during the research experience.*

The research participant also has an ethical responsibility to behave in an appropriate manner—for example, by paying attention to instructions and by performing tasks in the manner requested by the researcher. *In other words, lying, cheating, or otherwise fraudulent behavior by research participants violates the scientific integrity of the research situation.*

Ethical research practice requires that research participants be informed of all features of the research that might be expected to influence their willingness to participate. The researcher must respond to any questions individuals have about the research. By doing this, participants can make an *informed* decision about their participation. Participants should also be informed that they are free to withdraw their consent at any time without penalty or prejudice. Consent must be given freely, without undue inducement or pressure. *Written informed consent is absolutely essential when participants are exposed to more than minimal risk.*

Box 3.2

SAMPLE INFORMED CONSENT FORM

[DATE]

I, [NAME OF PARTICIPANT], state that I am over 18 years of age and that I voluntarily agree to partici-pate in a research project conducted by [NAME OF PRINCIPAL INVESTIGATOR, TITLE, INSTITU-TIONAL AFFILIATION]. The research is being conducted in order to [BRIEF DESCRIPTION OF THE GOALS OF THE RESEARCH]. The specific task I will perform requires [DETAILS OF THE RESEARCH TASK, INCLUDING INFORMATION ABOUT THE DURATION OF PARTICIPANT'S INVOLVEMENT. ANY POSSIBLE DISCOMFORT TO PARTICIPANT MUST ALSO BE DESCRIBED].

I acknowledge that [NAME OF PRINCIPAL INVESTIGATOR OR RESEARCH ASSISTANT] has ex-plained the task to me fully; has informed me that I may withdraw from participation at any time with-out prejudice or penalty; has offered to answer any questions that I might have concerning the research procedure; has assured me that any information that I give will be used for research purposes only and will be kept confidential. [PROCEDURE FOR PROTECTING CONFIDENTIALITY OF RESPONSES SHOULD BE EXPLAINED].

I also acknowledge that the benefits derived from, or rewards given for, my participation have been fully explained to me—as well as alternative methods, if available, for earning these rewards—and that I have been promised, upon completion of the research task, a brief description of the role my specific performance plays in this project. [THE EXACT NATURE OF ANY COMMITMENTS MADE BY THE RE-SEARCHER, SUCH AS THE AMOUNT OF MONEY TO BE PAID TO INDIVIDUALS FOR PARTICIPA-TION, SHOULD BE SPECIFIED HERE.]

_____   _____
[Signature of researcher]   [Signature of participant]

Box 3.2 presents a sample informed consent form for use with a normal adult population.

True informed consent cannot be obtained from certain individuals, such as the mentally impaired or emotionally disturbed, young children, and those who have limited ability to understand the nature of research and the possible risks. In these cases, consent must be obtained from the participants' parents or legal guardians. They, too, must be informed fully about the nature of the research, they must be allowed to withdraw consent without any negative consequences, and their con-sent must be given freely without any undue inducement or pressure.

In some situations it is not necessary to obtain informed consent. For exam-ple, informed consent is not required when researchers simply observe individ-uals' behavior in public places and do not identify specific individuals. An investigator, for instance, may gather evidence about race relations on a college campus by observing the frequency of mixed-race vs. unmixed-race groups sit-ting at tables in the college cafeteria. Such student behavior can be considered public, and the method is naturalistic observation (see Chapter 4). However, de-ciding what is public or private is not always easy (see Box 3.3 for examples).

Box 3.3

INFORMED CONSENT: WHAT DO YOU THINK?

Although the APA Code of Ethics suggests that informed consent is not necessarily required in studies involving naturalistic observation of public behavior or "similar research" (see Standard 6.10), deciding what is public is not always easy. Consider the following research scenarios and decide whether you think the participants' informed consent should be required. It may be that you want more information from the researcher. If so, what additional information might you want before deciding? You will see that requiring informed consent can change a research situation dramatically, making it difficult, for example, for a researcher to record behavior under "natural" conditions. Such are the dilemmas of ethical decision making.

1. In a study of the drinking behavior of college students, an undergraduate working for a faculty member attends a fraternity party and records the amount drunk by other students at the party.

2. As part of a study of the gay community, a gay researcher joins a gay baseball team with the goal of recording behaviors of the participants in the context of team competition during the season. (All games are played outdoors and may be watched by the public.)

3. The public bathroom behavior (e.g., flushing, hand washing, littering, graffiti writing, etc.) of men and women is observed by male and female researchers concealed in the stalls of the respective washrooms.

4. A graduate student investigates the cheating behaviors of college students by concealing himself in a projection booth in an auditorium during an exam. From his vantage point, he can see with the aid of binoculars the movements of most students. He records head movements, paper switching, note passing, and other suspicious exam behaviors.

Privacy is the right of individuals to decide how information about them is communicated to others. Diener and Crandall (1978) identify three major dimensions to consider when deciding what information is private: sensitivity of the information, setting, and dissemination of the information. Clearly, some information is sensitive. Individuals interviewed about their sexual practices, religious beliefs, or criminal activities are likely to be very concerned about how their information will be used.

The setting also plays a role in deciding whether behavior is public or private. Some behaviors, such as attending a baseball game, can reasonably be considered public. In public settings, individuals give up a certain degree of privacy. Some behaviors that occur in public settings, however, are not easily classified as public or private. When you ride in your car, use a public bathroom, or enjoy a family picnic in the park, are these behaviors public or private? Decisions about ethical research in these situations depend on the sensitivity of the information being gathered and the manner in which the information will be disseminated. When information is disseminated using statistical averages or proportions, it is unlikely to reveal much about specific individuals' behaviors. In other situations, code systems can be used to protect participants' confidentiality. *Dissemination of sensitive information about individuals or groups without their permission is a serious breach of ethics.*

As in other areas when ethical dilemmas arise, researchers must seek advice from knowledgeable individuals regarding the appropriateness of their procedures. Decisions regarding what is public *vs.* private behavior and procedures for obtaining informed consent should always be made with the goal of protecting the rights of research participants.

FALSE CONFESSIONS: INFORMED CONSENT

Before participating, student volunteers in Kassin and Kiechel's (1996) study signed a *consent form*. This consent form described the typing task students would perform to assess their reaction time. It did not mention anything about false confession, the true purpose of the research. The consent form also stated that participants' responses would be confidential, that participants could withdraw from the study at any time without penalty, and that they would receive extra credit for participating.

Did participants give their *informed consent?* The ethical standard that applies here is that individuals must be provided any information that may influence their willingness to participate. Usually, investigators and IRBs consider what individuals are asked to *do* in the study when considering factors that may influence their willingness to participate. In fact, participants in Kassin and Kiechel's study *did* perform a typing task, as described in the consent form. A serious ethical breach would occur if Kassin and Kiechel had exposed individuals to serious physical or emotional pain during their procedures without the participants' consent.

Kassin and Kiechel (1996) noted that for ethical reasons, participants "were accused merely of an unconscious act of negligence, not of an act involving explicit criminal intent" (p. 127). It could reasonably be argued that accusations of "negligence" are part of many people's everyday lives—for instance, when they forget an appointment or accidentally bump into someone. Thus, by accusing participants of negligence, the researchers sought a compromise between achieving their research goals (i.e., learning more about false confessions) and protecting individuals from undue risk. As you can see, the ethical issues raised in psychological research are not easy to resolve, and compromises that protect both the individual participants and the integrity of the research are necessary.

DECEPTION IN PSYCHOLOGICAL RESEARCH

The most controversial ethical issue related to research is deception. **Deception** can occur when information is withheld from participants or when participants are intentionally misinformed about an aspect of the research. Some people argue that research participants should *never* be deceived because ethical practice requires that the relationship between experimenter and participant be open and honest (e.g., Baumrind, 1985). Deception contradicts the principle of informed consent. Despite the increased attention given to deception in research over the past couple of decades, the use of deception in psychological research has not declined and remains a popular research strategy (Sharpe, Adair, & Roese, 1992). Table 3.3 presents the pros and cons of deception in psychological research.

How is it that deception is still widely used, despite ethical controversies? One reason is that it is impossible to conduct certain kinds of research without

Table 3.3 Pros and Cons of Deception

Pros

- Deception allows researchers to study individuals' natural behavior.
- Deception allows opportunities to investigate behaviors and mental processes not easily studied using nondeceptive methods.

Cons

- Deception contradicts the principle of informed consent.
- The relationship between researcher and participant is not open and honest.
- Frequent use of deception may make individuals suspicious about research and psychology.

withholding information about some aspects of the research. In other situations, it is necessary to misinform participants in order to have them adopt certain attitudes or behaviors. This was true in Kassin and Kiechel's (1996) study of false confession. If participants had known that the procedures were trying to elicit their false confessions, they probably would not have confessed. It is important to remember that although deception is sometimes justified on methodological grounds, deceiving participants for the purpose of getting them to participate in research in which they would not normally take part, or research that involves serious risk, is *always* unethical.

A goal of research is to observe individuals' normal behavior. A basic assumption underlying the use of deception is that sometimes it's necessary to conceal the true nature of an experiment so that participants will behave as they normally would, or so they will act according to the instructions provided by the experimenter. A problem occurs, however, with frequent and casual use of deception (Kelman, 1967). If people believe that researchers often mislead participants, they may expect to be deceived when participating in a psychology experiment. Individuals' suspicions about the research may prevent them from behaving as they normally would. This is exactly the opposite of what researchers hope to achieve.

Therefore, it's important that researchers use deception only in very special circumstances. Deception is justified only when the study is very important, when no other methods for conducting the research are available, and when the deception would not influence individuals' decision to participate (Kelman, 1972). *When deception is used, the researcher must inform participants after the experiment of the reasons for the deception, discuss any misconceptions they may have, and remove any harmful effects of the deception.* One goal of this *debriefing* is to educate the participant about the need for deception in the study. Research on deception in psychological research has shown that, on the average, participants do not appear to react negatively to being deceived (e.g., Christensen, 1988; Epley & Huff, 1998; Kimmel, 1996) and that, although suspiciousness about psychological research may increase, the overall effects seem to be small (see Kimmel, 1998). This seems to be the case in Kassin and Kiechel's (1996) study, as participants reported that the study was meaningful and their own contribution was valuable.

Beginning researchers sometimes believe that unless they tell participants *exactly* what they expect to find (that is, the hypothesis being tested), they are deceiving participants. This is not necessarily the case. Information about the specific hypothesis being tested is often withheld from participants in order not to bias them to behave in a certain way. In most situations, good research procedures include *not* telling participants exactly what the researcher is testing. Of course, *the researcher can never ethically withhold information that might seriously influence a participant's willingness to participate* (APA Ethical Standard 6.15). Debriefing provides an opportunity to inform participants about the specific goals of a study and to educate them about the need to do psychological research.

FALSE CONFESSIONS: DECEPTION

As we've already noted, Kassin and Kiechel (1996) used *deception* in their study of false confessions. Participants were unaware that the other "student" was actually working with the experimenter (called a "confederate"), that they did not hit the "Alt" key, that the confederate lied when providing false evidence against the participant, and that the study was really about false confession.

When evaluating the use of deception, investigators and IRBs consider whether there are *alternative methods* to answer the research question. Could the same study be done without deception? That is, what if Kassin and Kiechel had told participants that the other person was a confederate who would provide false evidence against them? Would they have been able to document evidence for false confessions?

The likely answer to this question is no. If participants had known the whole time that the entire procedure was "rigged," Kassin and Kiechel probably would have learned nothing about false confessions. They used deception so that individuals would behave as they normally would. Could they have used other procedures? One alternative is "naturalistic observation" of actual (or videotaped) interrogations that occur naturally in police settings. In fact, Kassin and his colleagues have conducted many such observations—this is the multimethod approach to conducting research we discuss throughout this book. However, an advantage of using the control technique of manipulation (i.e., the different conditions in their study) is that Kassin and Kiechel were able to state that individual vulnerability and false evidence *caused* individuals to submit false confessions. Obtaining this type of causal evidence is possible only with experimental methods. Thus, the use of deception seemed justified in this study—but remember that this is a subjective decision, and reasonable people disagree about the use of deception in psychological research.

THE RESEARCHERS' POINT OF VIEW

Question to Lee Kiechel: Deception can often be hard on the experimenters. Did you find this to be true in your study?

I served as a confederate (the provider of "incriminating evidence") in this study, and a friend served as the experimenter. The use of deception was hard on us only in that it required considerable stamina and acting ability. Including pilot work, we ran over 100 sessions, each of which lasted well over a half hour. We had to ensure that every participant's experience was exactly the same. This required us to act (and react) in a consistent manner across sessions—our words, gestures, and facial expressions were all scripted. To do this we had to maintain a high energy level, regardless of how we may have felt at the time.

ADDITIONAL RESPONSIBILITIES TO RESEARCH PARTICIPANTS

Over the years, many researchers have fallen into the trap of viewing human participants in research as "objects" from which to obtain data in order to meet their own research goals. Researchers sometimes have considered that their responsibility to participants ends when the final data are collected. A handshake or "thank-you" was frequently all that marked the end of the research session. Participants likely left with unanswered questions about the research situation and with only the vaguest idea of their role in the study. It is important when planning and conducting research to consider how the experience may affect the research participant *after* the research is completed, and to seek ways in which the participant will benefit from participation. These concerns follow directly from the moral principle of respect for individuals.

Earlier we discussed that protecting the confidentiality of a participant's responses benefits both the participant (e.g., by safeguarding him or her from social injury) and the researcher (e.g., by increasing the probability of honest responding). **Debriefing** participants at the end of a research session benefits both participants and researchers (Blanck et al., 1992). As we saw when discussing the use of deception, *debriefing is necessary to remove any harmful effects or misconceptions about participation, and to explain to participants the need for deception. Debriefing also has the important goals of educating participants about the research (rationale, method, results) and leaving them with positive feelings about their participation.* Researchers should provide opportunities for participants to learn more about their particular contribution to the research study and to feel more personally involved in the scientific process.

Debriefing is an opportunity for participants to learn more about research methods in general. Because the educational value of participation in psychological research is used to justify the use of large numbers of volunteers from college introductory psychology classes, researchers testing students have an important obligation to educate participants about psychological research. However, it is unethical to *require* research participation (e.g., as a course requirement). Therefore, psychology departments with a "subject pool" must also offer an alternative experience for students to learn about research in psychology.

Debriefing also helps researchers learn how participants viewed the procedures in the study. A researcher may wish to know whether a particular experimental procedure was perceived by the participant in the way the investigator intended (Blanck et al., 1992). For example, a study of how people respond to failure may include tasks that are impossible to complete. However, if participants don't judge their performance as a failure, the researcher's hypotheses cannot be

---

Box 3.4

SAMPLE QUESTIONS FOR DEBRIEFING

After completing a research project with a participant, the researcher may wish to learn how the participant perceived the procedures. The following general questions will help participants begin to talk about their experiences:

- What did you think about your experience in this research?
- What do you think we are trying to find out?
- Do you have any questions about the experiment—things we might not have explained fully?

These questions may be followed by more specific questions about the procedures.

After recording the participant's responses, the researcher should carefully explain the purpose of the experiment, reasons for any deception, and expected findings, and should provide a way for the participant to contact the researcher.

---

tested. Debriefing allows the investigator to find out how participants perceived their performance on the task.

When trying to learn participants' perceptions of the experiment, researchers shouldn't press them too hard. Research participants generally want to help with the scientific process, and they may fear that they will "ruin" the research if they reveal their guesses about the experiment. Thus, debriefing should be informal and indirect (see Box 3.4). The investigator should use general questions with an open-ended format (e.g., What do you think this study was about?). More specific questions can be used to follow up participants' responses, but these questions should not cue the participant about what responses are expected.

Debriefing also benefits researchers because it can provide clues to the reasons for participants' performance, which may help researchers interpret the results of the study or may provide ideas for another study. Errors in experimental materials such as missing information or ambiguous instructions are sometimes detected during debriefing. As previously mentioned, *debriefing is good for both the participant and the scientist.*

FALSE CONFESSIONS: DEBRIEFING

Because Kassin and Kiechel (1996) used *deception* in their research, it was absolutely essential that they fully *debrief* their research participants. Thus, at the completion of the study they explained to each participant the true nature of the research and why they felt their use of deception was justified. Kassin and Kiechel reported the following about their debriefing:

> Most subjects reacted with a combination of relief (that they had not ruined the experiment), amazement (that their perceptions of their own behavior had been so completely manipulated), and a sense of satisfaction (at having played a meaningful role in an important study). Subjects were also asked not to discuss the experience with other students until all the data were collected. Four subjects reported during debriefing that they were suspicious of the experimental manipulation. Their data were excluded from all analyses. (1996, p. 127)

Thus, it seems that participants in Kassin and Kiechel's study felt good about their participation, despite the deception. Note, too, that Kassin and Kiechel learned some valuable information during the debriefing: They learned that some individuals were suspicious. It's likely these individuals responded differently than the others to the procedures, so their data were not included in the analyses.

THE RESEARCHERS' POINT OF VIEW

Question to Dr. Kassin: How did participants respond to debriefing?
These debriefing sessions told us what was "right" about this study. I think the word participants used most to describe their experience (particularly those who internalized guilt) was *awesome*.

RESEARCH WITH ANIMALS

Each year millions of animals are tested in laboratory investigations aimed at answering a wide range of important questions. New drugs are tested on animals before they are used with humans. Substances introduced into the environment are first given to animals to test their effects. Animals are exposed to diseases so that investigators can observe symptoms and test various cures. New surgical procedures—especially those involving the brain—are often first tried out on animals. In the process, however, many animals are subjected to pain and discomfort, stress and sickness, and death. Although rodents, particularly rats and mice, are the largest group of laboratory animals, researchers use many species, including monkeys, fish, dogs, and cats. Specific animals are chosen because they are good models for human responses. For example, psychologists interested in hearing processes sometimes use chinchillas because their auditory processes are very similar to those of humans.

The use of animals as laboratory subjects has often been taken for granted. In fact, the biblical reference to humans' "dominion" over all lesser creatures is sometimes invoked to justify using animals as laboratory subjects (see, for example, Johnson, 1990; Rollin, 1985). More often, however, research with animal subjects is justified by the need to gain knowledge without putting humans in jeopardy. Most cures, drugs, vaccines, and therapies have been developed through experimentation on animals (Rosenfeld, 1981).

Many questions have been raised about the role of animal subjects in laboratory studies (see, for example, Novak, 1991; Shapiro, 1998; Ulrich, 1991). The most basic question is whether animals should ever be used in scientific investigations. Other questions concern the care and protection of animal subjects. Clearly, according to the APA principles, *the researcher who uses animal subjects in an investigation has an ethical obligation to look out for their welfare and to treat them humanely.* Only individuals qualified to do research and to manage and care for the particular species being used should be allowed to work with animals. When research exposes animals to pain or discomfort, it must be justified by the potential scientific, educational, or applied goals. As noted earlier, animal review committees (IACUCs) are now in place at research facilities receiving funds from the Public

Health Service. These committees determine the adequacy of procedures for controlling pain, carrying out euthanasia, housing animals, and training personnel. IACUCs also determine whether experimental designs are sufficient to gain important new information, and whether the animal model is appropriate or whether nonanimal models could be used (Holden, 1987).

Partly in response to concerns expressed by members of animal-rights groups during the 1980s, investigators must satisfy many federal and state requirements, including inspection of animal facilities by veterinarians from the U.S. Department of Agriculture (see, for example, Landers, 1987a, 1987b). These regulations are often welcomed by members of the scientific community, and many animal researchers belong to groups, such as the APA Committee on Animal Research and Experimentation (CARE), that seek to protect laboratory animals.[2] As with any ethically sensitive issue, however, compromises must be made. For example, until alternatives to animal research can be found, the need to conduct research using animal subjects in order to battle human disease and suffering must be balanced against the need to protect the welfare of animals in laboratory research (see, for example, Goodall, 1987).

REPORTING PSYCHOLOGICAL RESEARCH

As we discussed in Chapter 2, once a psychological investigation is complete, the investigator usually prepares a manuscript to submit to a psychology-related scientific journal. Ethical issues arise when considering publication credit and plagiarism.

Conducting a research study often involves many people. Colleagues offer suggestions about a study's design, graduate and undergraduate students assist an investigator by testing subjects and organizing data, technicians construct specialized equipment, and expert consultants give advice about statistical analyses. When preparing a research manuscript, should all of these people be considered "authors" of the research? *"Publication credit"* refers to the process of identifying as authors those individuals who have made significant contributions to a research project. Because authorship of published scientific studies frequently is used to measure an individual's competence and motivation in a scientific field, *it is important to acknowledge fairly those who have contributed to a project.*

It's not always easy to decide whether an individual should be credited by being an author of a scientific paper or whether an individual's contribution should be acknowledged in a less visible way (such as in a footnote). Also, once authorship is granted, then the order of authors' names must also be decided. "First author" of an article generally indicates a greater contribution than does "second author" (which is greater than third, etc.). Authorship decisions should be based mainly on the scholarly importance of the contribution (e.g., aiding the conceptual aspects of a study), not by the time and energy invested in the study (Bridgewater, Bornstein, & Walkenbach, 1981; Fine & Kurdek, 1993).

[2]CARE has developed a list of specific guidelines to be followed when animal subjects are used in psychological research. A copy of these guidelines can be obtained by writing CARE, c/o Science Directorate, American Psychological Association, 750 First Street, N.E., Washington, DC 20002-4242.

A rather troublesome area of concern, not only for some professionals but frequently for students, is **plagiarism.** Again, the ethical standard seems clear enough: Don't present substantial portions or elements of another's work as your own. But what constitutes "substantial portions or elements," and how does one avoid giving the impression that another person's work is one's own?

Sometimes acts of plagiarism are due to sloppiness (for example, failing to double-check a source). Errors of this kind are still plagiarism; *ignorance and sloppiness are not legitimate excuses.* On other occasions, especially among students, plagiarism can result from failure to use quotation marks around passages taken directly from a source. *Whenever material is taken directly from a source, it must be placed in quotation marks and the source must be properly identified.* It's important to note, too, that when material from a source is *paraphrased,* or put into your own words, you must also cite the source. *The ethical principle is that you must cite the sources of your ideas when you use the exact words and when you paraphrase* (see Table 3.4 for an example of plagiarism and a correct citation).

Plagiarism also occurs when individuals fail to acknowledge secondary sources. A *secondary source* is one that discusses other (original) work. Most textbooks can be considered secondary sources because they describe research done by others. Rather than citing a secondary source, you should try to locate and read the original source. If that's not possible, inform the reader that you did not read the original work (for example, by using the phrase "as cited in . . ." when referring to the original work). This tells the reader you are presenting another person's interpretation of the original material. Again, ignorance

Table 3.4 Example of Plagiarism and Correct Citation

Actual Text (an Example of a Correctly Cited Direct Quote)

"Informed by developments in case law, the police use various methods of interrogation—including the presentation of false evidence (e.g., fake polygraph, fingerprints, or other forensic test results; staged eyewitness identifications), appeals to God and religion, feigned friendship, and the use of prison informants" (Kassin & Kiechel, 1996, p. 125).

Example of Plagiarism (No Citation Accompanying Paraphrased Material)

Research investigations of deceptive interrogation methods to extract confessions are important because police use false evidence (e.g., fake test results) and false witnesses when interrogating suspects. Interrogators also pressure suspects by pretending to be their friends.

Paraphrased Material with Correct Citation

Research investigations of deceptive interrogation methods to extract confessions are important because police use false evidence (e.g., fake test results) and false witnesses when interrogating suspects (Kassin & Kiechel, 1996). Kassin and Kiechel also state that interrogators also pressure suspects by pretending to be their friends.

concerning the proper form of citation is not an acceptable excuse, and on unfortunate occasions researchers—professors as well as students—have seen their careers ruined by accusations of plagiarism.

Mistakes are easily made. For example, what constitutes a "substantial" element of another's thinking? Often, individuals assume that "substantial" refers only to the quantity of words and that sources should be cited when "a lot of words" are used or a large portion of someone's material is paraphrased. However, a key idea or concept, even if it is expressed using a single word or short phrase, may be considered a substantial element. "Substantial" refers to the importance of the idea. A simple rule to follow is this: *If the idea you are presenting is not your own, you must cite the source of the idea.*

FALSE CONFESSIONS: REPORTING PSYCHOLOGICAL RESEARCH

Kassin and Kiechel (1996) reported their findings in the psychology journal, *Psychological Science.* As the two authors for the study, they are credited for making the important scientific contributions reported in the article. The *order* of the two authors' names indicates the nature of their contributions. Lee Kiechel conducted the study as part of her honor's thesis in psychology, and Dr. Saul Kassin was her mentor. Kassin has worked in the area of false confession and psychology of law for many years, and he guided Kiechel in her work. Kassin's scientific contribution to this research project warrants "first" authorship because he contributed the most to the conceptual development, interpretation of the study, and preparation of the manuscript. Note that an experimenter and additional confederate were involved in the procedure. These individuals' contributions, although important for actually running the study, were not part of the *conceptual* development of the research. Therefore, they did not earn *publication credit.*

Kassin and Kiechel (1996) cited 27 *sources* in their article; the full references for their sources can be found in the "References" section at the end of their article. Most often, they *paraphrased* information from their sources. Each time they paraphrased they included a *citation* to the appropriate source. They also used *quotation marks* when using a phrase directly from a source. For example, when citing a U.S. Supreme Court ruling, they used quotation marks around the words *harmless error.* They regarded this concept to be a *substantial element* because it referred to a very important Supreme Court judgment that it is sometimes acceptable for courts to allow coerced confessions to be admitted as evidence against a defendant.

Throughout our discussion of Kassin and Kiechel's research, we cited their research using *paraphrases, direct quotes,* and a *secondary source* (see the first citation in the introduction to this research example for a citation of a secondary source). We also contacted the authors and requested permission to print their responses to our questions about their research. When writing about research, the writer is responsible for making clear to the reader the source of the ideas that are presented.

THE RESEARCHERS' POINT OF VIEW

Question to Lee Kiechel: It's not often that students publish their research in a prominent psychology journal. What was this process like for you?

I graduated within several weeks of completing my honor's thesis. Dr. Kassin then condensed and revised my thesis so that it would be suitable to submit to a journal. When he informed me that it had been accepted for publication, I was thrilled. It wasn't until I was a graduate student, however, that I realized how difficult it actually is to publish a research study. Now I'm even more grateful for the experience.

THINKING CRITICALLY ABOUT ETHICAL ISSUES

Should research participants be placed at risk of serious injury to learn about bystander apathy? Should psychologists use deception to learn about false confessions? Is it acceptable to make animals suffer in order to learn about human drug addiction? These questions require answers; however, you know by now that the answers are not easy. It's often not clear what the "right" answer is or even if there *is* a right answer.

What are the steps to take when making ethical decisions about research? By following a series of steps, researchers can think critically about the ethical issues involved in conducting research. Critical thinking about these issues will help protect the rights and welfare of humans and participants. The following are steps based on reading the ethics literature, and discussions with philosophers involved in ethical decision making.[3]

STEPS FOR ETHICAL DECISION MAKING

1. Find out all the facts of the situation. In other words, determine exactly what is involved in terms of procedure, nature of participants, and so on.
2. Identify the ethical issues that are relevant. An important part of this inquiry will be consulting ethical guidelines that are available, such as the APA Ethics Code, as well as policy statements from various professional organizations. Also, make sure that you are aware of state and federal regulations or laws in this area.
3. Decide what is at stake for all parties involved (participants, researchers, institutions). This will mean taking different viewpoints—for example, by asking what is at stake from a scientific point of view, from society's viewpoint, from the view of participants, and from an overall moral viewpoint.
4. Identify alternative methods or procedures, discussing the consequences of each alternative, including their ethical implications. As part of this discussion, consider the consequences of *not* doing the proposed research. Examine the practical constraints of each alternative.
5. Decide on the action to be taken. Judge the "correctness" of the decision not in terms of whether it makes you feel happy (you may not) but, rather, in

[3]The authors wish to acknowledge the contributions in this section of various members of the Loyola University of Chicago Center for Ethics, especially David Ozar, Mark Waymack, and Patricia Werhane.

terms of the process that was followed. Is it the best that can be done given the circumstances?

DISCUSSION OF THE RESEARCH EXAMPLE: FALSE CONFESSIONS

As you have seen, many ethical issues were involved in Kassin and Kiechel's (1996) study of false confessions. You probably have learned that ethical decision making is not easy. As we described Kassin and Kiechel's research in this chapter we tried to follow the steps for ethical decision making. First we learned the details of their methods (the participants, procedures), paying particular attention to procedures that placed participants at risk or protected participants from risk. We discussed the ethical issues in their study: risk, informed consent, deception, and debriefing. We also identified the stakes involved: the risks and benefits of the study for participants, researchers, and society. We discussed alternative methods, and whether these methods would allow the researchers to gain the same information with less risk.

If you were a member of the IRB that evaluated their proposal, would you have approved the research? Would you have required any modifications to their procedures?

THE RESEARCHERS' POINT OF VIEW

Questions to Dr. Kassin: Were you surprised by any of the findings?
I was shocked by our results. I was not surprised that so many participants signed a confession. This simply indicated that we had created a situation, as police often do, where the immediate benefits of confessing, such as terminating an unpleasant experience, outweighed the long-term negative costs. What was most surprising was the number of participants who came to internalize their guilt. These, after all, were bright college students—not highly suggestible, and not under the kinds of stress typical of suspects who are badgered for hours in an isolated interrogation room.
In retrospect, is there anything you would have done differently in this experiment?
If I could re-do one aspect of this study it would have been to ensure that we videotaped the sessions. On paper, the results are impressive. Up close and personal, they have impact.
What most would you like people to learn from this study?
More than anything, I'd like people to learn that each and every one of us is vulnerable to manipulation by social pressure, more so than we realize. Many people think they could never be induced to confess to a crime they did not commit. I want this study to plant a seed of doubt and to show that it is possible, at least in a small way.
Are you conducting any follow-up studies?
Currently, my students and I are testing the troubling proposition that when the police believe someone is guilty, they conduct more coercive interrogations, cause the person to behave more defensively, and in a way procure support for the conclusion that the suspect is guilty.

Question to Lee Kiechel: What did you learn about conducting psychological research while completing your honor's thesis?

I cannot even begin to describe all the things I learned while completing my honor's thesis. I definitely gained a true appreciation of all the work that goes into conducting a laboratory study. Conceiving an appropriate experimental design is just the beginning. I also learned how to standardize data collection procedures, conduct appropriate statistical analyses, and write an American Psychological Association (APA)–style paper.

Question to Lee Kiechel: What are you doing now?

I am currently enrolled in a Ph.D. program in Industrial/Organizational Psychology at George Mason University (Fairfax, Virginia).

READ MORE ABOUT IT

You can read about Kassin and Kiechel's research in the following article:

Kassin, S. A., & Kiechel, K. L. (1996). The social psychology of false confessions: Compliance, internalization, and confabulation. *Psychological Science, 7,* 125–128.

Information about additional research on false confession can be found in Dr. Kassin's review article:

Kassin, S. A. (1997). The psychology of confession evidence. *American Psychologist, 52,* 221–233.

Information about how prosecutors use confession evidence may be found in the following book:

McCormick, C. T. (1972). *Handbook of the law of evidence* (2nd ed.), St. Paul, MN: West.

If you would like to learn more about the growing area of psychology of law, you may wish to consider reading:

Wrightsman, L., Nietzel, M., & Fortune, W. (1998). *Psychology and the legal system* (4th ed.). Pacific Grove, CA: Brooks/Cole.

KEY CONCEPTS

risk/benefit ratio

minimal risk

informed consent

privacy

deception

debriefing

plagiarism

KEY POINTS TO LEARN

Ethical Standards

- Research projects must be reviewed to determine if they meet ethical standards.

The Risk-Benefit Ratio

- A subjective evaluation of the risks and benefits of a research project determines whether the research should be conducted.

- Potential risks in psychological research include the risk of physical, social, and psychological injury.
- Risks must be evaluated in terms of potential participants' capabilities, everyday activities, and physical and mental health.
- When a research study involves procedures or activities that are similar to those experienced by participants in their everyday life, the study is described as having minimal risk.
- Whether at risk or at minimal risk, research participants must be protected. More safeguards are needed as risks become greater.
- To protect participants from social risks, the information they provide should be anonymous, or, if that is not possible, their information should be kept confidential.

Informed Consent

- Researchers and participants enter into a social contract, often using an informed consent procedure.
- Researchers are ethically obligated to describe the research procedures clearly, identify any potential risks that might influence individuals' willingness to participate, and answer any questions participants have about the research.
- Research participants are ethically obligated to behave appropriately during the research by not lying, cheating, or engaging in other fraudulent behavior.

Deception in Psychological Research

- Deception in psychological research occurs when researchers withhold information or intentionally misinform participants about the research.
- By its nature, deception may seem to violate the ethical principle of informed consent, yet it is a widely used research strategy.

Additional Responsibilities to Research Participants

- Researchers are ethically obligated to seek ways to benefit participants even after the research is completed—for example, by using debriefing procedures.

Research with Animals

- Animals are used in research to gain knowledge that will benefit humans—for example, by helping cure diseases.
- Researchers are ethically obligated to protect the welfare of research animals.
- The use of animals in research is widely debated and involves complex issues.

Reporting Psychological Research

- Investigators attempt to communicate their research findings in peer-reviewed scientific journals, and the APA Code of Ethics provides guidelines for this process.
- Decisions about who should receive publication credit are based on the scholarly importance of contributions.
- The ethical reporting of research requires recognition of the work of others, using proper citations and references; failure to do so may result in plagiarism.

Thinking Critically about Ethical Issues
- Because ethical dilemmas may have no right or wrong answers, individuals need to follow guidelines for ethical decision making.

CHECKING THE ESSENTIALS

1. When should a researcher consult with the proper authorities about the appropriate procedure for institutional review of a research project?
2. What role does the risk/benefit ratio play when an Institutional Review Board (IRB) considers a research proposal?
3. Describe how researchers should treat the information obtained from participants in their research in order to protect the participants from social injury.
4. Under what conditions is it absolutely essential to obtain written informed consent from the participants in a research study?
5. Identify and briefly describe the three major dimensions that researchers should consider in deciding what information is private.
6. What three elements should be included in the debriefing that follows a research study in which deception has been used?
7. Under what conditions is it *always* unethical to deceive research participants?
8. Explain how the use of debriefing is beneficial for both the participant and the researcher.
9. According to APA ethical principles, what two responsibilities do researchers have when they test animal subjects in their research?
10. Indicate how material taken directly from a source should be identified in a research report and indicate how material that is paraphrased from a source should be presented.

APPLYING YOUR KNOWLEDGE

Assume you are a member of an Institutional Review Board (IRB). Besides you, the committee includes a clinical psychologist, a social psychologist, a social worker, a philosopher, a Protestant minister, a history professor, and a respected business executive in the community. The following is a summary of a research proposal that has been submitted to the IRB for review. (An actual research proposal submitted to an IRB would include more details than presented here.) After reading the proposal, you are to respond to each of the five steps for ethical decision making, which are presented following the proposal.

Proposed Research

Psychological conformity occurs when people accept the opinions or judgments of others in the absence of significant reasons to do so or in the face of evidence to the contrary. Previous research has investigated the conditions under which conformity is likely to occur and has shown, for example, that conformity increases when people anticipate unpleasant events (e.g., shock) and when the pressure to conform comes from individuals with whom the individuals identify. The proposed research examines psychological conformity in the context of discussions about alcohol consumption among teenage students. The goal of the research is to identify factors that contribute to students' willingness to attend social events where alcohol is served to minors and to allow obviously intoxicated persons to drive an automobile. This research seeks to investigate conformity in a natural setting and in circumstances where unpleasant events (e.g., legal penalties, school suspension, injury, or even death) can be avoided by not conforming to peer pressure.

Method

The research will involve 36 high school students between the ages of 16 and 18 who have volunteered to participate in a research project investigating "beliefs and attitudes of today's high school students." Participants will be assigned to four-person discussion groups. Each person in the group will be given the same 20 questions to answer; however, they will be asked to discuss each question with members of the group before writing down their answers. Four of the 20 questions deal with alcohol consumption by teenagers and with possible actions that might be taken to reduce teenage drinking and driving. One member of the group will be appointed discussion leader by the principal investigator. Unknown to the participants, they will be assigned randomly to one of three groups. In each group, there will be either zero, one, or two students who are actually working for the principal investigator. Each of these confederates has received prior instructions from the investigator regarding what to say during the group discussion of the critical questions about teenage drinking. Specifically, confederates have been asked to follow a script. The script presents the argument that most people who reach the legal driving age (16) and all individuals who are old enough (18) to vote in national elections and serve in the armed forces are old enough to make their own decisions about drinking alcohol. The script goes on to argue that it is up to each individual to make this decision about drinking alcohol and that other individuals do not have the right to intervene if someone under the legal age chooses to drink alcohol. Each of the confederates "admits" to drinking alcohol on at least two previous occasions. Thus, the experimental manipulation involves either zero, one, or two persons in the four-person groups suggesting they do not believe students have a responsibility to avoid situations where alcohol is served to minors or to intervene when someone chooses to drink and drive. The effect of this argument on the written answers given by the actual participants in this experiment will be evaluated. The researchers plan to make tape recordings of the sessions without participants' knowledge, and the contents of these tapes will be analyzed. Following the experiment, the nature of the deception and the reasons for making the tape recordings of the discussions will be explained to the participants.

Steps for Ethical Decision Making

1. Find out all the facts of the situation.
2. Identify ethical issues that are relevant.
3. Decide what is at stake for all parties involved (participants, researchers, institutions, society).
4. Identify alternative methods or procedures, discussing the consequences of each alternative, including their ethical implications.
5. Decide on the action to be taken (approve the proposal, request modifications, or fail to approve the proposal).

4 OBSERVATIONAL RESEARCH

INTRODUCTION

All of us observe behavior every day. At the grocery store, in the classroom, while shopping or taking public transportation, and in our homes, we can learn a lot by observing people's behavior. Scientists, too, rely on their observations to learn about behavior. However, scientific and our "everyday" kind of observation differ in many ways. When we observe casually we may not be aware of factors that bias our observations, and we rarely keep formal records of our observations. Instead, we depend on our memory about an event (and psychologists have observed that memory is not perfect!). Scientific observation, on the other hand, is made under precisely defined conditions, in a systematic and objective manner, and with careful record keeping.

In this chapter, we will examine observational methods used to investigate behavior. We will focus on observation in natural settings, but you should remember that the principles of good observation apply equally well in natural settings and in laboratories. As you will see, the scientist-observer is not always passively recording behavior as it occurs. Researchers sometimes intervene to create special situations for their observations. We'll also look at methods that do not require direct observation of people's behavior. By examining archival records (e.g., marriage licenses and high school yearbooks) and physical traces (e.g., graffiti and textbook underlining), scientists obtain important insights into people's behavior.

The goal of observational methods is to describe behavior. Scientists wish to describe behavior *fully* and as *accurately* as possible. You may have realized a problem, however. It's impossible for scientists to observe *all* of a person's behavior. Unlike *The Truman Show,* a popular 1998 movie in which the title character, Truman Burbank, was filmed 24 hours a day with thousands of cameras, scientists must rely on observing *samples* of people's behavior. But how do we know whether the *sample* accurately describes an individual's *usual* behavior? In this chapter we'll address how scientists select samples of behavior. We'll also explore methods for making observations and recording data, and techniques for analyzing data using quantitative and qualitative approaches. Finally, we'll discuss some problems associated with observations. Throughout this chapter, we will consider an observational study conducted in a natural setting—on a college campus. The investigators of this study, Drs. Daniel Simons and Daniel Levin, observed whether people noticed significant changes in their environment. You may be surprised by what they learned in their observational study.

LEARNING OBJECTIVES

By the end of this chapter you should know how to
- *sample behavior;*
- *identify different types of observational methods; and*
- *record, analyze, and interpret observational data.*

INTRODUCTION TO THE RESEARCH EXAMPLE:
DETECTING CHANGES IN THE REAL WORLD

How tuned-in are you to changes in your environment? Would you notice if someone were to change a lamp in your room (not the lightbulb—the *entire* lamp)? How soon would you notice a friend's new hairstyle? When giving directions to a stranger, would you notice if the person were changed—*replaced* by a different stranger in the middle of your conversation? The last question may seem ludicrous, but this is exactly what Simons and Levin (1998) investigated by observing people's awareness of changes in their environment.

It turns out that people often fail to notice changes in their environment, a phenomenon psychologists call *change blindness*. One explanation for this is that we simply do not pay much attention to some aspects of our environment. In fact, with so much going on around us, it would be *impossible* to pay attention to everything and notice every little change. This may certainly be true for objects that remain in the background—lamps, for instance—but do we also fail to notice changes even when we are paying attention?

In an initial attempt to answer this question Levin and Simons (1997) asked participants in their research lab to watch films in which an actor was replaced by a different person during the film. Even though participants were paying attention to the film, only 13 of the 40 participants noticed the change (Levin & Simons, 1997). Levin and Simons reasoned that noticing changes in our environment must involve more than simply paying attention. However, these researchers also pointed out that people may not notice changes when passively viewing a film. Perhaps to detect changes we need to be more actively involved—more actively processing information from the environment. In addition, when we watch films and television the camera angle jumps around and zooms in and out, making it difficult for us to do the mental comparisons necessary to detect change. Based on their findings using films, Levin and Simons could not answer the question of whether people would notice changes when interacting in the real world. A follow-up study was needed. This is not unusual in science: No single study can answer research questions completely. Instead, scientists often rely on a series of studies to understand a phenomenon fully.

Simons and Levin wanted to learn whether change blindness occurs when people are actively participating in the real world. They designed two observational studies in which they observed whether participants—people walking on a university campus—would notice that the stranger they were talking to was replaced midway through the conversation. As we discuss observational methods in this chapter, we will return to Simons and Levin's research to learn more about observational methods.

THE RESEARCHERS' POINT OF VIEW

Question to Dr. Simons: How did you become interested in studying change blindness?

I had been looking at how we represent different categories of objects (animals, artifacts, etc.) and was interested in seeing how quickly people could code the category. I tried changing the category of objects in a brief animated display and found that people generally missed all the changes I tried, even when they were fairly obvious. After reading recent studies of object representations in infancy, Dan Levin and I wondered whether adults might not be all too different from infants in how they retain information from one view to the next. We also knew that people often miss large continuity errors in motion pictures, and we set out to explore what sorts of information people retain from one view of a scene to the next. Those were the primary motivations that led to our studies of person changes in motion pictures and the real world.

SAMPLING BEHAVIOR

Before conducting an observational study, researchers must make a number of important decisions about when and where observations will be made. In most observational studies the investigator cannot observe all behavior. Only certain behaviors occurring at particular times, in specific settings, and under particular conditions can be observed. In other words, behavior must be *sampled*. This sample is used to *represent* the larger population of all possible behaviors. By choosing settings, times, or conditions for their observations that are representative of a population, researchers can *generalize* their findings to that population. Results can be generalized only to participants, settings, and conditions *similar to* those in the study in which their observations were made. This is the key feature of *representative samples:* They are "like" the larger population of people, settings, and conditions from which they are drawn.

Researchers typically use a combination of time sampling and situation sampling to identify representative samples (see Figure 4.1). In **time sampling,**

Figure 4.1   Sampling behavior.

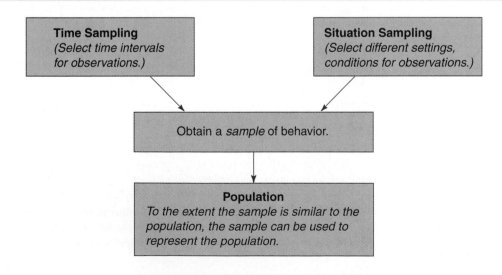

researchers seek representative samples by choosing various time intervals for their observations. Intervals may be selected systematically (e.g., observing the first day of each week), randomly, or both. For example, an observer may schedule observation intervals systematically (for example, every 2 hours), but then choose observation times randomly within the 2-hour time interval. However it is done, the goal of time sampling is to obtain a representative sample of behavior. That is, by sampling at different times, researchers seek to observe a sample of behavior that will represent an organism's usual behavior.

Situation sampling is used when behavior is observed in many different circumstances, locations, and conditions. By sampling various situations, researchers reduce the chance that their observations are unique to the specific circumstances or conditions. For example, animals do not behave the same in zoos as they do in the wild. If we were to observe animals only in zoos, we would not get an accurate description of their behavior. Stated more formally, animals' behavior in zoos may not represent their behavior in the wild. So, if we want to describe animals' behavior more fully and accurately, we should observe them in both situations—the zoo and the wild.

By sampling various situations, observers can also increase the diversity of the subject sample. As part of a naturalistic observation of racial differences in eye contact, LaFrance and Mayo (1976) sampled many situations. Pairs of individuals were observed in college cafeterias, restaurants, and waiting rooms. By observing in many situations, the investigators were more likely to obtain a representative sample of behavior of a diverse sample of individuals.

DETECTING CHANGES IN THE REAL WORLD: SAMPLING BEHAVIOR

Simons and Levin were interested in whether people detect changes when actively involved in their natural environment. To do this, they created an event in which change occurred and then noted whether participants detected the change. The change they created was rather dramatic: A person someone was speaking to "changed into" another person. This was accomplished by having two people carry a door between individuals in a conversation and then (while the door blocked the unsuspecting participant's view) quickly switch individuals. The participants in their study were people who happened to walk near the psychology building on a university campus. The researchers used this location because they had a video camera positioned nearby. In their first study there were 15 participants ranging in age from approximately 20 to 65. Someone working for the researchers approached them and asked for directions. Only individuals walking alone or with one other person (in two instances) were approached. In their second study they approached 12 students who were walking alone. While each participant was giving instructions, the door came through and a different person took the original questioner's place. Later, we'll explore more fully exactly how they pulled off this magic trick.

Simons and Levin sampled the behavior of various people at various times across the two studies. Although their report does not mention their method for selecting the times for observation, their goal in sampling was to ensure that the behavior of the individuals who were sampled could be used to describe the behavior of individuals in general.

THE RESEARCHERS' POINT OF VIEW

Question to Drs. Simons and Levin: How did pedestrians respond to the fact that they were unwittingly in a psychology study?

Dr. Dan Simons

Nobody seemed particularly upset by the event. Most found it interesting. [In the second study] people understood our intentions and most reacted positively.

Did your IRB have any trouble with your project, or did it require any modifications?

When we first ran the study, the IRB had no major objections. In this case, subjects couldn't give prior informed consent. However, the study represented a minimal imposition on their time, and the task they performed was something they would naturally do anyway (giving directions). After they gave directions, we asked them if they would be willing to answer a few questions. At that point, they could decline if they wanted to and we would have no data. The IRB felt that the potential benefits of the study outweighed the relatively minimal costs to subjects.

Dr. Dan Levin

This year they added the additional stipulation that subjects needed to have the option to tell us not to use their data once they had learned the full purpose of the study (because they had not given complete informed consent in advance). Nobody has wanted to do so yet, and most people are interested to hear about the study.

USING OBSERVATIONAL METHODS

Researchers often observe behavior while it occurs—that is, through *direct observation*. However, observations can also be made indirectly, as when researchers examine physical traces or archival records. This is *indirect (unobtrusive) observation*. Figure 4.2 illustrates the organization of observational methods. First we will discuss direct observational methods and then indirect (unobtrusive) methods.

Figure 4.2   Flow diagram of observational methods.

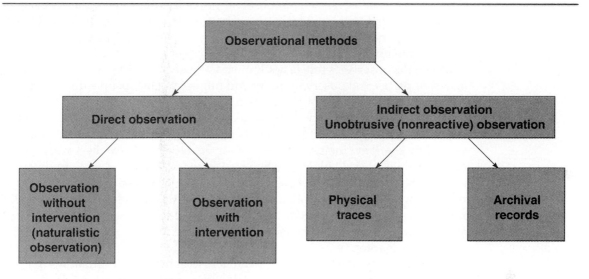

Direct Observational Methods

Observation Without Intervention ("Naturalistic Observation").   Direct observation of behavior in a natural setting, *without* any attempt by the observer to intervene, is frequently called **naturalistic observation.** An observer using this method acts as a passive recorder of what occurs. The events and behaviors occur naturally and are not manipulated or controlled by the observer. The major goals of observation in natural settings are to describe behavior as it ordinarily occurs and to investigate the relationships among variables that are present.

Researchers may choose to use naturalistic observation when moral or ethical considerations prevent them from controlling or manipulating the situation. For example, researchers may be interested in childhood aggression. We would not want researchers to create a situation in which children are intentionally harassed and picked on simply to record their reactions. Naturalistic observation is an appropriate method for studying children's aggression. As anyone knows who has observed children, there is plenty of naturally occurring aggression!

Observation with Intervention.   Let's face it. Scientists like to "tamper" with nature. They like to intervene and observe the effects. Intervention rather than nonintervention characterizes most psychological research. Three important methods of observation with intervention are participant observation, structured observation, and the field experiment.

In **participant observation,** observers play a dual role: They observe people's behavior *and* participate in a natural setting. You are familiar with participant observers in the classroom. Teachers are active participants in the classroom, but they also observe their students' behavior (e.g., students' responses to questions). In *undisguised* participant observation, individuals know the observer is recording their behavior. This method is used frequently by anthropologists who seek to understand the culture and behavior of groups by living and working with members of the group.

When the observer's role is not known to those being observed, we speak of *disguised* participant observation. As you might imagine, people do not always behave as they ordinarily would when they know they are being watched. As we'll discuss later in this chapter, a major problem with observational methods is **reactivity.** Reactivity occurs when people react to the fact they are being observed by changing their normal behavior. Remember, researchers want to describe people's *usual* behavior. Therefore, researchers may decide to disguise their role as observers when they believe people will change their behavior if they know they're being watched. Disguised participant observation typically raises the ethical issues of privacy and informed consent. Researchers must address how they will protect individuals' welfare prior to implementing the study (see Chapter 3).

Participant observation allows researchers to gain access to situations that are not usually open to scientific observation. For example, disguised participant observers in Rosenhan's (1973) classic study on psychiatric diagnosis and hospitalization allowed researchers to learn more about what it's like to be in a psychiatric hospital. The participant observers in this study reported hearing voices so they could be hospitalized. Once hospitalized, they recorded their observations. Because disguised participant observers may have the same experiences as the people under study, they gain important insights into and understanding of individuals or groups. Rosenhan reported on what it was like to be "sane in an insane place."

A participant observer's role in a situation can produce certain problems. By identifying with the individuals they are observing, observers may lose their scientific objectivity. Another problem with participant observation is that the observer can influence the behavior of people being studied. By participating in the situation, do observers change the participants and events? If people's normal behavior is changed by the participant observer, it is difficult to generalize results to other situations.

There are a variety of observational methods using intervention that are not easily categorized; such procedures are called **structured observation.** Often, the observer intervenes in order to cause an event to occur or to set up a situation so that events can be more easily recorded. Simons and Levin (1998) used structured observation to study change blindness. They created a significant change in people's environment and then observed whether people noticed the change. Structured observations are also frequently used by developmental psychologists. Perhaps most notable are the methods of Jean Piaget (1896–1980). In many of Piaget's studies, a child was first given a problem to solve, then was given several variations on the problem to test the limits of the child's understanding. These structured observations provided a wealth of information

An Example of Structured Observation

THE FAR SIDE by Gary Larson

"**And now we'll see if it attacks its own reflection.**"

regarding children's cognition and were the basis for Piaget's "stage theory" of intellectual development.

Structured observation is a middle ground between the passive nonintervention of naturalistic observation and the systematic control and manipulation of variables in laboratory methods. This compromise allows researchers to make observations in settings that are more natural than the lab setting. Nevertheless, there may be a price to pay. If observers fail to follow similar procedures each time they make an observation, it is difficult for other researchers to obtain the same results. Uncontrolled, and perhaps unknown, variables in natural settings may influence the behavior under observation.

In a **field experiment,** the researcher manipulates (controls) one or more variables in a natural setting in order to determine their effect on behavior. The field experiment represents the most extreme form of intervention in observational methods (see Figure 4.3). In a field experiment researchers typically manipulate a variable to create two or more conditions. The essential difference between field experiments and other observational methods is that researchers exert more control in field experiments. This control allows researchers to compare people's behavior in different conditions and to gain valuable knowledge

Figure 4.3   Extent of researcher control in different methods of observation with intervention.

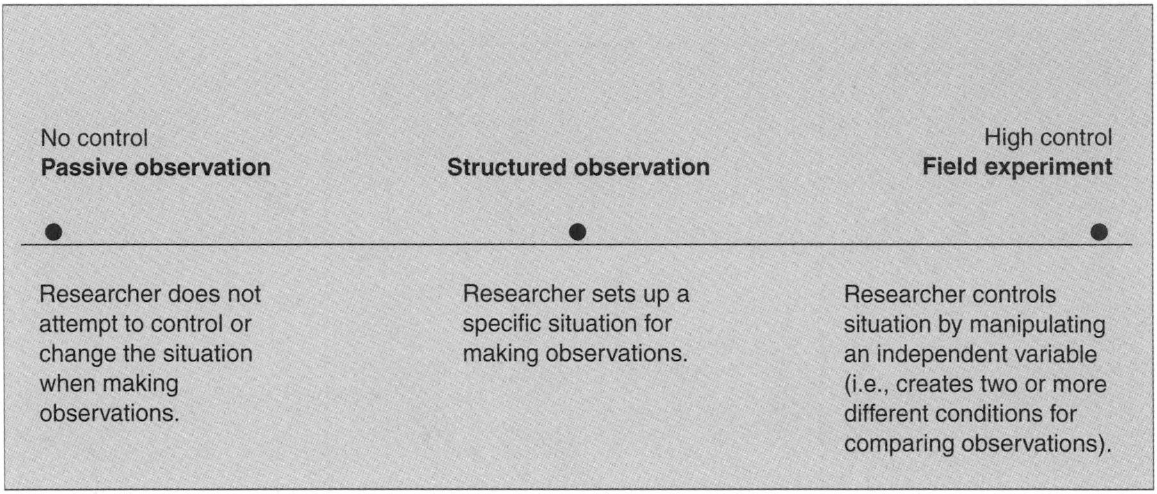

about the causes of people's behavior in natural settings. Field experiments are frequently used in social psychology. You may note that Simons and Levin's (1998) observational study was not a field experiment because there was only one condition: All participants experienced the same structured change situation.

Researchers also typically make use of **confederates** in field experiments and structured observations. As mentioned in Chapter 3, a confederate is someone in the research situation who is instructed to behave in a certain way in order to produce a situation for observing behavior. In Simons and Levin's (1998) study of change blindness, several confederates were needed to create the observation situation. Individuals were approached by one person, a confederate; midway through their conversation this confederate was replaced by a different confederate. Do you think you would have noticed the change?

Indirect (Unobtrusive) Observational Methods

We have been discussing observational methods in which an observer directly observes and records behavior in a setting. However, behavior can also be observed indirectly through records and other evidence of people's behavior. These methods are often called **unobtrusive methods** because the researcher does not intervene in the situation; in fact, the people being observed often are no longer present in the situation. An important advantage of these methods is that they are **nonreactive.** Because these observations are made indirectly, it's impossible for people to react, or change their behavior, while researchers observe. We will now turn to these indirect methods, which involve the observation of physical traces and archival records (see Table 4.1).

Table 4.1   Indirect (Unobtrusive) Measures

Physical Traces	Archival Records
1. *Use traces:* physical evidence that results from the use (or nonuse) of an item *Examples:* cans in a recycling bin, pages colored in a coloring book 2. *Products:* creations, constructions, or other artifacts of behavior *Examples:* petroglyphs (ancient rock paintings), MTV, *Star Wars* action figures	1. *Running records:* public and private documents that are produced continuously *Examples:* records for sports teams, stock market prices 2. *Records for specific episodes:* documents that describe specific events *Examples:* birth certificates, marriage licenses, college degrees

Based on distinctions made by Webb et al. (1981).

Physical Traces.   As everyone who has read a few detective stories knows, examining physical evidence of past behavior can provide important clues about the characteristics of individuals and events. For example, the size of footprints in the ground says something about the size and age of the person who stepped there. The distance between footprints can indicate whether the person was walking or running. **Physical traces** are the remnants, fragments, and products of past behavior. Two categories of physical traces are "use traces" and "products." *Use traces* are what the label implies—the physical evidence that results from the use (or nonuse) of an item. Remains of cigarettes in ashtrays, aluminum cans in a recycling bin, and fingerprints on a murder weapon are examples of use traces. The degree to which a young child's dolls show signs of wear is another example. This use trace might indicate which dolls the child likes best, just as the amount of wear and tear in students' textbooks may indicate which classes they like the best (or, at least, study the most).

Products are the creations, constructions, or other artifacts of earlier behavior. Anthropologists are often interested in the surviving products of ancient cultures. By examining vessels, paintings, and other artifacts, anthropologists can often describe patterns of behavior from thousands of years ago. MTV, the World Wide Web, and the many items on store shelves are examples of products that allow us to describe our modern-day culture and behavior. For example, Mooney and Brabant (1987) collected a random sample of birthday cards to examine deviant messages in interpersonal communication. They found that 16% of the cards had some reference to obesity, violence, marital infidelity, or mental illness. In the words of the researchers, these cards may be appropriate when "you care enough to send the very worst" (p. 386).

Physical measures offer a researcher valuable and sometimes novel means to study behavior, and the measures available are limited only by the ingenuity of the investigator. However, the validity of physical traces must be examined carefully and verified through independent sources of evidence. Validity refers to the truthfulness of a measure. Do physical traces truthfully inform us about people's behavior?

Biases can occur in the way physical-use traces are laid down and how traces survive over time. Does a well-worn path to the right in a museum indicate people's interest in objects in that direction or simply a natural human tendency to turn right? Does the number of cans found in recycling containers at a university reflect students' preferences for certain brands or simply what is available in campus vending machines?

Whenever possible, researchers need to obtain supplementary evidence for the validity of physical traces (see Webb et al., 1981). Alternative hypotheses for changes in physical traces must be considered. Care must also be taken when comparing results across studies to make sure that measures are defined similarly. A research study can be strengthened considerably by including several different measures of behavior, such as physical traces *and* surveys. A *multimethod approach* to hypothesis testing reduces the likelihood that research findings are due to problems associated with a single measurement procedure.

Archival Records.   **Archival records** are the public and private documents describing the activities of individuals, institutions, governments, and other groups (see Webb et al., 1981). The many records of sports teams are good examples of *running records* that are produced continuously. Other records, such as personal documents (e.g., marriage licenses), are more likely to describe specific episodes. The news media are yet another important source of archival information. Various records, ranging from stock market reports to crime statistics, are published in newspapers and reported on television.

Researchers may examine archives to assess the effect of a *natural treatment*, which is a naturally occurring event that significantly impacts society or individuals. Assassinations of world leaders, drastic changes in the stock market, and the passage of new laws may have important effects on behavior and can be investigated using archival data. Also, individuals experience naturally occurring events in their lives, such as death or divorce of parents, chronic illness, or marital difficulties. The effects of these events can be explored using archival data. For example, a researcher may examine school records of absenteeism or grades to investigate children's responses to parental divorce.

Researchers gain several practical advantages by using archival records. Archival data are plentiful and researchers can avoid an extensive data-collection stage. Also, because archival information is often part of the public record and usually does not identify individuals, ethical concerns are less worrisome. As more and more archival sources become available through the Internet, researchers will find it even easier to examine behavior in this way.

Researchers, however, need to be aware of the problems and limitations of archival records. Two problems are *selective deposit* and *selective survival*. These problems occur because there are biases in how archives are produced. The problem of selective deposit occurs when some information is selected to be deposited in archives, but other information is not. For example, think about that great archive, the high school yearbook. Not all activities, events, and groups are selected for the yearbook. Who decides what clubs and organizations, events, and photos are prominently displayed in the yearbook? When some events, activities, or groups have a better chance to be selected than others, bias exists. Or consider the fact that politicians and others who are constantly exposed to reporters know how to "use" the media. This can be seen as a problem of selective deposit—only certain information is "for the record."

Selective survival arises when records are missing or incomplete (something an investigator may not even be aware of). Researchers must consider whether some records "survived," whereas others did not. Documents that are particularly damaging to certain individuals or groups may vanish. Family photo albums may "mysteriously" lose photos of individuals now divorced or pictures from "fat years." The only way to control for these problems in using archival data is to be aware that they may exist and, when possible, seek other forms of supporting evidence.

DETECTING CHANGES IN THE REAL WORLD: THE OBSERVATIONAL METHOD

 Simons and Levin (1998) used *direct observation* because they observed participants' ability to notice change while the change was occurring. Their method was *structured observation* because they created a situation involving change in people's environment and then observed people's reactions. We saw in general what happened, but let's examine exactly how they created this change. Research often involves creativity and ingenuity, and Simons and Levin's research provides an excellent example of both.

In their first study, pedestrians were approached by an individual, a *confederate,* carrying a campus map. The researchers designed the encounter so that the pedestrian could view the confederate for about 20 meters before they met. The confederate asked the pedestrian for directions to a campus building. After about 10 to 15 seconds of conversation, the change took place. Two other confederates carrying a door rudely passed between them. As the door passed, the first confederate switched places with one of the confederates who was carrying the door (see Figure 4.4). After the door had passed, the pedestrian continued to provide directions, typically making eye contact with the new confederate. The entire interaction took 2 to 5 minutes. Simons and Levin noted that the two experimenters wore different clothing, differed slightly in height, and had different voices.

Their second observational study used the same procedure to switch the confederates during the interaction. However, in this study the two confederates dressed as construction workers (we'll learn why when we discuss their findings), but with clear differences in the color of their clothing and details of their construction hats and toolbelts (see Figure 4.5). As before, the first confederate asked pedestrians for directions to a campus building and then switched places with the second confederate when the passing door interrupted the conversation.

In both studies the second confederate continued the conversation with the pedestrian and observed whether the pedestrian noticed the change. After the pedestrians finished providing directions, the confederate explained they were conducting a psychology study on "the sorts of things people pay attention to in the real world" and asked the pedestrians whether they noticed "anything unusual at all when that door passed by a minute ago" (Simons & Levin, 1998, p. 645). The confederate recorded their

Figure 4.4   Frames from a video of a subject from Experiment 1. Frames a–c show the sequence of the switch. Frame d shows the two experimenters side by side.

(a)

(b)

(c)

(d)

responses, and when pedestrians didn't mention the change, they were asked directly, "Did you notice that I'm not the same person who approached you to ask for directions?" (p. 646). At the end of the interaction the pedestrians were told about the purpose of the study.

Videos of Simons and Levin's procedure can be viewed at Simons' lab web page: http://www.wjh.harvard.edu/~viscog/lab/ in the Demonstrations section.

THE RESEARCHERS' POINT OF VIEW

Question to Drs. Simons and Levin: How did you come up with the idea for these studies?

The original impetus for doing the real-world study came from a discussion with Ron Rensink during a break from a workshop on scene perception. Ron mentioned seeing an old television humor show that did

Figure 4.5   The experimenters dressed as construction workers for Experiment 2.

something like the task we eventually used. Based on the arguments we had been making, we had to predict that people would miss the person change in the real-world as well.

What were the difficult aspects of conducting this research?

The pragmatics of handing off the door from one confederate to the next took a bit of practice. Keeping a straight face after the change also took practice. Probably the most difficult problem we encountered was trying to find an optimal location to run the study. We needed to find a location with the right amount of traffic (enough people that we weren't always waiting, but not so many that we'd have trouble moving with the door). We also needed a location where we could hide the door, but still have it close enough to the initial confederate to be able to interrupt the conversation before it was over. That also meant that the people with the door had to be able to see the first confederate, but not be seen by the subject.

RECORDING BEHAVIOR

Observational methods also differ in the manner in which behavior is recorded. Sometimes researchers seek a *comprehensive* description of behavior and the situation in which it occurs. At other times they focus on only certain behaviors or events. Whether all behavior in a setting or only *selected* aspects are observed depends on the observers' goals. The choice of how behavior is recorded determines how the results are eventually measured, summarized, analyzed, and reported. (See Table 4.2.)

Comprehensive Records of Behavior

Researchers use **narrative records** when they seek a more or less faithful reproduction of behavior as it originally occurred. To create a narrative record, an observer can write descriptions of behavior or use audiotape recordings, videotapes, and films. After obtaining narrative records observers can study, classify, and organize the records at their convenience. Researchers test their hypotheses, or expectations about behaviors, by examining the record. An important advantage of narrative records is that observers can return to the records as many times as needed to test their hypotheses. For example, observers can view a videotape over and over, each time looking at different aspect of individuals' behavior.

Records of Selected Behaviors

Often researchers are interested only in certain behaviors or specific aspects of individuals and settings. They may have specific hypotheses about the behaviors they expect and clear definitions of the behaviors they are investigating. In this type of observational study, researchers typically measure the occurrence of the specific behavior while making their observations. For example, Simons and Levin (1998) selected the behavior of whether people detected the change in the confederate. As they observed this specific behavior, they quantified their observations. Observers can record their observations on paper-and-pencil forms or use an electronic recording device, such as a portable computer.

Suppose you wish to observe people's reactions to individuals with obvious physical disabilities. First you would need to define what constitutes a "reaction" to a physically disabled individual. Are you interested in helping behaviors, approach/avoidance behaviors, eye contact, length of conversation, or in another behavioral reaction? Next you would need to decide how to measure these behaviors. Assume you choose to measure people's reactions by observing eye contact between individuals with and without physical disabilities. Exactly how should you measure eye contact? Should you simply measure whether an individual does or does not make eye contact, or do you want to measure the duration of any eye contact? Your decisions will depend on the hypotheses or goals of your study, and will be influenced by information gained by reading previous studies that used the same or similar behavioral measures. (Unfortunately, previous research indicates that reactions to physically disabled

Table 4.2   Recording Behavior

Narrative Records	Records of Selected Behaviors
A comprehensive record that reproduces behavior as it originally occurred; audiotapes and videotapes are methods for obtaining narrative records of behavior.	A record of certain behaviors or specific aspects of individuals and settings; observers may record the occurrence of particular behaviors or measure the extent to which certain behaviors occur.

individuals frequently can be classified as unfavorable. See, for example, Thompson [1982].)

Measurement Scales

When researchers decide to measure and quantify specific behaviors they must decide what scale of measurement to use. There are four levels of measurement, or **measurement scales,** that apply to both physical and psychological measurement (see Table 4.3). The lowest level, or scale, is called a *nominal scale;* it involves categorizing ("classifying") events into discrete categories. When studying people's reactions to individuals with obvious physical disabilities, a researcher might use a nominal scale by measuring whether individuals make eye contact or do not make eye contact.

The second level of measurement, called an *ordinal scale,* involves ordering or ranking events to be measured. Ordinal scales add the arithmetic relationships "greater than" and "less than" to the measurement process; that is, ordinal scales indicate the magnitude of something. One common example of an ordinal scale is class rank. We can order students in a class from highest to lowest, but if we know only their ranks we have no information about how far apart the students are in academic performance.

The third level, an *interval scale,* involves specifying how far apart two observations are on a dimension. On an interval scale the differences between values on the scale are of equal size. Consider, for example, three scores on a verbal ability test: 75, 80, and 85. An interval scale assumes the difference in verbal ability between 75 and 80 (5 points) is the same as the difference in verbal ability between 80 and 85 (5 points). What is missing from an interval scale is a meaningful zero point. For instance, an individual's score of "zero" on the verbal aptitude test does not mean he or she has zero verbal ability. An advantage of interval scales is that addition, multiplication, subtraction, and division can

Table 4.3   Characteristics of Measurement Scales

Type of Scale	Key Feature	Goal of Measurement (Examples)
Nominal	Discrete categories	Sort stimuli into discrete categories (e.g., gender, college majors).
Ordinal	Differentiate stimuli according to magnitude	Rank-order stimuli on a single dimension (e.g., class rank).
Interval	Distance between scale values has meaning	Specify the distance between stimuli on a given dimension (e.g., test scores, self-report questionnaire of depression symptoms).
Ratio	Same as interval, plus value of "zero" has meaning	Specify the distance between stimuli and obtain ratios of scale values (e.g., reaction time measure for which someone responds twice as fast as another person).

be performed. Whenever possible, therefore, psychologists try to measure psychological dimensions using interval scales.

The fourth level of measurement is a *ratio scale*. A ratio scale has all the properties of an interval scale with the important additional quality of an absolute zero point. That is, a "score" of zero is meaningful. In terms of arithmetic operations, a zero point makes the ratio of scale values meaningful. For example, if time to complete a test is measured, 5 minutes is half the time of 10 minutes. Physical scales measuring time, weight, and distance can usually be treated as ratio scales.

Table 4.4 illustrates how the four major scales of measurement might be used to measure students' study behavior. You will need to keep these four types of scales in mind as you select statistical procedures for analyzing the results of the research you will be doing (see Appendix A).

DETECTING CHANGES IN THE REAL WORLD: RECORDING BEHAVIOR

Simons and Levin (1998) used both recording methods, *comprehensive* and *selected behaviors,* in their two studies on people's ability to detect changes when interacting in their environment. They obtained a *narrative record* of people's responses to the change of confederates using a hidden videotape camera. This allowed them to review the videotaped exchanges to determine how much eye contact occurred between the pedestrians and the

Table 4.4   Illustration of Measurement Scales: Measuring Students' Study Behavior

Scale	Question and Measurement Scale	Example	
Nominal	Do students study? Categories are yes and no.	Melissa—yes Gina—yes Neil—yes	Charles—yes Rose—no Jeff—no
Ordinal	Who studies more? Scale adds "more than" (or "less than").	Melissa studies more than Neil, who studies more than Gina. Gina studies more than Neil, and Neil studies more than Charles. Charles studies more than Rose and Jeff.	
Interval	Who studies more? An observer can rate their studying on a 5-point scale (*Never* to *Always*).	Melissa—5 (*Always*) Gina—4 (*Usually*) Neil—3 (*Often*) Charles—2 (*Sometimes*) Rose—1 (*Never*) Jeff—1 (*Never*)	
Ratio	Who studies more? Measure the amount of time students spend studying.	Melissa—12 hours a day Gina—8 hours a day Neil—2 hours a day Charles—1 hour a day Rose—0 hours a day Jeff—0 hours a day	

confederates. Their goal was to measure both the occurrence of eye contact *(nominal scale)* and the duration of eye contact *(ratio scale)*. They noted, however, that one problem with their recording method was that the position of the camera didn't allow a precise analysis of the effect of eye contact on pedestrians' ability to detect the change (the door got in the way).

Simons and Levin also selected a particular behavior to record: whether pedestrians noticed the switch of the confederates. Whether pedestrians detected the change (yes or no) is a nominal scale of measurement. The researchers recorded pedestrians' responses to the direct questions and recorded individuals' reactions when they learned about the switch. Finally, Simons and Levin recorded other features of the pedestrians. For example, they recorded the pedestrians' approximate ages to determine whether age is related to people's ability to detect change.

ANALYZING OBSERVATIONAL DATA

After recording their observations of behavior, researchers analyze observational data in order to summarize people's behavior and to determine the reliability of their observations. When summarizing their observations researchers use *quantitative data analysis* or *qualitative data analysis.* The type of data analysis that researchers choose depends on the data they've collected. For example, when researchers record selected behaviors using a measurement scale, the preferred method for data analysis is quantitative. When comprehensive records are obtained, researchers may choose either qualitative or quantitative data analysis.

Quantitative Data Analysis

The goal of **quantitative data analysis** is to provide a *numerical, or quantitative, summary* of the observations. An important step is to calculate *descriptive statistics.* Descriptive statistics are used to summarize observational data numerically. There are several types of descriptive statistics. The type of descriptive statistics the researcher should use depends on the scale of measurement used to code the data (Table 4.5).

When a nominal scale is used, events and behaviors are classified into mutually exclusive categories. The most common descriptive statistic for nominal data is *relative frequency.* The proportion, or percentage, of times that a behavior occurs in a category is expressed in terms of the total frequency of events observed. For example, suppose that 100 individuals are observed to determine whether they make eye contact with a physically disabled individual. If 30 of the 100 individuals make eye contact, the relative frequency is 30%.

When behavior is recorded on an interval or a ratio scale of measurement, researchers report measures of central tendency. The most common measure is the *arithmetic mean*, or *average*. The mean describes the "typical" score in a group of scores and is an important summary measure of group performance. In order to describe group performance more completely, researchers also report measures of variability or dispersion of scores around the mean. The *standard deviation* approximates the average distance of a score from the mean. (Measures of central tendency and variability are discussed in Appendix A, as are additional guidelines for data summary and description.)

Researchers should also determine the *reliability* of the observations. You may recall that reliability refers to consistency, and an analysis of reliability in an observational study asks if another observer viewing the same events would obtain the same results. The degree to which two independent observers agree about their observations is called **interobserver reliability.**

Consider an observational study in which two observers make their observations but never agree about the behaviors. When observers disagree we become uncertain about what is being measured and what behaviors and events actually occurred. This is called *low* interobserver reliability. Low interobserver reliability can be due to characteristics of the observers (e.g., boredom, amount of experience) or to the procedures and methods of observing. Interobserver reliability is generally increased by training observers and giving them specific feedback about discrepancies in their observations (Judd, Smith, & Kidder, 1991).

Low interobserver reliability can occur when events and behaviors to be recorded are not clearly defined. Without a clear definition of what they're supposed to observe and record, observers simply choose what they think is important based on their personal opinions. In addition to providing precise verbal definitions, researchers should provide concrete examples about what to observe to increase reliability among observers.

The way in which interobserver reliability is assessed depends on how behavior is measured. When events are classified according to mutually exclusive categories (nominal scale), interobserver reliability is generally assessed using a percentage agreement measure. The following is a formula for calculating percentage agreement between observers:

Table 4.5 Quantitative Data Analysis of Observational Data: A Summary of Descriptive Statistics

Relative Frequency	Mean	Standard Deviation	Interobserver Reliability
The proportion or percentage of times a behavior occurs during an observation period; typically used with nominal data.	The average score among a group of scores (the sum of all scores divided by the total number of scores); researchers typically calculate means when they have measured behavior using interval and ratio scales.	Describes the variability of a set of scores (calculated as the average distance of scores from the mean); researchers typically calculate standard deviations when they use interval and ratio scales.	The degree to which two independent observers agree about their observations. When a nominal scale is used, interobserver reliability is generally assessed using a percentage agreement measure; with interval and ratio scales, interobserver reliability is measured using a correlation coefficient.

$$\frac{\text{Number of times two observers agree}}{\text{Number of opportunities to agree}} \times 100$$

Although there is no hard-and-fast percentage of agreement that defines low interobserver reliability, researchers generally seek estimates of reliability that exceed 85%.

When subjective ratings are made or when a variable such as time is measured (interval and ratio scales, respectively), interobserver reliability can be measured using a Pearson Product-Moment Correlation Coefficient, *r*. (Correlational measures are discussed more fully in Chapter 5.) Good agreement between observers (reliability) is indicted by high correlation coefficients. Generally, researchers want the correlation between observers to be greater than .80. These high standards for interobserver reliability indicate how important it is for scientists to have reliable observations.

Qualitative Data Analysis

As you might imagine, observational studies that use narrative records or archival data provide a wealth of information—sometimes piles and piles of papers, videotapes, and audiotapes. Once collected, how do researchers summarize all of this information? Using **qualitative data analysis,** researchers seek to provide a *verbal* summary of their observations and to develop a theory that explains behavior in the narrative records. This is called the *grounded theory method* of qualitative data analysis (Strauss & Corbin, 1990). That is, the researcher seeks to develop a *theory* about behavior that is *grounded* in observations from the narrative records.

As shown in Table 4.6, qualitative data analysis has three main steps: data reduction, data display, and conclusion drawing/verification (Miles & Huberman, 1994). In qualitative analyses, *data reduction* occurs when researchers

Table 4.6   Steps for Qualitative Data Analysis

Step	What Is Accomplished
Data reduction	Researchers *code* observations to identify themes, categorize different pieces of information, and record their own observations about the narrative records.
Data display	Researchers use graphs, charts, matrices (rows and columns), networks (nodes connected by links), and other types of visual displays to organize and condense the vast amounts of narrative data.
Draw and verify conclusions	Researchers build a logical chain of evidence and a coherent theory about behavior in the narrative record based on the coding and data displays.

Miles & Huberman (1994)

verbally summarize information, identify themes, categorize information, group various pieces of information, and record their own observations about the narrative records. This type of data reduction involves *coding,* as researchers "tag," or label, parts of the narrative records to describe the content or make inferences about parts of the record. Researchers identify patterns, causes and explanations, relationships among people, and other theoretical constructs in their narrative records. For example, a qualitative analysis of the minutes from meetings of an organization might code the content of what was said (e.g., requests for information, praise, directives), the status of those who spoke (e.g., boss, subordinate), and inferences about the meetings (e.g., emotional tone, group cohesion, sources of conflict).

The second major step of qualitative analysis is *data display.* Researchers use graphs, charts, matrices (rows and columns), networks (nodes connected by links), and other types of visual displays to organize and condense the often vast amounts of narrative material from their study. Data displays can include the verbal codes, quotes from narrative records, and phrases used to summarize the records. Researchers choose from many different display methods depending on the goals of their analysis. Thus, displays may show the context or components of behavior seen in narrative records, the time sequence of events, relationships among people's roles in a setting, or relationships among concepts and variables. In our example of minutes from meetings, the researcher may display the behaviors that occurred during conflict, or the sequence of events that occurred as conflict was resolved.

The final step in qualitative data analysis is to *draw and verify conclusions.* You may recognize that throughout the analysis researchers interpret narrative data and form preliminary conclusions as they code and display the data. However, as researchers form theories from their narrative data, they seek to explain the meaning of behavior in the records. As they seek understanding, qualitative researchers try to build a logical chain of evidence and a coherent theory about behavior in the narrative record. In our example of minutes from meetings, the researcher may develop a theory about how the organization's hierarchical structure influences conflict resolution. Qualitative researchers then seek to verify their findings to determine the validity, or accuracy, of their observations. This involves examining the quality of their data, reviewing exceptions to identified patterns, and approaching their conclusions with scientific skepticism (Miles & Huberman, 1994).

The issue of the validity of qualitative analyses is controversial. Many researchers argue that qualitative data analyses are highly subjective. Individual researchers who code narrative records may have biases that influence their interpretations and conclusions. As we've previously seen, the best defense against bias in research is to use a *multimethod approach* to data collection and analysis. By using different methods and analyses, researchers seek agreement in their findings across different studies. To the extent that research findings are repeated, or replicated, across different studies and methods, we have greater confidence in the findings and conclusions.

DETECTING CHANGES IN THE REAL WORLD: THE DATA ANALYSIS

Simons and Levin's (1998) *quantitative* data analysis was straightforward. Their main interest was whether pedestrians detected the change in confederates (yes or no). This is a *nominal scale*. For their *descriptive statistics* they calculated the *relative frequency* of how many people detected the change. In their first study, 7 of the 15 pedestrians noticed the change; thus, the relative frequency was 7/15, or 47%. In their second study only 4 of the 12 (33%) pedestrians detected the change when asked if they had noticed anything unusual.

Simons and Levin also examined the relationship between the approximate age of the pedestrians in their first study and whether they detected the change. They classified the pedestrians into two age groups: (1) roughly the same age as the confederates (ages 20–30) and (2) older than the confederates (approximately 35–65 years old). Thus, "age" had two categories, same-age and older. They also had two categories for whether pedestrians detected the change, yes or no. Their frequency counts can be presented in a "2 × 2 contingency table" (read "2 by 2") to show the relationship between age and detection of the change:

		Detected Change	
		Yes	No
Age	Same Age	7	0
	Older	0	8

The 2 × 2 table shows that all of the pedestrians who were approximately the same age as the confederates detected the change and that the pedestrians who did not detect the change were older than the confederates.

Simons and Levin also described a *qualitative* data analysis of their observations. Recall that they were unable to code eye contact using the videotape because of the obstructed location of the camera. However, they were able to provide the following qualitative summary of pedestrians' eye contact: "In all cases, subjects made extensive eye contact after completing their directions, and most pedestrians did make eye contact immediately before and after the arrival of the door, suggesting that eye contact does not guarantee successful detection of the change" (Simons & Levin, 1998, p. 649).

THE RESEARCHERS' POINT OF VIEW

Question to Drs. Simons and Levin: Were you surprised by any of the findings?

We were surprised by the magnitude of the effects. We had expected that a few people might miss the change, but were surprised that nearly 50% did.

In many cases, we've created displays or changes that we thought wouldn't work. We would look at a video or the people switching and think "This time we've gone too far—100% of our subjects are going to see this." In fact, that is one of our most interesting findings—people (ourselves included) intuitively think that these changes should be plainly visible, even though they are not. We are currently studying this phenomenon, trying to document this metacognitive error: When we show people stills from movies in which changes occur and point out the changes, people massively overestimate how certain they were that they would have seen the change. We have found that up to 90% of subjects believe they would notice the very changes that 0% of subjects actually detect. They are very confident as well, often citing cases where they have seen unexpected changes (e.g., continuity errors in movies), or simply stating that they typically pay attention to things that change.

THINKING CRITICALLY ABOUT OBSERVATIONAL RESEARCH

Conducting a good observational study involves choosing how to sample behavior and events to observe, choosing the appropriate observational method, and choosing how to record and analyze observational data. Now that you know the basics of observational methods, you also need to know the problems that can occur. We've touched on these problems but now will cover them in greater detail. The first problem occurs because people often change their behavior when they know they're being observed: This is called *reactivity*. A second problem occurs when observers' *biases* influence what behavior they choose to record.

Reactivity

Did your parents ever ask you to be "on your best behavior" when entertaining guests? Your parents may have been worried that their guests would observe (and judge) your behavior. Often parents want their children to change their usual behavior when guests are present so that the guests have a favorable impression of the family.

As previously discussed, the presence of an observer can lead people to change their behavior because they know they're being observed. This problem is called *reactivity*. Generally, reactive research situations are situations in which individuals "react" to the presence of an observer. As a result, observers record behaviors that may not represent people's usual behavior. Although parents may want their children to change their usual behavior, a researcher's goal is to record people's *normal* behavior. Therefore, reactivity can be a major problem for researchers.

Individuals often react to the presence of an observer by trying to behave in ways they think the researcher wants them to behave. Knowing they are part of a scientific investigation, individuals usually want to cooperate and be "good" participants. Research participants often try to guess what behaviors are expected, and they may use cues and other information to guide their behavior (Orne, 1962). These cues in the research situation are called **demand characteristics.** Orne suggests that individuals generally ask themselves the question, What am I supposed to be doing here? To answer this question, participants pay attention to cues present in the setting, the research procedure, and implicit cues given by the researcher. As research participants try to guess what is expected, they may change their behavior accordingly.

How do researchers control the problem of reactivity? One answer to this question comes from our understanding of the different observation methods. Reactivity can be eliminated if research participants do not know an observer is present. Disguised participant observation achieves this goal because individuals are not aware that an observer is present in the setting. We can presume, then, that individuals behave as they normally would. Simons and Levin (1998) used this procedure, and we can assume that people in their study were giving directions and otherwise behaving as they normally would—including detecting or not detecting changes as they normally would. Observers can also conceal themselves while making observations, or they can use hidden cameras or tape recorders to make their observations (but they must be aware of ethical concerns related to privacy; see Chapter 3).

An important advantage of indirect observation, or unobtrusive methods, discussed earlier is that these observations are nonreactive. Researchers observe physical traces and archival records to learn about people's past behavior. Because the individuals do not know they are being observed by the researcher, they cannot change their behavior.

Another way of dealing with reactivity is to *adapt* participants to the presence of an observer. We can assume that as participants get used to an observer's presence, they will eventually behave normally in that person's presence. Researchers studying animals in their natural habitat often use various methods to adapt the animals to the presence of an observer, as do researchers observing children in a classroom. See Table 4.7.

Table 4.7   Questions and Answers About Reactivity

What is reactivity?
Reactivity occurs when individuals change their usual behavior when they know they are being observed.

How do individuals know what their behavior should be like in an observational study?
Research participants often pay attention to the *demand characteristics* of the situation: the cues and information available in the situation that tell individuals how they "should" behave.

How do researchers control problems of reactivity?
Researchers can control reactivity using the following methods:
1. Conceal the observer.
2. Use disguised participant observation.
3. Use indirect (unobtrusive) observation.
4. Adapt participants to the presence of the observer.

Observer Bias

As an example of disguised participant observation, recall Rosenhan's (1973) classic study in which observers were admitted to mental hospitals. Once in the hospital they observed and recorded the behavior of hospital staff. Rosenhan's research identified a serious bias on the part of the staff. Once the observer-patients (called "pseudopatients") were labeled schizophrenic, staff members interpreted their behavior solely according to this label. Behaviors that might have been considered normal were interpreted by the staff as evidence of the pseudopatients' illness. For instance, the pseudopatients soon learned they could record their notes openly—no one paid much attention to what they were doing. When Rosenhan later checked the medical records for the pseudopatients, he found that staff members had cited the note taking as symptoms of their illness. (Don't worry—note taking is not a sign of mental illness!) Because staff members interpreted the pseudopatients' behavior in terms of the schizophrenic label, their sanity was never detected. This example clearly illustrates the danger of **observer bias,** the systematic errors in observation that result from an observer's expectations. In this case, the staff demonstrated observer bias.

In many scientific studies the observer has some expectations about what behavior should be like in a particular situation or following a specific psychological treatment. For example, when researchers design an observational study they review the previously published research literature to help them develop their hypotheses. This knowledge can lead observers to form expectancies about what should occur in a research situation. Expectancies can be a source of observer bias—*expectancy effects*—if they lead to systematic errors in observation (Rosenthal, 1966, 1976). Expectancy effects can also occur in our everyday life. Box 4.1 offers some illustrations of expectancies you can try on your friends.

An observer's expectancies regarding the outcome of a study may not be the only source of observer bias. You might think that using automated equipment such as video cameras would eliminate observer bias. Although automation reduces the opportunity for observer bias, it does not necessarily eliminate it. Consider the fact that, in order to record behavior on film, the observer must determine the angle, location, and time of filming. To the extent that these aspects of the study are influenced by the observer's personal biases, such decisions can introduce systematic errors into the results. We've already seen how the obstructed angle of the video camera in Simons and Levin's (1998) study on change blindness influenced their analyses because participants' behavior was not fully recorded. Furthermore, using automated equipment generally only postpones the process of classification and interpretation, and it is possible for the effects of observer bias to be introduced when narrative records are coded and analyzed.

We usually cannot eliminate observer bias, but we can reduce it in several ways. As mentioned, the use of automatic recording equipment can help, although the potential for bias is still present. *Probably the most important factor in dealing with observer bias is being aware that it might be present.* That is, an observer who knows about this bias should take steps to reduce its effect.

Box 4.1

ILLUSTRATIONS OF OBSERVER BIAS

Observer bias refers to systematic errors in observation when an observer expects certain behaviors or events to occur. The observer "sees" these events, even if they don't accurately reflect the behavior or events that are observed.

Illustrations

To illustrate how easy it is to develop expectancies about events, see if you can get your friends to develop expectancies and then make an error in their "observations":

1. Ask a friend to say aloud the following words one at a time as you spell them: *folk, joke, poke, soak.* Then ask, "What is the

white of an egg called?" (Most likely, he or she will say *yolk*, which is not correct). Your friend should develop an expectancy for "oak" words, which will lead to an error in answering a simple question.

2. With another friend, spell aloud—slowly—the following words one at a time and ask your friend to say aloud the word you are spelling: *M-A-C-D-O-N-A-L-D, M-A-C-B-E-T-H, M-A-C-I-N-T-O-S-H*, and finally, *M-A-C-H-I-N-E-R-Y.* Most likely, your friend will mispronounce the word "machinery" because he or she has developed an expectancy for "Mac" words.

One important way researchers reduce observer bias is by limiting the information provided to observers. When observers and coders do not know the hypotheses of a study they cannot form expectancies about behavior. In a manner of speaking, observers can be kept "blind" to certain aspects of the study. Observers are blind when they do not know reasons for the observations or the goals of the study. Using blind observers greatly reduces the possibility of introducing systematic errors due to observer expectancies.

DISCUSSION OF THE RESEARCH EXAMPLE: DETECTING CHANGES IN THE REAL WORLD

 Simons and Levin (1998) used structured observation to demonstrate that people sometimes fail to detect important changes in their environment, even while they are actively participating and paying attention. Their findings in a real-world setting—on a campus sidewalk—extend their laboratory findings on change blindness. However, are there alternative explanations for participants' failure to notice the change in confederates? Could they have *reacted* to being observed? Did they behave as they normally would?

First, it's likely that Simons and Levin's pedestrians didn't know they were participants in a research study while giving directions to the confederate. We can assume they probably were behaving as they normally would. However, recall that near the end of the interaction the confederate told them they were in a psychology study, and asked whether they noticed anything unusual when the door went by. Here, the *demand characteristics* were quite high. Imagine yourself as a participant in this study. Wouldn't you now want to say, "Well, yes, of course, I did notice something," because the experimenter just told you that something unusual happened?

How did the pedestrians respond to this question? Simons and Levin (1998) noted that "most pedestrians reported that the people carrying the door were rude" (p. 646). The confederate then raised the demand characteristics even higher when he asked the pedestrians whether they noticed "that I'm not the same person who approached you to ask for directions" (p. 646). Think about what it would be like to be a pedestrian in this study now. What would you say? Wouldn't you want to look as if you "knew it all along"? Simons and Levin reported that in their first study only one person then claimed to notice the change, and in their second study three individuals claimed to have noticed. Thus, even when the demand characteristics to report the change were quite high, most participants who missed the change continued to claim nothing unusual had happened. This gives us more confidence that the participants really did not detect the change in the confederates.

How did Simons and Levin (1998) interpret their findings? Remember that Levin and Simons (1997) found in their laboratory studies that simply paying attention is not enough to detect changes. They suggested that to detect change, individuals must use effort to encode or process information in their environment. But what factors determine *when* people will use effort to process information?

Simons and Levin developed an answer to this question based on their findings that the participants' age was related to their detection of the change. Using findings from social psychology, they suggested that one of the first things individuals do in a social interaction is to categorize the other individual as a member of an "in-group" or an "out-group." In-group members are people of one's own social group, and out-group members are people belonging to social groups different from one's own. Simons and Levin reasoned that older pedestrians in their first study perceived the confederates to be out-group members, and same-age pedestrians perceived the confederates to be in-group members. Once we categorize someone as an out-group member we tend to perceive the individual as simply a member of the out-group and "tune out" the individual's specific characteristics. Thus, the older pedestrians simply may not have processed information about the confederates and, as a result, failed to detect the change. In contrast, social psychological research indicates that we may do more work to identify in-group members' distinguishing features. Thus, we would expect the same-age pedestrians (in-group) to notice the change in the confederates more often—precisely what Simons and Levin observed.

Perhaps now you may guess why the confederates dressed as construction workers in Simons and Levin's (1998) second study. The students who were approached for directions were in the same age group as the confederates, but because the confederates were "construction workers," they were probably categorized as out-group members. Therefore, based on the in-group/out-group explanation, we wouldn't expect students to expend much effort processing specific details about the two "construction workers." And, in fact, these students were less likely to detect the change than were the students in the first study. What this finding also shows us is that the critical variable is not simply the age of the pedestrian. After all, we could have interpreted the findings from the first study as indicating that younger individuals detect change more readily than older individuals. However, the young participants in the second study didn't detect the change very often, suggesting that in-group/out-group membership might be the critical variable.

THE RESEARCHERS' POINT OF VIEW

Questions to Drs. Simons and Levin: What kept you from concluding that older people simply don't detect change? That is, how did you decide to pursue the idea of in-group/out-group status?

The older subjects for the most part weren't much older than the confederates, and we would have hated to think that aging effects would start influencing performance by the mid-thirties. Most aging effects don't start that early. More important, many of the older subjects reported encoding the scene as "some student asking questions." Given other research on categorization and on cross-race recognition and perception, their description strongly reminded us of in-group/out-group coding effects. Ideally, we would have been able to run a version of the study with older confederates to see if we could reverse the effect. However, that was pragmatically too difficult. Instead, we thought it would be easier to use the same two people but to change their category membership in relation to the younger subjects.

We hoped that aging was not the reason, and thought that social categories were the more likely explanation. The changes themselves are pretty obvious at a perceptual level, and the in-group/out-group explanation seemed parsimonious.

What most would you like people to learn from your research?

1. People miss surprisingly large changes, even to attended objects.

2. Depending on how people categorize an object or event (i.e., determine the meaning of a scene), they will be more or less likely to notice changes. Change detection is most likely when the change appears to alter the meaning of a scene.

The metacognitive question is also important. Our intuitions often suggest that changes should be easy to detect, but when we actually conduct the study, we often find that these intuitions are completely wrong.

Are you conducting studies to follow up your findings?

We're conducting a number of follow-up studies. Most of them have to do with the specificity of the memory for the changed object and what sorts of changes people will and will not notice.

CONCLUSION

Simons and Levin's (1998) careful and systematic observation of change blindness in the real world contributes important information about how and when we process information in our environment. We started this chapter by noting that casual, everyday observation is likely to have biases. Simons and Levin demonstrated that one such bias may occur when we evaluate others in our environment who are part of in-group versus out-group relationships. (The elderly, for instance, may be examples of out-group members when viewed by traditional college-aged students.) Our casual observations of out-group members may lead us to make errors in our judgments and prevent us from really "seeing" out-group members as individuals. It is precisely these types of biases that psychologists must try to avoid in their scientific observations.

READ MORE ABOUT IT

Details about Simons and Levin's two studies of change blindness in the real world can be found in the journal article that describes their findings:

Simons, D. J., & Levin, D. T. (1998). Failure to detect changes to people during a real-world interaction. *Psychonomic Bulletin and Review, 5,* 644–649.

Information about these investigators' laboratory studies on failure to detect changes in film actors may be found in the following journal article:

Levin, D. T., & Simons, D. J. (1997). Failure to detect changes to attended objects in motion pictures. *Psychonomic Bulletin and Review, 4,* 501–506.

If you would like to learn more about in-groups and out-groups, you may wish to consult these sources:

Judd, C. M., & Park, B. (1988). Out-group homogeneity: Judgments of variability at the individual and group levels. *Journal of Personality and Social Psychology, 54,* 778–788.

Linville, P. W., Fischer, G. W., & Salovey, P. (1989). Perceived distributions of the characteristics of in-group and out-group members: Empirical evidence and a computer simulation. *Journal of Personality and Social Psychology, 57,* 165–188.

Rothbart, M., & John, O. P. (1985). Social categorization and behavioral episodes: A cognitive analysis of the effects of intergroup contact. *Journal of Social Issues, 41,* 81–104.

KEY CONCEPTS

time sampling	**physical traces**
situation sampling	**archival records**
naturalistic observation	**narrative records**
participant observation	**measurement scales**
reactivity	**quantitative data analysis**
structured observation	**interobserver reliability**
field experiment	**qualitative data analysis**
confederate	**demand characteristics**
unobtrusive (nonreactive) methods	**observer bias**

KEY POINTS TO LEARN

Sampling Behavior

- When a complete record of behavior cannot be obtained, researchers seek to obtain a representative sample of behavior.

- The extent to which observations can be generalized depends on how behavior is sampled.
- Time sampling refers to researchers' choosing time intervals systematically or randomly for making representative observations.
- Situation sampling involves studying behavior in different circumstances, locations, and conditions, and often with different participants.

Using Observational Methods

- Behavior can be observed directly or indirectly.
- Direct observational methods can be classified as observation without intervention (naturalistic observation) or observation with intervention.
- The goals of naturalistic observation are to describe behavior as it normally occurs and to examine relationships among variables.
- The three methods of observation with intervention are participant observation, structured observation, and the field experiment.
- Participant observation may be disguised or undisguised.
- Structured observations are created to record behaviors that may be difficult to observe using naturalistic observation.
- In a field experiment, researchers manipulate variables in a natural setting to determine the effect on behavior.
- Indirect, or unobtrusive, observations can be obtained by examining physical traces and archival records.

Recording Behavior

- Researchers choose whether to obtain a comprehensive behavioral record or to record selected behaviors depending on the goals of the observational research.
- The way in which the results of a study are ultimately summarized, analyzed, and reported depends on how the behavioral observations are recorded and measured.
- Narrative records in the form of written descriptions of behavior, audiotapes, and videotapes are comprehensive records of observed behavior.
- When researchers seek to describe *specific* behaviors or events, they often obtain quantitative measures of behavior, such as the frequency of occurrence or duration of a behavior.
- Quantitative measures of behavior use one of the four levels of measurement scales: nominal, ordinal, interval, and ratio.

Analyzing Observational Data

- Researchers choose quantitative data analysis or qualitative data analysis to summarize observational data.
- In quantitative data analysis researchers summarize the data statistically.
- Descriptive statistics, such as relative frequency, mean, and standard deviation, help researchers summarize data numerically.
- Interobserver reliability is the degree to which independent observers agree about their observations.

- In qualitative data analysis researchers provide a verbal summary and grounded theory for observations from narrative records.
- The three main steps in qualitative data analysis are data reduction, data display, and conclusion drawing/verification.

Thinking Critically About Observational Data

- When individuals change their behavior because they are being observed (reactivity), their behavior may no longer represent their normal behavior.
- Research participants may use demand characteristics in the research situation to guide their behavior.
- Methods to control reactivity include concealing the observer, disguised participant observation, unobtrusive (nonreactive) measurement, and adaptation.
- Observer bias occurs when observers' expectations about behavior lead to systematic errors in identifying and recording behavior, as well as when researchers' biases determine which behaviors they choose to observe.
- Expectancy effects can occur when observers are aware of the hypotheses for the outcome of the study or the outcome of previous studies.
- The first step in controlling observer bias is to recognize that it may be present.
- Observer bias can be reduced by keeping observers unaware (blind) of the goals and hypotheses of the study.

CHECKING THE ESSENTIALS

1. What are researchers trying to accomplish when they use a combination of time sampling and situation sampling?
2. Identify the major goals of research that involves observation in natural settings without any attempt by the observer to intervene.
3. What two ethical issues arise when researchers do a study involving disguised participant observation?
4. Compare the amount of control researchers exert in a study involving structured observation with the amount of control they exert in a field experiment.
5. Identify an important (perhaps the most important) advantage of using unobtrusive methods and explain why this advantage occurs when unobtrusive methods are used.
6. Identify and briefly describe two problems that can arise because of biases in the ways in which archival records are produced.
7. Describe the relationships between comprehensive and selective recording of observations and the use of qualitative and quantitative data analysis.
8. Describe briefly the roles that the grounded theory method and data display play in qualitative data analysis.
9. Identify at least two ways that researchers can control for the problem of reactivity.
10. What is probably the most important factor in dealing with observer bias?

APPLYING YOUR KNOWLEDGE

1. The following description is based on a study that was done as an assignment in a research methods class. Use this description to answer the questions that follow it.

   The study was conducted to investigate one aspect of the pace of life at a small college. The measure of pace of life was the time it took a person to walk a distance of 70 feet. Researchers observed people walking along the main path in front of the administration building and continuing through the path that leads past the admissions office. The researchers measured the walking speeds of people who passed another person on the path (called passers). They compared the walking speeds of the passers with the walking speed of the person who was closest to the passer on the path but who did not pass anyone (called nonpassers). The passers and nonpassers were identified as they walked through an area on the path designated as the passing zone. The participants' walking speeds were measured from the time the participants passed a marker that indicated the start of the timing zone until they reached the end of the timing zone, which was 70 feet long. Observers worked in pairs, with one observer timing the passer and the second observer timing the nonpasser. There were 24 pairs of observers, who made a total of 83 paired observations (passer/nonpasser pairs). The observers positioned themselves so that they could see the passing zone and the timing zone. But the observers could not be seen by the people walking along the path. The observers recorded the gender of each observed person, the context in which the observation took place (e.g., how crowded it was, weather conditions), and the date and time of the observation. Observations were distributed across the days of the week during which the study was done, with more observations on Monday, Wednesday, and Friday than on Tuesday and Thursday. The results indicated that the passers' times through the 70-foot timing zone were faster than the times for the corresponding nonpassers.

A. Identify the type of observational method used in this study.

B. What is the operational definition of the dependent (measured) variable in this study?

C. What aspects of the sampling used in this study would increase the representativeness of the observed behavior?

D. Identify one aspect of the procedures in this study that would likely decrease the reactivity of the observations in this study.

E. There are many possible interpretations for the finding that passers walked faster than did nonpassers. Try to identify at least one interpretation based on a characteristic of the people in each category (an individual differences variable) and at least one based on characteristics of the situation.

2. A friend of yours is absolutely convinced that he has a positive influence on the friendliness of conversations in which he is a participant. He has reached this conclusion on the basis of his everyday observations. You convince him that a systematic study is needed to confirm his hypothesis. Your friend (still smiling) carefully develops an operational definition of the friendliness of a conversation and records a rating for each of the next 50 conversations in which he is a participant. His results show that 75% of these conversations are rated "very friendly," 20% are rated "friendly," and 5% are rated neutral. Your friend returns to you—now convinced beyond a shadow of a doubt that he has a positive effect on the friendliness of a conversation.

A. Identify the type of observational method used in this study.

B. Do you accept your friend's conclusion about his having a positive effect on the friendliness of a conversation? Be sure to consider the issues of sampling and observer bias as you respond to your friend.

Chapter Five

CORRELATIONAL RESEARCH: SURVEYS

Outline

INTRODUCTION

What are your favorite foods? How much sleep do you get? What brand of car do you drive? Do you use the library on campus? Are you satisfied with your life at this point? At some time, you've probably been asked questions like these as part of a survey. Psychologists, sociologists, political scientists, market researchers, magazine editors, and others use surveys to gain information about people's opinions, attitudes, and preferences. Surveys are used to achieve two goals of research in psychology: description and prediction. The results of a survey are often used to *describe* people's opinions, feelings, and preferences. For example, the results of pre-election polls describe potential voters' preferences for the candidates or their opinions about election issues. Survey researchers also seek to make *predictions* about people's behavior. For example, a market researcher may try to predict which households are likely to use a new product. A psychologist may design a questionnaire that identifies people who are at risk for suicide.

Survey research represents a more general approach to psychological research called **correlational research.** When researchers conduct correlational research they assess relationships among naturally occurring variables. An example of a naturally occurring variable is intelligence—people naturally vary in their level of intelligence. Other examples of naturally occurring variables are height, weight, athletic ability, grades, moral values, attitudes, preferences, and personality characteristics. Psychologists use surveys and other measures to assess people's scores on a wide range of variables—the list of variables is endless. Researchers identify relationships between variables in order to make predictions. For example, there is a correlation between the number of hours spent watching television (a variable researchers can measure) and school test scores (another variable researchers can measure). Therefore, we can predict student test scores if we know how much television a student watches. (In case you didn't guess, the correlation tells us that, the more TV watching, the lower the test score.)

Researchers compute a *correlation coefficient* to determine the strength and direction of the relationship between two naturally occurring variables. As we'll see, researchers first measure the variables (e.g., using questionnaires), and then calculate a correlation coefficient to determine the predictive relationship between two variables. Correlation coefficients range from −1.0 to 0.0 (negative correlations) and from 0.0 to +1.0 (positive correlations). The size of a correlation indicates the strength of the predictive relationship (the closer to −1.0 or +1.0, the better the predictive power). The sign (minus or plus) indicates the direction of the relationship. A positive correlation indicates that, as the values for one measure increase, the values for the other measure also increase (as might be the relationship between hours spent studying and test scores). A negative correlation indicates that, as the values for one measure increase, the values for the other measure decrease (as in our example of TV watching and test scores).

Throughout this chapter we will examine how researchers use correlation co-efficients to describe relationships between variables and make predictions. On the surface, survey research is deceptively simple. If you want to know what people are thinking, just ask them! As you will see, survey research involves much more than simply asking people questions.

Although surveys differ according to whether they are conducted over the phone, in personal interviews, or in a mail survey, all surveys have some characteristics in common. First, surveys generally involve sampling, a concept introduced in our discussion of observational methods (Chapter 4) and which we will discuss more in this chapter. Surveys also use a set of predetermined questions for all respondents in the form of a questionnaire. Oral or written responses to these questions constitute the principal data obtained in a survey. By using the same phrasing and ordering of questions, it is possible to summarize the views of all respondents using statistical analyses.

To help illustrate the survey method, we will examine an interesting article that appeared in the *Journal of Abnormal Psychology* in 1997. The authors were Dr. Todd Heatherton, Fary Mahamedi, Meg Striepe, Alison Field, and Pamela Keel. The topic was eating attitudes and behaviors of college students and young adults.

LEARNING OBJECTIVES

By the end of this chapter you will

- *be familiar with questionnaires and measurement issues of reliability and validity,*
- *know how to obtain a sample and implement a survey design, and*
- *be able to analyze and interpret survey data.*

INTRODUCTION TO THE RESEARCH EXAMPLE: CHANGES IN EATING BEHAVIOR AND ATTITUDES

Have you ever heard a friend complain about her body? Have you ever heard any of your friends say, "I'm on a diet"? Chances are the answer to both these questions is yes. Our society seems to be obsessed with how we look and what we eat. All of this attention to dieting and appearance doesn't escape the attention of our youth. Girls often report first dieting before adolescence, and by the time they are in high school, are dieting constantly (Heatherton & Polivy, 1992). Adolescents and young adults are most at risk. Eating disorders are most likely to be identified around the age of 18 (Thelen, Mann, Pruitt, & Smith, 1987).

A great deal of research has focused on disordered eating among college students. For example, research findings suggest that 30% of college women and 10% of college men report current or past problems with binge eating (Heatherton, Nichols, Mahamedi, & Keel, 1995). Other research has focused not on eating disorders, but on body dissatisfaction and dieting—eating "problems." Results from these studies indicate that body dissatisfaction and chronic dieting are very common among college students.

But what happens *after* college? Although much is known about eating attitudes and dieting behaviors in adolescents and college students, do these attitudes and behaviors change over time? Do young women and men experience fewer problems with eating and body dissatisfaction as they get older? Heatherton and his colleagues (1997) sought

Table 5.1 Survey Design for Heatherton et al.'s (1997) Study of Eating Attitudes and Behaviors

Heatherton et al. used a *longitudinal design* in which the same individuals were surveyed in 1982 and 1992. They asked respondents to complete measures at both times to assess changes in eating attitudes and behaviors, and they used responses at Time 1 to predict eating attitudes and behaviors 10 years later.

Time 1 (1982) Measures	Time 2 (1992) Measures
Height, weight	Height, weight
General eating patterns	General eating patterns
Dieting history	Dieting history
Abnormal eating behaviors	Abnormal eating behaviors
Eating Disorder Inventory	Eating Disorder Inventory
	Marital status, children
	Career, income

to answer this question. They reasoned that as individuals move away from college—where there is an emphasis on physical appearance—eating problems should decrease. They also reasoned that during their twenties, individuals settle down, marry, establish careers, begin families, and gain a stronger sense of identity that is less dependent on physical appearance. Therefore, Heatherton and colleagues hypothesized that the prevalence of eating-disordered behaviors and attitudes should decrease as individuals grow older.

To test their hypothesis, the researchers conducted a *longitudinal survey*. In 1982 they asked a *randomly selected sample* of 800 women and 400 men from a private northeastern college to complete a survey about eating and dieting. In 1992 they contacted these individuals again (with the help of the alumni office) and asked them to complete a survey about their eating attitudes and behaviors. As we discuss survey research during this chapter, we will focus on the procedures and results of Heatherton et al.'s study on changes in eating disorders among adult women and men (see Table 5.1 for an outline of the Heatherton et al. [1997] study).

THE RESEARCHERS' POINT OF VIEW

Questions to Dr. Heatherton: How did you become interested in studying eating behavior and eating disorders?

I became interested in eating behavior while in graduate school. My initial interests were how and why diets failed. More specifically, I was interested in situational factors that led people to break their diets. Along the way I discovered that low self-esteem dieters were especially likely to break their diets when they were emotionally upset. This led me to become interested in assessing whether low self-esteem was involved in eating disorders. I developed a theoretical model (the spiral model) that linked perfectionistic attitudes, low self-esteem, and dieting to the development of disordered eating.

Were any of your co-authors graduate or undergraduate students while conducting this study? What were their roles in the project?

Almost all of my co-authors were graduate and undergraduate students. The study could not have been conducted without them. Viveca Aghassi was an undergraduate research assistant in my lab who first discovered the 1982 archival data. [She, and others who assisted in the research, are acknowledged in a footnote to the report.] Pamela Keel was an under-

Dr. Todd Heatherton

graduate in my lab who became very interested in eating disorders. She went on to graduate school in clinical psychology and has recently joined the faculty at Harvard University. Fary Mahamedi and Meg Striepe were graduate students working in my lab. Alison Field was a graduate student in epidemiology who joined us in the project.

With a lot of collaborators on a project it's often hard to determine order of authorship. How did you make these decisions for this project?

I always determine authorship according to the role the person played in writing the manuscript and conducting the research. The first author is always the person who writes the first credible draft of the paper. To be an author, a person has to make a substantial contribution to the research and to writing the paper.

MEASURES IN CORRELATIONAL RESEARCH

Questionnaires

The value of correlational research (and any research) ultimately depends on the quality of the researchers' measurements. The quality of these measurements, in turn, depends on the quality of the instruments used to make the measurements. Questionnaires are the primary research instrument in survey research. Questionnaires may not look like high-tech, modern research instruments, but, when constructed and used properly, a questionnaire is a powerful scientific instrument for investigating behavior.

Questionnaires frequently measure *demographic variables*. Demographic variables allow researchers to describe the characteristics of the people who complete the survey. Examples of demographic variables include race, ethnicity, age, religious affiliation, occupation, and socioeconomic status (see Box 5.1 for sample demographic questions). Whether we decide to measure these variables depends on the goals of our study. For example, we may be interested in learning whether age is related to satisfaction with life. As people become older, do

---

Box 5.1

EXAMPLES OF DEMOGRAPHIC QUESTIONS

Please check each box that applies to you:

1. Your gender:
   ❏ female   ❏ male

2. Your ethnic background:
   ❏ Hispanic/non-White   ❏ Black/African American   ❏ Asian/Pacific Islander
   ❏ Caucasian/White   ❏ Native American   ❏ Other _____

3. Your marital status:
   ❏ single   ❏ married/joined   ❏ divorced/separated   ❏ widowed
   ❏ engaged   ❏ long-term dating relationship   ❏ other _____

Note: Researchers select demographic items and response options based on the goals of their study.

---

they become more or less satisfied with life? To answer this question a researcher would need to include a question that asks respondents' age.

Researchers also assess individuals' *preferences and attitudes* using surveys. For example, a marketing researcher may be interested in consumers' preferences for various brands of coffee, or a political group may be interested in potential voters' attitudes regarding controversial issues. Psychologists measure people's thoughts and feelings on a vast array of topics, and often develop *self-report scales* for people to provide verbal or written responses to items on the scale.

Self-report scales can be used to measure people's judgments about items on the scale. A market researcher, for example, may ask consumers to rate various chocolate desserts according to how "rich" they taste. Psychologists have used self-report scales to learn how individuals experience stressful life events (e.g., the death of a loved one, divorce, illness, exams). For example, respondents may be asked to report how often during the past year they experienced various stressful life events listed on a scale. A total stress score can be obtained for each individual by summing responses to the items on the scale. Individuals can then be compared according to the amount of stress they've experienced during the past year.

The most frequently used method to measure differences among individuals is quite simple. A researcher constructs a scale that respondents can use to identify their self-reported feelings, attitudes, or opinions. For example, a researcher may be interested in individuals' general willingness to forgive others. A rating scale is provided for individuals to respond by circling a number on the scale. The following is one item that could be used to measure forgiveness:

When people hurt me or make me angry, I can usually forgive them.

$$1 \text{------} 2 \text{------} 3 \text{------} 4 \text{------} 5$$

Strongly   Strongly
disagree   agree

Examples of other self-report questionnaire items appear in Box 5.2.

Self-report measures, often in the form of a questionnaire, are important tools for the research psychologist. Given their importance, these measures must be developed carefully.

Reliability and Validity

As we learned in Chapter 1, reliability and validity are important characteristics of all psychological measurement, so it makes sense that measurements in survey research must be reliable and valid. In this section we will examine some procedures researchers use to determine whether measures are reliable and valid.

Reliable measures, like reliable observers, are *consistent*. There are several ways to determine a measure's **reliability** (see Table 5.2). One common method is to compute *test-retest reliability*. Usually, test-retest reliability involves administering the measure to a large sample of people at two different times (hence,

---

Box 5.2

EXAMPLES OF QUESTIONNAIRE ITEMS THAT ASSESS ATTITUDES ABOUT ONESELF

Please circle the appropriate number to indicate the extent to which you agree or disagree using the following scale:

1 = Strongly disagree
2 = Disagree
3 = Neutral
4 = Agree
5 = Strongly agree

On the whole, I am satisfied with myself. (From Self-Esteem Inventory [Rosenberg, 1965])	1	2	3	4	5
I find it difficult to be alone. (From Dependency Beliefs Scale [Persons et al., 1993])	1	2	3	4	5
People will think less of me if I make a mistake. (From Achievement Beliefs Scale [Persons et al., 1993])	1	2	3	4	5
I always look on the bright side of things. (From Life Optimism Test [Scheier & Carver, 1985])	1	2	3	4	5

test and retest). A reliable measure yields similar (consistent) results each time it is taken. However, an individual doesn't need to obtain identical scores each time he or she completes the measure. Instead, a person's relative *position* in the distribution of scores should be similar at the two test times. That is, to be consistent, a person scoring "high" the first time should also score "high" the next time the test is given (although the scores may not be exactly the same). Researchers compute a correlation coefficient using the two scores for each person in the sample to establish the consistency of individuals' relative position. These correlations are called "reliability coefficients" because they are used to describe the reliability of the measure. Test-retest reliability coefficients should be .80 or above for the measure to be considered reliable.

The second common method for establishing a measure's reliability is called *internal consistency reliability.* The goal of this method is to determine whether all the items within a measure consistently measure the same thing. For example, a researcher with a 10-item measure of "forgiveness" would want to make sure that all 10 items measure forgiveness. If all the items are related to forgiveness, the measure is said to be internally consistent. A common approach for calculating internal consistency reliability is to compute the correlation between responses for each item and every other item (a lot of interitem correlations, so this is best done using a computer), and then calculate the average of all these correlations. Researchers generally consider average interitem correlations above .80 to indicate acceptable internal consistency reliability.

The size of a reliability coefficient is influenced by several factors (Table 5.3). One important factor is the number of items on the measure; *more items is better.* Our measures would be unreliable if we tried to measure students' understanding of material based on a single test item, a baseball player's hitting ability based on a single time at bat, or a person's attitude toward the death penalty based on a single question on a survey. The reliability of measures increases greatly if we average the behavior in question across a large number of observations—many test items, many at bats, and many survey questions.

Measurements are also more reliable when individuals completing the measure differ substantially on the factor being assessed. A sample of individuals

Table 5.2   Assessing the Reliability of Measures

Reliability refers to the consistency of measures, and is assessed in two ways:

1. *Test-retest reliability.* The consistency of individuals' responses over time. A sample of individuals completes a measure twice (separated by weeks or months). The correlation between individuals' two sets of scores assesses the measure's reliability.
2. *Internal consistency reliability.* The consistency of items within a measure—that is, how consistently all the items measure the same construct. A sample of individuals completes the measure (once). Internal consistency is represented by the average of all the correlations among the items of the measure.

Table 5.3   Methods for Increasing Reliability

Researchers increase the reliability of their measurement by

1.   Increasing the number of items used to assess a construct
2.   Administering the measure to a diverse sample rather than to a restricted sample of individuals
3.   Making sure the testing situation is free of distractions and the measure has clear instructions

who vary greatly from one another are easier to differentiate reliably. Consider the following example. Suppose we wish to assess soccer players' ability to pass the ball effectively to other players. We will be able to differentiate more reliably good players from poor players if we include in our sample a wider range of players—for example, professionals, high school players, and peewee players. It would be much harder to differentiate players reliably if we test only professional players—they would all be good players. Therefore, a measure is often more reliable when administered to a diverse sample than when given to a restricted sample of individuals.

A third and final factor affecting reliability is the actual administration of the measure. Measures are more reliable when the testing situation is free of distractions and when the measure has clear instructions. (You may wish to think about times when your own test performance was hindered by noise or when you weren't sure what a question was asking.)

The reliability of a measure is easier to determine and to achieve than the validity of a measure. The definition of **validity** is deceptively straightforward—a valid measure assesses what it is intended to measure. For example, a valid test of your research methods knowledge might ask you about the terms *reliability* and *validity*. You probably would question the validity of a research methods test that asked you to define "off sides in a soccer game." Have you ever heard students complain that questions on a test didn't seem to address the material covered in class? This is an issue of validity.

At this point we will focus on construct validity, which is just one of many ways researchers assess the validity of a measure. The *construct validity* of a measure represents the extent to which the instrument measures the theoretical construct it is designed to measure. Psychologists assess many theoretical constructs, including intelligence, arousal, prejudice, self-esteem, memory, and depression (you can probably think of many other constructs). One approach to determining the construct validity of a measure relies on two other kinds of validity: *convergent validity* and *discriminant validity* (see Figure 5.1).

Convergent validity reflects the degree to which two measures of the *same* construct converge, or go together. When researchers attempt to assess the construct validity of their measure, they use their measure *and* one or more additional measures that assess the same construct. If their measure has convergent validity, individuals' scores on the measures should be similar—that is, their

Figure 5.1 Convergent validity and discriminant validity.

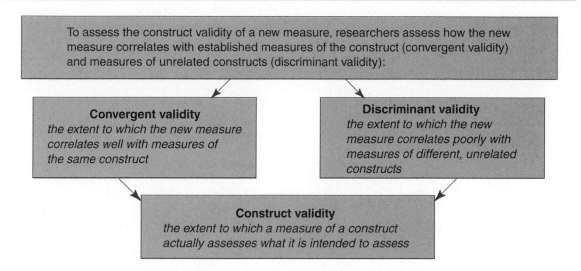

To assess the construct validity of a new measure, researchers assess how the new measure correlates with established measures of the construct (convergent validity) and measures of unrelated constructs (discriminant validity):

Convergent validity
the extent to which the new measure correlates well with measures of the same construct

Discriminant validity
the extent to which the new measure correlates poorly with measures of different, unrelated constructs

Construct validity
the extent to which a measure of a construct actually assesses what it is intended to assess

scores on the measures should converge. For example, researchers measuring children's coping ability may rely on a paper-and-pencil measure of coping, but to demonstrate convergent validity, they may also ask teachers to rate the children's ability to cope. Presumably, the two measures should be correlated if the paper-and-pencil questionnaire of coping is indeed measuring coping ability. If they do correlate significantly, then the researchers have demonstrated convergent validity.

The case for the construct validity of a measure is stronger when it also has discriminant validity. The idea here is to show what constructs the measure *does not* assess. For example, the researchers studying children's coping would want to demonstrate that the coping measure does not assess another theoretical construct, such as intelligence. To demonstrate discriminant validity, the researchers would administer the coping measure and a measure of intelligence. Individuals' scores on the two measures should correlate poorly—that is, scores on the coping measure should have little relation to scores on the intelligence measure if coping and intelligence are different constructs. This would provide evidence for *discriminant* validity of the coping measure for children (see Table 5.4).

Our ability to identify general psychological principles depends on whether measures of people's thoughts and behaviors are reliable and valid. However, another critical aspect of psychological research concerns sampling. Typically, researchers cannot measure the thoughts, feelings, and opinions of an entire population; instead, they use a sample to represent a population. We will next turn to issues associated with selecting a sample for survey research.

Table 5.4   Correlation Matrix to Illustrate Convergent Validity and Discriminant Validity

Correlations among measures are often presented in a "correlation matrix." The following hypothetical correlations demonstrate the construct validity of the "Coping Measure."

	Coping Measure	Teachers' Coping Rating	Intelligence Measure
Coping Measure	1.00	———	———
Teachers' Coping Rating	.80	1.00	———
Intelligence Measure	.10	.15	1.00

1. The correlation between "Coping Measure" and "Coping Measure" simply indicates that a measure correlates with itself perfectly (1.00); researchers typically ignore the diagonal line of 1.00 in a correlation matrix.
2. The correlation between "Coping Measure" and "Teachers' Coping Rating" (.80) indicates the convergent validity of the Coping Measure: It correlates well with another coping rating.
3. The correlation between "Coping Measure" and "Intelligence Measure" (.10) indicates the discriminant validity of the Coping Measure: It correlates poorly with a measure of a different construct, intelligence. That is, the "Coping Measure" seems to assess coping, not intelligence.
4. "Teachers' Coping Rating" and "Intelligence Measure" correlate poorly (.15), indicating that these two measures are not related.

CHANGES IN EATING BEHAVIOR AND ATTITUDES: MEASURES

In order to learn about changes in individuals' eating attitudes and behaviors, Heatherton et al. (1997) asked study participants to complete several questionnaires in 1982 and again in 1992. Their 1982 survey included *demographic* items that asked about height, weight, general eating patterns (e.g., meal frequency), dieting history, and abnormal eating behaviors (binge eating, vomiting, laxative and diuretic use, and fasting). The 1992 survey included questions about those topics and additional questions about marital status, education, career, income, exercise history, and children. These questions allowed the investigators to describe the demographic characteristics of their sample and the prevalence of eating-disordered behaviors.

Heatherton et al. (1997) also measured eating disorder *attitudes* using a *self-report scale* called the Eating Disorder Inventory (EDI; Garner, Olmstead, & Polivy, 1983). Heatherton et al. used five subscales from the EDI: Drive for Thinness, Bulimia, Maturity Fears, Perfectionism, and Interpersonal Distrust. Each subscale measures a different *construct* related to eating attitudes and behaviors. Respondents rated the extent to which each of the items applied to them on a 6-point scale (from *always* to *never*). Sample items from each scale are as follows:

Drive for Thinness: I am terrified of gaining weight.
Bulimia: I stuff myself with food.

Maturity Fears: I feel that people are happiest when they are children.

Perfectionism: Only outstanding performance is good enough in my family.

Interpersonal Distrust: I am open about my feelings. [This item is "reverse-scored."]

What can be said about the *reliability* and *validity* of these measures? For example, is the EDI a reliable and valid measure of eating-disordered attitudes? Heatherton et al. did not address this question directly in their research; instead, they relied on the research conducted by the psychologists who developed the measure. Garner et al. (1983) computed *internal consistency reliability* for each subscale of the EDI using a sample of 113 female patients diagnosed with anorexia nervosa and a comparison sample of 577 female university students. Consider, for example, the items that make up the Drive for Thinness subscale, which assesses excessive concern with dieting and weight:

I eat sweets and carbohydrates without feeling nervous. [reverse-scored]

I think about dieting.

I feel extremely guilty after overeating.

I am terrified of gaining weight.

I exaggerate or magnify the importance of weight.

I am preoccupied with the desire to be thinner.

If I gain a pound, I worry that I will keep gaining.

The reliability coefficient for the Drive for Thinness subscale for each sample was .85, indicating that the items within each subscale reliably (consistently) measured the construct, Drive for Thinness.

Garner et al. (1983) also reported evidence for the *construct validity* of the EDI. To establish *convergent validity* they examined correlations between EDI subscales and other eating-disorder questionnaires. For instance, scores on the Drive for Thinness subscale were positively correlated with scores on another measure, the Eating Attitudes Test. These findings indicate good convergent validity of the Drive for Thinness scale. To assess *discriminant validity*, Garner and colleagues asked respondents to complete questionnaires that assessed constructs that are theoretically distinct from eating-disorder attitudes. Considering just the Drive for Thinness scale again, Garner and colleagues found that attitudes related to thinness correlated poorly with self-esteem, locus of control, and depression. These findings contribute to the construct validity of the Drive for Thinness subscale because the items on the measure seem to measure specific attitudes related to eating, not general negative attitudes about the self.

OBTAINING A SAMPLE

Samples Are Used to Describe Populations

Assume you've decided to use a survey to answer your research question, and you know what population you're interested in studying. The next step is to select a sample of respondents to represent the population. Whether you are describing a national population or a much smaller one (e.g., the students at one university), the procedures are the same. A **population** is the set of all cases of interest. For example, if you are interested in the attitudes of students on your campus toward services provided by the library, your population is all students on your campus. But contacting everyone in a large population, such as all students at a school, is often practically impossible. Therefore, researchers usually select a **sample,** a subset of the population to represent the entire population.

Our ability to describe the population using results from the sample depends critically on the **representativeness** of the sample: How well do individuals in the sample represent the entire population? Clearly, individuals in a population differ in many ways, and populations differ from each other. For example, one population might be 40% men and 60% women, whereas in another population the distribution might be 75% women and 25% men. *A sample represents the population when it exhibits the same characteristics as the population.* If a sample of 200 individuals has 80 males and 120 females, which of the preceding two populations does it represent? (Box 5.3 has more examples for you to match the representative sample to the population.)

Box 5.3

IDENTIFYING REPRESENTATIVE SAMPLES

Presented on the left side are descriptions of four populations. Find the sample on the right side that represents each population.

Populations	Samples
1. 60% women, 40% men 90% ages 18–22, 10% age >22 70% freshman/sophomore, 30% junior/senior	A. 132 women, 44 men 114 ages 18–22, 62 age >22 141 freshman/sophomore, 35 junior/senior
2. 80% women, 20% men 60% ages 18–22, 40% age >22 70% freshman/sophomore, 30% junior/senior	B. 244 women, 61 men 183 ages 18–22, 122 age >22 213 freshman/sophomore, 92 junior/senior
3. 75% women, 25% men 65% ages 18–22, 35% age >22 80% freshman/sophomore, 20% junior/senior	C. 48 women, 12 men 54 ages 18–22, 6 age >22 42 freshman/sophomore, 18 junior/senior
4. 80% women, 20% men 90% ages 18–22, 10% age >22 70% freshman/sophomore, 30% junior/senior	D. 150 women, 100 men 225 ages 18–22, 25 age >22 175 freshman/sophomore, 75 junior/senior

Answers

1. D   2. B   3. A   4. C

The major threat to representativeness is bias. A **biased sample** is one in which the characteristics of the sample differ *systematically* from those of the target population. A sample of 100 individuals that included 80 women and 20 men would be biased if the population were to contain 60% women and 40% men. In this sample, women would be overrepresented and men would be underrepresented.

There are two sources of bias: selection bias and response bias. **Selection bias** occurs when researchers use selection procedures that overrepresent or underrepresent a segment of the population. For example, a researcher interested in surveying parents with young children may sample parents from local preschools. This selection procedure could lead to bias because parents who don't enroll their children in preschool may not be sampled. They are systematically excluded because of the researcher's "system" for selecting a sample.

Response bias threatens the representativeness of a sample when not all sample respondents complete the survey. There are many reasons why this may occur. For example, respondents with literacy problems or vision problems may not complete the questionnaire; therefore, people with these characteristics may not be represented well in the final sample of respondents. Often, people included in the initial sample are too busy or not interested enough in the study to return a completed questionnaire. Low response rate (i.e., failure to complete and return the survey) is the major factor leading to response bias in mail surveys.

Approaches to Sampling

"Sampling" refers to the procedures used to select a sample to represent the population. The two basic approaches to sampling are nonprobability sampling and probability sampling (Figure 5.2). In *nonprobability sampling,* there is no guarantee that each member of the population has a chance of being included and no way to estimate the probability of each member's being included in the sample. The most common form of nonprobability sampling is convenience

When evaluating a survey, be sure to find out how the sample was selected.

Figure 5.2 The two primary approaches to sampling are nonprobability sampling and probability sampling.

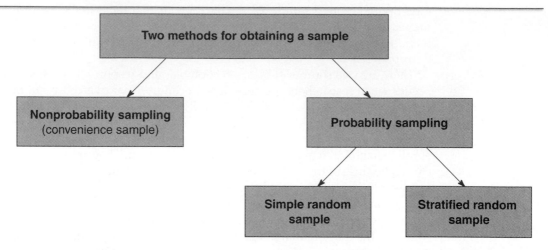

sampling. *Convenience sampling* involves selecting respondents who are available and willing to respond to the survey. In a campus survey of library services, we could select the first 25 students in the library on a Monday morning to complete our survey. This is an example of convenience sampling. Not all students would be equally likely to be at the library at that particular time, and some students would have essentially no chance of being included in the sample (e.g., if they were in class at the time of the survey). Convenience sampling is also involved when people respond to surveys in *Cosmopolitan* or other magazines because the magazine has to be available (and purchased), and people must be willing to send in their responses.

In *probability sampling* all members of a population have an equal chance of being included in the sample. In our library survey, if we were to select 25 students randomly from the registrar's list of enrolled students, we would be using probability sampling. Probability sampling allows researchers to estimate the likelihood that their sample findings differ from the findings they would have obtained by studying the whole population. Probability sampling is much better than nonprobability sampling in ensuring that selected samples represent the population. Our sample of 25 students randomly selected from the registrar's list of students is more likely to represent the population than is a sample of the first 25 students entering the library.

Two common types of probability sampling are simple random sampling and stratified random sampling. **Simple random sampling** is the basic technique of probability sampling. The most common definition of *simple random sampling* is that every member of the population has an equal chance of being included in the sample.

In **stratified random sampling,** the population is divided into subpopulations called *strata* (singular, *stratum*), and random samples are drawn from each of these strata. The representativeness of a sample can often be increased by using stratified random sampling. To obtain a representative sample, we want to draw individuals for the sample on a proportional basis. Consider a population of undergraduate students made up of 30% freshmen, 30% sophomores, 20% juniors, and 20% seniors (class years are the strata). A stratified random sample of 200 students drawn from this population would include 60 freshmen, 60 sophomores, 40 juniors, and 40 seniors.

CHANGES IN EATING BEHAVIOR AND ATTITUDES: THE SAMPLE

Heatherton et al. (1997) wanted to describe changes in eating-disordered attitudes and behaviors as college students mature through their twenties. Thus, their first step was to survey college students. As you might imagine, it would be very costly and time-consuming to survey the entire *population* of college students. Furthermore, it would be costly and time-consuming to obtain a *sample* from the *entire* population of college students. So, Heatherton et al. did the next best thing: They selected a *stratified random sample* of college students close to home—at their own college. They randomly selected 800 women and 400 men to complete the survey; half of each group were seniors and half were freshmen. Because their sample came from one college (described by the researchers as "a selective northeastern college"), it is reasonable to wonder whether their sample was *representative* of the entire population of college students. Note, too, that they did not survey sophomores and juniors. Thus, we may ask if this *selection bias* affects our ability to *generalize* their findings from the sample to the population of college students or to adults in general.

One way that their sample differed from the general adult American population was in terms of weight. Although recent studies indicate that 20 to 35% of American adults are overweight or obese (Kuczmarski et al., 1994), less than 4% of their sample was characterized as overweight or obese in 1982. In fact, almost one-third of the women in their sample were *underweight*. These differences indicate that we must be cautious when generalizing findings from this sample to all adults.

Heatherton et al. also reported that not all students who received the survey completed it; this was more true for the men than for the women, suggesting a possible *response bias*. The response rate was 78% for women ($n = 625$) and 69% for men ($n = 276$). Given that women tend to experience more problems with eating attitudes and behaviors, it's possible they were more interested in the survey than were the men.

THE RESEARCHERS' POINT OF VIEW

Questions to Dr. Heatherton: What procedures did you use to sample students in 1982?

The first wave of data was collected by Anne Colby. [She] had the registrar at Harvard/Radcliffe write a program to randomly sample among first-year and senior students. The registrar then provided the list to researchers.

You indicated that the respondents in your study may not have been representative of the larger population of college students. How did this affect your thinking about your results?

We know that eating disorders are especially common among high-achieving and perfectionistic young women. In many ways, therefore, ours was the perfect sample to study for disordered eating. However, it is plausible that various selection factors might have influenced our findings. For instance, it might have been the case that women prone to eating disorders were more likely to attend the school we studied. Alternatively, it might have been that the school was highly competitive and stressful, thereby exacerbating disordered eating. Therefore, the slight decline in disordered eating [over time] may reflect a change from a particularly stressful environment. Of course, this finding is interesting in its own right.

SURVEY RESEARCH DESIGNS

One of the most important decisions survey researchers must make is the choice of a research design. A survey research design is the overall plan or structure used to conduct the entire study. There are three general types of survey designs: the cross-sectional design, the successive independent samples design, and the longitudinal design. Researchers choose a design based on the goals of the study (Table 5.5).

The cross-sectional design is one of the most commonly used survey research designs. In a **cross-sectional design** one or more samples are drawn from the population *at one time.* Information for different variables is collected from the sample(s) and is used to describe the population(s) at that point in time, and researchers can make predictions based on the correlational survey data.

Cross-sectional designs are not necessarily simple and quick. For example, in a study of mental disorders in children and adolescents, a total of 1,285 parent-youth pairs from Connecticut, Georgia, New York, and Puerto Rico completed surveys and were interviewed in their homes (Goodman et al., 1997)—quite a massive effort. Cross-sectional designs are ideally suited for the descriptive and predictive goals of correlational research. However, these survey designs do not

Table 5.5   Three Survey Research Designs

Survey Designs	Characteristics	Goals
Cross-sectional	One or more samples are drawn from the population *at one time.*	To describe the population at that time, make predictions about the population
Successive independent samples	A series of cross-sectional surveys are drawn from the population over time; different representative samples are selected each time.	To describe changes in the population over time
Longitudinal	The same sample of individuals is surveyed more than once.	To describe changes in individuals over time

allow researchers to assess *changes* in attitudes or behaviors over time. To assess changes over time, researchers choose either the successive independent samples design or the longitudinal design.

In the **successive independent samples design,** researchers conduct a series of cross-sectional surveys over time (successively). The samples are independent because a *different* sample of respondents completes the survey at each point in time. There are two key ingredients: (1) the same set of questions should be asked each time, and (2) the different samples should be drawn from the same population. If these two conditions are met, researchers can compare survey responses over time. This design is most appropriate when the major goal of a study is to describe changes in attitudes or behaviors of a population over time. For example, public opinion researchers frequently ask independent samples of Americans the extent to which they approve of the U.S. president (referred to as the president's "approval ratings"). Changes in approval ratings over time are used to characterize Americans' opinions of the president's actions.

The successive independent samples design has some limitations. First, we have to remember that the samples are independent, so we don't know how specific individuals change over time. The purpose of the successive independent samples design is to describe changes over time in *population* characteristics, not changes in *individual* respondents.

A second potential problem with the successive independent samples design arises when the successive samples are not representative of the same population. This can happen when researchers mistakenly draw samples from *different* populations at the various times of the survey. This is called the problem of *noncomparable samples*. For example, if a public opinion researcher were to sample mostly Republicans in one sample and mostly Democrats in a second sample, it's likely the researcher would observe changes over time in the approval ratings. If this were to happen it would be very difficult to determine whether changes in survey responses over time were due to true changes in the population's opinion about the president or to the different populations that were sampled. Researchers can detect changes in the population across time only when the successive independent samples are drawn from the *same* population.

In the **longitudinal design,** the *same* sample of respondents is surveyed more than once. As we've seen, the Heatherton et al. (1997) research on changes in eating-disordered attitudes in behaviors over time used a longitudinal survey design. Using a longitudinal design, the researcher can determine the direction and extent of change for *individual* respondents. This was a critical consideration for Heatherton and his colleagues. One potential problem with longitudinal survey designs is that it is difficult to pinpoint the exact *causes* for individuals' changes over time. For example, a researcher who observes changes in people's emotions after divorce cannot be sure what caused these changes. Remember that survey designs represent correlational research. Although researchers may be able to observe correlations between changes in individuals' responses and specific variables, these correlations do not allow researchers to identify the causes of those changes.

Another potential problem with longitudinal designs is that it can be difficult to obtain a sample of respondents who will agree to participate in a longitudinal study, which often means a long-term commitment. Even when the respondents do agree to participate, they may later drop out of the study for various reasons (e.g., they move or are no longer interested). This problem is called *respondent mortality* (or attrition). When people drop out of the study, the final sample may no longer represent the original population. It is usually possible, however, to determine whether the final sample is different from the original sample. Researchers know the characteristics of the people who drop out because they participated in the original sample. Therefore, researchers look at their original responses to see how these individuals may differ from the people who continued their participation.

Paradoxically, problems can also arise in longitudinal designs precisely because the same respondents are surveyed more than once. One possible problem is that respondents may strive heroically to be consistent across interviews. Although their attitudes may have actually changed, people may report their original attitudes in an effort to appear consistent (perhaps they don't want to appear wishy-washy). Another potential problem is that the initial survey may sensitize respondents to be more aware of the issue under investigation. Consider a longitudinal design used to assess students' concerns about crime on campus. Once the study starts, participants may pay more attention to crime reports than they normally would. You might recognize this as an illustration of reactive measurement—people behaving differently because they know they are participating in a study (see Chapter 4).

CHANGES IN EATING BEHAVIOR AND ATTITUDES: THE SURVEY DESIGN

 Heatherton and colleagues (1997) used a *longitudinal survey design* to examine changes in individual respondents' eating attitudes and behaviors. Individuals completed the first survey in 1982 (while in college) and were contacted again in 1992 to complete the survey again. They hypothesized that eating-disordered attitudes and behaviors would decrease as individuals matured after college.

In 1982, 901 participants completed the survey. However, in 1992, only 715 (79%) of the original participants returned a useable survey. To examine this problem of *respondent mortality*, Heatherton and colleagues compared the 1982 survey responses of those who dropped out with the responses of those who continued their participation. They found that women were more likely to continue than men and that participants who reported frequent dieting or symptoms of eating difficulties in college were more likely to continue than were those who reported never dieting. These findings suggest that the 1992 sample comprised more individuals with eating problems than the 1982 sample—something to keep in mind when considering the results of the study.

Heatherton and colleagues (1997) also considered the *reliability* of respondents' answers to the survey questions over time. Did the respondents try to make their answers consistent across the two surveys? Rather than trying to be heroically consistent in their eating attitudes and behaviors over time, the participants may have been reluctant to report they were experiencing the same eating problems as when they were in college. Thus, any decreases in problem eating during the 10-year period may be due to the fact that "women who are approaching their thirties may be embarrassed to admit they are experiencing problems typically associated with adolescence" (p. 124).

THE RESEARCHERS' POINT OF VIEW

Question to Dr. Heatherton: What were the difficulties you experienced while conducting this longitudinal research?

One of the major difficulties was paying for the research. The first wave of data was collected by Anne Colby at the Henry Murray Research Center, and she had a grant to collect those data. Fortunately, most of what we needed to do was not inherently expensive. Tracking down the people after 10 years was effortful, but not costly. Finding the people after 10 years was somewhat challenging, especially people who moved around a great deal. The one tremendous benefit that we had was that the data from the 1982 study were archived at the Murray Center and were set up in a way that we could conduct the longitudinal study. We also had the assistance of the Harvard/Radcliffe Alumni Association, who provided addresses for most of the study participants. Thus, we were the happy beneficiaries of many cooperative researchers and administrators.

ANALYZING SURVEY DATA

Researchers use surveys to describe a population. This is often done by observing the frequency of various responses (for nominal data) or by calculating measures of central tendency and dispersion (interval and ratio data). Researchers also use survey data to identify relationships—correlations—between variables. The primary method of analyzing survey data, therefore, is to calculate correlations. Also, because results from a sample are used to represent a population, we need to know how well the findings for the sample describe the population; this is called the "margin of error."

Correlation Coefficients and Scatterplots

We introduced the concept of correlation briefly at the beginning of this chapter. A **correlation** exists when two measures of the same people, events, or things vary together or go together. For example, obesity and heart disease covary, or go together. The more overweight a person is, the more likely he or she is to have symptoms of heart disease. Obesity and heart disease are correlated. We can determine the *direction* and *strength* of a correlation by computing a **correlation coefficient,** a quantitative index of how well we are able to predict one set of scores (e.g., symptoms of heart disease) using another set of scores (e.g., percentage overweight).

Recall that the direction of a correlation coefficient can be either positive or negative. A positive correlation indicates that, as the values for one measure increase, the values for the other measure also increase. As we've seen, measures of obesity and heart disease are positively correlated (more overweight, more heart disease). Another predictive relationship concerns Scholastic Aptitude Test (SAT) scores: SAT scores and college students' first-semester GPAs are positively correlated. Thus, we can predict that students with higher SAT scores will have higher first-semester GPAs, and that students with lower SAT scores will have lower first-semester GPAs. With correlations, the "reverse" prediction can be made too. If we know only the first-semester GPAs of students, we can "predict" what their SAT scores were prior to entering college. Students with higher GPAs are more likely to have higher SAT scores, and students with lower GPAs are likely to have lower SAT scores.

In a negative correlation, as the value of one measure increases, the value of the other measure *decreases*. A national survey of high school seniors showed a negative correlation between the amount of time spent watching TV and the number of correct answers on an academic achievement test (Keith, Reimers, Fehrmann, Pottebaum, & Aubrey, 1986). Students who spent *more* time watching TV answered *fewer* questions correctly on an achievement test. What about the reverse prediction? Based on this finding, if you knew that a student scored very high on the achievement test, would you predict that the student had spent a "a lot" of time or "a little" time watching TV? (Box 5.4 has more examples of positive and negative correlations.)

The strength of a correlation coefficient can range in absolute values from 0.0 to 1.00. A value of 0.0 indicates there is no correlation and no basis for making predictions. The relationship between intelligence and mental illness, for example, has a zero correlation. We cannot predict the likelihood that a person will

---

Box 5.4

ILLUSTRATIONS OF POSITIVE AND NEGATIVE CORRELATIONS

For each of the following relationships between two variables, identify whether the correlation is positive or negative.

1. As the number of years in which individuals smoke cigarettes increases, the likelihood of lung cancer increases.
2. As the frequency of participating in volunteer activities increases, occasions of depressed mood decrease.
3. As perceptions of parental support during college decreases, measures of psychological adjustment in college decrease.
4. As a woman's age increases, the incidence of self-reported eating-disordered attitudes and behaviors decreases.

5. As arousal level increases, the likelihood of retaliation following an offense increases.
6. As measures of self-reported life satisfaction decrease, measures of self-reported depression increase.

Answers

1. positive
2. negative
3. positive
4. negative
5. positive
6. negative

become mentally ill by knowing the person's IQ (nor can we predict a person's IQ based on his or her mental health). A value of +1.00 indicates a perfect positive correlation, and a value of −1.00 indicates a perfect negative correlation. When a correlation coefficient is either +1.00 or −1.00, we can make predictions with absolute confidence. Values between 0.0 and 1.00 indicate predictive relationships of intermediate strength and, therefore, we have less ability to predict confidently. The stronger the correlation, the better the predictive power. The sign of the correlation tells us its direction; the value of the correlation tells us its strength. A correlation coefficient of −.46 indicates a stronger (more predictive) relationship than one of +.20. (In practice, the sign is included for a correlation only when it is negative; a coefficient without a plus or minus sign is treated as positive—that is, +.20 = .20.) A formula for calculating a correlation coefficient appears at the end of this chapter.

Correlations also can be represented using a scatterplot. Scores for the two variables are represented on the x-axis and y-axis. Each individual has a value (or score) for each variable (e.g., SAT score and first-semester GPA). A scatterplot shows the intersecting points for each pair of scores. Hypothetical examples of scatterplots showing strong positive, practically zero, and moderate negative correlations are shown in Figure 5.3. The strength of a correlation is seen in a scatterplot by looking at how well the points form a straight line; stronger correlations seem to form a straight line of points. The correlation is stronger in the first example (a) than in the other two examples; however, the correlation represented in the third example (c) is stronger than in the second example (b). The direction of a correlation can be seen in the scatterplot by noting how the points are arranged. When the pattern of points seems to move from the lower left corner to the upper right (a), then the correlation is positive.

Figure 5.3 Three scatterplots illustrating a strong positive (a), a zero (b), and a moderate negative (c), correlation between scores on two variables x and y.

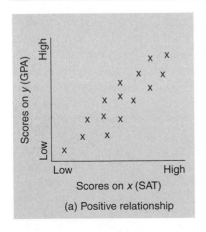

(a) Positive relationship

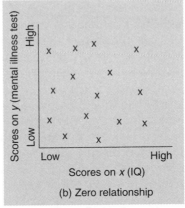

(b) Zero relationship

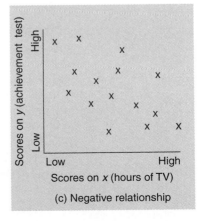

(c) Negative relationship

When the pattern of points is from the upper left to the lower right (c), the correlation is negative. Whether represented in a scatterplot or in a correlation coefficient, a correlation is used to determine how well we can predict one measure based on its covariation with another measure.

Margin of Error

Researchers often report survey results in terms of the percentage of respondents who prefer a certain candidate, agree or disagree with a certain position, or possess a particular demographic characteristic. Well-selected samples will provide good descriptions of the population, but it's unlikely that the results for a sample will describe the population *exactly*. We expect some "slippage" due to sampling, some "error" between the actual population values and the estimates from the sample. At issue, then, is how accurately the responses from the sample represent the larger population.

Researchers can estimate the **margin of error** between the sample results and the true population values. Rather than providing a precise estimate of a population value (e.g., "Sixty-five percent of the population prefer the present mayor"), the margin of error presents a *range* of values with the idea that the true population value is likely to be within the range (e.g., "Between 60 and 70% of the population prefer the present mayor in the next election"). What, specifically, is this range?

The margin of error gives us the range of population values we can expect due to sampling error. Suppose a newspaper editor conducts a poll of many voters prior to a mayoral election and gives the following report: "Results indicate that 63% of those sampled favor the incumbent, and we can say with 95% confidence that the poll has a margin of error of 5%." The reported margin of error with the specified level of confidence (usually 95%) indicates that the percentage of the *actual* population who favor the incumbent is estimated to fall somewhere between 58% and 68% (5% is subtracted from and added to the sample value of 63%). Figure 5.4 displays this margin of error; the bars in this figure represent the range of values when estimating the percentage of a population that supports the incumbent.

The margin of error is primarily determined by the size of the sample—the larger the sample size, the smaller the margin of error. This is because a larger sample is more likely to provide a better estimate of the population characteristics. Thus, in order to reduce the margin of error (and more precisely describe the population), an obvious decision is to increase the size of the sample. This may make sense in some situations, but increasing sample sizes can sometimes make the cost of doing a survey too high.

The goal of many surveys is to state, "with a margin of error," what the true population value is. However, knowing the margin of error for a survey does not assure that the survey results can be interpreted. Interpretable results also depend on factors such as how the survey sample was selected, whether those

Figure 5.4   Bars are used to represent the margin of error for the estimate of the population value.

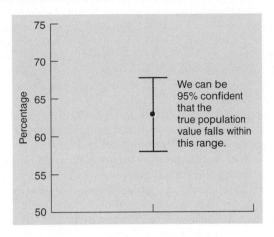

selected for the sample actually responded to the survey, how the questions on the questionnaire were worded, and how the interviewers who administer the questionnaire were trained (Converse & Traugott, 1986). Unfortunately, these important aspects of survey research usually are not reported in the media. Thus, we should be cautious in accepting interpretations of survey results unless we are well informed about critical characteristics of the survey.

CHANGES IN EATING BEHAVIOR AND ATTITUDES: THE DATA ANALYSIS

 Heatherton et al.'s (1997) longitudinal study involved a massive effort. The benefit of their effort, however, was that they were able to examine changes within individuals over time. Their results indicated different changes in eating and weight gain for women and men—two *strata* within their sample of respondents. The following summary highlights some of the *descriptive* and *predictive* data found in their study.

What happened to respondents' weight over the 10-year period? Both the women and men gained weight: an average of 4 pounds for women and almost 12 pounds for men. Heatherton and colleagues used *correlational analyses* to identify variables from the 1982 survey that would predict weight gain in 1992. One variable, scores from the Drive for Thinness scale of the EDI, predicted weight gain for both the women and men, but with opposite relationships. For women, a *negative* correlation indicated that *lower* scores on this scale (low concern about being thin) were associated with *greater* weight gain. In contrast, the men's Drive for Thinness scores were *positively* correlated with weight gain: The *more* concerned men were about being thin, the *more* weight they gained.

Heatherton and his colleagues also examined changes in individuals' responses to questions that asked about their body satisfaction, desire to lose weight, and dieting. In

1982, most of the women described themselves as *overweight* or *very overweight* (recall that this sample was predominantly *underweight* when compared with the population). They reported they wanted to lose weight and dieted *sometimes* or *often*. By 1992, however, these women were less likely to describe themselves as overweight, less likely to diet frequently, and less likely to desire weight loss, compared with 1982 (although the majority still reported a desire to lose weight). Men, in contrast, were more likely to describe themselves in 1992 as overweight, wishing to lose weight, and reported more frequent dieting, compared with 1982 (but remember also that these men gained weight during the 10-year period).

Finally, Heatherton and colleagues (1997) examined changes in the respondents' eating-disordered attitudes (assessed using the Eating Disorder Inventory) and symptoms (assessed using a symptom checklist). Women decreased their bulimic attitudes and their drive for thinness over the 10-year period. These changes were paralleled by changes in eating-disordered symptoms. Compared with 1982, the women were less likely in 1992 to report binge eating, fasting, and laxative use. Men also decreased their bulimic attitudes over the 10 years, but *increased* their drive for thinness attitudes (related, perhaps, to their weight gain and dieting). Men were less likely than women to experience symptoms of eating disorders in 1982 and 1992, and men's symptoms did not change significantly over time. Using correlational analyses, Heatherton and colleagues (1997) found that changes in eating disorders and attitudes toward eating could be predicted by changes in the respondents' dieting frequency, body dissatisfaction, and weight change.

THE RESEARCHERS' POINT OF VIEW

Question to Dr. Heatherton: Were you surprised by any of the findings?
I was surprised that the men gained so much weight in the 10 years following college. It was also extremely interesting to note that as they increased dieting (to compensate), they started to experience many of the problems reported by the women while the women were in college (and dieting). I was somewhat surprised at the extent to which disordered eating subsided for women.

THINKING CRITICALLY ABOUT CORRELATIONAL RESEARCH

Correlation and Causation

Researchers use correlational studies when their goals are description and prediction. It's very important to remember that correlations cannot be used to make statements about the causes of relationships between variables. Recall the phrase "Correlation does not imply causation." This means that simply because two variables are related, one doesn't necessarily cause the other. The third goal of psychological research, understanding, is not met through correlational research.

Consider, for example, Heatherton et al.'s (1997) findings for weight gain among men in their sample. They found that men's Drive for Thinness scores were positively correlated with weight gain: Greater concern about being thin was associated with more weight gain. Based on this correlation, we could *not* argue that being concerned about thinness *causes* men to gain weight. With any correlation, any one of three possible causal relationships may be correct, and it's impossible to determine which is correct based on the correlation alone:

1. A causes B (concern about being thin causes weight gain).
2. B causes A (weight gain causes concern about being thin).
3. C causes A and B.

What third variable (C) could cause the correlation between concern for thinness and weight gain? One possibility is that men may become less physically active (e.g., sports, workouts) in their years after college. Less physical activity may lead to weight gain and a concern about thinness. A correlation that can be explained by a third variable is called a *spurious relationship* (Kenny, 1979). This doesn't mean that the original positive correlation between concern about thinness and weight gain doesn't exist (it certainly does); it just means that other variables (e.g., physical activity) may explain *why* the relationship exists. These problems with understanding causal relationships based on correlations should make it clear *that correlational evidence is not sufficient for making causal statements.*

Reactivity in Survey Research

Regardless of how carefully survey data are collected and analyzed, the value of these data depends on the truthfulness of the respondents' answers to the survey questions. Should we believe that survey responses reflect people's *true* thoughts, opinions, feelings, and behavior? Researchers have debated extensively about the truthfulness of people's self-reports, and no clear-cut conclusion has emerged. Judd, Smith, and Kidder (1991) note, however, that in everyday life we regularly accept the verbal reports of others as valid. If a friend tells you she enjoyed reading a certain novel, you do not usually question whether the statement accurately reflects your friend's feelings. However, in everyday life there are some situations in which we *do* have reason to suspect the truthfulness of someone's statements. When shopping for a used car, for instance, we might not always trust the sales pitch. Generally, however, we accept people's remarks as valid unless we have reason to suspect otherwise. We apply the same standards to the information we obtain from survey responses.

Survey research involves reactive measurement because respondents know their responses are being recorded. Pressures may be strong for people to respond as they think they "should" rather than what they actually believe. The term often used to describe these pressures is **social desirability** ("politically correct" refers to similar pressures). For example, if respondents are asked whether they favor giving help to the needy, they may respond "yes" because they believe this is the most socially acceptable attitude (see Table 5.6 for examples

Table 5.6   Examples of Questions with Socially Desirable Responses

The following items, taken from the Marlowe-Crowne (1964) Social Desirability Scale, are used to assess whether individuals tend to respond to items in a socially desirable manner. For each item, can you tell whether "True" or "False" represents a socially desirable response?

1.	No matter who I'm talking to, I'm always a good listener.	T	F
2.	I like to gossip at times.	T	F
3.	I'm always willing to admit it when I make a mistake.	T	F
4.	I have almost never felt the urge to tell someone off.	T	F

Answers: Socially desirable responses to these questions would be T, F, T, and T. That is, individuals who respond in this manner may be trying to "look good" or respond in a socially desirable manner.

Source: Crowne and Marlowe (1964)

of questionnaire items with socially desirable responses). Similarly, when Heatherton et al. (1997) asked people about their weight gain, we can presume that some respondents would be hesitant to describe large weight gains. As suggested in Chapter 4, the best protection against reactive measurement is to be aware of its existence and control for it as best we can. Heatherton et al. promised respondents that their responses would be kept confidential and treated only in the aggregate (i.e., as a group) so that individuals could not be identified. No doubt this procedure helped reduce reactivity in their study.

DISCUSSION OF THE RESEARCH EXAMPLE: CHANGES IN EATING BEHAVIOR AND ATTITUDES

Using a longitudinal survey design, Heatherton and colleagues (1997) found that during the decade following college, women's eating-disorder symptoms, frequent dieting, and body dissatisfaction decreased, as hypothesized. However, despite these decreases, women's dissatisfaction with their body and their desire to lose weight remained high (and were always higher than men's). Men, in contrast, rarely had problems with eating and weight during college. Ten years later, however, they experienced weight gain, increased dieting, and changes in their attitudes about eating (i.e., greater drive for thinness).

Heatherton and colleagues (1997) made some interesting observations that are relevant to our understanding of longitudinal surveys. They proposed that decreases in women's eating problems reflect their maturation during their twenties, changes in their life roles, and moving away from the college campus (and the pressures to be thin that occur on college campuses). That is, these factors may *cause* changes in women's eating attitudes and behaviors. However, as we've seen, survey research—and correlational research more generally—does not allow researchers to make statements about the causes of behavior. It's possible that other factors or processes may account for changes in individuals across the 10 years of the survey.

One possible alternative explanation is that eating attitudes and behaviors were changing at the *societal* level during this time period. Heatherton et al.'s explanation focuses on the individual: *individual* maturation or changes in roles over time. Could it be that decreases in women's eating problems were caused by changes in society that occurred between 1982 and 1992?

Heatherton et al. (1997) addressed this question by reporting the results of a *successive independent samples* survey design conducted during the same 1982–1992 period (see Heatherton et al., 1995). In this design, *separate* samples of college students were surveyed in 1982 and 1992. Heatherton and his colleagues noted that eating-disordered symptoms and body dissatisfaction were lower for the college students in the 1992 sample compared with the 1982 sample. These findings suggest that decreases in eating-disordered attitudes and behaviors may reflect changes that occurred at a societal level, not an individual level. That is, because different samples of individuals from the same population were surveyed over time, the observed decreases occurred at the population level, not necessarily within the individuals.

Heatherton et al. (1997) suggested that greater information about eating disorders in the media (e.g., accounts of the late Princess Diana's struggle with bulimia) may explain decreases in eating-disorder attitudes and behaviors within society. However, Heatherton and colleagues also noted that decreases in problem eating were larger among individuals in the longitudinal survey than in the successive independent samples survey. Based on the different findings for the two survey designs, they reasoned that maturational processes, in addition to societal changes, were likely operating to decrease individuals' problem eating over time.

As you can see, establishing the causes of individuals' behavior and attitudes (in this case, their problem eating) is not an easy task. Heatherton and his colleagues relied on two survey designs, the longitudinal design and the successive independent samples design, to help them make inferences about changes in eating attitudes and behavior. One goal of this book is to show you that researchers select from a variety of research methods as they try to answer their research questions—this is the *multimethod approach* to research. In the next two chapters of this book we will discuss the most frequent type of research that psychologists use to understand behavior and mental processes—experimental methods. As you will learn, experimental research designs are best suited for helping researchers identify the causes of behavior.

THE RESEARCHERS' POINT OF VIEW

Questions to Dr. Heatherton: What most would you like people to learn from this study?

I think there are a few important lessons. First, researchers should use secondary data [archival] sources whenever possible. [See Chapter 4 for information about archival data.] We were extremely fortunate to find the study from 1982 and to be able to follow up that original study. Longitudinal studies are expensive and time-consuming, but if we can find older data that allow for follow-up, half of the work has been done (and the study can be done more quickly). A second lesson is that one has to be sensitive to changes in item meaning over time. We were very concerned that the questions might have had a different meaning for participants [in 1992] and therefore change might have been more apparent than real. Thus, it was important to have subsidiary measures that reflected disordered attitudes.

Finally, I hope that the take-home message is that disordered eating can resolve itself over time for most people. Our findings fit in nicely with other research showing that eating disorders typically remit over time.

Why do you think women's eating-disordered attitudes were still high in 1992?

North American culture continues to place a strong emphasis on body weight and attractiveness. Cultural norms, at least for Caucasians, emphasize a thin ideal that is difficult to obtain. Media and other pressures encourage dieting at young ages, which can lead to disordered eating in some individuals.

You suggested in your conclusions that both societal changes and individual maturational processes contributed to changes over time in eating-disordered attitudes and behaviors. Which may be more important in causing change?

I believe that maturational changes are the most important. For instance, we are still seeing very high rates of disordered eating among young women, and we still see those patterns before the students arrive at college. The years following college involve many important transitions and new life meanings (job, marriage, family) that change the relative priorities given to physical attractiveness.

Are you conducting any follow-up studies to this research? Do you intend to survey these students again?

We are following up this research in a number of ways. Clinical psychologist Thomas Joiner has become a frequent collaborator on models of eating disorders. Together with Dr. Lyn Abramson and graduate students Kathleen Vohs and Anna Bardone, we have developed a more thorough model of the development of eating disorders that we are testing. We have recently conducted a large longitudinal study of students at Dartmouth College, in which we assessed their eating behavior before they arrived at Dartmouth (while they were in high school). We found that disordered eating was firmly in place before they arrived at college and did not change much during the first year at college.

Thomas Joiner, Pam Keel, and I plan to conduct a 20-year study of our sample in 2002. The data will be archived at the Henry Murray Center so that other researchers can use the data to answer their empirical questions about long-term changes and stability in eating patterns.

READ MORE ABOUT IT

A full description of Heatherton et al.'s longitudinal study can be found in the following journal article:

Heatherton, T. F., Mahamedi, F., Striepe, M., Field, A. E., & Keel, P. (1997). A 10-year longitudinal study of body weight, dieting, and eating disorder symptoms. *Journal of Abnormal Psychology, 106,* 117–125.

To learn more about their successive independent samples survey, read

Heatherton, T. F., Nichols, P., Mahamedi, F., & Keel, P. K. (1995). Body weight, dieting, and eating disorder symptoms among college students 1982 to 1992. *American Journal of Psychiatry, 152,* 1623–1629.

Details about the Eating Disorders Inventory can be found in

Garner, D. M., Olmstead, M. P., & Polivy, J. (1983). Development and validation of a multidimensional eating disorder inventory for anorexia nervosa and bulimia. *International Journal of Eating Disorders, 2,* 15–34.

KEY CONCEPTS

correlational research
reliability
validity
population
sample
representativeness
biased sample
selection bias
response bias
simple random sampling

stratified random sampling
cross-sectional design
successive independent samples design
longitudinal design
correlation
correlation coefficient
margin of error
social desirability

KEY POINTS TO LEARN

Measures in Correlational Research

- Most survey research relies on questionnaires to measure variables.
- Demographic variables describe the characteristics of people who are surveyed.
- Self-report scales are used to assess people's judgments or to identify individual differences among respondents.
- Reliability is the consistency of measurement and is frequently assessed using the test-retest reliability method or internal consistency reliability.
- Reliability is increased by including many similar items on a measure, by testing a diverse sample of individuals, and by using uniform testing procedures.
- Validity is the truthfulness of a measure: Does it measure what it intends to measure?
- Construct validity is the extent to which a measure assesses the theoretical construct it is designed to assess; construct validity is determined by assessing convergent validity and discriminant validity.

Obtaining a Sample

- Careful selection of a survey sample allows researchers to generalize findings from the sample to the population.

- The identification and selection of individuals who will make up the sample are at the heart of all sampling techniques.
- A representative sample has the same characteristics as the population from which it was drawn.
- Biased samples decrease researchers' ability to generalize from the sample to the population.
- Selection bias and response bias are two sources of biased samples.
- Two approaches to selecting a survey sample are nonprobability sampling and probability sampling.
- With nonprobability sampling techniques, there is no guarantee that every member of the population has an equal chance of being included in the sample.
- With probability sampling techniques (simple random sampling and stratified random sampling), researchers can estimate the likelihood that their findings for the sample differ from the population.
- Probability sampling is the best method for obtaining a representative sample.

Survey Research Designs

- The three types of survey design are the cross-sectional design, successive independent samples design, and longitudinal design.
- Cross-sectional designs are used to describe characteristics of a population at one point in time, successive independent samples allow researchers to describe changes in populations over time, and longitudinal designs are used to describe changes within individuals over time.

Analyzing Survey Data

- A correlation assesses the extent to which two variables covary; the correlation coefficient is a quantitative index of the direction and magnitude of this relationship.
- The direction of a correlation coefficient can be negative or positive.
- The magnitude of a correlation coefficient ranges from -1.00 (a perfect negative relationship) to $+1.00$ (a perfect positive relationship); a correlation coefficient of 0.00 indicates no relationship.
- Scatterplots are graphical displays of the relationship between two variables.
- The margin of error represents a quantitative estimate regarding the difference between sample results on a measure and the likely population values.
- Although the margin of error indicates how well survey results may describe a population, whether these results can be interpreted depends on the quality of the survey research methods.

Thinking Critically About Correlational Research

- When two variables are related (correlated), we can make predictions for the variables; however, we cannot make inferences about the cause of the relationship.
- Survey research involves reactive measurement because individuals are aware that their responses are being recorded.
- Social desirability refers to pressure respondents sometimes feel to respond as they "should" believe rather than how they actually believe.

CHECKING THE ESSENTIALS

1. Describe an example to illustrate the way in which psychologists use self-report scales to measure people's thoughts and feelings.
2. Identify three factors that influence the reliability of measurements in survey research.
3. Explain how convergent validity and discriminant validity are used in determining the construct validity of measurements in survey research.
4. Briefly explain why probability sampling is more likely than nonprobability sampling to yield a sample that is representative of the population.
5. Identify two conditions that must be met before researchers using the successive independent samples design can compare survey responses over time.
6. What information can be gained when researchers use a longitudinal design that cannot be gained from either the cross-sectional design or the successive independent samples design?
7. Describe the relationship (direction and strength) between the measures of TV viewing time and school test performance if the correlation coefficient for this relationship is $-.64$.
8. What is the primary factor that determines the size of the margin of error for the results of a particular survey, and what factor may limit the researcher's ability to reduce the size of the margin of error?
9. Briefly explain how spurious relationships illustrate the more general principle that correlational evidence is not sufficient for making causal statements.
10. What is the best protection researchers have against the reactive measurement that is inherent in survey research?

APPLYING YOUR KNOWLEDGE

1. Because of your expertise in research methods, one of the representatives from Student Congress comes to you with some questions about a survey she is planning to conduct. She is interested in determining students' opinions on the recent policy statements by the administration regarding restrictions on off-campus housing for students. You look over her questionnaire and see that it is a very good one—likely to yield reliable and valid descriptions of students' opinions. You are concerned, however, about her sampling plan. She intends to administer her questionnaire to the first 100 students who arrive for dinner at the dining hall on campus.
   A. Identify the type of sampling your student representative plans to use, and briefly describe the most serious limitation of this approach.
   B. Suggest how the sampling *should* be done. Your student representative is willing to administer as many as 200 questionnaires. Consider whether there might be reasons to use stratified random sampling in this situation.
2. A physician from an inner-city hospital wrote a critique of a newspaper article describing a survey that reported a low incidence of child abuse in the past year. The sample for the survey was 1,400 families, most of which were intact and economically advantaged. What do you think was the survey research problem that was the basis of the physician's critique?
3. Dual-income couples now outnumber those with single incomes, and this has led researchers to examine how dual-career demands affect relationships. The researchers found that among dual-career couples there was a positive correlation such that couples who spent greater amounts of time together found their relationship more

satisfactory. Presume that this finding is a reliable one. What alternative explanations would you propose to explain why there is a positive correlation between the time dual-career couples spend together and their degree of satisfaction with their relationship? Try to identify at least one alternative explanation that involves a third variable (spurious relationship).

Pearson Product-Moment Correlation Coefficient *r*

We can determine the degree of relationship between two variables for the same sample of subjects by calculating a correlation coefficient. If the two measures both represent at least an interval scale of measurement (see Chapter 4), then the Pearson Product-Moment Correlation Coefficient *r* is used. The computational formula for the Pearson *r* is as follows:

$$r = \frac{\Sigma XY - \dfrac{(\Sigma X)(\Sigma Y)}{n}}{\sqrt{\left(\Sigma X^2 - \dfrac{(\Sigma X)^2}{n}\right)\left(\Sigma Y^2 - \dfrac{(\Sigma Y)^2}{n}\right)}}$$

where
　　X = raw scores for the first variable
　　Y = raw scores for the second variable
　　Σ = sum of scores
　　n = number of pairs of scores

6 EXPERIMENTAL RESEARCH DESIGNS

INTRODUCTION

In Chapter 1, we introduced you to the four goals of research in psychology: description, prediction, understanding, and creating change. Psychologists use observational methods (Chapter 4) to develop detailed descriptions of behavior, often in natural settings. Survey research methods (Chapter 5) allow psychologists to describe people's attitudes and opinions. Psychologists are able to make predictions about behavior and mental processes when they discover measures and observations that covary (correlations). Description and prediction are essential to the scientific study of behavior, but they are not sufficient for understanding the causes of behavior. Psychologists also seek understanding—the "why" of behavior. We achieve understanding when we identify the causes of a phenomenon. Chapters 6 and 7 focus on the best available research method for identifying causal relationships—the experimental method.

In this chapter, we will discuss different types of experimental research designs. We will examine the underlying logic of experimental research and the procedures for comparing different conditions in experimental designs. We will also address issues of internal and external validity of experiments, as well as the ways in which data from experimental designs are analyzed.

LEARNING OBJECTIVES

By the end of this chapter, you will be able to

- *understand the logic of experimental designs and control techniques,*
- *identify the types of experimental research designs,*
- *evaluate the internal validity and external validity of experimental designs, and*
- *understand the basic steps of analyzing data from experimental designs.*

INTRODUCTION TO THE RESEARCH EXAMPLE: WRITING ABOUT EMOTIONAL EXPERIENCES

Popular wisdom tells us that we shouldn't keep our emotions and thoughts about negative events "bottled" within us, that it's good to "get things off our chest." In fact, the emotional release of catharsis was one of Freud's therapeutic techniques, and continues to be an important ingredient in many modern-day psychotherapies. Until recently, however, little research examined the psychological and physical health consequences of directly confronting traumatic emotional experiences.

Pennebaker (1989) theorized that keeping thoughts and feelings about painful experiences bottled up might take a physical toll—that is, it's hard on the body to keep these experiences inside. According to this "inhibition theory," inhibiting the expression of painful thoughts and feelings increases autonomic nervous system (ANS) activity. This prolonged activation of the ANS, in turn, was theorized to have long-term negative health consequences.

Pennebaker and his colleagues conducted many experiments to test the inhibition theory. In several of their experiments, participants were assigned to one of two groups. One group of participants was asked to write about traumatic emotional events, and another group was asked to write about superficial topics. The researchers assessed health outcomes for both groups using measures such as number of physician visits, immune functioning (e.g., T-helper cell activity), and ANS activity. Results of these experiments indicated that participants who wrote about emotional events had better health outcomes than participants who wrote about superficial topics. Thus, disclosing emotional thoughts and feelings—rather than inhibiting them—seemed to produce beneficial health outcomes.

Despite this supportive evidence for inhibition theory, Dr. James Pennebaker and Martha Francis (1996) argued that other evidence indicates that inhibition theory cannot fully explain the positive health outcomes associated with writing about traumatic experiences. For example, students asked to dance expressively about a trauma did not experience the same benefits as students who danced *and* wrote about the trauma. Pennebaker and Francis suggested a new theory: Cognitive changes that occur as individuals write about traumatic experiences may help explain the beneficial health outcomes. As individuals write about their emotional experiences, they try to understand the meaning and significance of the events and their emotional responses. Therefore, the purpose of Pennebaker and Francis' study was to determine if cognitive processes associated with writing about emotional events could account for the positive health outcomes that occur when thoughts and feelings are expressed. First-semester college students in their experiment were asked to write about their thoughts and feelings associated with coming to college *or* about superficial topics. Pennebaker and Francis asked whether students who disclose their emotional experiences will have better health and academic outcomes than students who do not. Most important, they wanted to know if cognitive changes that occur through writing can account for these outcomes.

THE RESEARCHERS' POINT OF VIEW

Question to Dr. Pennebaker: How did you become interested in studying disclosure? It was a confluence of forces. Over the years, I have been interested in a number of seemingly random things—religious conversion, lie detection, traumatic experiences, psychosomatic problems, and why therapy appears to work. Beginning in the late 1970s and early 1980s, I slowly realized that all of these themes were intuitively related. I noticed, for example, that traumas were almost always associated with later health problems, that keeping secrets was linked to greater physiological arousal, and, finally, that disclosing or confessing (whether as a part of a religious ceremony or in the FBI polygrapher's office) made people feel better. It all began to fit together like a complex puzzle.

Dr. James Pennebaker

EXPERIMENTAL RESEARCH

In a true experiment the researcher *manipulates* one or more factors and *measures* (observes) the effects of this manipulation on behavior. The factors the researcher controls or manipulates are called **independent variables**. The simplest experiment has an independent variable with two levels (conditions). A condition in which the treatment is present is commonly called the *experimental condition;* the condition in which the treatment is absent is called the *control condition* (or "comparison condition"). The measures of behavior used to observe the effect (if any) of the independent variables are called **dependent variables**. The independent variable in Pennebaker and Francis' experiment was "type of writing," with two conditions: emotional writing and superficial writing. The primary dependent variable in Pennebaker and Francis' experiment was health outcome—for example, as measured by the number of physician visits (see Table 6.1).

The logic of experimental research is straightforward. Researchers design experiments so that the only factor allowed to vary is the independent variable. For example, if the *only* factor that differs between the emotional-writing group and the superficial-writing group is the type of writing these individuals complete, then any health differences at the end of the experiment must necessarily be caused by the type of writing. As you'll see, the trick to conducting good experiments is making sure that the independent variable is the *only* factor that varies, and that other factors are controlled (i.e., not allowed to vary).

WRITING ABOUT EMOTIONAL EXPERIENCES: THE EXPERIMENT

In the emotional writing condition of Pennebaker and Francis' (1996) experiment, students were asked to "write about your very deepest thoughts and feelings about coming to college" (p. 607). In the superficial writing condition, students were asked to "describe in writing any particular object or event of your choosing . . . as objectively and as dispassionately as you can . . . without mentioning your emotions, opinions, or beliefs" (p. 607). New college students ($N = 72$, 44 females, 28 males) in an introductory psychology class participated during the fall academic semester. Students in each condition wrote for 20 minutes on 3 consecutive days during the last week of October.

As is true for most psychology experiments, Pennebaker and Francis measured several dependent variables to assess the effect of the independent variable manipulation. They hypothesized that students who wrote about their emotional experiences associated with attending college would have better health and academic outcomes than students who wrote about superficial topics. Therefore, Pennebaker and Francis chose dependent variables that would allow them to assess students' health and academic outcomes: number of health center visits and grade point average (GPA). These measures were obtained from archival records at the health center and the university registrar, respectively, seven months after the writing manipulation.

Pennebaker and Francis also hypothesized that students who wrote about emotional events, compared with students who wrote about superficial topics, would demonstrate various cognitive changes. Although Pennebaker and Francis included many dependent variables to assess cognitive change, we will focus here on one of their dependent

Table 6.1   Independent Variables and Dependent Variables

Independent Variable	Dependent Variable(s)
• Manipulated (controlled) by experimenter • At least two different conditions (e.g., "treatment" and "control")	• Measured by the experimenter • Used to determine effect of independent variable
Example from Pennebaker and Francis (1996)	
• *Type of writing* was controlled by the experimenter • Two conditions: *emotional writing* ("treatment") and *superficial writing* ("control")	• *Health outcome*, measured by number of physician visits • *Academic outcome*, measured using grade point average • *Cognitive change*, measured using language use (number of "insight" and "understand" words)

measures: language use. They developed a computerized text analysis program called Linguistic Inquiry and Word Count (LIWC) to determine the extent to which students' essays contained specific types of emotional and cognitive words. In particular, they were interested in students' use of words indicating insight or understanding of the causes of their experiences. Examples of insight words are *realize, see,* and *understand,* and examples of causal words are *because, why,* and *thus.* The LIWC program counted the number of times students used insight and causation words in their essays. Pennebaker and Francis hypothesized that students' essays in the experimental condition would contain more insight and causation words than students' essays in the control condition.

CONTROL AND INTERNAL VALIDITY

An experiment has **internal validity** when we are able to state confidently that the independent variable *caused* differences between groups on the dependent variable. Three conditions must be met in order to make a causal inference: co-variation, time-order relationship, and elimination of plausible alternative causes (see Table 6.2). The covariation condition is met when we observe a relationship between the independent and dependent variables. For example, when Pennebaker and Francis (1996) manipulated the type of writing students completed, they observed different health outcomes for the students. Students who wrote about their emotional experience of attending college had better health outcomes than students who wrote about superficial topics. Thus, the health outcomes were related to (covaried with) the type of writing (emotional or superficial). Establishing a covariation between independent and dependent variables is the first step for making a causal inference.

Typically, we make a causal inference when the cause precedes the effect. Imagine bumping your head and experiencing a headache (a covariation). The time-order relationship is usually one in which you bump your head and *then*

Table 6.2   Requirements for Causal Inference

1. Covariation	We observe a relationship between the independent and dependent variables. *Example:* Participants who write about emotional events have better health and academic outcomes than participants who write about superficial events.
2. Time-order relationship	The presumed cause precedes the effect. *Example:* Writing about emotional events (cause) comes before the beneficial health and academic outcomes (effect).
3. Elimination of plausible alternative causes	Using control techniques, we rule out other possible causes for the outcome. *Example:* One plausible alternative explanation is that individuals in the emotional-writing group were healthier and more academically successful than individuals in the superficial-writing group *before* the writing exercise. We can eliminate this alternative explanation because participants were randomly assigned to the two groups (random assignment forms comparable groups, on average).

experience the headache, so you infer that bumping your head caused the subsequent headache. If you had a headache before you bumped your head, you wouldn't say the bump caused your headache. Similarly, in an experiment, researchers satisfy the second condition for causal inference, a time-order relationship, when they manipulate an independent variable and *then* observe a subsequent difference in behavior.

The most challenging condition for making causal statements is the third one: eliminating plausible alternative explanations. To infer that a factor caused an effect on behavior, we must be sure that other explanations are not possible. How did Pennebaker and Francis determine that the students in their experiment differed *only* in terms of what they wrote about? Was it possible that one group was healthier to begin with? How do we know that students in the emotional-writing condition also didn't receive more attention from the experimenters? If experimental and control groups differ on a factor *other than* the independent variable, then the results of the experiment cannot be interpreted; the experiment doesn't have internal validity. When the independent variable of interest and a different, potential independent variable are allowed to covary, a **confounding** is present.

Researchers seek to eliminate alternative hypotheses—confoundings—for their results by using various control techniques. Two important control techniques are *holding conditions constant* and *balancing*. Let's see how Pennebaker and Francis used these control techniques in their experiment.

WRITING ABOUT EMOTIONAL EXPERIENCES: CONTROL AND INTERNAL VALIDITY

 In their experiment, Pennebaker and Francis (1996) sought to make the causal inference that writing about emotional experiences *causes* beneficial health and academic outcomes. They manipulated the independent variable, type of writing, to determine the causal effect of this manipulation on health and academic outcomes. They observed a

Calvin is correct in saying that it's hard to know what *causes* violence.

difference between the two groups on their dependent variables. That is, health and academic outcomes covaried with writing conditions. Also, because differences in number of health center visits and GPA occurred *after* the writing manipulation, they established a time-order relationship between the different writing conditions and the different outcomes. Thus, they met the first two conditions for making a causal inference, covariation and time-order relationship. However, in order to infer that the writing conditions caused different outcomes, there must be no alternative explanations for their findings.

One alternative explanation is that simply writing about *anything* improves people's health and academic outcomes. However, Pennebaker and Francis used the control technique of *holding conditions constant* to eliminate this alternative explanation. For example, both groups of participants were asked to write about something (although the *content* of the writing differed). By asking the control group to write about superficial topics, Pennebaker and Francis could rule out the alternative explanation that the simple act of writing (anything) causes better health and academic outcomes. They also held other conditions constant for the experimental and control groups. For example, both groups wrote on the same 3 consecutive days for 20 minutes, and both groups wrote at the same time of day and as a large group in the same classroom.

There are some factors we often want to control but we cannot hold constant. The most important factors in psychological research that we cannot hold constant are the characteristics of the participants who are tested. Here's the problem: Often when we conduct an experiment with two or more conditions, we assign *different* people to participate in the two conditions. If we observe a difference in behavior, how do we know that the differences are caused by the independent variable and not simply by the fact that there were *different people in the conditions?* We might ask, Is it possible that students in the emotional-writing condition were healthier when they started the experiment, compared with students in the superficial-writing condition?

Individual differences among participants cannot be held constant—we simply can't make everyone exactly the same. Experimenters must find a way to make sure these individual differences do not confound the independent variable being investigated. They use the control technique of *balancing* to control for the different characteristics of the participants in their conditions. The goal of balancing is to make sure that, *on average,* the participants in each condition are essentially the same. Experimenters must make sure that one group is not healthier, smarter, more motivated, or more conscientious; does not contain more females; does not have fewer psychology majors; and so forth than another group. To accomplish this, Pennebaker and Francis assigned participants *randomly* to the two conditions.

Randomly assigning participants to the two conditions *balances* their individual characteristics across the conditions. Thus, the two groups can be assumed to be equivalent, *on average*, prior to writing—that is, participants in the two groups are unlikely to differ in ways that could affect the dependent variable outcomes. For example, the groups were probably equivalent in terms of their average overall health, their academic ability, the degree to which their adjustment to college had been stressful, whether they live close to home or far from home, and so on. The beauty of random assignment is that *any* subject characteristic you can think of (and even ones you don't think of) will be balanced, or averaged, across the groups of the experiment.

THE RESEARCHERS' POINT OF VIEW

Question to Dr. Pennebaker: What aspects of your procedure do you think are most critical for protecting the internal validity of the experiment—that is, to allow you to infer that emotional writing causes beneficial outcomes?

Simple answer: People are randomly assigned to a condition in our writing studies—half of the people are asked to write about traumatic experiences, and the other half write about superficial topics for the same amount of time. Everyone is treated the same outside of the writing task. We then collect measures from the student health center to see how frequently people go to the doctor for illness in the months before writing compared with the months after writing. We can assume, then, that something about the writing task is producing health effects.

Complex answer: Whether or not there are confounds depends on your unit of analysis. If you are looking at a disclosure study from a very broad perspective, you may be inclined to say that this type of study has virtually no confounds. But, if you are looking at this from the view of a cognitive or even social psychologist, you might shake your head in disgust. The reason is that the writing manipulation actually manipulates a lot more than just writing for a few minutes a day. It is very possible (even likely) that people in our experimental group talk with their friends differently after writing, have different types of thoughts and dreams, and even change their diets during and after the experiments. Perhaps our health effects are the result of social changes rather than any cognitive changes. Yes, the writing manipulation ultimately resulted in better health, but there are dozens of potential pathways that may have affected the health.

RESEARCH DESIGNS

There are two major types of experimental research designs: independent groups designs and repeated measures designs. In **independent groups designs,** separate groups of individuals participate in the different independent variable

Figure 6.1   Diagram of experimental research designs.

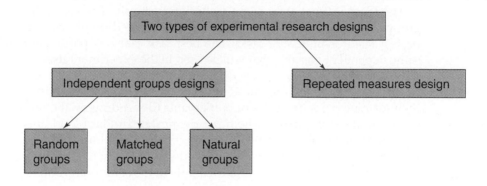

conditions. In **repeated measures designs,** each individual participates in each condition of the experiment. Figure 6.1 displays a diagram of the types of experimental designs. We will first consider three types of independent groups designs and then we will address the repeated measures design.

Independent Groups Designs

Random Groups Design.   You may see that Pennebaker and Francis' (1996) experiment used an independent groups design because some individuals participated in the emotional-writing condition and other individuals participated in the superficial-writing condition. More specifically, they used an independent groups design called the *random groups design* because participants were randomly assigned to the two conditions of their experiment.

Clearly, one key to the logic of the experimental method is to begin with similar groups at the start of the experiment. The most common technique to create equivalent groups is **random assignment;** consequently, studies using this technique are called random groups designs. Researchers use a random procedure, such as a flip of a coin, to determine which condition each individual will participate in. Pennebaker and Francis used the last digit of students' social security number to assign them to conditions. Students with a social security number that ended with an even digit were assigned to the experimental group, and students with a number that ended with an odd digit were assigned to the control group. After being assigned to conditions, participants received the different instructions for writing about emotional or superficial topics. Box 6.1 offers a simple exercise using a deck of cards for you to see how random assignment works to create equivalent groups.

Matched Groups Design.   The random groups design is by far the most common type of independent groups design. To work effectively, however, researchers must have sufficient numbers of participants for random assignment to balance individual differences across the conditions of the experiment. However, some psychologists study small samples (e.g., infants, elderly people).

Randomly assigning small numbers of individuals to different groups usually will not make the groups equivalent.

The logic of the matched groups design is simple. The researcher makes the groups equivalent by matching participants in the different conditions using a pretest task (or matching task). The best task matches participants using the same dependent variable that will be used in the experiment itself. For example, if the dependent variable in the experiment is blood pressure, a researcher could match participants by first measuring the blood pressure of all individuals and then forming pairs or triples of participants (depending on the number of conditions in the experiment) who have identical or similar blood pressures. After these matched sets are formed, the investigator randomly assigns participants in each set to the different conditions of the experiment (i.e., treatment, control). Thus, at the start of the study, participants in the different groups will have, *on*

Box 6.1

DOES RANDOM ASSIGNMENT CREATE EQUIVALENT GROUPS?

The purpose of this exercise is to use random assignment to form equivalent groups. You will need a deck of cards. You will use different features of the cards to represent different subject characteristics.

1. Shuffle the deck of cards to place them in random order.
2. Deal the cards into two piles of 26 each (you can think of these two piles as the "treatment" and "control" groups).

Checking the Random Assignment

1. Separate the red cards from the black cards in your treatment group; then do the same for the control group. Think of the red cards as women and the black cards as men. How many women and men are in each group? Are the treatment and control groups approximately equivalent in the number of women and men?
2. For both the treatment group and the control group, divide the cards into hearts, diamonds, clubs, and spades. You may think of these suits as representing freshmen, sophomores, juniors, and seniors,

respectively. Do your treatment and control groups have approximately equivalent numbers of these four student groups?
3. Sum the face value of the 26 cards in the treatment group and the 26 cards in the control group (count the ace as 1 and the king, queen, and jack as 10 each). Obtain the mean value for each group by dividing each sum by 26. You can think of these values as representing a measure of how "healthy" each card is. Is the mean for the treatment group approximately equivalent to the mean for the control group? (*Note:* There are 340 points total in the deck of cards. You could sum one group's cards and then subtract this value from 340 to obtain the sum for the second group.)

Random Assignment with Small Sample Size

Do the same exercise as above, except deal only 10 cards into each pile. Did this random assignment create equivalent treatment and control groups? The most likely answer is no. This is because random assignment requires a larger sample size to create equivalent groups.

average, equivalent blood pressure. Researchers can then reasonably attribute any group differences in blood pressure at the end of the study to the treatment (presuming other potential variables have been held constant or balanced).

Natural Groups Design.   Researchers in many areas of psychology are interested in independent variables that are called *individual differences variables* or *subject variables.* An individual differences variable is a characteristic or trait that varies across individuals. Religious affiliation is an example of an individual differences variable. Researchers can't control this variable by randomly assigning people to Catholic, Jewish, Muslim, Protestant, or other groups. Instead, the researcher "controls" the religious affiliation variable by systematically selecting individuals who *naturally* belong to these groups. Table 6.3 has other examples of individual differences variables.

An experiment that has an independent variable with selected levels of an individual differences variable is called a *natural groups design.* Researchers use natural groups designs when ethical and practical constraints prevent them from directly manipulating independent variables. For example, no matter how interested we are in the effects of major surgery on depression symptoms, we cannot ethically perform major surgery on a randomly assigned group of introductory psychology students and then compare their depression symptoms with symptoms of students who have not received surgery. Similarly, if we are interested in the relationship between divorce and emotional disorders, we cannot randomly assign some people to get divorced. The natural groups design allows us to compare people who have had surgery with those who have not. People who have chosen to divorce can be compared with those who have chosen to stay married.

Table 6.3   Examples of Individual Differences (Subject) Variables

Individual differences variables are characteristics that describe how people differ:

Physical Characteristics	Social (Demographic) Characteristics	Personality Characteristics	Mental Health Characteristics
Race	Ethnicity	Agreeableness	Depression
Sex	Religious affiliation	Extroversion	Anxiety
Height	Economic status	Conscientiousness	Disordered thinking
Weight	Marital status	Emotional stability	Substance abuse
Age	Geographical region		
Handedness (left, right, ambidextrous)			

Can you think of others?

Researchers use natural groups designs to meet the first two objectives of the scientific method: description and prediction. For example, we can describe divorced and married individuals in terms of emotional disorders, and we can predict which group is more likely to experience emotional disorders. However, we cannot use natural groups designs to make causal inferences. For instance, the finding that divorced persons are more likely than married persons to receive psychiatric care shows that these two factors covary. But, before we can conclude that divorce *causes* emotional disorders, we must assure ourselves that the time-order condition for a causal inference has been met. Does divorce precede the emotional disorder, or does the emotional disorder precede the divorce? A natural groups design does not tell us.

The natural groups design also poses problems when we try to satisfy the third condition for demonstrating causality, eliminating plausible alternative causes. The individual differences studied in a natural groups design are usually confounded—groups of individuals are likely to differ in many ways *in addition to* the variable used to classify them. For example, individuals who divorce and individuals who stay married may differ in ways other than their marital status. They may differ in their religious practices or financial circumstances. Any differences observed between divorced and married individuals may be caused by these other characteristics, not divorce.

You may see that the natural groups design is very similar to correlational research, which we discussed in Chapter 5. In fact, you may consider experiments that use natural groups variables a type of correlational research. When we observe a difference on a dependent variable between natural groups of subjects, we can say that a covariation is present. This allows us to describe differences between groups and make predictions for the natural groups, but we cannot make causal inferences about *why* the groups differ because we frequently lack good evidence about a time-order relationship and natural groups are naturally confounded.

Repeated Measures Design

We've seen that individuals in an independent groups design participate in just one condition of the experiment. They are randomly assigned to one condition in random groups and matched groups designs, or they are selected to be in one group in natural groups designs. In contrast, individuals in a *repeated measures design* (or *within-subjects design*) participate in the study more than once—specifically, they participate in *each* condition of the experiment. You may be able to see why this type of experiment is called "repeated measures." Each time individuals participate in the conditions of the experiment, they complete the dependent variable measure—thus, the measure is repeated.

Earlier we saw that an alternative explanation for group differences on the dependent variable in a random groups design is that individuals in the groups may naturally differ. Researchers use random assignment to the different conditions to rule out this alternative explanation by balancing individual differences across the conditions of the experiment. However, when researchers use a

Figure 6.2 Repeated measures design.

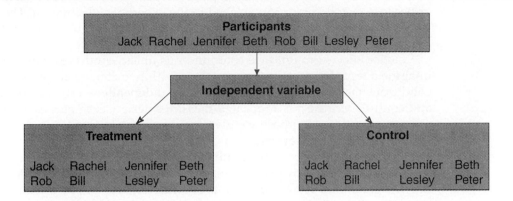

repeated measures design, they don't have to worry about this alternative explanation. Why not? Because the *same* people participate in each condition of the experiment. It's impossible for one group to be smarter, healthier, or more motivated than the other because the same people participate in all conditions of the experiment (see Figure 6.2).

Researchers gain several additional advantages when they use a repeated measures design. First, repeated measures designs require fewer participants, so these designs are ideal for situations in which only a small number of participants is available. Second, repeated measures designs often are more convenient and efficient. This is especially true when experimental conditions take only a few seconds or minutes for participants to complete. It makes more sense to have individuals participate in several brief conditions than to recruit many individuals to participate in the different conditions.

Another important advantage of repeated measures designs is that they are generally more *sensitive* than an independent groups design. A sensitive experiment is one that can detect the effect of an independent variable on the dependent variable even if the effect is a small one. An experiment is more sensitive when there is less variability in participants' responses within a condition of an experiment. That is, in any one condition, participants will not all respond the same way; there will be some variability (called "error variation"). Error variation can be caused by several factors, including variations in the procedure each time the experiment is conducted and individual differences in the participants. Repeated measures designs have less error variation than independent groups designs because the error variation due to individual differences across conditions is reduced.

Repeated measures designs have great advantages, but they also have disadvantages. As we'll see, researchers need to worry about practice effects when they use the repeated measures design. **Practice effects** arise because participants change as they are repeatedly tested. Even though the *same* people participate in each condition, each individual can change over time. Individuals may improve with practice, for example, because they learn more about the task or because they become more relaxed in the experimental situation. They also may get worse with practice—for example, because of fatigue, boredom, or reduced motivation.

Practice effects can produce confoundings unless controlled. For example, imagine a repeated measures experiment with two conditions: A and B. The conditions may represent two levels of an independent variable, treatment and control. Because it is a repeated measures design, each participant serves in both conditions. Suppose we give each participant Condition A first and then Condition B. Performance on Condition B is likely to be affected by the participant's experience with Condition A. Participants might be more tired, more excited, less motivated, happier, or more skilled at the task after doing the first condition. Thus, participants are different due to practice when they get to Condition B. Any differences in behavior may be due to the differences due to practice effects, not to the effect of the independent variable (treatment *vs.* control).

Researchers cannot eliminate the practice effects participants experience due to repeated testing, but they can *balance* practice effects across the conditions. The key is to make sure that one condition of the independent variable doesn't end up with all the practice effects—for example, by always presenting it last. We don't want to always present A followed by B. Balancing works by *averaging* practice effects across all the conditions in the experiment. By doing this, we avoid confounding practice effects with the conditions of the independent variable.

Thus, it is essential in the repeated measures design that the researcher control the *order* in which subjects participate in the conditions. Researchers balance practice effects across the conditions by **counterbalancing** the order of the conditions. Let's take a closer look at exactly how this is done. Suppose that a researcher chooses a repeated measures design to have participants judge the "honesty" of faces in photographs that vary on a certain dimension, such as facial expression. Five conditions of the independent variable, facial expression, might be *smiling, frowning, puzzled, surprised,* and *bored* faces (see Figure 6.3). Assume further that the participants are asked to judge the honesty of five smiling faces, five frowning faces, and so on. Thus, they would experience each condition of the experiment *more than once* (i.e., five times each) and make a total of 25 ratings of honesty. The dependent variable is participants' average honesty ratings for each of the five conditions.

Practice effects would be confounded with the independent variable (type of facial expression) if the researcher were to administer the five smiling faces first, then the five frowning faces, and so on. To avoid confounding practice effects with the conditions of the experiment, the researcher should administer the five conditions in different orders. For example, the researcher could first present a random order of the five conditions, such as bored, smiling, frown-

Figure 6.3   Five types of facial expression.

ing, surprised, and puzzled. The next five faces would appear in a new random order of the conditions, and so on. With many trials, practice effects would be balanced across the different conditions of the experiment. This counterbalancing technique is called a *block randomization*. The counterbalancing might look like this (with A, B, C, D, and E representing the five different conditions):

1	2	3	4	5
BCADE	ADCBE	DCBAE	ABDEC	CAEDB

Note that there are five blocks, each with a different order of the five conditions.

When each individual participates in each condition *only once,* a different counterbalancing strategy must be used. A researcher may choose this repeated measures design when the different conditions of the independent variable are too time-consuming to repeat many times with each individual. Consider the situation facing a researcher who asks individuals to participate in both the experimental (E) and control (C) conditions of an experiment. The first participant might be tested first in the control condition (C) and then in the experimental condition (E). But we have already seen that this produces a confounding due to practice effects. To break this confounding, the researcher can administer different orders of the conditions to *different* participants. For example, the researcher could administer the conditions of the experiment to a second participant in the EC order, testing the experimental condition first and the control condition second. Generally, the researcher would want to test half the participants in the CE order and half in the EC order. In this way, the researcher could balance the effects of order across the two conditions using different participants. For half the participants, practice effects would affect condition E; for the other half, practice effects would affect condition C. Thus, the practice effects would be balanced across the conditions. The counterbalancing would look like this:

One-half of the participants: C then E
One-half of the participants: E then C

The general rule for balancing practice effects in this situation is simple: *Each condition of the experiment must appear in each ordinal position (i.e., first, second, third) equally often.* Although several counterbalancing techniques satisfy this general rule, the best technique is to use *all possible orders* of the conditions. Each participant is randomly assigned to one of the orders. With only two conditions (A and B) there are only 2 possible orders (AB and BA); with three conditions, there are 6 possible orders (ABC, ACB, BAC, BCA, CAB, CBA); with four conditions, there are 24 possible orders (see Table 6.4). The number of required orders increases dramatically with increasing numbers of conditions. For instance, for five conditions, there are 120 possible orders of the conditions; for six conditions, there are 720 possible orders. Because of this, researchers generally use all possible orders if they have four or fewer conditions in the experiment, and they use selected orders when there are more than four conditions (see Shaughnessy, Zechmeister, & Zechmeister [2000] for techniques for selecting particular orders from all possible orders). In all cases, however, participants should be randomly assigned equally to the various orders of conditions.

An obvious limitation of repeated measures designs is that they cannot be used to study individual differences variables (e.g., age, gender). Experimenters cannot make a person male, then female, and then male again. Second, researchers avoid repeated measures designs when each condition takes a great deal of time to implement. For example, if treatment and control conditions each requires a year of participation, the experiment would take years to complete.

Finally, repeated measures designs should be avoided when "differential transfer" across conditions is likely to occur. *Differential transfer* occurs when the effects of the manipulation for a condition persist ("carry over") and influence performance in subsequent conditions. For example, suppose a researcher examines the effect of alcohol on individuals' problem solving using two conditions: alcohol present and alcohol absent. In a repeated measures design, some participants would receive an alcoholic drink first, followed by a nonalcoholic beverage. Other participants would receive the reverse order. What can we say about the performance of participants who receive an alcoholic drink first? Would the effects of the alcohol vanish when they participate soon after that in

Table 6.4   Counterbalancing Using All Possible Orders

Levels of the Independent Variable	All Possible Orders
Two: A, B	AB, BA
Three: A, B, C	ABC, ACB, BAC, BCA, CAB, CBA
Four: A, B, C, D	ABCD, ABDC, ACBD, ACDB, ADBC, ADCB, BACD, BADC, BCAD, BCDA, BDAC, BDCA, CABD, CADB, CBAD, CBDA, CDAB, CDBA, DABC, DACB, DBAC, DBCA, DCAB, DCBA

the alcohol-absent condition? Probably not. The effects of the alcohol-present condition would carry over, or *transfer,* to the alcohol-absent condition. Is the same true for participants who receive the order alcohol-absent then alcohol-present? No, there is not likely to be a problem of transfer across conditions for this order. Thus, differential transfer is likely in this experiment.

If differential transfer occurs in an experiment, the researcher will have a very difficult time interpreting the effects of the independent variable. Therefore, whenever the effects of an independent variable manipulation could persist differently across conditions, researchers should choose an independent groups design to study the variable.

EXTERNAL VALIDITY

As you can see, researchers have a lot of options to consider when they choose to conduct an experiment. The researcher's goal is to conduct an experiment that has internal validity. That is, researchers hope that by conducting a controlled experiment that eliminates confoundings, they will be able to make a causal inference about the effect of the independent variable on the dependent variable.

In addition to internal validity, we can also evaluate an experiment's **external validity,** the extent to which findings from an experiment can be generalized to individuals, settings, and conditions beyond the scope of the specific experiment (see Table 6.5). A frequent criticism of highly controlled experiments is that they *lack* external validity. That is, the findings observed in a controlled laboratory experiment may describe what happens only in that *specific* controlled setting, with the *specific* conditions that were tested, and with the *specific* individuals who participated. The issue of external validity raises the question, if the findings of laboratory experiments are so *specific,* what good are they to society?

One answer to this question is a bit unsettling, at least initially. Quite simply, for some experiments researchers do not worry about external validity. When the purpose of an experiment is to test a specific hypothesis derived from a psychological theory, the external validity of the findings is irrelevant (Mook, 1983). That is, experiments may be done to determine whether subjects *can* be induced to behave in a certain way, as predicted by a theory. Whether subjects *do* behave

Table 6.5   Questions of External Validity

---

1. Would the same findings occur in different *settings* (e.g., the "real world" rather than the lab or in different laboratories)?
2. Would the same findings occur with different *conditions* (e.g., different levels of treatment or different operational definitions of the independent and dependent variables)?
3. Would the same findings hold true for different *participants* (e.g., a different sample of participants from the same population or members of a different population)?

---

that way in their natural environment is secondary to the theoretical question raised in the experiment (and, as we discussed in Chapter 1, theoretical questions are important to society).

Of course, researchers often do wish to generalize findings beyond the boundaries of the experiment itself. There are several ways to proceed. Most obviously, you should include in your experiment characteristics of the situation or people to which you wish to generalize. For example, if you wish to generalize your findings to describe men and women, you should include both men and women in your study.

Researchers often use replication to establish the external validity of their findings. **Replication** involves repeating the procedures used in a particular experiment to determine whether the same results are obtained a second time with different participants. Findings are "replicated" when the effect of an independent variable is present in both the original study and the replication study.

Sometimes external validity is established at the "conceptual level" of an experiment. What we wish to generalize from any one study are *conceptual relationships* among variables, not the *specific* conditions, manipulations, settings, samples, and so on (see Banaji & Crowder, 1989; Mook, 1983). An example provided by Anderson and Bushman (1997) illustrates the idea of generalizing at the level of conceptual relationships. We could conduct a study with 5-year-old children to determine if a specific insult ("pooh-pooh head") induces anger and aggression, then conduct a replication study to determine if the same insult produces the same results with 35-year-old adults. As Anderson and Bushman state, the findings for 5-year-olds probably wouldn't be replicated with the 35-year-olds because "'pooh-pooh head' just doesn't pack the same 'punch' for 5- and 35-year-old people" (p. 21). However, if we wish to generalize the general psychological process "insults increase aggressive behavior," we can use different words that are meaningful insults for each population. When Anderson and Bushman (1997) examined variables (such as insults) at the conceptual level, the findings for laboratory and real-world studies were very similar. These findings indicate that results from laboratory studies often can be generalized to the real world.

WRITING ABOUT EMOTIONAL EXPERIENCES: EXTERNAL VALIDITY

We can refer again to the Pennebaker and Francis (1996) study on the effect of emotional writing on physical health to illustrate problems of external validity. By itself, the experiment has little *external validity*. It was conducted on a single college campus, with one sample of college freshmen and transfer students, at one time in these students' lives (i.e., when they were adjusting to college). Based on this one study, it's hard to *generalize* their findings beyond this one sample and setting. We can ask, does writing about emotional events improve health outcomes for other populations in other settings, and for people who experience different types of stressful or traumatic experiences?

We can answer this question by examining the findings for similar studies on emotional writing. Pennebaker and Francis (1996) *replicated* the procedures used in several other experiments on the effects of emotional writing. These other experiments involved different samples (e.g., other college students, adults in the community) and different types of trauma (e.g., lay-off from a job). The findings from these different studies were all similar. In each case, emotional writing, compared with superficial writing, caused better outcomes. Therefore, we can say that the findings for emotional writing are *reliable* and that they have external validity. It is important to note that across these various studies, Pennebaker and his colleagues did not always ask participants to write about their adjustment to college life (indeed, this would not have made sense for people who were recently unemployed). Because they were interested in the *psychological processes* involved in emotional writing, Pennebaker and his colleagues developed *operational definitions* that best represented the *concept*, emotional writing, for the particular population they studied.

THE RESEARCHERS' POINT OF VIEW

Question to Dr. Pennebaker: Experiments involving college student samples often are criticized because of external validity concerns. You've addressed this concern by replicating your procedures with other samples and traumatic events (e.g., job lay-offs). Are you now pretty confident about the reliability of the emotional writing effect?

This is something that I am most excited by. There have now been dozens of studies by researchers around the world that demonstrate that writing about upsetting experiences can influence physical and mental health. These studies find comparable effects across age, sex, social class, language, culture, and health status.

ANALYSIS OF EXPERIMENTAL DESIGNS

Researchers conduct experiments to determine whether an independent variable affects behavior (as indicated by the dependent variable). They collect data for the different conditions of their experiment and then seek to determine whether individuals' responses on the dependent variable differ across the conditions of the experiment. The analysis of an experiment follows three distinct stages. Researchers first check the data; then summarize the data; and, finally, confirm what the data reveal (see Table 6.6). We will examine these steps here; more information about these steps is presented in the Statistics Appendix (Appendix A).

Check the Data

The first step in the analysis of an experiment is to *check the data*. At a basic level, we can look to see if the numbers in the data set make sense. Errors can occur if responses are not recorded correctly and if data are entered incorrectly into computer statistical software for analysis. Researchers also look at the distribution of scores. This can be done by generating a frequency distribution (e.g., a histogram) for the dependent variable. When examining the distribution of scores, researchers may discover "outliers." Outliers are data values that are

Table 6.6   Steps for Data Analysis

Step	What to Do
1. Check the data.	Identify errors (e.g., out-of-range values). Identify outliers.
2. Summarize the data.	Compute values for central tendency (e.g., mean) and variability (e.g., standard deviation). Compute effect size.
3. Confirm what the data reveal.	Compute inferential statistics (e.g., confidence intervals, null hypothesis testing). Consider Type I and Type II errors.

markedly different from the rest of the distribution of scores. Outliers sometimes occur when a participant has not followed instructions or if equipment in the experiment did not function properly. When outliers are identified, researchers may decide to exclude the data from the analyses. However, it is essential that they report the deletions and the criteria used to exclude outliers when describing the research project.

Summarize the Data

The second step in data analysis is to summarize the data in a meaningful way. **Descriptive statistics** begin to answer the question, what happened in the experiment? Researchers first describe data for the dependent variable using measures of central tendency and variability. When data are measured on an interval or ratio scale, two common descriptive statistics are the *mean* and *standard deviation.* The mean represents the average score on a dependent variable. The standard deviation tells us about the variability of participants' scores— approximately how far, on the average, scores vary from a group mean.

Suppose a researcher learns that the mean number of health center visits is 5.0 for participants in a superficial-writing group and 3.0 for participants in an emotional-writing group. The critical question is, did the independent variable (type of writing) have a *reliable* effect on participants' health center visits?

One answer to this question considers the size of this difference. Is a mean difference of 2 health center visits a *large* effect? We use measures of *effect size* to describe whether mean differences are small, medium, or large. Measures of **effect size** indicate the strength of the relationship between the independent and the dependent variables. However, calculating an effect size requires more than obtaining a difference between the means. The mean difference between two groups is always *relative to* the average variability in participants' scores (see Appendix A for computing both the standard deviation and effect size).

Effect size is calculated by dividing the mean difference by the variability. This effect size is called Cohen's *d.* The mean difference in our hypothetical emotional-writing study is 2.0 (5 − 3). Suppose further that the average standard deviation for our hypothetical study is 4.0. The effect size, *d,* is .50 (2.0 ÷

4.0 = .50). According to accepted criteria for interpreting effect sizes, *d* values of .20, .50, and .80 represent *small, medium, and large* effects of the independent variable, respectively (Cohen, 1988). An effect size of .50 indicates that emotional writing, relative to superficial writing, has a *medium* effect on participants' health center visits.

Sometimes participants' responses on the dependent variable (e.g., health center visits) are extremely variable. Suppose our average variability is 10.0 instead of 4.0, and the average difference in health center visits between groups remains the same (2.0). Now our conclusion is that emotional writing has a *small* effect on health center visits (2.0 ÷ 10.0 = .20). An important goal in all research is to decrease variability in participants' responses on the dependent variable. Researchers accomplish this by being consistent in their procedures, by maintaining an environment free of distractions, and by using measures that are reliable (consistent) indicators of the dependent variable.

Confirm What the Data Reveal

An important approach to identifying whether an independent variable has produced a reliable effect uses inferential statistics to determine whether group differences are *statistically significant*. When researchers use inferential statistics they consider issues of sampling and the fact that the observed group differences can occur simply by chance. Thus, the two means for emotional writing (5.0) and superficial writing (3.0) might differ *simply by chance*, not because of any effect of the independent variable.

Researchers use **inferential statistics** in the third stage of data analysis—confirming what the data reveal. Inferential statistics help us test whether differences between group means can be attributed to an effect of the independent variable, not to chance factors. Researchers use two types of inferential statistics, confidence intervals and null hypothesis testing, to make this decision. Both types are described briefly in the following sections; Appendix A has a more detailed discussion of both methods.

Confidence Intervals.   When researchers test the effect of an independent variable on a dependent variable, they conduct their research with a sample of participants. Scores on the dependent variable for the *sample* are used to estimate a characteristic of the *population*, such as the population mean. We would have to assess all members of the population on our dependent variable to measure the population mean directly. It's unlikely that the estimate based on our sample will correspond exactly to the population value. We can expect some slippage when estimating the population values. A **confidence interval** gives us information about the probable range of values we can expect for the population characteristic, given our sample results (see also "margin of error" in Chapter 5).

In a random groups design such as our hypothetical experiment, we have two sample means for number of health center visits, one for the emotional-writing condition and one for the superficial-writing condition. With two sample means we can estimate the range of expected values for the *difference between two population means* based on our experimental results.

The confidence interval tells us the likelihood (usually set at .95) that the confidence interval contains the actual population mean difference. Confidence intervals are particularly important when we wish to determine the likely range of possible effects for our independent variable. Suppose, for example, that the .95 confidence interval for our hypothetical study is 0.56 to 3.44. We can say with 95 percent confidence that this interval contains the true difference between population means represented by the emotional-writing condition and the superficial-writing condition. The difference between population means could be as small as the lower boundary of the interval (i.e., 0.56) or as large as the upper boundary of the interval (i.e., 3.44). Although we don't know the "real" effect of the independent variable for the population, the evidence we have (based on the confidence interval) suggests strongly that there was *some* effect of the independent variable. That is, the difference between emotional writing and superficial writing at the population level is likely to fall within 0.56 and 3.44 health center visits.

Suppose, however, that the confidence interval includes zero (e.g., a range of values from 0 to 4). A "zero difference" indicates that there is no difference in the number of health center visits for emotional-writing and superficial-writing conditions at the population level. When the confidence interval includes zero, the results for the effect of the independent variable are inconclusive. We can't conclude that the independent variable *did not* have an effect. After all, the confidence interval tells us that the effect could be zero, or anywhere up to a difference of 4 health center visits. There are situations in which it is important for researchers to confirm that an independent variable does not have an effect (for example, a treatment, relative to a control condition, does not have aversive side effects). When these situations arise, researchers conduct several replications of the experiment to determine if the confidence intervals in each experiment include zero. In general, inferential statistics (such as confidence intervals) are used as an efficient substitute for the more cumbersome, but more effective, process of replication.

Null Hypothesis Testing. A more common approach to deciding whether the independent variable has a reliable effect on the dependent variable is **null hypothesis testing**. In this approach researchers begin by assuming that the independent variable has *no* effect, called the *null hypothesis*. For example, the null hypothesis for our hypothetical writing experiment states that the population means for emotional-writing and superficial-writing are *not* different. Under this assumption, any observed difference between sample means is attributed to chance.

However, sometimes the difference between sample means seems too large to be simply due to chance if we assume the population means don't differ. Null hypothesis testing asks the question, how likely is the difference between sample means observed in our experiment, assuming there is no difference between the population means? In other words, what is the likelihood of a difference this large (e.g., 2 health center visits), given the null hypothesis (no difference in the population) is assumed to be true? If the probability of obtaining the mean difference in our experiment is small, then we reject the null hypothesis and conclude that the independent variable *did* have an effect on the dependent variable. As we discuss null hypothesis testing, you may wish to refer to Table 6.7, which outlines the steps.

How do we know the probability of obtaining the mean difference observed in our experiment? Most often, researchers use inferential statistics such as the *t* test and analysis of variance (ANOVA, or *F* test). Each value of *t* and *F* has a probability value associated with it when the null hypothesis is assumed. Once the researcher has computed the statistic, he or she can determine the probability of the outcome. (See Appendix A for how to do *t* and *F* tests.)

We have two possible conclusions when we do null hypothesis testing: We either reject the null hypothesis or we fail to reject the null hypothesis. Outcomes (i.e., observed differences between means) that lead us to reject the null

Table 6.7 Steps for Null Hypothesis Testing

Goal: To determine if the independent variable has a statistically significant (reliable) effect on the dependent variable. In our example the independent variable is type of writing (emotional, superficial), and the dependent variable is number of health center visits.

Step	Example
1. Assume the null hypothesis is true.	Population mean for emotional-writing group = population mean for superficial-writing group.
2. Use sample means to estimate population means.	Mean for emotional-writing group = 3.0. Mean for superficial-writing group = 5.0. Mean difference = 2.0
3. Statistical question: Is the observed mean difference greater than what is expected based on the assumed difference of zero (i.e., null hypothesis)?	Is the observed mean difference of 2.0 statistically different from zero?
4. Compute the appropriate inferential statistic.	A *t* test is used to test the difference between between two groups' means.
5. Identify the probability associated with the inferential statistic.	The probability (or *p* value) is printed in computer output or can be found in a table.
6. Compare the observed probability with the predetermined level of significance (alpha).	Compare the observed *p* value with the alpha level, which is usually .05.
7. If the observed *p* value is less than .05, reject the null hypothesis of no difference.	If the *p* value is <.05, conclude that type of writing had a reliable (statistically significant) effect on health center visits.
8. If the observed *p* value is greater than .05, do not reject the null hypothesis of no difference.	If the *p* value is >.05, conclude that type of writing did not have a reliable (statistically significant) effect on health center visits.

hypothesis are said to be **statistically significant**. *A statistically significant outcome indicates that the difference between observed means in the experiment is larger than would be expected by chance if the null hypothesis is true.* We conclude that the independent variable caused the difference between means (presuming, of course, that the experiment is internally valid).

A statistically significant outcome is one that has only a small likelihood of occurring if the null hypothesis is true. That is, when we look at the results of our statistical test, the probability value associated with the statistic is small. But just how small does this probability value have to be? Scientists tend to agree that outcomes associated with probabilities of less than 5 times out of 100 (or .05) are judged to be statistically significant. Thus, if we obtain a probability value that is lower than .05, we conclude that the effect of the independent variable is statistically significant. The probability value we use to decide that an outcome is statistically significant is called the *level of significance.* The level of significance is indicated by the Greek letter alpha (α). Thus, researchers speak of the .05 level of significance, reported as $\alpha = .05$.

When researchers conduct an experiment and observe that the effect of the independent variable is not statistically significant, they do not reject the null hypothesis. However, they do not *accept* the null hypothesis of no difference either. The results are inconclusive (similar to when the confidence interval for the mean difference includes zero). There may have been a factor in the experiment that prevented the researchers from observing an effect of the independent variable (e.g., few subjects, poor operationalization of the independent variable).

Because researchers rely on probabilities to make a decision about the effects of the independent variable, there is always some chance of making an error. The two possible "true states of the world" and the two possible decisions an experimenter can make are listed in Table 6.8. The two "true states of the world" are that the independent variable either has an effect on behavior or it does not. The two possible correct decisions the researcher can make are represented by the upper-left and lower-right cells of the table. If the independent variable does have an effect, the researcher should reject the null hypothesis; if it does not, the researcher should fail to reject the null hypothesis.

The two potential errors are represented by the other two cells of Table 6.8, and these two types of errors have the highly descriptive names of Type I error and Type II error. A *Type I error* occurs when researchers reject the null

Table 6.8   Possible Outcomes of Decision Making with Inferential Statistics

Decision	States of the World	
	Null Hypothesis is False	Null Hypothesis is True
Reject null hypothesis.	Correct decision	Type I error
Fail to reject null hypothesis.	Type II error	Correct decision

hypothesis when it is true. When a researcher makes a Type I error, he or she claims that the independent variable had a reliable effect on behavior, when the "true state of the world" is that the variable does not affect behavior. A *Type II error* occurs when a researcher fails to reject the null hypothesis when it is false. When an experimenter makes a Type II error, he or she claims that the independent variable does not affect behavior, when the "true state of the world" is that the variable does affect behavior.

The problem of Type I errors and Type II errors should not immobilize researchers. But you may see why researchers rarely use the word *prove* when they describe the results of an experiment that involved inferential statistics. Instead, they say the results "are consistent with the hypothesis" or "support the hypothesis." These more tentative statements acknowledge the possibility of making a Type I or Type II error. The problem of Type I and Type II errors also reminds us that statistical inference can never replace replication as the ultimate test of the reliability of an experimental outcome.

WRITING ABOUT EMOTIONAL EXPERIENCES: THE DATA ANALYSIS

We're now in a position to look carefully at the results of Pennebaker and Francis' (1996) experiment. Although they analyzed data for several dependent variables, we will consider only their findings for the number of health center visits, GPA, and language use (i.e., insight and causation words).

Using archival data, Pennebaker and Francis first determined that the number of health center visits for students in the emotional-writing (experimental) and superficial-writing (control) groups was equivalent prior to the writing manipulation, as we'd expect because of the random assignment procedures. However, the average number of health center visits for illness in the two months after writing was lower for the experimental group ($M = .14$) than for the control group ($M = .30$). *The effect size, d,* for the effect of writing on health center visits in their study was 0.52, which represents a medium effect, according to Cohen's (1988) criteria. Pennebaker and Francis also conducted *null hypothesis testing* to determine if the difference between the two groups was *reliable.* Using a *level of significance* of $\alpha = .05$, Pennebaker and Francis found that the difference in average health center visits between the experimental and control groups was *statistically significant.*

Pennebaker and Francis (1996) conducted similar analyses for the students' GPA. Although the experimental and control participants' GPA did not differ in the fall semester, results indicated that the average second-semester GPA for the experimental group ($M = 3.08$) was greater than the average GPA for the control group ($M = 2.86$). The effect size for the effect of writing on GPA was 0.48, and the outcome of null hypothesis testing indicated that this was a statistically significant difference.

Finally, we can address Pennebaker and Francis' hypothesis that the beneficial outcomes associated with emotional writing are related to cognitive changes. Using their LIWC program, Pennebaker and Francis determined the percentage of insight and causation words in students' essays. Across the three days of writing, students' essays in the experimental condition comprised, on average, 3.39% insight words and 1.09% causation words. In contrast, control students' essays had 1.21% insight words and 0.64% causation words. Using tests of statistical significance, Pennebaker and Francis observed these differences between emotional writing and superficial writing to be statistically significant. They suggested that as students attempt to understand and find causal meaning when writing about their college experiences, they are more likely to experience beneficial physical and psychological health consequences.

THE RESEARCHERS' POINT OF VIEW

Question to Dr. Pennebaker: Were you surprised by any of the findings in the experiment?

Honestly? Yes. The first study was the one that blew me away. I still have a flashbulb memory of walking across campus from the student health center looking at the health center records, knowing who was in what condition. I couldn't believe it—the study actually worked! Now [after many experiments], I've become jaded. And a bit of a true believer.

CONDUCTING A GOOD EXPERIMENT: A SUMMARY

We can identify four important characteristics of good experiments: internal validity, reliability, sensitivity, and external validity (see Table 6.9). An experiment has *internal validity* when the cause-and-effect relationship is interpretable—that is, we can conclude that manipulating the independent variable *caused* a change in the dependent variable, and we can rule out other plausible causes for the outcome. We want our experiments to have internal validity because only then can we make claims about the causes of behavior (causal inferences).

Second, the purpose of an experiment is to produce a difference in behavior between conditions of the experiment; a *reliable experiment* is one in which this difference is likely to be observed again if the experiment is repeated. When our experiments are reliable we can state confidently that our conclusions are not arbitrary or based on events that are likely to happen by chance.

Table 6.9   Four Characteristics of Good Experiments

Internal validity	An experiment has internal validity when we can conclude that manipulating the independent variable caused a change in the dependent variable, and when we can rule out other plausible causes for the outcome.
Reliable	An experiment is reliable when we can conclude that the outcome is not due to chance factors.
Sensitive	A sensitive experiment is likely to detect the effect of an independent variable even when the effect is small.
External validity	An experiment has external validity when we can generalize the findings to individuals, settings, and conditions beyond the scope of the experiment.

Third, independent variables differ in terms of how large an effect they have on behavior; a *sensitive experiment* is likely to detect the effect of an independent variable even when the effect is small. Our goal is to design sensitive experiments that allow us to observe the effects of our manipulation, even when those effects might be small. Finally, when an experiment has *external validity* we can generalize the findings to individuals, settings, and conditions beyond the scope of the specific experiment. That is, questions of external validity ask whether the findings observed in an experiment will be observed when other individuals participate, and when researchers use other settings and conditions.

Researchers try to enhance each of these characteristics in their experiments. However, this may not be easy because these four important characteristics of a good experiment cannot always be maximized simultaneously. For instance, procedures that increase the sensitivity of an experiment can reduce its external validity. Thus, planning an experiment is a balancing act that requires careful consideration of many factors. But this shouldn't stop us. Science is a self-correcting process. When you do your research, you will be able to compare your results with those of other researchers. The best overall approach to research is a multimethod approach. Psychologists try to answer a research question using different methods and look to see if similar answers are obtained using the various methods. If the answers are similar we gain confidence in the answer to the question. The conclusions we form have *convergent validity.* That is, we hope the findings from various studies converge to allow us to form a conclusion—an answer to the research question.

It's important to remember that each research strategy has strengths and weaknesses. An advantage of the multimethod approach is that the strengths of one research method may overcome the weaknesses of a different research method. We have seen that a weakness of observational and survey methods is that they don't allow researchers to identify the causes of relationships between variables. The special strength of the experimental method is that it is especially effective for identifying cause-and-effect relationships. But it is always supplemented by other methods.

THINKING CRITICALLY ABOUT EXPERIMENTAL RESEARCH

Throughout this chapter we focused on techniques researchers use to conduct internally valid experiments and to correctly analyze and interpret the outcomes of their experiments. We've already discussed problems that can affect the internal validity of repeated measures designs: practice effects and differential transfer. There are several circumstances, however, that can threaten the internal validity of independent groups experiments. These include testing intact groups, the presence of extraneous variables, subject loss, and expectancy effects (see Table 6.10). We will discuss each of these in turn.

Sometimes, for the sake of convenience, researchers randomly assign "intact groups," rather than individual participants, to the conditions of their experiment. Remember that researchers randomly assign participants to create

Table 6.10   Some Threats to Internal Validity in Experiments

Threat	Description
Intact groups	Groups formed prior to the start of the experiment (rather than individuals) are assigned to the different levels of the independent variable.
Extraneous variables	Extraneous variables occur when practical decisions about implementing the independent variable lead to confound-ings (e.g., size of sessions, different experimenters).
Subject loss	Some participants fail to complete the experiment, which can ruin the group equivalence established at the beginning of the experiment.
Expectancies	Participants' performance may be influenced by demand characteristics; experimenters' performance may be influenced by their expectations and biases.

equivalent groups in the random groups design. In contrast, *intact groups* are formed prior to the start of the experiment, but not through random assignment. For example, the various sections of an introductory psychology class are intact groups and, for convenience, a researcher may randomly assign different *sections* of the class to the different conditions of the experiment.

However, students often choose to be in a particular section because of the time the class meets, friends who will be in the class, and any number of other factors. Problems arise, then, because individuals likely differ across the intact groups. For example, students who choose to attend an 8:00 A.M. section may differ from students who prefer a 1:00 P.M. section. Random assignment of these intact groups to experimental conditions will not balance these differences across the conditions of the experiment. These individual differences, then, are almost guaranteed to confound the independent variable under investigation. The solution to this problem is simple—do not use intact groups in a random groups design.

Researchers typically are not interested in variables such as the size of the group in which participants are tested and differences among experimenters who implement the experiment. These potential confounding variables are called *extraneous variables*. Don't let the term fool you—an experiment confounded by an extraneous variable is uninterpretable—as is any other experiment with a confounding. Researchers should take steps to balance extraneous variables across conditions of the experiment. For example, a researcher might decide to have several experimenters test small groups of participants to complete the experiment more quickly. The different-size groups and the experimenters themselves become potentially relevant variables that could confound the experiment, making the results uninterpretable. For example, if all the individuals in the experimental group are tested by one experimenter and all those in the control group are tested by another experimenter, the levels of the intended independent variable become confounded with the different experimenters. To avoid confounding, each experimenter should test the same number of subjects in each condition of the experiment.

Another problem occurs when subjects begin an experiment but fail to complete it successfully. If *subject loss* occurs because of inadvertent mistakes or equipment failures, the internal validity of the experiment isn't threatened. However, the internal validity of an experiment *is* threatened if individuals drop out of one condition of an experiment more than others. For example, this can occur if individuals "don't like" a particular condition. Subject loss can occur in treatment studies when subjects don't like the side effects of a drug and drop out of the study. If subject loss occurs in one condition more than others, the group equivalence established at the start of the study (e.g., through random assignment) is likely ruined. If the groups are no longer equivalent, individual differences in the people who remain in the study become alternative explanations for the study outcome.

The final challenge to internal validity arises because of *expectations* held by both participants and experimenters. *Demand characteristics* are the cues and other information used by individuals to guide their behavior in a psychological study (see also Chapter 4). For example, if research participants know they have been given alcohol, they may expect certain effects, such as relaxation or giddiness, and behave accordingly. Researchers use *placebo control* groups to deal with the problem of demand characteristics. A *placebo* is a substance that looks like a drug or another active substance but is actually *inert*, or inactive. When the different groups in an experiment receive a treatment (e.g., either the treatment being tested *or* a placebo), the demand characteristics are the same for the groups—all participants expect to experience beneficial treatment effects. Any differences between the experimental groups and the placebo control group can be attributed to the *actual* effect of the experimental treatment, not the participants' expectations about receiving an effective treatment.

Experimenters' expectations can also bias a study. The general term used to describe these biases is *experimenter effects* (Rosenthal, 1963). Experimenter effects may lead experimenters to treat individuals differently in the different groups of the experiment (other than those required to implement the independent variable). In addition, experimenters' observations may be biased if they expect certain effects to occur.

Placebo control groups can be used in combination with a technique that controls for both demand characteristics *and* experimenter effects. The technique is called a *double-blind* procedure because both the participant *and* the observer are blind to (unaware of) what treatment is being administered. Two researchers are needed to accomplish the double-blind procedure. For example, in a drug study, the first researcher prepares the drug capsules and codes each capsule in some way; the second researcher distributes the drugs to the participants, recording the code for each drug as it is given to an individual. This procedure ensures there is a record of which drug each person received, but neither the participant nor the experimenter who actually administers the drugs (and observes their effects) knows which treatment the participant received. Thus, experimenter expectancies about the effects of the treatment are controlled because the researcher who makes observations is unaware of who received the treatment and who received the placebo. Similarly, demand characteristics are controlled because participants remain unaware of whether they received the drug or a placebo.

There are special ethical concerns whenever researchers use placebo control groups because research participants who expect to receive a drug may instead receive a placebo. Typically, researchers address the ethics of this procedure in the informed consent procedure before the experiment. Participants are told they may receive a drug or a placebo. Only individuals who consent to receiving the placebo or the drug participate in the research.

DISCUSSION OF THE RESEARCH EXAMPLE: WRITING ABOUT EMOTIONAL EXPERIENCES

Pennebaker and Francis (1996) attempted to conduct an internally valid experiment to assess the causal effects of emotional writing on health and academic outcomes. Were they successful?

We've already addressed their use of the control techniques of manipulation, holding conditions constant, and balancing through random assignment. These techniques are required to establish covariation and a time-order relationship, as well as to eliminate plausible alternative explanations for the findings. We also know from their procedures that they *randomly assigned individuals* to the two conditions rather than *intact groups*, thus protecting the internal validity of their study. Furthermore, because they conducted both conditions in the same room at the same time by the same person, we can be confident that *extraneous variables* probably did not influence their results.

Pennebaker and Francis reported that *subject loss* occurred in the experiment. Data for 18 students were excluded because some students did not complete the three days of writing, some dropped the course, and some had dropped out of school by the end of the second semester. Pennebaker and Francis also reported, however, that subject loss was not related to the conditions of the independent variable. Thus, we can be reasonably confident that subject loss did not threaten the internal validity of the study.

Finally, did participants' and experimenters' expectations influence the different health and academic outcomes for the emotional-writing group and superficial-writing group? For this to be a plausible alternative explanation, participants would need to be aware of the experimental hypothesis and adjust their health center visits and GPA to be consistent with the hypothesis (e.g., lower their GPA if in the superficial-writing group). Pennebaker and Francis asked students directly whether they were aware of the hypotheses—that is, whether they were paying attention *to demand characteristics* in the experiment. Only 2 of the 72 participants accurately guessed that the study was about the relationship between writing and health, suggesting this is not a plausible alternative explanation for the overall findings.

Did the experimenters' expectations and behaviors influence the outcome of the study? The procedures for this experiment replicated the procedures used in several other studies, so it's likely the experimenters had a good idea about the expected results. However, we can look at their procedures to determine if experimenters' expectancies could have influenced the results. First, students participated in groups that comprised both conditions (with written instructions for the two conditions appearing in their packets), and the experimenters didn't know which type of writing individuals were assigned to complete (i.e., they were *blind* to individuals' conditions). Thus, the experimenters probably didn't treat individuals in the two groups differently. Also, the health and academic outcome dependent variables were measured using archival data, and the essays were analyzed using a computer program, making it unlikely that the experimenters influenced the dependent variables in any way. Thus, we can be confident that the experimenters' expectations did not threaten the internal validity of the findings.

Our analysis of Pennebaker and Francis' (1996) experiment suggests it is internally valid. We can confidently conclude that writing about emotional experiences associated with beginning college, compared with superficial writing, *causes* better health outcomes (in terms of health center visits for illness) and better academic outcomes (in terms of GPA).

THE RESEARCHERS' POINT OF VIEW

Questions to Dr. Pennebaker: Your theory about disclosure has changed over time, first focusing on inhibition and then moving more toward language processes. Can you explain how the theory has developed over time?

More than anything, it is important to realize that all theories are flawed. No one gets it right the first time. At the beginning, I made the connection that not talking about a traumatic experience was associated with greater incidence of health problems. A number of studies confirmed this and hence the inhibition theory was born: The more you inhibit your thoughts, behaviors, and emotions, the more physiological work it takes. And this physiological work is later linked to stress-related health problems.

But then, I realized that there was more to the story than just inhibition. We found out that writing or talking about the problem improved health. But, more important, *HOW* people wrote or talked about it mattered. And this led me to begin to study the nature of language more closely. Eventually, we found that healthy writing was associated with a linguistic "fingerprint." That is, people who benefited from writing were gradually putting a story together about their trauma.

And this has now led us to go back to the beginning. I'm now convinced that writing about an upsetting experience ultimately allows us to interact with other people in more normal, healthy ways. Just as inhibition and not talking causes health problems, it also distances us from our friends and loved ones. If we can resolve upsetting experiences by talking with others or even writing about them, we can then reestablish our friendships with others.

What most would you like people to learn from your research?

I think two things: First, that writing or talking about emotional upheavals can have a profound effect on health and well-being. Second, I'd like them to appreciate the joy of scientific investigation.

Are you conducting studies to follow up these findings?

I'm actually going down several paths right now. The one that is particularly intriguing concerns the role of social integration: How does writing about an emotional experience affect social behavior?

READ MORE ABOUT IT

To read more about Pennebaker and Francis' (1996) experiment, you can consult their research report in the following journal article:

Pennebaker, J. W., & Francis, M. E. (1996). Cognitive, emotional, and language processes in disclosure. *Cognition and Emotion, 10,* 601–626.

To learn more about emotional disclosure research, we recommend Dr. Pennebaker's highly readable and popular book:

Pennebaker, J.W. (1997). *Opening up: The healing power of expressing emotion.* New York: Guilford.

KEY CONCEPTS

independent variables	external validity
dependent variables	replication
internal validity	descriptive statistics
confounding	effect size
independent groups designs	inferential statistics
repeated measures design	confidence interval
random assignment	null hypothesis testing
practice effects	statistically significant
counterbalancing	

KEY POINTS TO LEARN

Experimental Research

- Researchers manipulate an independent variable in an experiment to observe the effect on behavior, as assessed by the dependent variable.
- Researchers conduct experiments to test hypotheses about the causes of behavior.

Control and Internal Validity

- Control is the essential ingredient of experiments; experimental control is gained through manipulation, holding conditions constant, and balancing.
- Experimental control allows researchers to make the causal inference that the independent variable *caused* the observed changes in the dependent variable.
- An experiment has internal validity when it fulfills the three conditions required for causal inference: covariation, time-order relationship, and elimination of plausible alternative causes.
- Manipulation of an independent variable is used to establish covariation and a time-order relationship.
- When confounding occurs, a plausible alternative explanation for the observed covariation exists; therefore, the experiment lacks internal validity.
- Plausible alternative explanations are ruled out by holding conditions constant and balancing.

Research Designs

- In an independent groups design, each group of participants in the experiment represents a different condition of the independent variable.
- The logic of the random groups design allows researchers to make causal inferences about the effect of the independent variable on the dependent variable.
- Random assignment to conditions is used to form equivalent groups by balancing, or averaging, subject characteristics across the conditions of the independent variable manipulation.
- A matched group design can be used to create equivalent groups when there are not sufficient numbers of subjects available for random assignment to work effectively.
- Individual differences variables (or subject variables) are selected rather than manipulated to form natural groups designs.
- The natural groups design represents a type of correlational research in which researchers look for covariations between natural groups variables and dependent variables.
- Researchers may decide to use a repeated measures design when few participants are available, to be more efficient when conducting the experiment, to increase the sensitivity of the research, or to study differences within participants over time or across stimuli.
- In repeated measures designs, confoundings due to individual differences variables are eliminated because the same individuals participate in each condition of the independent variable manipulation.
- In repeated measures designs, participants' performance may change across conditions simply because of repeated testing, not because of the independent variable manipulation; these changes are called practice effects.
- Practice effects may threaten the internal validity of a repeated measures experiment when the different conditions of the independent variable are presented in the same order to all participants; counterbalancing eliminates this confounding.
- Differential transfer occurs when the effects of the manipulation for a condition persist and influence performance differently in subsequent conditions.

External Validity

- When findings from an experiment can be applied to other individuals, settings, and conditions, the experiment has external validity.
- In some investigations (e.g., theory testing), researchers may choose to emphasize internal validity over external validity; other researchers may choose to increase external validity using replication.
- Replication is an important method for establishing the reliability and external validity of research findings.
- Researchers often seek to generalize results about conceptual relationships among variables rather than specific conditions, manipulations, settings, and samples.

Analysis of Experimental Designs

- The first step in data analysis is to check the data for errors and outliers.
- The second step in data analysis is to describe the outcome of the experiment using measures of central tendency (e.g., mean) and variability (e.g., standard deviation).
- Measures of effect size indicate the strength of the relationship between the independent and dependent variables.
- Inferential statistics, such as confidence intervals and null hypothesis testing, are used to determine whether an independent variable has a reliable effect on a dependent variable.
- Confidence intervals identify the range of values which we can expect to contain a population value with a specified level of confidence.
- Null hypothesis testing is used to determine whether mean differences among groups in an experiment are greater than the differences that are expected simply by chance.
- The first step in null hypothesis testing is to assume that the groups do not differ—that is, that the independent variable did not have an effect (the null hypothesis).
- Probability theory is used to estimate the likelihood of the experiment's observed outcome, assuming the null hypothesis is true.
- A statistically significant outcome is one that has a small likelihood of occurring if the null hypothesis is true.
- Because decisions about the outcome of an experiment are based on probabilities, Type I or Type II errors may occur.

Conducting a Good Experiment: A Summary

- Good experiments can be identified by their internal validity, reliability, sensitivity, and external validity.
- The multimethod approach to research allows psychologists to use the strengths of different research methods to answer their research questions.

Thinking Critically About Experimental Research

- Randomly assigning intact groups to different conditions of the independent variable creates a potential confounding due to individual differences among participants in the intact groups.
- Factors having to do with the practical considerations of conducting an experiment are called extraneous variables; internal validity is threatened if these factors vary across the different conditions of the independent variable.
- Subject loss threatens the internal validity of an experiment when individuals are more likely to drop out of one condition of the experiment more than others.
- Placebo control groups are used to control for the problem of demand characteristics, and double-blind experiments control both demand characteristics and experimenter effects.

CHECKING THE ESSENTIALS

1. Describe the logic of experimental research in terms of the variation of the independent variable and of other factors that could lead to different outcomes on the dependent variable.
2. Identify the three conditions that must be met in order to state confidently that the independent variable *caused* differences in the dependent variable between groups.
3. What two important control techniques do researchers use when they seek to eliminate alternative hypotheses for the results of their experiments?
4. What do researchers want to achieve when they use random assignment to form the groups in a random groups design experiment?
5. Briefly describe why researchers cannot use the results of natural groups designs to make causal inferences about independent variables that involve selected levels of an individual differences variable.
6. What is the general rule for balancing practice effects in repeated measures designs?
7. What role does the external validity of a finding play when an experiment is done to determine whether people *can* be induced to behave in a certain way, as predicted by a theory?
8. Briefly explain why researchers interested in establishing the external validity of research findings from laboratory experiments focus on the *conceptual relationships* among variables rather than on the *specific* conditions, manipulations, settings, or samples in the experiments.
9. Identify the three distinct steps that researchers follow when they analyze the results of an experiment.
10. Describe how researchers use measures of effect size, inferential statistics, and confidence intervals to answer the critical question posed in any experiment: Did the independent variable have a *"significant* effect" on the dependent variable?

APPLYING YOUR KNOWLEDGE

1. Students in a research methods class were the confederates and observers in a random groups design experiment in which they examined people's responses when their personal space was invaded. The confederates invaded personal space by staring at the people they were observing. The students observed other students as they walked past a bench along a path near the center of campus. The research methods students worked in pairs, with one member of the pair (the confederate) sitting on the bench and the other member (the observer) observing and timing the participants. There were 25 teams of research methods students; each team observed one participant in each condition of the experiment. Participants were selected to be included in the study if they were walking along the path alone. Participants were randomly assigned to one of the three conditions in the experiment. The three conditions all related to what the confederate sitting on the bench did. The confederates were either reading a newspaper held up in front of them, or they stared at the participant as the participant approached the bench. In a third condition, participants were observed with no one sitting on the bench. The observers measured the time it took the participant to walk up to the bench and away from the bench. The research methods students predicted that participants would walk faster when the confederate stared at them. Contrary to their predictions, the research methods students found that

participants walked more slowly toward the bench in the staring condition than in the other two conditions. There was no difference in the three conditions in the walking speeds away from the bench.

A. What aspect of their experiment did the students control by using manipulation?

B. What aspect of their experiment did the students control by holding conditions constant?

C. What aspect of their experiment did the students control by using balancing?

D. The student researchers found that participants walked more slowly toward the bench in the staring condition than in the other two conditions. What aspect of the experiment makes it possible to reach this conclusion, even though the people in the three groups in the experiment were likely very different from one another?

E. Identify one factor that likely would increase the external validity of the findings of this experiment and one factor that likely would decrease external validity.

2. An experiment was done to test the effectiveness of a drug being considered for possible use in the treatment of people who experience chronic anxiety. Fifty chronically anxious people were identified through a local health clinic, and all 50 people gave their informed consent to participate in the experiment. Twenty-five people were randomly assigned to the experimental group, and they received the drug. The other 25 people were randomly assigned to the control group, and they received a placebo. The participants in both groups were monitored by a physician and by a clinical psychologist during the 6-week treatment period. After the treatment period, the participants provided a self-rating on a reliable and valid 20-point scale, indicating the level of anxiety they were experiencing (higher scores indicated greater anxiety). The mean self-rating in the control group was 13.5 ($SD = 2.8$) and the mean rating in the experimental group was 10.2 ($SD = 2.4$) The confidence interval for the difference between these two means does not include zero. The effect size for this drug is .37 in this experiment.

A. Explain why a double-blind procedure would be useful in this experiment and describe how the double-blind procedure could be carried out in this experiment.

B. What information from the description of this experiment would you use to decide whether the drug had a reliable effect on the level of anxiety that the participants experienced?

3. A researcher wants to use a repeated measures design in an experiment investigating people's abilities to solve problems. The problems vary in difficulty at three levels (high, medium, and low). Each problem takes several minutes to solve, but all three can be solved in the 30-minute sessions the researcher plans to use for testing participants. The researcher asks you to prepare the orders of the conditions for testing each of the participants. The researcher wants to use all possible orders of the conditions in this experiment. Prepare a table showing the orders of the conditions for the first six participants in this experiment.

7

COMPLEX DESIGNS

Outline

INTRODUCTION

In Chapter 6, we examined the basic experimental designs psychologists use to study the effect of an independent variable. We discussed how an independent variable could be implemented with a separate group of participants in each condition (independent groups designs) or with each participant experiencing all the conditions (repeated measures design). We limited our discussion to experiments involving only one independent variable to concentrate on the basics of experimental research. Experiments involving only one independent variable are not, however, the most common type of experiment in current psychological research. Instead, researchers most often use **complex designs,** in which two or more independent variables are studied simultaneously in one experiment.

In Chapter 6 we learned how Pennebaker and Francis (1996) examined how the type of writing influences health and academic outcomes. To continue this example, suppose a researcher is interested in the effect of type of writing (emotional, superficial) *and* the effect of instructions that ask participants to focus on the causes of the events. (Recall that Pennebaker and Francis (1996) theorized that beneficial health outcomes are related to gaining insight into the causes of emotional experiences.) Thus, an independent variable manipulation could be type of instructions with two levels, "insight instructions" (e.g., "Please focus on the *causes* of the events you describe") and "no-insight instructions" (e.g., "Please focus on the *details* of the events you describe"). Let's assume both variables are manipulated using an independent groups design and health outcomes are measured as the dependent variable. An efficient way to study the effect of both these independent variables is to conduct a single study using a complex design. The design would look like this:

Type of Writing

	Emotional	Superficial
Insight (Causes)	Participants in this condition would write about an emotional event with insight instructions.	Participants in this condition would write about a superficial event with insight instructions.
No-insight (Details)	Participants in this condition would write about an emotional event with no-insight (details) instructions.	Participants in this condition would write about a superficial event with no-insight (details) instructions.

Type of Instructions (label at left of table)

In a typical complex design researchers combine the levels for each of the two independent variables *factorially*. Factorial combination involves creating conditions of the experiment by pairing each level of one independent variable with each level of a second independent variable. In this example we are factorially combining the two independent variables, type of writing and type of instructions: (1) emotional writing—insight instructions, (2) emotional writing—no-insight instructions, (3) superficial writing—insight instructions, and (4) superficial writing—no-insight instructions.

This complex design has four conditions (the "cells" in the diagram). The number of conditions in a complex factorial design is always equal to the product of the number of levels for each independent variable. That is, there are two levels of the type of writing independent variable (emotional, superficial), and two levels of the type of instructions independent variable (insight, no-insight). The number of conditions, then, is four ($2 \times 2 = 4$). This is called a "2×2 factorial design" (read "2 by 2").

When researchers use factorial combination in complex designs they can assess the effect of each independent variable alone (the *main effect* of an independent variable) and the effect of the independent variables in combination (an *interaction* between the independent variables). An *interaction effect* can be discovered only when two or more independent variables are included in the same experiment. In general, an interaction occurs when the effect of one independent variable differs depending on the level of a second independent variable. For example, if the effect of type of writing (emotional vs. superficial) depended on the type of instructions (insight vs. no insight), an interaction would be present. The ability to detect interactions between independent variables is the special strength of complex designs.

Complex designs may seem a bit complicated at this point, but the concepts will become clearer as you progress through this chapter. In what follows, we will examine the procedures for producing, analyzing, and interpreting main effects and interactions. To do this we will turn to a topic from social psychology: the perceived attractiveness of potential dating partners. We will then review the guidelines for manipulating independent variables in a complex design. Because complex designs are best understood using an example, we will refer to the research example throughout the chapter.

LEARNING OBJECTIVES

By the end of this chapter, you should be able to
- *identify main effects and interactions in complex designs,*
- *understand how complex designs are analyzed, and*
- *interpret the meaning of interactions in complex designs.*

THE RESEARCH EXAMPLE: ATTRACTIVENESS OF POTENTIAL DATING PARTNERS

Clearly, the close relationships we have with other people, particularly our romantic partners, are very important aspects of our lives. We work hard to maintain these relationships and feel sadness and loss when these relationships end. Social psychology researchers have demonstrated that individuals in committed romantic relationships maintain their relationship by sharing tasks (e.g., Dainton & Stafford, 1993), by affiliating with couples in good relationships, and by behaving positively toward a partner during conflicts (e.g., Rusbult & Buunk, 1993).

Another potential way that individuals maintain their relationship with a romantic partner is by seeing other potential relationship opportunities as undesirable or unattractive (Bazzini & Shaffer, 1999). This occurs when individuals put on "blinders" so they don't even notice attractive alternative partners or, more consciously, when individuals evaluate potential partners negatively. When individuals derogate, or put down, a potential partner, their current relationship isn't threatened. In fact, several experiments have demonstrated that individuals in committed relationships rate attractive prospects less favorably than individuals not in relationships. This finding has been interpreted as evidence that individuals in committed relationships derogate potential partners in order to maintain their relationship with their current partner.

Drs. Doris Bazzini and David Shaffer (1999) argued, however, that this finding could be interpreted in a different way: Rather than committed-relationship individuals putting down an attractive alternative, it may be that individuals not in relationships *enhance* their ratings of the desirability of an attractive prospect. That is, these individuals may evaluate a potential partner more favorably because they're unattached and perhaps looking to become attached to this person. Bazzini and Shaffer noted there's no clear standard to determine which group is accurate when rating the desirability of an attractive potential partner. So, rather than members of the committed group derogating a potential partner, they hypothesized that non-committed individuals rate a potential partner more favorably because they're seeking a relationship. This finding would cast doubt on the idea that we maintain relationships by putting others down.

The purpose of Bazzini and Shaffer's experiment was to determine whether *relationship maintenance* (by individuals in committed relationships) or *relationship seeking* (by individuals not in committed relationships) can explain attractiveness ratings of potential dating partners. These investigators also sought to establish an objective standard for evaluating the desirability of an attractive prospect—someone who is equally attractive to individuals in committed relationships and individuals not in relationships. As we'll see, they did this using a complex design.

THE RESEARCHERS' POINT OF VIEW

Questions to Dr. Bazzini: How did you become interested in studying people's evaluations of potential dating partners?

I was a junior in college and already a declared psychology major when I took my first course in social psychology. Within a few weeks I knew the material was making an impact on my career decisions, but it wasn't until we learned about Dion's work on the beautiful-is-good stereotype that I found a research focus—attraction and dating. At the time, I was living in a coed dorm and was very attentive to the soap-opera-

Dr. Doris Bazzini

like happenings of my dormmates and was thrilled to finally have labels for the phenomena that were occurring around me. My decision to go to the University of Georgia was influenced by the fact that David Shaffer (who became my adviser) was also interested in interpersonal processes.

Previous research in this area seemed to provide strong support for the relationship maintenance hypothesis. What led you to question this evidence and conduct your own experiments?

Dr. David Shaffer

Around the time I was seeking a dissertation topic, two important things happened. First, a long-time friend of mine asked me on a date while I was engaged to be married to another man. I accepted the date and later married that same friend. Second, I was taking a methodology course designed to teach critical analysis of published research (e.g., propose alternative hypotheses for the findings, etc.). I came across one of the articles that supported the relationship maintenance hypothesis and that had used nonexclusive daters as the objective-observer control group. Two questions immediately came to mind: "Why did relationship-maintenance mechanisms not prevail in my engagement?" and "Why wouldn't nonexclusive daters be as motivated to seek out a relationship as exclusive daters would be motivated to protect a relationship?"

MANIPULATING INDEPENDENT VARIABLES IN A COMPLEX DESIGN

In Chapter 6 we learned that the simplest possible experiment involves one independent variable manipulated with two levels. Similarly, the simplest possible complex design involves two independent variables, each with two levels. A 2 × 2 design identifies the most basic complex design. Conceptually, there is an unlimited number of complex designs because researchers can study any number of independent variables and each independent variable can have any number of levels. In practice, however, researchers rarely test more than four or five independent variables; it's more common to test just two or three independent variables in a complex design.

Regardless of the number of independent variables, we can determine the number of conditions in a complex design by multiplying the number of levels of the independent variables. For example, in a 3 × 3 design there are two independent variables, each with three levels. Thus, there would be nine conditions

(3 × 3) in the experiment. In a 3 × 4 × 2 design there are three independent variables with three, four, and two levels, respectively, and a total of 24 conditions.

As mentioned earlier, the conditions in a complex design typically are created using *factorial combination*. To create a factorial design, researchers pair each level of an independent variable with each level of the other independent variable(s). In Bazzini and Shaffer's (1999) experiment on attractiveness ratings of potential dating partners, college students first completed a questionnaire about their current dating status. Based on their responses to several questions, Bazzini and Shaffer classified participants as "exclusive daters" (individuals in a committed romantic relationship) or "nonexclusive daters" (individuals not in a committed relationship). Thus, this independent variable of "dating status" had two levels: exclusive daters (*n* = 50) and nonexclusive daters (*n* = 48). Note that this is an independent groups design because individuals were placed in only one group (they could not participate in both groups, as in a repeated measures design). You should also recognize that dating status is a natural groups variable because whether or not individuals are in an exclusive dating relationship is an individual differences variable. The groups were formed "naturally." The levels were selected, not manipulated.

In a separate session, Bazzini and Shaffer asked these college students to read a hypothetical scenario in which they imagined themselves at a restaurant with their best same-sex friend. The scenario described a situation in which they encounter an "extremely attractive member of the opposite sex" who was described as either attracted to the participant or attracted to the participant's best friend (all of the participants were heterosexual). Students were randomly assigned to read one of the two scenarios. Thus, Bazzini and Shaffer manipulated a "type of scenario" independent variable using two levels: (1) the stranger is attracted to them (i.e., the participant) and (2) the stranger is attracted to the friend. The scenario variable was manipulated using independent groups—more specifically, random groups.

Bazzini and Shaffer reasoned that individuals in exclusive relationships would experience the scenario in which the attractive stranger was attracted to them as a potential *threat* to their current relationship. However, these individuals would not be threatened when the stranger was attracted to the friend. In contrast, Bazzini and Shaffer believed that nonexclusive daters would experience the scenario in which the attractive stranger was attracted to them as an *opportunity* for a new relationship. In contrast, no opportunity would be present when the stranger was described as interested in the participants' friend.

The following diagram shows the factorial design resulting from the combination of these variables. Because it was a 2 × 2 design there were four conditions, each representing a combination of levels of the two independent variables.

Type of Scenario

Dating Status		Stranger Attracted to Friend	Stranger Attracted to Participant
	Exclusive Daters	These participants were in an exclusive relationship and read the scenario in which the stranger was attracted to their friend (n = 24).	These participants were in an exclusive relationship and read the scenario in which the stranger was attracted to them (n = 26).
	Nonexclusive Daters	These participants were not in an exclusive relationship and read the scenario in which the stranger was attracted to their friend (n = 23).	These participants were not in an exclusive relationship and read the scenario in which the stranger was attracted to them (n = 25).

Bazzini and Shaffer (1999) examined several dependent variables to determine whether exclusive daters put down the attractive stranger (relationship-maintenance hypothesis), or whether nonexclusive daters enhanced ratings of the attractive stranger (relationship-seeking hypothesis). For example, they assessed participants' "romantic interest" in the stranger by asking, "All things considered, how likely is it that one could have a satisfying relationship with this person?" (p. 166). Bazzini and Shaffer used participants' responses to this question (and others) to determine the effects of the independent variables.

Recall that one of Bazzini and Shaffer's goals was to establish an objective standard for evaluating the desirability of an attractive potential partner—someone who is equally attractive to individuals in committed relationships and individuals not in relationships. They reasoned that exclusive daters and nonexclusive daters would rate the desirability of the stranger equally when the stranger was interested in the friend. That is, participants' motivations to maintain their current relationship or seek a new relationship should not influence their ratings of someone who is not interested in them. The researchers' hypotheses, therefore, were framed in terms of this "neutral" person.

Exclusive daters were predicted to rate the desirability of the attractive stranger *lower* when the stranger was interested in them, compared with when the stranger was interested in their friend. This would support the idea that exclusive daters put down potential dating partners in order to protect their current relationship. In contrast, nonexclusive daters were predicted to rate the desirability of the attractive stranger *higher* when the attractive stranger was interested in them, compared with when the stranger was interested in their friend. These hypotheses are outlined in Table 7.1.

Table 7.1   Attractiveness of Potential Dating Partners: The Research Hypotheses

Relationship-Maintenance Hypothesis: Effect of Scenario	
Exclusive daters (in a committed relationship)	Mean romantic interest ratings should be greater when the stranger is attracted to the friend, compared with when the stranger is attracted to the participant. That is, to maintain their relationship, exclusive daters will "put down" the potential dating partner when he or she is interested in them.

Relationship-Seeking Hypothesis: Effect of Scenario	
Nonexclusive daters (not in a committed relationship)	Mean romantic interest ratings should be greater when the stranger is attracted to the participant, compared with when the stranger is attracted to the friend. That is, when seeking a relationship, nonexclusive daters will "enhance" the potential dating partner when he or she is interested in them.

THE RESEARCHERS' POINT OF VIEW

Question to Dr. Bazzini: An important part of your procedure was developing an objective standard to compare participants' evaluations of an attractive suitor who was interested in the participant. How did you come up with your ideas?

Dr. Shaffer and I spent quite some time considering how we would establish an objective standard, or "control group," against which to judge evaluations of a dating alternative. The bottom line is that people are either exclusive or nonexclusive daters and are motivated by their respective needs. We wanted the first study to be more similar to other research paradigms that had been used [to replicate previous findings], so we knew we could use a hypothetical situation. We started considering dating norms that we felt most people would not violate and decided that one such norm involved an alternative [person] that showed interest in dating a friend—a "hands-off" situation for uncommitted individuals who might be seeking a relationship and, at the same time, a clear nonthreat to a committed, exclusive dater. We believed people could be objective in making an evaluation of a person who wanted to date a friend of theirs.

IDENTIFYING MAIN EFFECTS AND INTERACTIONS

The nature of main effects and interactions is essentially the same in all complex designs, but they're easiest to see in a 2 × 2 design. In any complex factorial design researchers can test predictions regarding the overall effect of each independent variable in the experiment while ignoring the effect of the other independent variable(s). The overall effect of an independent variable in a complex design is called a **main effect**. You can think of main effects as a way researchers can examine the effect of a single independent variable *as if* they had studied *only* that variable in the experiment. However, before researchers can examine the effect of an independent variable, they need to identify a dependent variable.

Although Bazzini and Shaffer had several dependent variables, we will focus on participants' ratings of the stranger's romantic appeal. Bazzini and Shaffer summed participants' responses to three items (each rated on a 5-point scale) to derive a total "romantic interest" score for each participant (maximum = 15). The mean romantic interest ratings for participants in each condition were as follows:

Means for "Romantic Interest"

Type of Scenario

Dating Status	Stranger Attracted to Friend ($n = 51$)	Stranger Attracted to Participant ($n = 47$)	Means for Dating Status
Exclusive Daters ($n = 50$)	9.77 ($n = 26$)	9.25 ($n = 24$)	9.52
Nonexclusive Daters ($n = 48$)	10.00 ($n = 25$)	11.13 ($n = 23$)	10.54
Means for Type of Scenario	9.88	10.17	

Source: Bazzini and Shaffer (1999)

We can examine the *main effects* of the type of scenario and dating status independent variables on participants' romantic interest ratings by examining the *means* for the columns and rows. The main effect of the scenario independent variable is represented by the overall means for the stranger-attracted-to-friend condition ($M = 9.88$) and stranger-attracted-to-participant condition ($M = 10.17$), collapsed across the dating status independent variable. These means are similar, suggesting that, on average, romantic interest ratings did not differ for the two scenario conditions.

We can also look at the main effect of the dating status independent variable. Collapsed across type of scenario, the mean romantic interest rating by nonexclusive daters ($M = 10.54$) was greater than the mean romantic interest rating by exclusive daters ($M = 9.52$). Thus, on average, nonexclusive daters rated their romantic interest in the stranger higher than exclusive daters (i.e., regardless of who the stranger was attracted to). We must rely, however, on the results of a statistical test to tell us whether these differences are statistically significant, that is, greater than what would be expected by chance.

Main effects represent the effect of each independent variable considered separately; interactions represent how independent variables work together to influence behavior. An **interaction** between independent variables occurs when the effect of one independent variable differs depending on the level of the second independent variable. To look for an interaction in the Bazzini and Shaffer study we need to look at the effect of dating status at each level of the scenario independent variable.

Means for "Romantic Interest"

Type of Scenario

Dating Status	Stranger Attracted to Friend	Stranger Attracted to Participant
Exclusive Daters	9.77	9.25
Nonexclusive Daters	10.00	11.13
Difference Between Means	9.77 – 10.00 = –0.23	9.25 – 10.00 = –1.88

Source: Bazzini and Shaffer (1999)

In the condition in which the stranger was attracted to the friend, exclusive daters and nonexclusive daters were approximately equal in their romantic interest ratings (Ms = 9.77 and 10.00, respectively). The difference between these means is very small (–0.23).

Recall that Bazzini and Shaffer wished to use this condition as an objective standard for evaluations of an attractive potential dating partner. Because exclusive and nonexclusive daters agreed in their romantic interest for the stranger when he or she was attracted to the friend, Bazzini and Shaffer suggested that ratings in the stranger-attracted-to-friend condition provide a good standard for comparison.

In contrast, a larger difference between exclusive daters and nonexclusive daters seemed to emerge in the condition in which the stranger was attracted to the participant. Nonexclusive daters rated their romantic interest in the stranger higher than did exclusive daters (Ms = 11.13 and 9.25, respectively). The difference between the means, –1.88, is greater in this condition. Thus, in the stranger-attracted-to-participant condition, the dating status independent variable had a larger effect than it did in the stranger-attracted-to-friend condition. Remember, an interaction is indicated when the effect of one independent variable varies as a function of the level of the second independent variable. These data, therefore, suggest there was an interaction between the two independent variables for participants' romantic interest in the stranger.

Detecting interactions this way, by using the difference between means, is called the "subtraction method." When the results of subtraction between means for the conditions lead to very different values (e.g., –0.23 and –1.88), an interaction is likely present in the data.

Let's summarize the interaction: The dating status independent variable had little or no effect when participants read that the stranger was attracted to their friend, but it had an effect in the condition in which participants read that the stranger was interested in them. The effect of the dating status independent variable differed *depending on* the level of the type of scenario independent variable.

When one independent variable interacts with a second independent variable, the second independent variable must interact with the first one (that is, the order of the independent variables doesn't matter). The way in which researchers choose to describe the results of an interaction depends on which aspect of the interaction they want to emphasize. By looking at the interaction another way, Bazzini and Shaffer (1999) tested their hypotheses for whether exclusive daters put down an alternative dating partner and whether nonexclusive daters enhance their ratings of a potential dating partner. To do this they examined the effect of the type of scenario independent variable separately for exclusive daters and nonexclusive daters.

Means for "Romantic Interest"

Dating Status	Type of Scenario		
	Stranger Attracted to Friend	Stranger Attracted to Participant	Difference Between Means
Exclusive Daters	9.77	9.25	9.77 − 9.25 = 0.52
Nonexclusive Daters	10.00	11.13	10.00 − 11.13 = −1.13

Source: Bazzini and Shaffer (1999)

These are exactly the same means as before; we're simply now going to compare the means across the columns instead of the rows. First we'll consider the effect of the type of scenario independent variable just for exclusive daters. The mean romantic interest rating for exclusive daters who read that the stranger was attracted to their friend was 9.77. However, when exclusive daters read that the stranger was attracted to them, their mean romantic interest rating was slightly lower ($M = 9.25$). Although in the predicted direction, the difference between these two means was small (0.52), and results of a statistical test indicated the difference between these means was not statistically significant. Thus, exclusive daters seemed to rate their romantic interest in an attractive stranger similarly when the stranger was attracted to someone else and when the stranger was attracted to them. This is not what Bazzini and Shaffer predicted based on the relationship maintenance hypothesis. According to the hypothesis, exclusive daters should have put down the stranger who was attracted to them to a greater extent in order to protect their relationship.

A different result emerged for the nonexclusive daters. Their mean romantic interest rating for the stranger who was attracted to their friend was 10.00. However, their mean romantic interest rating for the stranger who was attracted to them was 11.13. The difference between means for the two scenario conditions was −1.13. This finding suggests that nonexclusive daters rated their romantic interest for an attractive stranger higher when the stranger was attracted to them rather than someone else. Results of a statistical test indicated this difference was statistically significant. This finding is consistent with the relationship-seeking hypothesis. Based on this hypothesis, Bazzini and Shaffer had predicted that nonexclusive daters would enhance their ratings of a potential dating partner when the person was interested in them.

A graph of the mean romantic interest ratings for each condition can help us see the results more clearly. When graphing results for an experiment we always place the dependent variable on the *y*-axis (vertical axis). One independent variable (in this case, type of scenario) is graphed on the *x*-axis (horizontal axis), and the second independent variable (dating status) is plotted as two separate lines (one for each dating-status group) within the space of the graph (see Figure 7.1).

An interaction between variables can be detected easily on a graph. When an interaction is present the lines of the graph are not parallel—the lines either intersect, converge, or diverge (as in Figure 7.1). When independent variables do not interact the lines are approximately parallel (i.e., the lines do *not* cross, converge, or diverge). Because the presence of interactions is easily detected using a graph of the means, a good first step when analyzing the results of a complex design is to graph the means for your conditions to "see" what happened in your experiment. You should then follow up this descriptive analysis of your data with inferential tests, such as confidence intervals or null hypothesis testing (see Analyzing Complex Designs section).

As you can see, a lot of information is gained when researchers use a complex design. Bazzini and Shaffer (1999) were able to learn how individuals evaluate potential relationship partners and test hypotheses regarding relationship maintenance and relationship seeking. The only way they could answer their

Figure 7.1   Interaction between dating status and type of scenario independent variables for participants' romantic interest ratings (Bazzini & Shaffer, 1999).

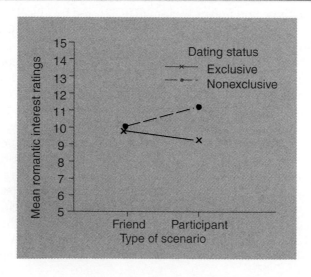

research questions was to use a complex design. Mastering the concepts of main effects and interactions requires practice in identifying the various types of outcomes that can arise in a complex design. Box 7.1 provides an exercise that gives you an opportunity to practice identifying main effects and interactions in 2×2 designs using only descriptive statistics (i.e., means for the conditions). Inferential statistics such as F tests would be required to confirm the statistical significance of any obtained effects, but the effects themselves can best be seen in a table or graph of the means for the conditions of the experiment.

The power, complexity, and efficiency of complex designs increase substantially when the number of independent variables in the experiment increases from two to three. A two-factor design has only one interaction, but in a three-factor design (e.g., $2 \times 2 \times 2$) each independent variable can interact with each of the other two independent variables, and all three independent variables can interact. Thus, changing from a two-factor to a three-factor design introduces the possibility of obtaining four different interactions—and much more information about the effects of the independent variables. The possible effects in two-way and three-way factorial designs are identified in Table 7.2.

ANALYZING COMPLEX DESIGNS

The analysis of complex designs builds on the logic used in the analysis of experiments with only one independent variable (see Chapter 6). The first step is to check the data for errors and to see if the distribution of scores is relatively normal (bell-shaped) rather than skewed. If the distribution is skewed, researchers

Table 7.2   Effects In Factorial Designs

Two-Factor Experiment: Independent Variables *A* and *B*

Main effect of *A*: compare levels of *A* (collapsed across levels of *B*)
Main effect of *B*: compare levels of *B* (collapsed across levels of *A*)
A × *B* interaction: compare all conditions of the experiment

Three-Factor Experiment: Independent Variables *A*, *B*, and *C*

Main effect of *A*: compare levels of *A* (collapsed across levels of *B* and *C*)
Main effect of *B*: compare levels of *B* (collapsed across levels of *A* and *C*)
Main effect of *C*: compare levels of *C* (collapsed across levels of *A* and *B*)
A × *B* interaction: compare cells that combine levels of *A* and *B* (collapsed across *C*)
A × *C* interaction: compare cells that combine levels of *A* and *C* (collapsed across *B*)
B × *C* interaction: compare cells that combine levels of *B* and *C* (collapsed across *A*)
A × *B* × *C* interaction: compare all conditions of the experiment

---

Note: When using this table to understand complex designs, substitute the names of independent variables for *A*, *B*, and *C*. Make sure you use the names of independent variables (e.g., dating status), not individual levels of independent variables (e.g., exclusive daters).

Box 7.1

HERE AN INTERACTION, THERE AN INTERACTION, EVERYWHERE AN INTERACTION

In the spirit of practice makes perfect, let us now turn our attention to an exercise to help you learn to identify interactions. Your task is to identify main effects and interactions in each of six complex design experiments (A through F). In each table or graph in this box, you are to determine whether the effect of each independent variable differs depending on the level of the other independent variable. In other words, is there an interaction? After checking for the interaction, you can also check to see whether each independent vari-

able produced an effect when collapsed across the other independent variable. That is, is there a main effect of one or both independent variables? The exercise will be most useful if you also practice translating the data presented in a table (Figure 7.2) into a graph and those presented in graphs (Figures 7.3 and 7.4) into tables. The idea of the exercise is to become as comfortable as you can with the various ways of depicting the results of a complex design.*

Figure 7.2   Mean number of correct responses as a function of task difficulty and anxiety level.

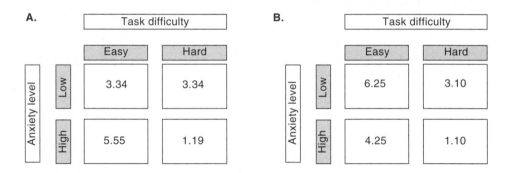

*Answer key for exercises in this box: An interaction occurs in A, D, and E.

may examine the data for outliers. The next step is to summarize the results using descriptive statistics. Researchers calculate the means and standard deviations for the conditions of the experiment, as well as the effect sizes for the independent variables. As mentioned earlier, it's very useful to display the means in a graph to get a sense of what happened in the experiment. We've already done this for Bazzini and Shaffer's (1999) experiment (review Figure 7.1).

As we examine the means in Figure 7.1, we can see some differences among the means. Another way to say this is that there is *variability* across the groups on the dependent variable. We use the third step in data analysis, the confirmatory stage, to determine whether the independent variables are responsible for the variability among group means. That is, we ask whether the independent

Figure 7.3   Mean number of errors as a function of type of task and brain hemisphere tested.

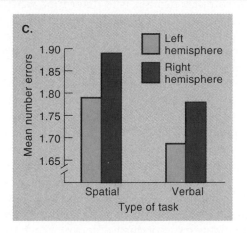

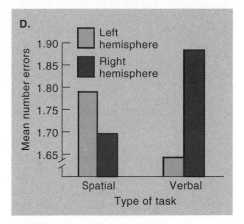

Figure 7.4   Mean reaction time as a function of set size and response type.

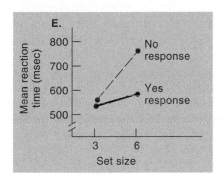

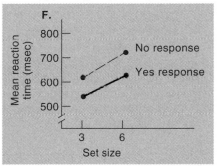

variables reliably influenced participants' responses on the dependent variables. The most common method for testing the effects of independent variables in complex designs is *null hypothesis testing*, which was described in Chapter 6.

In a complex design, each independent variable may lead to *overall* differences in the way in which individuals respond on a dependent variable (independently of the other independent variable). These are called the main effects of each independent variable. Similarly, the combined effect of independent variables may influence participants' responses on the dependent variable. In any experiment it's possible for independent variables to influence behavior as main effects or when interacting with another variable, or both. Another way of saying this is that it is possible, in a complex design with two variables

(*A* and *B*), to have a main effect of *A*, a main effect of *B*, a main effect of both *A* and *B*, and an interaction (*A* × *B*). In short, any combination of effects is possible, including no statistically significant effects.

The goal of statistical tests for complex designs is to determine whether the effect associated with each independent variable is greater than chance. The statistical analysis most commonly used for complex designs is *analysis of variance (ANOVA)*, which makes use of the *F* test. ANOVAs for complex designs are most easily computed using a statistics software package. The output of the statistics program will include an *ANOVA summary table*. A summary table for a 2 × 2 complex design presents three *F* tests: one *F* test associated with each main effect for the two independent variables and the *F* test associated with the interaction between the two independent variables. The ANOVA summary table also includes the probability value associated with each *F* test. As mentioned in Chapter 6, we use the observed probability value associated with a test statistic to decide whether an outcome is "statistically significant." Most often, our *level of significance* is α (alpha) = .05. When our observed probability value is less than .05, we claim that the effect of the independent variable on the dependent variable is statistically significant, or reliable (i.e., not due to chance). When the probability value associated with the *F* test is greater than .05, we state that the effect of the independent variable is not statistically significant; that is, any observed difference between means is most likely due to chance. An ANOVA summary table can also provide information about the effect size of each main effect and interaction. Thus, in addition to deciding whether an independent variable has had an effect, researchers can also determine the size of the effect.

The analysis of variance summary table for participants' romantic interest ratings in Bazzini and Shaffer's (1999) experiment appears in Table 7.3. There are three statistical effects in this analysis: the main effect of dating status, the main effect of type of scenario, and the interaction between the dating status and scenario independent variables. An *F* test is presented for each effect. The

Table 7.3   ANOVA Summary Table For Romantic Interest Ratings

Source	df	SS	MS	*F*	*p*	eta*
Type of Scenario	1	2.28	2.28	0.74	.300	.09
Dating Status	1	27.24	27.24	8.78	.001	.29
Type of Scenario X Dating Status	1	16.63	16.63	5.36	.020	.23
Error	94	291.72	3.10			
Total	97	335.96				

Source: Data provided by Doris G. Bazzini.

*Eta is a measure of effect size that represents the strength of the relationship between the independent variable and the dependent variable. Guidelines for interpreting the size of the effect are as follows (Rosenthal & Rosnow, 1991)—small: eta = .10, medium: eta = .30, large: eta = .50. Some statistical software packages may present results for eta^2, which is simply the squared value of eta.

specific probabilities for each of the F tests were part of the computer output for this analysis.

The results of the F test indicate that the main effect of dating status on participants' romantic interest ratings was statistically significant. The value for the F test was 8.78 and the probability value (p) associated with this statistic was .001. Because this p value is less than .05, we conclude that the main effect of dating status was statistically significant. The computer output also presents an index of effect size, *eta,* which tells us the strength of the relationship between the independent variable and dependent variable. The value of eta, .29, represents a medium effect of dating status on participants' romantic interest ratings.

In contrast, the outcome of the F test for the main effect of the type of scenario independent variable was not statistically significant. The value for the F test was 0.74 and the p value was .30, which is greater than our criterion for significance, $\alpha = .05$. The effect size, *eta = .09,* indicates that the type of scenario had only a small effect on participants' romantic interest ratings.

Finally, the value of the F test for the Dating Status X Scenario interaction was 5.36, and the p value associated with this outcome was .02. Because this p value is less than .05, we conclude the interaction was statistically significant. The effect size, *eta = .23,* indicates a small-to-medium effect of the interaction on participants' ratings.

The information in the ANOVA summary table is useful only in conjunction with the means displayed in Figure 7.1. That is, we can interpret the meaning of the F tests *only* by looking at the means for the effect. For example, the F test for the main effect of dating status doesn't tell us whether the romantic interest ratings were higher for exclusive daters or nonexclusive daters. To determine the direction of the statistically significant effect *we must look at the means.* As we saw earlier, the means for the main effect of dating status indicated that, on average, nonexclusive daters were more romantically interested in the stranger than were exclusive daters.

Similarly, the statistically significant F test for the interaction indicates that the effect of the dating status independent variable differs depending on the level of the scenario independent variable. The F test does not allow us to describe *how* these variables interact; the F test tells us only whether the independent variables interact reliably to influence responses on the dependent variable. In order to describe the interaction, we need to look at the means in Figure 7.1. As we've seen, the means reveal a larger difference between exclusive and nonexclusive daters when the stranger was interested in the participant than when the stranger was interested in the friend.

The initial overall analysis of the experiment is called an *omnibus* analysis of variance. The omnibus statistical test produces outcomes for each main effect and interaction in the experiment. Often in complex designs, follow-up analyses are needed to interpret the initial omnibus tests. This is especially true when a statistically significant interaction is present in the data. For example, a *simple main effect* is the effect of one independent variable at *one level* of a second independent variable. In fact, one definition of an interaction is that the simple main effects across levels are different. Thus, in order to identify the source of an

Looks like an interaction is present.

© 1989 by Sidney Harris-'Einstein Simplified'.
Rutgers University Press.

interaction, researchers examine the effect of one independent variable at each level of the second independent variable (see Keppel, 1991). When an interaction effect is *not* statistically significant, the next step is to examine the main effects for each independent variable. Therefore, "follow-up" analyses for complex designs differ, depending on whether or not a statistically significant interaction is present.

INTERPRETING INTERACTIONS

Theories play a critical role in the scientific method. For example, Bazzini and Shaffer (1999) examined hypotheses about the attractiveness of potential dating partners derived from a theory of interpersonal relationships. Prior to their study, research on the attractiveness of potential dating partners seemed to support the relationship-maintenance hypothesis. Because they used a complex design, Bazzini and Shaffer's (1999) data provided evidence to test both the relationship-maintenance hypothesis and the relationship-seeking hypothesis. The data for participants' romantic interest in the attractive stranger provided evidence regarding the relationship-maintenance hypothesis (for exclusive daters) and the relationship-seeking hypothesis (for nonexclusive daters). Bazzini and Shaffer (1999) predicted that exclusive daters may put down an attractive stranger who is attracted to them in order to maintain and protect their current relationship. Contrary to this prediction, however, exclusive daters rated the stranger similarly when the stranger was described as attracted to them or to their friend. Bazzini and Shaffer stated that this finding "is not consistent with the notion that exclusive daters would seek to maintain or protect their existing relationship by devaluing the attributes of an attractive stimulus person who might pose a threat to their relationship" (p. 167). Thus, the relationship-maintenance hypothesis was not supported in their experiment.

In contrast, the findings for nonexclusive daters indicated support for the relationship-seeking hypothesis. Nonexclusive daters rated their romantic interest higher when the stranger was attracted to them rather than to their friend. As Bazzini and Shaffer stated, "they seemed to be bolstering their evaluations of the available target as if they were intrigued by the possibility of establishing a new relationship" (p. 168). Bazzini and Shaffer's experiment illustrates how interactions allow us to make more sophisticated tests of psychological theories.

Why did Bazzini and Shaffer's results contradict the findings of previous research, which supported the relationship-maintenance hypothesis? Recall that a problem with previous research was that there had not been an objective standard to determine whether exclusive daters were putting down a potential partner or whether nonexclusive daters were enhancing their ratings of a potential partner. By including an independent variable manipulation of who the stranger was interested in, Bazzini and Shaffer were able to shed light on why studies in this area have produced different results. That is, by including a condition in which the attractive stranger was interested in a friend, Bazzini and Shaffer created a comparison ("control") condition. They compared participants' ratings in this condition with ratings when the stranger was interested in them. Previous research compared exclusive and nonexclusive daters only when potential partners were interested in the participants. By adding the comparison condition in a complex design, Bazzini and Shaffer's experiment helped resolve the contradictory findings regarding relationship maintenance.

Complex design experiments also help researchers establish the *external validity* of research findings. In Chapter 6 we noted that researchers often use replication to establish external validity (i.e., to generalize their research findings). Interactions in complex designs help researchers determine the external validity of findings in a complex design.

When *no* interaction occurs, the effects of each independent variable can be generalized across the levels of the other independent variable. Let's see why this is true by considering Bazzini and Shaffer's results for a different dependent variable, participants' physical attractiveness ratings of the stranger. The participants also rated whether they thought the stranger in the scenario was physically attractive and "sexy." The Dating Status X Type of Scenario interaction was not statistically significant for these ratings, but the main effect of the scenario independent variable was statistically significant. Participants rated the stranger as more physically attractive when he or she was interested in them than when he or she was interested in the friend. This finding was true for *both* exclusive and nonexclusive daters (i.e., dating status and scenario independent variables did not interact). Therefore, we can say that the effect of the scenario variable *generalizes* across the levels of dating status for attractiveness ratings.

Of course, we cannot generalize findings beyond the boundaries or conditions that were included in the experiment. For example, the absence of an interaction between the dating status and scenario independent variables does not allow us to conclude that *married individuals* would also rate the stranger's physical attractiveness higher when the stranger was interested in them. Married individuals weren't tested in Bazzini and Shaffer's experiment, so we can't generalize the findings to the population of married individuals. Similarly, Bazzini and Shaffer tested only two specific conditions in which a stranger expressed interest. It's possible that other scenarios of interpersonal attraction may produce different results.

As we have seen, the *absence* of an interaction increases the external validity of the effects of each independent variable in the experiment. Perhaps what is more important, the *presence* of an interaction identifies limits for the external validity of a finding. For example, Bazzini and Shaffer (1999) observed a statistically significant interaction between dating status and scenario independent variables for participants' romantic interest ratings. One way we interpreted this interaction was to note that exclusive daters rated their romantic interest for an attractive stranger similarly when the stranger was interested in someone else and when the stranger was interested in them. In contrast, nonexclusive daters rated their romantic interest higher when the stranger was interested in them, compared with someone else. Given this finding, the best way to respond to someone's query regarding romantic interest in potential dating partners is to say that *it depends*. In this case, romantic interest depends on whom the potential dating partner is interested in *and* whether someone is in a committed relationship. The presence of the interaction limits external validity but also specifies what those limits are.

THE RESEARCHERS' POINT OF VIEW

Question to Dr. Bazzini: In your article, you addressed the external validity issue that married individuals' responses to an attractive suitor may differ from the responses of exclusive daters in your experiments. How do you think married individuals' responses to this situation would differ?

Had our participants been married, it seems questionable that a momentary meeting with an attractive stranger would be a sufficient temptation to risk disrupting a relationship that one can assume has involved a substantial investment of time and resources. Therefore, in the same situation, we would predict that married individuals may show more derogation of the attractive alternative than did the individuals in our study. On the other hand, estimates of the incidence of infidelity in marriages are higher than one might imagine, and about half of all marriages end in divorce. Thus, we may well be wrong if we assume that marrieds wouldn't succumb to similar temptations to those faced by our exclusive daters. As Aronson and Linder point out in their gain-loss theory of attraction, positive evaluations from strangers can be a potent source of esteem building for us. The question that arises is whether married individuals who encounter an attractive and interested alternative on a more continuous basis can continue to evade the temptation. This remains to be tested empirically and may be difficult to do so in an ethical and ecologically valid way.

THINKING CRITICALLY ABOUT COMPLEX DESIGNS

There are two more important things to know about interpreting interactions, which we cover in this section. First, we will examine a problem that occurs when interactions appear to be present in an experiment, but they occur because of problems with the way in which dependent variables are measured. This problem may lead to floor effects or ceiling effects. Second, we will consider how to interpret interactions that involve natural groups independent variables.

Floor and Ceiling Effects

Consider the results of a hypothetical experiment somewhat similar to the one conducted by Bazzini and Shaffer (1999), but using a different manipulation of the scenario independent variable. Suppose exclusive and nonexclusive daters rated their romantic interest in one of three scenario conditions: unattractive stranger, "average" attractive stranger, and very attractive stranger interested in them (the "attracted-to-friend" condition is not tested in this experiment). Suppose the rating scale appears like this:

Please rate the extent to which you would try to meet the stranger described in the scenario:

0—1—2—3—4—5—6—7—8—9—10—11—12—13—14—15
No   Definitely
interest   try to meet

The results for this hypothetical experiment are presented in Figure 7.5.

The pattern of results in Figure 7.5 looks like a classic interaction; the effect of the dating status independent variable differs depending on the attractiveness of the stranger. There's no difference between exclusive and nonexclusive daters in the unattractive condition, but the difference between the dating-status groups increases as the attractiveness of the stranger increases. If a researcher were to analyze these data using analysis of variance, the interaction effect would very likely be statistically significant (and we can see that the lines diverge in the figure). Unfortunately, this interaction would be essentially *uninterpretable*. The ratings of romantic interest are at the minimum level (zero) for exclusive daters who rated the unattractive stranger. However, it's possible that the rating scale in the experiment couldn't detect their actual feelings of romantic interest, which may have been *less than zero* (e.g., actively spurning the potential partner rather than simply having zero interest).

Figure 7.5   Mean romantic interest ratings for hypothetical 3 × 2 design (illustrates floor effect in ratings).

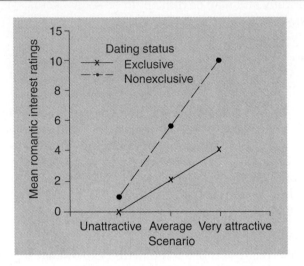

The preceding hypothetical experiment illustrates the general measurement problem referred to as a **floor effect.** Whenever participants' scores reach a minimum in any condition of an experiment, there is danger of a floor effect. The corresponding name given to this problem when performance reaches a maximum (i.e., the highest scores on a measure) is **ceiling effect.** In general, we can avoid ceiling and floor effects by selecting dependent variables that allow ample "room" for differences to be measured across conditions. For example, suppose the measure in our hypothetical study allows participants to rate their romantic interest and their romantic "repulsion" on the rating scale, the latter represented by negative romantic interest ratings. The new rating scale may appear as follows:

−10	−8	−6	−4	−2	0	2	4	6	8	10
Definitely										Definitely
avoid this										try to meet
person										

The hypothetical data for this new rating scale appear in Figure 7.6.

When participants are given a broader scale to rate their romantic interest in this hypothetical experiment, the interaction disappears. In these data it's likely that the main effects of stranger attractiveness and dating status would be statistically significant, but the interaction would not. Thus, the danger of floor and ceiling effects is that they may lead researchers to believe an interaction is present in the data, when in fact the interaction occurs because the measurement scale does not allow the full range of responses that participants could make.

Figure 7.6 Mean romantic interest ratings for revised hypothetical 3 × 2 design (revised scale eliminates floor effects).

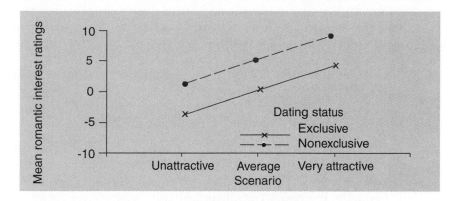

Interactions and the Natural Groups Design

The natural groups design, which we described briefly in Chapter 6, is one of the most popular research designs in psychology. Groups of people are formed by selecting individuals who differ on a characteristic such as gender, age, introversion-extroversion, aggressiveness, or dating status (e.g., exclusive and nonexclusive daters). Researchers then look for systematic relationships between these individual differences variables and other aspects of behavior. The natural groups design is effective for establishing *correlations* between individuals' characteristics and their performance. As we also noted in Chapter 6, however, the natural groups design is perhaps the most challenging design when it comes to drawing conclusions about the *causes* of behavior.

The difficulty in interpreting the natural groups design arises when we try to conclude that differences in performance are caused by the characteristics of the people used to define the groups. For instance, we cannot say that dating status *caused* differences in how participants evaluated potential dating partners in Bazzini and Shaffer's (1999) experiment. Why not? There are probably many additional ways in which people who are in committed dating relationships differ from individuals who are not. For example, the groups may differ in relationship history, religious background, maturity, and various personality characteristics. Any one of these potential differences could influence how participants evaluated potential dating partners. In short, many possible alternative explanations other than individual differences in dating status could account for differences in how participants evaluated potential dating partners in Bazzini and Shaffer's experiment.

There is a potential solution to the problem of drawing causal inferences based on the natural groups design (Underwood & Shaughnessy, 1975). The key to this solution is to develop a theory regarding the critical individual difference variable. Thus, we develop a theory for *why* the natural groups differ. This is nicely illustrated by the Bazzini and Shaffer (1999) experiment. Remember, they argued that exclusive daters, relative to nonexclusive daters, seek to maintain and protect their current relationship. If relationship maintenance is the critical difference between exclusive and nonexclusive daters, then an independent variable that specifically manipulates participants' motivation to maintain their relationship would allow researchers to make more definitive statements about the causes of differences between natural groups. And that is exactly what Bazzini and Shaffer did by manipulating the interest or noninterest of a stranger.

To summarize, the three steps researchers must follow in drawing causal inferences based on the natural-groups design are as follows:

- *Step 1: State your theory.* The first step is to develop a theory explaining *why* a difference in performance should occur between groups that are differentiated using an individual differences variable. In the Bazzini and Shaffer experiment, the researchers theorized that exclusive daters are different from nonexclusive daters *because* they are motivated to put down, or derogate, a potential dating partner.
- *Step 2: Identify a relevant manipulated variable.* The second step is to manipulate an independent variable that is presumed to influence the likelihood that this theoretical process will occur. Bazzini and Shaffer manipulated the extent to which relationship maintenance concerns may be activated by varying the interest of a potential dating partner.
- *Step 3: Look for an interaction.* The most critical aspect of this approach is to produce an interaction between the manipulated variable and the individual differences variable. Bazzini and Shaffer predicted an interaction such that the effect of the scenario variable (potential date interested or not interested) would differ depending on the level of dating status.

The key to making a causal inference about a natural groups variable when using this procedure is that the manipulated independent variable must reveal the theoretical process presumed to differentiate the natural groups, and an interaction between the natural groups independent variable and the manipulated independent variable should occur. Based on this interaction we can begin to make causal inferences about *why* individuals differ—one of the primary goals of the scientific method in psychology. As you can see, complex designs are essential for achieving this goal.

DISCUSSION OF THE RESEARCH EXAMPLE: ATTRACTIVENESS OF POTENTIAL DATING PARTNERS

Using a complex design, Bazzini and Shaffer (1999) examined college students' evaluations of potential dating partners. They tested the hypothesis, based on theories of interpersonal relationships and previous research, that exclusive daters (individuals in committed relationships) would evaluate potential dating partners negatively in order to maintain and protect their current relationship. They also tested the hypothesis that individuals not in committed relationships (nonexclusive daters) would enhance their ratings of a potential dating partner because of their motivation to seek relationships. The results of their 2 (dating status) × 2 (type of scenario) complex design provided support for the relationship-seeking hypothesis, but did not support the relationship-maintenance hypothesis.

One criticism of this research (and previous research in this area) is that participants responded to hypothetical scenarios. It's possible that their responses to the different scenarios may not *generalize* to how they would respond to actual situations in which someone expressed an interest in them. To test whether their findings would generalize, Bazzini and Shaffer (1999) conducted a second experiment. In their second experiment, they wanted to know how individuals would evaluate the desirability of potential dating partners when they anticipated *actually meeting* the person. They created an experimental situation in which exclusive and nonexclusive daters were led to believe that another person in the experiment was available and interested in dating them *or* unavailable because he or she was dating someone else. Bazzini and Shaffer were able to demonstrate again that exclusive daters did not try to protect their relationship. Of course, Bazzini and Shaffer (1999) asked participants only to rate potential dating partners and did not ask them to do anything that may harm their current relationships. Asking college students to engage in behaviors that could jeopardize the students' current relationships would be unethical.

THE RESEARCHERS' POINT OF VIEW

Questions to Dr. Bazzini: A major contribution of your second experiment is that participants anticipated actually meeting an attractive, potential dating partner. How did you go about devising a believable procedure?

Creating a believable procedure was a major concern for us. Gail Williamson, who had done work on communal and exchange relationships, suggested we use an anticipation-of-future-interaction paradigm. We knew that suspicion about the presence of the "other participant" would seriously undermine the study. We considered using a confederate who would actually interact with the participant, but decided we could accomplish our goal more simply by administering the "proposition for a date" via a sealed envelope delivered by the experimenter. We included several additional details that increased the credibility of the procedure. First, all of the participants were photographed with a Polaroid camera. This eliminated any suspicion regarding how we came to have a photograph of the target person (i.e., the experimenter told participants that he or she had just photographed the other participant in a room down the hall). Second, and believe me this was a bit humiliating for the experimenter, at one point in the experiment, prior to walking into the real participant's room, the experimenter had a brief conversation with the fictitious target person [i.e., outside the door so the participant could hear the "conversation"]. If the real participant had been suspicious up to this point, the suspicion was eliminated after that.

Did your IRB have any problems with your experiment?
Once I submitted the study's description to the IRB, the chair of the review committee contacted me and asked if I could address some specific issues about the design. Her major concern was for exclusive daters who might experience guilt or anxiety after receiving the proposition (if they were in that condition). In addition to fully debriefing participants, she suggested we offer the university's counseling center number to all of the participants. (As it turned out, most of the students laughed when I offered the number.) However, I believe it was a good precaution.

Were you surprised by any of the findings in your experiments?
Particularly in Study 2, we were surprised to find so little evidence for relationship maintenance by exclusive daters. Throughout the planning of the study, Dr. Shaffer and I kept discussing the likelihood that we would see evidence for both relationship seeking by nonexclusive daters and relationship maintenance by exclusive daters. What we found instead was a demonstration of how flattering it may be for us to have an attractive stranger showing interest in us, despite involvement in a committed relationship. Even the exclusive daters didn't seem to want to derogate that individual.

What most would you like people to learn from your research?
From a research standpoint, we'd like for our study to show how crucial it is to establish an appropriate control group when conducting research. When a theory is being shaped, particularly one that is as socially appealing as relationship maintenance, it is tempting to focus on one explanation of the results when another is just as viable.

On a more practical level, the study emphasizes the difference between imagining a situation and experiencing it. When we consider what we might do in a setting which clearly evokes social desirability concerns, we are more likely to focus on norms regarding how we *should* behave in the set of circumstances. However, when faced with the actual experience (attractive stranger is flirting with us), our ability to resist the temptation may be seriously weakened. More reality-based research on romantic relationships needs to be done.

Are you conducting studies to follow up your findings?
At this point, Dr. Shaffer and I have not conducted follow-up studies. However, we've discussed some possible directions that we'd like to explore. One possibility would be to obtain behavioral measures of relationship maintenance by having participants interact with an attractive confederate. A study like this would be more involved to plan, but again, the rewards would be a more realistic assessment of how people actually behave in these interpersonal dilemmas.

Do you have any advice for students in exclusive dating relationships based on your findings?

It's difficult to give advice based on these two studies only. However, as stated earlier, it may be important to recognize the potency of flattery. Although we may be motivated to maintain our romantic relationships, knowledge of an interested alternative provokes curiosity. Exclusive daters who are strongly committed to their relationship may still overestimate how easily such unsolicited attention (and here we are giving them the benefit of the doubt) can be disregarded. Exclusive daters should be a bit more wary of these seemingly minor flirtations if their goal is to remain committed to their partner.

READ MORE ABOUT IT

To learn more about the details of Bazzini and Shaffer's two experiments on the attractiveness of potential dating partners, you should read their article:

Bazzini, D. G., & Shaffer, D. R. (1999). Resisting temptation revisited: Devaluation versus enhancement of an attractive suitor by exclusive and nonexclusive daters. *Personality and Social Psychology Bulletin, 25,* 162–176.

The following book, cited by Bazzini and Shaffer, has information about relationships:

Brehm, S. S. (1992). *Intimate relationships.* New York: McGraw-Hill.

The following two research articles describe relationship maintenance behaviors and processes:

Dainton, M., & Stafford, L. (1993). Routine maintenance behaviors: A comparison of relationship type, partner similarity and sex differences. *Journal of Social and Personal Relationships, 10,* 225–271.

Rusbult, C. E., & Buunk, B. P. (1993). Commitment processes in close relationships: A test of the investment model. *Journal of Social and Personal Relationships, 10,* 175–204.

KEY CONCEPTS

complex designs	interaction
main effect	floor (ceiling) effect

KEY POINTS TO LEARN

Manipulating Independent Variables in a Complex Design

- Researchers use complex designs to study the effects of two or more independent variables in one experiment.
- In complex designs, the independent variables can be independent groups designs or repeated measures designs.

Identifying Main Effects and Interactions

- The simplest complex design is a 2 × 2 design—two independent variables, each with two levels.

- The number of different conditions in a complex design can be determined by multiplying the number of levels for each independent variable (e.g., $2 \times 2 = 4$).
- Complex designs allow researchers to examine interactions between independent variables.
- The overall effect of each independent variable in a complex design is called a main effect, and represents the average performance for each level of an independent variable collapsed across the levels of the other independent variable.
- An interaction between independent variables occurs when the effect of one independent variable differs depending on the levels of the second independent variable.
- Evidence for interactions can be identified using descriptive statistics presented in graphs (nonparallel lines) or tables (subtraction method), and the presence of an interaction is confirmed using inferential statistics (analysis of variance).
- More powerful and efficient complex designs can be created by including more levels of an independent variable or by including more independent variables in the design.

Analyzing Complex Designs

- In a complex design with two independent variables, the statistical analysis examines the main effects for each independent variable and the interaction between the two independent variables.
- Descriptive statistics are needed to interpret the results of inferential statistics.

Interpreting Interactions

- Theories frequently predict that two or more independent variables interact to influence behavior; therefore, complex designs are needed to test theories.
- By testing for interactions between independent variables, often in the form of replications, researchers can identify reasons for contradictory findings in previous studies.
- When no interaction occurs in a complex design, the effects of each independent variable can be generalized across the levels of the other independent variable; thus, external validity of the independent variables increases.
- The presence of an interaction limits the external validity of a finding by specifying the conditions in which an effect of an independent variable occurs.

Thinking Critically About Complex Designs

- When participants' performance reaches a maximum (ceiling) or a minimum (floor) in one or more conditions of an experiment, results for an interaction are uninterpretable.
- Researchers use complex designs to make causal inferences about natural groups variables when they test a theory for why natural groups differ.

- Three steps for making a causal inference involving a natural groups variable are to state a theory for why group differences exist, to manipulate an independent variable that should demonstrate the theorized process, and to test whether the hypothesized interaction occurs between the manipulated independent variable and natural groups variable.

CHECKING THE ESSENTIALS

1. Describe how a main effect of an independent variable in a complex design compares with the effect of that same independent variable studied in an experiment with only one independent variable.
2. Describe the nature of the interaction effect obtained in the Bazzini and Shaffer (1999) experiment between their two independent variables (dating status and type of scenario) using participants' mean romantic interest ratings.
3. What patterns of results indicate the presence or absence of an interaction when the results of a 2 × 2 complex design experiment are plotted in a graph?
4. Identify three statistical effects that can occur in any complex design experiment involving two independent variables.
5. What information must be used to describe and interpret the meaning of statistically significant F tests in a complex design?
6. Describe the analyses that are done to identify the source of a statistically significant omnibus interaction and describe the analyses that are done when the interaction is not statistically significant.
7. Describe how testing for possible interactions in complex design experiments allows researchers to make more sophisticated tests of psychological theories.
8. Explain how the presence or absence of an interaction in a complex design experiment affects the external validity of the research findings.
9. Describe the three steps researchers can follow to be able to draw causal inferences based on the natural groups design.

APPLYING YOUR KNOWLEDGE

1. A doctor developed a simple training program to help people reduce stress. She wanted to determine how the effectiveness of the training program was influenced by the length of time a person spent in training and the severity of the person's initial stress level. She decided to do an experiment in which she selected people of high and of moderate stress level (50 of each). The investigator used a reliable and valid measure of stress level; scores on the stress measure ranged from 0 to 50. Ten people from each stress level were randomly assigned to from one to five hours of the training program. The data in the following table represent the mean stress scores following training for each of the 10 groups.

Stress Level	Hours of Training				
	1	2	3	4	5
Moderate	25	15	10	5	5
High	40	30	20	10	5

A. Is there evidence of an interaction in this experiment?

B. What means would you use to describe the main effect of the stress level variable?

C. Is there any reason that you might be hesitant to interpret the interaction in this experiment?

2. An experiment was done on vocabulary learning in which there were two independent variables. Each of 96 introductory psychology students was asked to learn 20 unfamiliar English vocabulary words. Participants studied the vocabulary words with a familiar synonym (synonym condition), with a dictionary definition (definition condition), with a literary passage in which the word was used correctly (passage condition), or without any accompanying information (control condition). In addition, half the participants were asked to write sentences using the new words during study (active processing), whereas the other half simply studied without writing (passive processing). Thus, there were eight groups of 12 participants in this 4×2 design. Participants were randomly assigned to the eight groups. The mean number correct for each group on the final vocabulary test is shown in the following table.

Processing	Condition			
	Control	Passage	Definition	Synonym
Active	9.5	18.0	16.0	14.0
Passive	10.0	13.0	15.0	13.5

A. Identify the three statistical effects that can be tested in this 4×2 design.

B. What values would you use to describe the main effect of the study condition variable? What would you conclude about these means if you were to find that the F test for the main effect was $F(3, 88) = 69.7, p < .001$?

C. The overall analysis of this experiment revealed that there was a statistically significant interaction of type of processing and study condition. What information in the table of means indicates that an interaction is present?

D. In light of the statistically significant interaction in this experiment, describe what further analyses you would do. Be sure to explain why you would do the analyses you propose.

8

SINGLE-CASE
RESEARCH DESIGNS

INTRODUCTION

So far this book has emphasized *group methodology*—research designed to examine the average performance of one or more groups of participants. In this chapter we will examine an alternative methodology that emphasizes a single individual or, at most, a few individuals. This approach is sometimes called "small *n* research." We use the name *single-case research designs* to identify this kind of psychological research.

Single-case research permits detailed observations that allow researchers to reveal various nuances and subtleties of behavior that a group approach may miss. In addition, results from single-case research designs can teach us about typical or average behavior by revealing what is *not* average.

In this chapter we will discuss two single-case research methodologies, the case study method and single-case experimental designs. Both approaches are frequently associated with clinical psychology, but psychologists from other branches of psychology also make use of these methods. For example, neurologist Oliver Sacks (1985, 1995) captivated millions with his vivid case studies of individuals with peculiar, and rather fascinating, brain disorders. One of Sacks' best-known books is *The Man Who Mistook His Wife for a Hat* (1985). In it, as the title indicates, we are introduced to a man who literally, when searching for his hat, seized his wife's head and tried to lift it off and put it on. These "clinical tales," as Sacks calls them, not only provide insights into the relationship between mind and brain, but also reveal how individuals adapt, cope, and succeed when faced with profound neurological deficits.

Case studies are frequently the source of valuable hypotheses about behavior and can be an important complement to more rigorously controlled approaches to understanding behavior. We will examine a case study and review the advantages and disadvantages of the case study method.

Single-case experimental designs, also frequently called "$N = 1$ experimental designs," often are used to analyze and treat behavior. $N = 1$ designs are more systematic and controlled than case studies. In order to understand the principles of single-case experimental designs, we will focus on a particular type of $N = 1$ experimental design, the multiple baseline design. Ms. Tamara Hartl and Dr. Randy Frost (1999) used a multiple-baseline research design as they treated a woman who compulsively hoarded. As we discuss $N = 1$ designs, we will refer to their research to examine the essential steps of these experiments.

LEARNING OBJECTIVES

After reading about single-case research, you should be able to
- *identify the advantages and disadvantages of case study research;*
- *understand $N = 1$ designs (ABAB, multiple baselines), including their limitations; and*
- *differentiate case studies from $N = 1$ experimental designs.*

THE CASE STUDY METHOD

A **case study** is an intensive description and analysis of a single individual. Case study researchers obtain their data from several sources, including naturalistic observation (Chapter 3), interviews and psychological tests and even archival records (Chapter 4). A case study frequently describes the application and results of a particular treatment. For example, a clinical report of a case study may describe an individual's symptoms, the methods used to understand and treat the symptoms, and evidence for the treatment's effectiveness. Thus, case studies provide a potentially rich source of information about individuals.

However, treatment variables are rarely controlled systematically in case studies. Instead, several treatments may be used simultaneously, and the psychologist may have little control over extraneous variables (e.g., home and work environments that influence the client's symptoms). Thus, a fundamental characteristic of case studies is that they often lack a high degree of control. Without control, it's difficult for researchers to make valid inferences about variables that influence the individual's behavior (including any treatment).

The case study method offers both advantages and disadvantages to the research psychologist (Bolgar, 1965; Hersen & Barlow, 1976; Kazdin, 1998). Before reviewing its advantages and disadvantages, however, we will illustrate the method with a summary of an actual case study reported by Kirsch (1978), which describes an attempt to implement "self-management training" with a woman experiencing low self-confidence and social inhibition. The case study, describing her treatment during nine therapy sessions and a five-month

Case studies have advantages and disadvantages.

© 1989 by Sidney Harris – 'Einstein Simplified'. Rutgers University Press.

follow-up, appeared in the journal *Psychotherapy: Theory/Research/Practice/Training*. It is important that you read this slightly abbreviated version of a case study carefully because we will review it when discussing the advantages and disadvantages of the methodology.

CAN CLIENTS BE THEIR OWN THERAPISTS?
A CASE STUDY ILLUSTRATION

This article reports on the use of Self-Management Training (SMT), a therapeutic strategy which capitalizes on the advantages of brief therapies, while at the same time reducing the danger of leaving too many tasks not fully accomplished. . . . The essence of this approach involves teaching the client how to be his or her own behavior therapist. The client is taught how to assess problems along behavioral dimensions and to develop specific tactics, based on existing treatment techniques, for overcoming problems. As this process occurs, the traditional client-therapist relationship is altered considerably. The client takes on the dual role of client and therapist, while the therapist takes on the role of supervisor.

The Case of Susan

Susan, a 28-year-old married woman, entered therapy complaining that she suffered from a deficient memory, low intelligence, and lack of self-confidence. The presumed deficiencies "caused" her to be inhibited in a number of social situations. She was unable to engage in discussions about films, plays, books, or magazine articles "because" she could not remember them well enough. She often felt that she could not understand what was being said in a conversation and that this was due to her low intelligence. She attempted to hide her lack of comprehension by adopting a passive role in these interactions and was fearful lest she be discovered by being asked for more of a response. She did not trust her own opinions and, indeed, sometimes doubted whether she had any. She felt dependent on others to provide opinions for her to adopt.

Administering a Wechsler Adult Intelligence Scale (WAIS), I found her to have a verbal IQ of about 120, hardly a subnormal score. Her digit span (scale score = 12, raw score = 13) indicated that at least her short-term memory was not deficient. The test confirmed what I had already surmised from talking with her: that there was nothing wrong with her level of intelligence or her memory. After discussing this conclusion, I suggested that we investigate in greater detail what kinds of things she would be able to do if she felt that her memory, intelligence, and level of self-confidence were sufficiently high. In this way, we were able to agree upon a list of behavioral goals, which included such tasks as stating an opinion, asking for clarification, admitting ignorance of certain facts, etc. During therapy sessions, I guided Susan through overt and covert rehearsals of anxiety-arousing situations, . . . structured homework assignments which constituted successive approximations of her behavioral goals, and had her keep records of her progress. In addition, we discussed negative statements which she was making to herself and which were not warranted by the available data (e.g., "I'm stupid"). I suggested that whenever she noticed herself making a statement of this sort, she counter it by intentionally saying more appropriate, positive statements to herself (e.g., "I'm not stupid—there is no logical reason to think that I am").

During the fifth session of therapy, Susan reported the successful completion of a presumably difficult homework assignment. Not only had she found it easy to accomplish, but, she reported, it had not aroused any anxiety, even on the first trial. . . . It was at this point that the nature of the therapeutic relationship was altered. During future sessions, Susan rated her progress during the week, determined what the next step should be, and devised her own homework assignments. My role became that of a supervisor of a student therapist, reinforcing her successes and drawing attention to factors which she might be overlooking.

After the ninth therapy session, direct treatment was discontinued. During the following month, I contacted Susan twice by phone. She reported feeling confident in her ability to achieve her goals. In particular, she reported feeling a new sense of control over her life. My own impressions are that she had successfully adopted a behavioral problem-solving method of assessment and had become fairly adept at devising strategies for accomplishing her goals.

Follow-up

Five months after termination of treatment, I contacted Susan and requested information on her progress. She reported that she talked more than she used to in social situations, was feeling more comfortable doing things on her own (i.e., without her husband), and that, in general, she no longer felt that she was stupid. She summarized by saying: "I feel that I'm a whole step or level above where I was."

I also asked her which, if any, of the techniques we had used in therapy she was continuing to use on her own. . . . Finally, she reported that on at least three separate occasions during the five-month period following termination of treatment, she had told another person: "I don't understand that—will you explain it to me?" This was a response which she had previously felt she was not capable of making, as it might expose her "stupidity" to the other person.

Three months after the follow-up interview, I received an unsolicited letter from Susan (I had moved out of state during that time), in which she reminded me that "one of [her] imaginary exercises was walking into a folk dancing class and feeling comfortable; well, it finally worked."

Source: Kirsch, I. (1978). Teaching clients to be their own therapists: A case-study illustration. *Psychotherapy: Theory, Research, and Practice, 15,* 302–305. (Reprinted by permission.)

Advantages of the Case Study Method

The case study method offers researchers several opportunities (see Table 8.1). First, case studies provide a rich source of information about individuals and insights into possible causes of people's behavior. These insights, when translated into research hypotheses, then can be tested using more controlled research methods. This aspect of the case study method was acknowledged by Kirsch (1978) in discussing the successful psychotherapy with the woman named Susan (review the case study). He stated that the study's "conclusions . . . should be viewed as tentative. It is hoped that the utility of [this technique] will be established by more controlled research" (p. 305).

In addition, the case study method provides an opportunity to "try out" new therapeutic techniques or to try unique applications of existing techniques. The use of self-management training (SMT) in psychotherapy was a clinical innovation because Kirsch changed the typical client-therapist relationship. The SMT approach is based on teaching clients to be their own therapists—in other

Table 8.1   Advantages of the Case Study Method

- Rich source of ideas for developing hypotheses
- Opportunity for clinical innovation
- Method for studying rare events
- Possible challenge to theoretical assumptions
- Tentative support for a psychological theory

---

words, to identify problems and design behavioral techniques for dealing with them. The client is both client and therapist, whereas the therapist acts as supervisor.

Case studies are also useful for studying rare events. Some events appear so infrequently in nature that we can describe them only through the intensive study of single cases. Many of the cases described by Oliver Sacks, for example, describe individuals with rare brain disorders. Because it is virtually impossible to obtain groups of individuals with these disorders, the case study method is the only way researchers can study these disorders.

Researchers also use case studies to provide evidence for psychological theories. First, case studies can provide evidence to challenge theoretical assumptions. For example, a theory that all Martians have three heads would quickly collapse if a reliable observer were to spot a Martian with only two heads. With the presence of a "counterinstance," a single case that violates a general proposition of a theory, the theory must be changed. Second, evidence from a case study can provide tentative support for a psychological theory. Although results of case studies are not used to provide *conclusive* evidence for a particular hypothesis, case studies can sometimes provide important evidence in support of a psychological theory. The results of a case study generally must be viewed as tentative and must await investigation via more carefully controlled procedures before they are accepted by the scientific community.

Disadvantages of the Case Study Method

Although there are several advantages of the case study method, researchers also must be aware of its limitations (see Table 8.2). Many scientists seek to discover the causes of phenomena—to reveal *unambiguously* the specific factors that produce particular events. However, researchers can rarely draw cause-and-effect conclusions using the case study method. The major limitation of the case study method is that researchers often are unable to control extraneous variables. Numerous plausible hypotheses are generally present to "explain" behavior change. As a result, case studies frequently leave us wondering about the causes of behavior and behavior change.

Consider, for instance, the treatment of Susan through SMT reported by Kirsch (1978). Although Susan apparently benefited from SMT therapy, can we be sure that SMT caused her improvement? First, we know that many illnesses and emotional disorders improve without treatment. Case study researchers

Table 8.2   Disadvantages of the Case Study Method

- Difficulty drawing cause-and-effect conclusions (limited internal validity)
- Possible biases when interpreting outcomes due to observer bias and biases in data collection
- Problem of generalizing findings for a single individual (limited external validity)

---

must always consider the alternative hypothesis that individuals may have improved *without* the treatment. In addition, numerous aspects of the situation may have been responsible for Susan's improvement. For example, her care was in the hands of a clinical psychologist who provided reassurance. Also, Susan may have changed her attitudes toward herself because of the insights of her therapist and the testing results, not because of SMT. The therapist also asked Susan, as part of her therapy, to rehearse anxiety-arousing situations. This technique is similar to rehearsal desensitization, which may itself be an effective treatment (Rimm & Masters, 1979).

Because several treatments were used simultaneously we cannot argue conclusively that SMT therapy "caused" Susan's improvement. As we have seen, Kirsch himself was sensitive to the limitations of his results and suggested the results should be considered tentative until the treatment can be investigated more rigorously.

A second major limitation of the case study method concerns *bias*. The outcome of a case study often depends on conclusions drawn by a researcher who is both participant and observer (Bolgar, 1965). That is, a therapist observes the client's outcome *and* participates in the therapeutic process. It's reasonable to assume that the therapist may be motivated to believe that his or her treatment helped the client. As a result, the therapist, even if well-intentioned, may not accurately observe the client's behavior. You may see this is a problem of *observer bias*.

The outcome of a case study may be based mainly on the "impressions" of the observer (Hersen & Barlow, 1976). For example, Kirsch (1978) described the client Susan's "feelings" about her ability to achieve her goals and that she reported a "sense of control" over her life. He stated that his "impressions are that she successfully adopted a behavioral problem-solving method of assessment and had become fairly adept at devising strategies for accomplishing her goals" (p. 304). A serious weakness of the case study method is that interpretation of the outcome often is based solely on the subjective impressions of the observer.

In addition, case studies often include several sources of information, including personal documents, psychological tests, and session notes. Researchers must examine each of these sources for possible biases. Archival records (see Chapter 4) are open to several sources of bias. Further, when individuals provide information about themselves (self-report), they may distort or falsify the information in order to "look good." This possibility existed in Susan's treatment: We have no way of knowing whether she exaggerated her self-reports of improvement. Another source of bias occurs when reports are based on individuals' memory. Cognitive psychologists have demonstrated repeatedly that memory can be inaccurate, particularly for events that happened long ago. When researchers rely on an individual's memory for a case study, the potential for bias exists.

A final problem of the case study method concerns *external validity*. To what extent can we generalize the findings for one individual to a larger population? Our initial response might be to state that the findings for one person cannot be generalized at all. However, the ability to generalize from a single case depends on the degree of variability in the population from which the case was selected. For example, psychologists who study visual perception are often able to generalize their findings based on the study of one individual. Vision researchers assume that visual systems in all humans are very similar. Therefore, only one or several cases may be used to understand how the visual system works. In contrast, other psychological processes are much more variable, such as learning and memory, emotions, personality, and mental health. When studying processes that vary greatly in the population, it is impossible to claim that what is observed in one individual will hold for all individuals.

Thus, even if we accept Kirsch's (1978) conclusion regarding the effectiveness of the SMT technique of psychotherapy, we do not know whether this particular treatment would be as successful for other individuals who might differ from Susan in any of numerous ways, including intelligence, age, family background, and gender. As with findings from group methodologies, the important next step is to *replicate* the findings with additional individuals.

The Case Study Method: Critical Thinking

Case studies sometimes offer dramatic demonstrations of "new" findings or provide evidence for the "success" of a particular treatment. Consider advertisements for products you see in the media (e.g., infomercials). How many people who worry about their weight can resist the example of a formerly overweight individual who is shown to have lost considerable weight through Product X? Evidence from case studies can be very persuasive. This is both an advantage and a disadvantage to the scientific community. Case study demonstrations of new or unusual findings may lead scientists to reconsider their theories, or may lead them to new and fruitful avenues of research. Case studies, then, can help advance science.

However, the disadvantage of dramatic case studies is that they are often accepted uncritically by nonscientists. Individuals eager to lose weight or be cured of an illness may not consider the limitations of case study evidence. Instead, the evidence offers a ray of hope for a cure. For people who have (or think they have) few alternatives, this grasping at straws may not be totally unreasonable. However, too often people do not consider (perhaps they do not want to consider) the reasons why a particular treatment would *not* work for them.

Individuals' failure to consider the limitations of case study evidence can have unfortunate consequences. For example, during the early 1980s considerable controversy surrounded the supposed cancer-curing drug Laetrile (Sun,

1981). Few respectable scientists or medical researchers considered this drug, which was made from apricot pits, to be beneficial in the treatment of cancer. Advocates of Laetrile, however, presented case study results indicating benefits of the drug. Largely because of public (not scientific) pressure, the government carried out systematic and expensive tests of the drug under controlled conditions. Researchers did not find any beneficial effects of the drug in controlled experiments. As others have commented, by using Laetrile instead of traditional therapies, many patients may have postponed or interrupted valid treatments and thus contributed to the spread of their cancer.

Because of the disadvantages associated with the case study method, researchers have developed more systematic and controlled techniques for studying individuals' behaviors: single-case ($N = 1$) experimental designs. As we discuss these designs, we will review the treatment carried out by Ms. Tamara Hartl and Dr. Randy Frost as they sought to help a woman control her compulsive hoarding.

INTRODUCTION TO THE RESEARCH EXAMPLE: TREATMENT OF COMPULSIVE HOARDING

If you have any experience with moving, did you wonder how you've accumulated so much "stuff"? Or do you remember your parents asking you to clean your room and organize your belongings? Maybe they even said something like, "I can't even walk across the floor in your room!" We all have tendencies to save things, and sometimes our organizational systems break down. Papers might accumulate in various scattered piles until we find time to organize and put things away or discard them. This is normal.

However, saving can become extreme. Such was the case with a woman, "D.," treated by Hartl and Frost (1999). As part of her obsessive-compulsive disorder, D. developed a problem with compulsive hoarding. Frost and Hartl (1996) described compulsive hoarding as "(1) the acquisition of, and failure to discard, a large number of possessions that appear to be useless or of limited value; (2) living spaces sufficiently cluttered so as to preclude activities for which those spaces were designed; and (3) significant distress or impairment in functioning caused by the hoarding" (p. 341).

Frost and Hartl (1996) developed a theoretical model that conceptualized compulsive hoarding in terms of cognitive, emotional, and behavioral problems. One cognitive problem is that compulsive hoarders have trouble making decisions about objects, such as categorizing things as "needed" or "not needed." Emotionally, compulsive hoarders may experience problems in forming attachments, which may translate to becoming attached to possessions. Behaviorally, in addition to hoarding things, compulsive hoarders may avoid occasions for sorting and discarding items. Based on this model, Hartl and Frost (1999) developed a cognitive-behavioral therapy to treat D.'s compulsive hoarding.

THE RESEARCHERS' POINT OF VIEW

Questions to Ms. Hartl and Dr. Frost: How did you become interested in the treatment and research of compulsive hoarding?
We had both been interested in the assessment and treatment of obsessive compulsive disorder (OCD) before hoarding sparked our interest. Perhaps

the two features of hoarding that contributed to our interest the most were its
complexity and the extremely debilitating impact it had on the lives of those
who suffered from it.

Ms. Tamara Hartl

Many hoarders seem to fluctuate in
terms of their insight into the problematic nature of their saving and cluttering;
it was not uncommon to hear hoarders
one day boast about their useful collec-
tions while cursing their clutter the next
day because it controlled their lives.

Perhaps the most significant feature
that incited our interest was the severe
impairment associated with hoarding
symptoms. Having visited several
homes of hoarders for research purposes, we were repeatedly surprised by
the circumstances under which many
hoarders live and suffer. In addition to
having only narrow pathways in the
house to move from room to room, there
were several homes that contained no
clear spaces to sit, eat, or wash dishes.
Many homes were so dirty, in part because it was impossible to dust or vacuum, that the hoarders and their
children suffered from severe allergies.
There was a great deal of social impairment as well, with many hoarders refus-

Dr. Randy Frost

ing to invite friends, family members, or their children's friends over.

*Previous treatment research produced equivocal results. How did your
treatment, based on your model, attempt to resolve contradictory findings?*
Few reports about the treatment of hoarding exist, and are usually brief
comments buried within treatment studies that focus on more general issues. Most of these comments or anecdotes suggested that hoarding was
more difficult to treat than other OCD symptoms. We assumed that an effective treatment would need to target the important cognitive features of
hoarding, such as indecisiveness.

Overall, we believed that a treatment would have to be as multifaceted
as the model and extremely intensive. Our primary goal was to see if we
could create a cognitive-behavioral treatment for hoarding that worked.
From there, we hoped to refine it to make it practical.

SINGLE-CASE (N = 1) EXPERIMENTAL DESIGNS

The **single-case (N = 1) experiment,** as its name suggests, typically focuses on the behavior of one individual. In a single-case experiment the researcher contrasts treatment conditions for one individual whose behavior is being continuously monitored. That is, the independent variable of interest (usually a treatment) is manipulated systematically for one individual. You can think of single-case experiments as a type of repeated measures design applied to one individual rather than a group (see Chapter 6).

The first stage of a single-case experiment is usually an observation stage, or **baseline stage.** During this stage researchers record the individual's behavior prior to any treatment. Clinical researchers typically measure the frequency of the target behavior within a unit of time, such as a day or an hour. For example, a researcher might record the number of times during a 10-minute interview an excessively shy child makes eye contact, the number of headaches reported each week by a migraine sufferer, or the number of verbal pauses per minute made by a chronic stutterer. Using the baseline record, researchers are able to *describe* behavior before they provide treatment and, importantly, they can *predict* what behavior will be like in the future without treatment (Kazdin, 1998). Of course, unless behavior is actually monitored, researchers don't know for sure what future behavior will be like, but baseline measures allow them to predict what the future holds. Figure 8.1 illustrates this function of the baseline record.

Once researchers observe that the individual's behavior is relatively stable during the baseline stage, they introduce an intervention (treatment). The next

Figure 8.1   Hypothetical example of baseline observations for the frequency of responses. Data in baseline stage (solid line) are used to predict the likely rate of responses in the future if treatment is not implemented (dashed line). (Adapted from Kazdin, 1998, p. 209.)

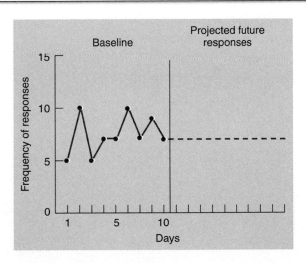

step is to record the individual's behavior with the same measures used during the baseline stage. By comparing the behavior observed immediately following an intervention with the baseline behavior, researchers are able to determine the effect of the treatment. The effect of the treatment is seen most easily using a graph of the behavioral record. Figure 8.2 illustrates a treatment to decrease the frequency of a behavior (e.g., decrease number of cigarettes per day). Keep in mind that we can predict what behavior would be like without treatment; this is represented by the dashed line in Figure 8.2 (see also Figure 8.1). By visually inspecting the difference between behavior following treatment and what was predicted would occur without treatment, we can infer whether treatment effectively changed the individual's behavior. Traditionally, single-case experimenters don't use tests of statistical significance to make decisions about the effect of treatment. Later in this chapter, however, we will discuss problems that arise when we rely on visual inspection to determine whether a treatment was effective (see also Kazdin, 1998).

Although researchers have many design possibilities available, the most common single-case designs are the ABAB and multiple-baseline designs (Kazdin, 1998).

The ABAB Design

Researchers use the **ABAB design** to demonstrate that behavior changes systematically when they alternate "no treatment" and "treatment" conditions. The procedure of an ABAB design is just as it sounds: An initial baseline stage (A) is followed by a treatment stage (B), next by a return to baseline (A), and then by another treatment stage (B). Because treatment is removed during the second A stage, and any improvement in behavior is likely to be reversed at this point, this design is also called a **reversal design.** The researcher using the

Figure 8.2   Simple illustration of treatment effect (solid line). Dashed line represents projected frequency of behavior in the absence of treatment.

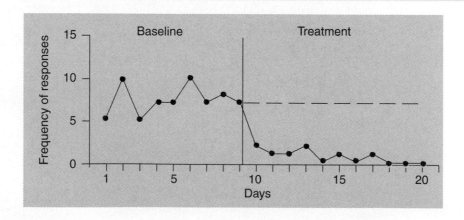

ABAB design observes whether behavior changes immediately upon introduction of a treatment variable (first B), whether behavior reverses when treatment is withdrawn (second A), and whether behavior improves again when treatment is reintroduced (second B). If behavior changes following the introduction and withdrawal of treatment, the researcher gains considerable evidence that the treatment caused the behavior change (see Figure 8.3 for an example in which the treatment is intended to decrease the frequency of a behavior).

A major methodological problem that sometimes arises in the context of an ABAB procedure is illustrated Figure 8.4. Assume a treatment is intended to decrease a behavior. Figure 8.4 illustrates that the first application of treatment (B) decreased the behavior. However, in the second baseline stage, when the treatment was withdrawn, the frequency of behavior remained low, rather than returning to the baseline level. What can the researcher conclude in this situation? Is the treatment effective?

One reason behavior may not revert back to the baseline level is that the behavior may not be expected logically to change once treated. This occurs in situations in which treatment involves teaching individuals new skills. For example, a researcher's treatment may involve teaching a developmentally disabled individual how to commute successfully to a job. Once the skill is learned, it's unlikely to be "unlearned" (reverse back to baseline) when treatment is withdrawn. The solution to this problem is straightforward. Researchers should not use the ABAB design when they can expect logically that the target behavior would not revert back to baseline when treatment is withdrawn.

What other reasons exist for the behavior not to reverse to baseline in Figure 8.4? One possibility is that a variable *other than* the treatment caused behavior to change in the first shift from baseline to treatment stages. For example, the

Figure 8.3 Illustration of treatment effect in ABAB design.

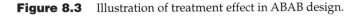

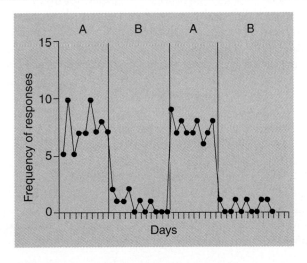

Figure 8.4   Illustration of ABAB design in which reversal does not occur.

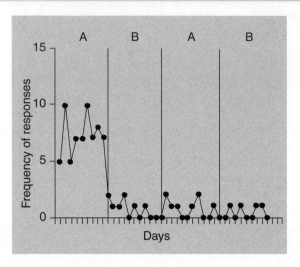

individual may receive increased attention from staff or friends during treatment. This increased attention—rather than the treatment—may cause behavior to improve. If the attention persists even though the specific treatment is withdrawn, the behavior change is likely to persist as well. This explanation suggests a *confounding* between the treatment variable and another, uncontrolled factor (such as attention).

It's also possible that, although the treatment caused behavior to improve, other variables took over to control the new behavior. Again, we can consider the effect attention has on behavior. When family and friends witness a change in behavior, they may pay attention to the individual. Think of the praise people get when they've lost weight or quit smoking. Positive reinforcement in the form of attention and praise may maintain the behavior change that was initiated by the treatment. If this occurs, we can expect behavior not to reverse to baseline levels when the treatment is withdrawn.

Thus, if behavior does not reverse back to baseline levels when treatment is withdrawn, researchers cannot conclude that the treatment caused the initial behavior change (Kazdin, 1980, 1998). The researcher must examine the situation carefully with the hope of identifying variables that might be confounding the treatment variable or must replicate the procedure with the same individual or different individuals (Hersen & Barlow, 1976).

Finally, single-case researchers also face an ethical problem when using the ABAB design. Suppose the treatment (B) seems to improve the individual's behavior relative to the baseline (A). Is it ethical to remove what appears to be a beneficial treatment to determine if the treatment caused the improvement? As you might imagine, withdrawing a beneficial treatment may not be justified in all cases. Some behaviors might be life-threatening or exceptionally debilitating, and it would not be ethical to remove treatment once a positive effect is observed. For example, some autistic children exhibit self-injurious behaviors such as head banging. If a clinical researcher succeeds in reducing the frequency of this behavior, it would be unethical to withdraw treatment to meet the requirements of the ABAB design. Fortunately, there is a single-case experimental design that does not involve withdrawal of treatment and that may be appropriate in such situations—the multiple-baseline design.

The Multiple-baseline Design

The **multiple-baseline design** also makes use of baseline (A) and treatment (B) stages, but not by withdrawing a treatment as in the ABAB design. As the name suggests, researchers establish several baselines when using a multiple-baseline design. For example, a clinical researcher may attempt to change a child's aggressive behavior at home, in the classroom, and at an after-school day care facility. The first step in the multiple-baseline design is to record aggressive behavior in each of these situations as it normally occurs (i.e., without treatment). In this way, the researcher establishes the baseline frequency of aggressive behavior in each situation (i.e., multiple baselines).

Next, treatment is introduced in one of the situations but not in the other situations. The researcher continues to monitor behavior in all of the situations. A critical feature of the multiple-baseline design is that treatment is applied in one situation at a time. This allows clinical researchers to compare the behavior in the treatment situation with the behavior in the situations that are still in the baseline stage. The behavior in the treated situation should improve; the behavior in the baseline situations should not improve.

The next step is to apply treatment in a second situation (treatment may continue in the first situation as well) and continue to monitor behavior. Again, researchers examine the behavioral records for treatment and baseline situations to determine the effectiveness of the treatment. If treatment is effective, behavior should change when the researcher introduces the treatment in the second situation. This procedure is continued until the treatment has been applied in each situation. You may see that the multiple-baseline design has *replications* built into the design. That is, by repeatedly introducing treatment across different situations one at a time, researchers are able to determine whether the results replicate. If they do, we gain confidence in the effectiveness of the treatment.

Clinical researchers can choose from among several variations of the multiple-baseline design. Our example considered one child's aggressive behavior in different situations (multiple baselines across situations). An alternative method is to consider a behavior in one situation for different individuals (multiple baselines across subjects). For example, a clinical researcher may treat the aggressive behavior of several children in one classroom. Finally, a third method can be used to treat different behaviors of one individual in one situation (multiple baselines across behaviors). For example, a researcher may treat one child's aggression, inattentiveness, and fidgeting in a classroom.

Often the first question to arise when doing a multiple-baseline experiment is, how many baselines do I need? As with many other aspects of single-case research, there are no hard-and-fast rules. The bare minimum is two baselines, but this is generally considered inadequate. Three or four baselines are recommended (Hersen & Barlow, 1976).

A problem sometimes seen in the multiple-baseline design occurs when changes in one behavior *generalize* to other behaviors or situations. Thus, clinical researchers may observe changes in baseline behavior *before* the treatment is introduced. For example, if a treatment decreases a child's aggressiveness in the classroom, his or her behavior may also change at home—before treatment in the home is introduced. As we have noted, unless behavior improves directly following an experimental intervention, it's hard to conclude that the treatment was effective. Two possibilities exist: Either the treatment was *very* effective and caused the child to change his or her behavior in all situations or a factor other than the treatment caused the behavior to change. Unfortunately, it's difficult for clinical researchers to sort out these alternative explanations.

TREATMENT OF COMPULSIVE HOARDING: MULTIPLE-BASELINE DESIGN

At the time of treatment, D. was a 53-year-old woman for whom hoarding was "a small problem that mushroomed" (Hartl & Frost, 1999, p. 453). The clutter in her house took up approximately 70% of the living space, and rooms could not be used for their intended purpose. Hartl and Frost (1999) described the following:

> The TV room was the most daunting. Letters, paid and unpaid bills, receipts, newspapers, and important documents were piled up to 3 ft high on the couch and streamed over onto the floor, completely burying a coffee table therapists did not know was there until unearthed in a later session. . . . Upstairs, the hallway was filled with hundreds of gifts that D. had bought with no recipient in mind, explaining that the buys were too good to pass up. . . . items in some places [were] piled as high as the ceiling . . . . She acknowledged that clutter was in large part responsible for the demise of her marriage. (pp. 453–454)

Hartl and Frost's (1999) treatment consisted of "training in decision-making and categorization, exposure and habituation to discarding, and cognitive restructuring . . . each woven into the context of weekly excavation sessions" (p. 454). They used a *multiple baseline design across situations* in D.'s treatment. The different situations were different rooms in her house, treated in the following order: kitchen (4 sessions), parlor (6 sessions), TV room (14 sessions), dining room (8 sessions), downstairs hallway (4 sessions), and upstairs hallway (9 sessions). The bedroom was maintained as a baseline "control" throughout the intervention in order to evaluate the effectiveness of the treatment.

To assess D.'s progress during the intervention, Hartl and Frost computed "clutter ratios" (CRs). They first measured the room dimensions and the square footage of surface space for each piece of furniture and then determined the portion of space covered by clutter. The larger the ratio, the greater the clutter. Hartl and Frost calculated CRs for each room before treatment and after 4, 10, 24, 32, 36, and 45 sessions.

Hartl and Frost (1999) reported that CRs "decreased substantially in each of the target rooms once treatment was applied" to the room (p. 456). Clutter did not change in the bedroom, the control room. In fact, as D. worked to unclutter the other rooms in the house, the bedroom became slightly more cluttered. Figure 8.5 displays the furniture clutter ratios. The dotted line that descends down the page indicates when intervention began and ended in each room. For example, treatment began in the TV room during Session 10 and ended at Session 24. At that time, they began working on the dining room. In each case, CRs did not change for a room until the treatment was applied, indicating the effectiveness of the treatment.

THE RESEARCHERS' POINT OF VIEW

Questions to Ms. Hartl and Dr. Frost: How did you decide to use "clutter ratios" as a measure of hoarding?

Looking around D.'s house, it was clear that the source of impairment was mainly the clutter that covered nearly all of her furniture and floor spaces. We hypothesized that a reduction in clutter would decrease distress in addition to decreasing obsessive-compulsive symptoms in general.

We believed treatment would be more effective if D. had hard evidence of the gains she made. Working on one room at a time allowed D. to quickly establish one "normal," clutter-free zone with which to compare to her other rooms. We hypothesized that increased use of the cleared room would result in habituation to the lack of clutter, and an appreciation for the mobility and increased accessibility that the room allowed.

Your article describes what must have seemed like an overwhelming amount of clutter. Did this influence your optimism for whether your treatment would be effective?

At the onset of treatment, there were definitely times when the road ahead seemed long and bumpy because there was just so much stuff in that one house. However, the decision to work on one room at a time ended up sustaining optimism for client and researchers alike. Once the kitchen was free of clutter, it was easy to believe that D. would eventually uncover the other rooms as well.

D.'s ability to maintain clear spaces made us even more optimistic. The fact that she could keep uncovered spaces clear suggested to us that in the process of sorting and uncluttering, D. had learned how to make decisions about possessions and how to deal with and talk herself through the discomfort associated with discarding. Given the amount of clutter in D.'s home, we knew treatment would be a long, intensive process. Nevertheless, D.'s success maintaining the kitchen area suggested that treatment would be effective.

What challenges did you face as you implemented the treatment?

There were several challenges, including D.'s patterns of avoidance and the time-intensive nature of treatment.

Several times D. phoned a couple of hours prior to our scheduled visit because she feared she did not have the energy or the will to work on sorting and discarding that day. Usually, she was able to trace her reluctance

Figure 8.5   Multiple baseline analysis of clutter ratios across five rooms (Hartl & Frost, 1999, p. 457).

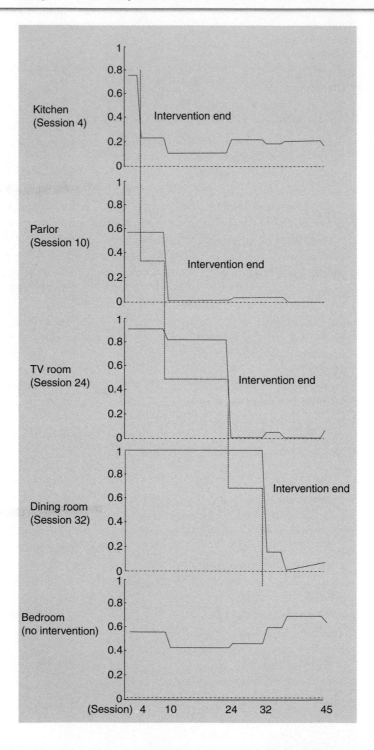

to other issues or difficulties she was having that day. In general, we were able to convince her that working on these difficult days would pay off the most for her in the end.

Over the course of a year and a half, we visited D.'s home three or four times per month for sessions that were 2 to 2½ hours long. Such a lengthy and involved treatment might not be feasible under the conditions of managed care or other reimbursement paradigms. Also, many clinicians may be unwilling to commit to such an intensive treatment protocol.

THINKING CRITICALLY ABOUT SINGLE-CASE RESEARCH DESIGNS

We've already noted some problems associated with interpreting ABAB designs and multiple-baseline designs. Other problems are common to all single-case designs: problems with the baseline record, external validity, and identifying interactions among variables. We will examine each of these limitations and then consider the ethical issues associated with single-case research designs.

Problems and Limitations Common to All Single-case Designs

Problems with Baseline Records.   It is difficult to evaluate the effects of an intervention when there are increasing or decreasing baseline trends or excessive variability in behavioral records. Panel A of Figure 8.6 shows an ideal baseline record and response to an intervention. Behavior during baseline is very stable, and behavior changes immediately following the introduction of treatment. If this were the outcome of the first stages of either an ABAB or a multiple-baseline design, we would be headed in the direction of showing that our treatment effectively changed behavior. However, consider the baseline and treatment stages shown in panel B of Figure 8.6. The baseline shows extreme variability, and, although the desired behavior appears to increase in frequency following an intervention, it is difficult to know whether the treatment produced the change or behavior just happened to be on an upswing. In this case, it would be hard to decide whether the intervention successfully increased the behavior.

How do clinical researchers deal with the problem of excessive baseline variability? One approach is to look for variables in the situation that might be producing the variability and remove them. For example, a particular staff member might be causing changes in the behavior of a psychiatric patient; researchers could ask that this staff member not work with the patient. Another approach is to wait it out—to continue taking baseline measures until behavior stabilizes. We cannot, of course, predict when behavior might stabilize, but introducing an intervention before behavior stabilized would not allow us to interpret the experimental outcome. Another approach researchers use is to average data points. By charting a behavioral record using averages of several points (e.g., across several days), researchers can sometimes reduce the appearance of variability (Kazdin, 1978).

Figure 8.6 Examples of behavioral records showing possible relationships between baseline and intervention phases of a behavior modification program.

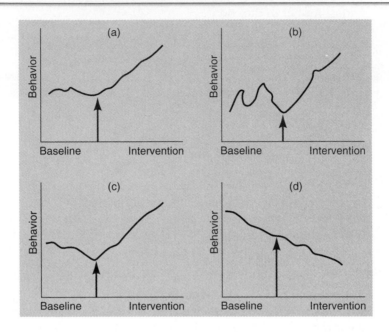

Another problem arises when the baseline record shows an increasing or a decreasing trend. In panel C of Figure 8.6, we see that the initial baseline is characterized by a trend for a behavior to decrease in frequency. If the goal of the intervention is to *increase* the frequency of behavior, the change illustrated in panel C is easy to interpret. When an intervention aimed at increasing a behavior *reverses* a decreasing trend, we can conclude that the treatment was effective. However, what if the goal of intervention was to *reduce* the frequency of behavior? With a decreasing trend in the baseline, it would be difficult to know whether the continued decrease in behavior following the intervention is due to the intervention or to continuation of the baseline trend. This situation is illustrated in panel D of Figure 8.6. It's difficult to know in this case whether the treatment had any effect. Because a treatment effect in a single-case design is usually judged by visually inspecting the behavioral record, we would have to see a very marked change in the behavioral record (see, for example, Parsonson & Baer, 1992).

Questions of External Validity. When an effect is demonstrated using a single-case design, a frequent criticism is that external validity is limited. Because each person is unique, we don't know whether treatment effects will generalize to other individuals. There are several reasons why this problem may not be as serious as it seems. First, the types of intervention used in single-case studies are often very potent and frequently produce dramatic and sizable changes in behavior (Kazdin, 1978). Consequently, these types of treatments are often found to generalize to other individuals. Other evidence for the generality of effects based on single-case studies comes from multiple-baseline designs. A multiple-baseline design across subjects, for example, shows that a particular intervention can successfully modify the behavior of *several* individuals. Similarly, multiple baselines across situations and behaviors attest to the external validity of a treatment effect.

A treatment effect can also be shown to generalize to other individuals when a single group of subjects is used in a single-case experiment. Researchers sometimes use the procedures associated with single-case designs with small groups of individuals. To the extent that the treatment is effective with a small group of individuals, researchers gain evidence for the external validity of the findings.

Interaction Effects.   One limitation of single-case research designs is not easily dismissed, and it illustrates again the lesson that no one research methodology can provide all the answers to psychologists' questions. The $N = 1$ experiment is not always appropriate for examining the effect of *interactions* among variables. Although a single-case design can provide evidence of the effect of one variable (a main effect) by showing, for example, that behavior changes between conditions of "no treatment" and "treatment," we have a hard time examining combinations of various treatments and individual differences variables (Kazdin, 1998). Thus, if a researcher wishes to determine whether treatment X in conjunction with treatment Y is more effective than treatment X or Y alone, a single-case research design would be difficult to implement. One way to do this might be to have one individual alternate between baseline, treatment X, baseline, treatment Y, baseline, treatment X + Y, baseline, and so on. Because of these difficulties, researchers may instead choose a group methodology in which some individuals receive treatment X, some receive treatment Y, and others receive treatment X + Y.

Ethical Issues in Single-case Designs

Two particularly salient ethical issues associated with single-case research should be mentioned. One of these we have already discussed briefly—namely, an effective treatment is sometimes withheld in the ABAB design. Clinical researchers are faced with ethical dilemmas when treatments aimed at reducing painful or harmful events are shown to improve behavior (for example, in the first treatment stage of an ABAB design) and then are withdrawn (in the second baseline stage). In these situations researchers face the dilemma between satisfying one goal of psychological research, understanding the causes of behavior, and the goal of creating change. Thus, in order to demonstrate unambiguously that a treatment *causes* improved behavior, the ABAB design requires that treatment be withdrawn. However, when researchers also seek to create change and improve people's lives, they may choose not to withdraw a treatment—

even if they don't know unequivocally whether the treatment is causing the improvement.

Another ethical problem sometimes associated with single-case research concerns the nature of the treatment. For example, behavior modification sometimes requires a noxious or aversive treatment. Lovaas, for example, has used mild electric shock with autistic and schizophrenic children in order to develop appropriate social responses (e.g., Lovaas, 1993; Lovaas, Schaeffer, & Simmons, 1965). This research has generated considerable controversy despite the fact that aversive treatments are used only when other methods have failed and the alternative (no treatment) appears even more harmful. That is, the success of these treatments apparently saved some individuals from permanent institutionalization, with little hope of successful therapeutic intervention. This type of research clearly illustrates the often difficult nature of ethical decision making. Is the risk to the participant outweighed by the benefit of the treatment?

Clinical researchers must carefully consider all relevant factors to determine whether a treatment is justified. As noted in Chapter 3, researchers must consult with knowledgeable others when the risk/benefit ratio is not easily determined. Of course, researchers must address these questions whenever research involves a potentially harmful treatment, not just when using single-case research designs.

DISCUSSION OF THE RESEARCH EXAMPLE: TREATMENT OF COMPULSIVE HOARDING

Hartl and Frost's (1999) treatment of D.'s compulsive hoarding appeared to be successful. They used a *multiple-baseline design* to apply treatment successively to different rooms in D.'s house. Each time treatment was applied in a room, the clutter on the floor and furniture decreased. *Baseline variability* or trends did not pose a problem because the behavior—hoarding—was consistent across time and across the rooms. *External validity* for the treatment was evidenced across the different situations—the rooms in her house. However, it remains to be seen whether the treatment would be effective for other hoarders.

Hartl and Frost's treatment had many components. In single-case research designs, it's impossible to determine systematically what aspect of a multifaceted treatment is effective or which components may *interact* to produce change. In applied research, as with D., the goal is to *create change*. Thus, although Hartl and Frost sought to demonstrate the effectiveness of their comprehensive treatment, they did not seek to identify which component was critical or whether treatment components interacted. In fact, they believed that all the components would be necessary to create change. Future research involving group methodology would be needed to isolate the effectiveness of various treatment components and interactions.

Finally, Hartl and Frost's research presented few *ethical dilemmas*. An advantage of the multiple-baseline design is that effective treatment is not withdrawn (as in ABAB designs). However, D. was required to work on one room at a time so that the effects of treatment could be easily evaluated. This may have been stressful for D., who was eager to see her entire house become uncluttered. Thus, a compromise was needed. In order to allow the researchers to evaluate the effectiveness of treatment, D. had to work on one room at a time.

THE RESEARCHERS' POINT OF VIEW

Questions to Ms. Hartl and Dr. Frost: Did the increased clutter ratio in the bedroom (control) influence your conclusion about treatment effectiveness or generalizability?

The increase in clutter in the bedroom was not very surprising, given that D. had few accessible storage places to put possessions she decided to keep. It would have been problematic if her bedroom had become a catch-all for possessions she had removed from other rooms, but we found that she moved only select items into her bedroom.

We consider the effectiveness of the treatment to depend on several characteristics. Overall, there was a substantial decrease in clutter in D.'s rooms. In turn, D. was able to use her rooms in ways they hadn't been used in years—for eating meals and working on school projects with her children, and for devising a filing system to maintain a more organized lifestyle.

It was extremely encouraging to get the sense from talking with her that it was not only the condition of her house that changed, but that she truly felt and behaved differently with regard to saving and cluttering.

Key components of multiple baseline designs are maintaining an appropriate baseline and implementing treatment in one setting at a time. Did you face any special problems as you tried to maintain the integrity of the research design?

There were several times when D. had to be persuaded to focus on the room that she was currently working on, rather than switching gears to tackle piles in other rooms. It seemed that once D. became confident that she could make decisions about possessions and discard them, she would identify sorting projects in other areas of the house that she was eager to initiate. We were thrilled that she was becoming so ambitious! But at the same time, we tried to channel her energy back into the room we were working on in order to maintain the integrity of the research design.

Have you been able to learn whether treatment gains have been maintained?

We have had only infrequent contacts with D. since the treatment. Approximately one year after we finished, she reported that her house was still significantly uncluttered, though she did report an increase in clutter from the time we stopped treatment.

You mentioned in your article that you are continuing to develop your treatment of compulsive hoarding. What is your current work in this area?

This study told us that changing hoarding behavior is possible. The next step is to build from this a treatment protocol that is both effective and practical. We are experimenting with various forms of delivery (such as group, paraprofessionals) that would make this approach more cost-effective.

READ MORE ABOUT IT

If you would like to learn more about Hartl and Frost's treatment of D., you should consult their article:

Hartl, T. L., & Frost, R. O. (1999). Cognitive-behavioral treatment of compulsive hoarding: A multiple baseline experimental case study. *Behaviour Research and Therapy, 37,* 451–461.

Hartl and Frost describe their theory of compulsive hoarding in the following article:

Frost, R. O., & Hartl, T. L. (1996). A cognitive-behavioral model of compulsive hoarding. *Behaviour Research and Therapy, 34,* 341–350.

More information about treating obsessive-compulsive disorder may be found in the following edited book:

Pato, M., & Zohar, J. (Eds.). (1991). *Current treatments of obsessive compulsive disorder.* Washington, DC: American Psychiatric Press.

KEY CONCEPTS

case study	**ABAB design (reversal design)**
single-case ($N = 1$) experiment	**multiple-baseline design**
baseline stage	

KEY POINTS TO LEARN

The Case Study Method

- Case studies, intensive descriptions and analyses of individuals, lack the degree of control found in experimental designs.
- Case studies provide new ideas and hypotheses, opportunities to develop new clinical techniques, a chance to study rare phenomena, and evidence to support or challenge scientific theories.
- Because extraneous variables are not controlled and several treatments may be applied simultaneously in case studies, researchers are unable to make valid causal inferences using this method.
- Observer bias and biases in data collection can lead to incorrect interpretations of case study outcomes.
- Whether results from a case study may be generalized depends on the variability within the population from which the case was selected; some characteristics (e.g., personality) vary more across individuals than others (e.g., visual system).
- When considering individuals' testimonials about the effectiveness of a particular treatment, we need to remember the limitations of the case study method.

Single-case (*N* = 1) Experimental Designs

- Researchers manipulate an independent variable in single-case experiments; therefore, these designs allow more rigorous control than case studies.
- In single-case experiments, baseline observations are first recorded to describe what an individual's behavior is like (and predicted to be like in the future) without treatment.
- In the ABAB design, baseline (A) and treatment (B) stages are alternated to determine the effect of treatment on behavior.
- Researchers conclude that treatment causes behavior change when behavior changes systematically with the introduction and withdrawal of treatment.
- Interpreting the causal effect of the treatment is difficult in the ABAB design if behavior does not reverse to baseline levels when treatment is withdrawn.
- In a multiple-baseline design, a treatment effect is shown when behaviors change following the introduction of a treatment.
- Interpreting the causal effect of treatment is difficult in a multiple-baseline design when changes are seen in a baseline *before* an experimental intervention; this can occur when treatment effects generalize.

Thinking Critically About Single-case Research Designs

- Interpreting the effect of a treatment can be difficult if the baseline stage shows excessive variability or increasing or decreasing trends in behavior.
- The problem of low external validity with single-case experiments can be reduced by testing small groups of individuals.
- Although psychologists can compare treatment and no-treatment conditions in single-case experiments, it is difficult to examine interactions among treatment variables using this method.
- Psychologists are sometimes faced with the ethical dilemma of removing an apparently effective treatment in order to demonstrate its efficacy.
- Psychologists must carefully consider the risk/benefit ratio when treatments are potentially harmful or aversive.

CHECKING THE ESSENTIALS

1. Identify five advantages of the case study method.
2. What is the major limitation of the case study method and what is the consequence of this limitation in terms of drawing causal inferences?
3. Comment critically on the question of the external validity of the findings from case studies.
4. What role does the baseline stage of a single-case experiment play in the description and prediction of behavior?
5. Describe the procedure of an ABAB design single-case experiment that is used to test the effectiveness of a treatment.
6. Describe at least one reason why behavior may not return to the original baseline level after the treatment is removed at the end of the first AB stage of an ABAB single-case experiment.

7. What ethical consideration would lead you to recommend against the use of an ABAB single-case experimental design? What single-case experimental design would you recommend in this situation?
8. What two alternative explanations are there for the problem that can arise in a multiple-baseline design when changes in behavior occur during the baseline before the treatment is introduced?
9. Comment critically on the question of the external validity of single-case design experiments.

APPLYING YOUR KNOWLEDGE

1. A case study showing how "mud therapy" was successful in treating an individual exhibiting excessive anxiety was reported in a popular magazine. The patient's symptoms included trouble sleeping, loss of appetite, extreme nervousness when in groups of people, and general feelings of arousal that led the individual always to feel tense and fearful. The California therapist who administered the mud therapy was known for this treatment, having appeared on several TV talk shows. He first taught the patient a deep relaxation technique and a "secret word" to repeat over and over in order to block out all disturbing thoughts. Then the patient was asked to lie submerged for two hours each day in a wooden "calm tub" filled with mud. During this time the patient was to practice the relaxation exercises and to concentrate on repeating the secret word whenever the least bit of anxiety was experienced. The therapy was very costly, but after six weeks the patient reported to the therapist that he no longer had the same feelings of anxiety that he had had before. The therapist pronounced him cured and attributed the success of the treatment to immersion in the calming mud. The conclusion drawn by the author of the magazine article describing this therapy was that "it is a treatment that many people could benefit from." On the basis of your knowledge of the limitations of the case study method, answer the following questions:
   A. What possible sources of bias were present in the study?
   B. What alternative explanations can you suggest for the successful treatment?
   C. What possible problem arises from studying only one individual?
2. Suppose during the summer months you find employment in a camp for mildly mentally impaired children. As a counselor, you are asked to supervise a small group of children, as well as to look for ways to improve their attention to various camp activities that take place indoors (e.g., craft making and sewing). You decide to explore the possibility of using a system of rewarding the children for "time on task." You realize that the camp director will want evidence of the effectiveness of your intervention strategy, as well as some assurance that it will work with other children in the camp. Therefore, you plan to do a single-case experiment to test your idea.
   A. Explain what behavioral records you will need to keep and how you will determine whether your intervention has produced a change in the children's behavior. You will need, for example, to specify exactly when and how you will measure behavior and to justify your use of a particular design to carry out your experiment.
   B. Describe the argument you will use to convince the director that your intervention strategy (assuming that it works) will work with other, similar children.

9 QUASI-EXPERIMENTAL DESIGNS AND PROGRAM EVALUATION

INTRODUCTION

Many experiments are conducted in natural settings to improve the conditions in which people live and work; we described this as "applied research" in Chapter 1. A government, for instance, may experiment with a new tax system or a new method of job training for the economically disadvantaged. Schools may experiment by changing lunch programs or after-school care. A business may experiment with new methods of delivering employee benefits or flexible work hours. In these cases, as in the laboratory, researchers must determine whether the "treatment" caused a change. Did a change in the way patients are admitted to a hospital emergency room cause patients to be treated more quickly and efficiently? Did a college energy conservation program cause a decrease in energy consumption? When we know whether a treatment was effective, we can make important decisions about continuing the treatment, about spending additional money, about investing more time and effort, and about changing the present situation on the basis of our knowledge of the results. Research that seeks to determine the effectiveness of changes made by institutions, government agencies, and other units of society, is called *program evaluation.*

Doing research in the real world comes at a cost: "True" experiments with the high degree of control necessary to identify cause-and-effect relationships are sometimes not feasible in the real world. In these cases, researchers use experimental procedures that only *approximate* the conditions of highly controlled laboratory experiments. These procedures are called **quasi-experiments** because they are like true experiments, but they lack the degree of control found in true experiments.

We begin our discussion of quasi-experimental techniques by examining research done by Drs. Tom Greenfield, Karen Graves, and Lee Kaskutas (1999) on the effects of warning labels on alcohol containers. They sought to determine whether the U.S. federally mandated alcohol warning labels influence people's alcohol-related behaviors. As we discuss quasi-experimental research designs and program evaluation, we will return to the work of Greenfield and his colleagues to illustrate quasi-experimental methods in natural settings.

INTRODUCTION TO THE RESEARCH EXAMPLE: THE EFFECTS OF ALCOHOL WARNING LABELS

 Since November 1989, the United States Congress has required that all alcohol containers sold in the United States carry the following message about the effects of alcohol on health:

> **GOVERNMENT WARNING:** (1) According to the Surgeon General, women should not drink alcoholic beverages during pregnancy because of the risk of birth defects. (2) Consumption of alcoholic beverages impairs your ability to drive a car or operate machinery, and may cause health problems.

As part of this mandate, Congress required that researchers evaluate the effects of the warning label. The U.S. National Institute on Alcohol Abuse and Alcoholism funded the

Alcohol Research Group to conduct a series of cross-sectional surveys in the United States and Ontario, Canada (Greenfield et al., 1999). Ontario was selected because it is demographically similar to the United States, but does not have a warning label law. Greenfield and his colleagues designed a quasi-experiment to determine if alcohol users in the United States differ from their Canadian counterparts in terms of their exposure to the warning label, memory for what the label says, and alcohol-related attitudes and behaviors.

As we discuss quasi-experimental designs, we will look at how Greenfield and his colleagues investigated the effectiveness of the U.S. government's "treatment." We will learn the answer to their research question, do warning labels on alcohol containers influence people's alcohol-related behaviors?

THE RESEARCHERS' POINT OF VIEW

Questions to Dr. Greenfield: How did you become interested in alcohol use and behaviors?

Actually, my earliest interest grew out of a fascination with the phenomenology of altered states of consciousness (my dissertation was on the psychology of meditation). As I moved into the study of addictions after my Ph.D., my interest in prevention policy interventions increased. I studied campus alcohol policies in the 1980s and then national ones when I took on the evaluation of the federal alcohol warning label policy.

Dr. Thomas Greenfield

How did you become involved in exploring the effects of alcohol warning labels?

I had been research director at an institute studying alcohol and other drug abuse prevention from an environmentally oriented public health perspective. When the possibility of directing the national evaluation which was mandated by Public Law No. 100-690 (1988) requiring container warnings as of November 1989 was offered to me, I jumped on it. Although I could see it would be difficult to detect effects, with so few national alcohol policies to study, the challenges of studying this one seemed unique and intriguing to me.

QUASI-EXPERIMENTS VS. TRUE EXPERIMENTS

A good way to appreciate the strengths and weaknesses of quasi-experimental techniques is to compare them with true experiments. Thus, before we discuss the type of quasi-experiment carried out by Greenfield et al. (1999), let's review briefly the characteristics of true experiments (Table 9.1).

Table 9.1   Characteristics of True Experiments and Quasi-Experiments

True Experiments	Quasi-Experiments	Characteristics
☒	☒	An intervention is implemented.
☒	☒	The experimenter includes a comparison.
☒	☐	The experimenter has a high degree of control over the experimental situation (most notably, random assignment).

Characteristics of True Experiments

True experiments exhibit three important characteristics:

1. In a true experiment, an intervention or a treatment is implemented.
2. True experiments are characterized by an appropriate comparison. Thus, in a true experiment the researcher compares a treatment condition and a control (comparison) condition to establish the effectiveness of the treatment. The simplest experiment has two groups that are treated alike, except for the independent variable of interest. Researchers can increase the complexity of experiments by increasing the number of conditions of an independent variable or by testing the effects of more than one independent variable in a complex design.
3. True experiments are marked by the high degree of control the experimenter has over the arrangement of experimental conditions, assignment of participants to conditions, systematic manipulation of independent variables, and choice of dependent variables. Researchers' ability to assign participants randomly to experimental conditions is often seen as the most critical defining characteristic of the true experiment (Judd, Smith, & Kidder, 1991).

When researchers meet these characteristics of a true experiment, they are in a position to attribute any differences in a dependent variable to the effect of the independent variable.

Obstacles to Conducting True Experiments in Natural Settings

Although experimental research is an effective tool for solving problems and answering questions about causes and effects, we face two major obstacles when we try to conduct experiments in natural settings. The first problem is obtaining permission to do the research from individuals in positions of authority. Unless they believe that the research will be useful, school board presidents and government and business leaders are unlikely to support research financially or otherwise.

The second, and often more pressing, obstacle to doing experiments in natural settings is obtaining access to participants. This problem can prove especially troublesome if we wish to assign participants randomly to either a treatment group or a control (no-treatment) group. Often, individuals don't wish to be randomly assigned because it seems unfair, and perhaps they've entered a research study seeking an experimental treatment. However, because random assignment is often the best way to ensure the average comparability of participants in treatment and control groups, it is the best method for researchers to determine the effectiveness of a treatment.

Often researchers use "waiting list" control groups in natural settings. Agencies and organizations create a waiting list if they cannot immediately provide services for all who seek them. One way to establish a control group is to consider people who are waiting as a waiting list control group. These people complete the measures (dependent variables) at the same time as people who receive treatment, then receive services after the research is over. It is essential, however, that people be assigned randomly to the waiting list or treatment groups. This will ensure that the people who receive treatment are similar, on average, to the people on the waiting list.

Researchers will always face circumstances in which random assignment simply cannot be used. As you will see, quasi-experimental designs can be used in these situations.

Threats to Internal Validity: Thinking Critically About Experiments

Throughout this book we've learned to evaluate an experiment by identifying whether alternative explanations for a phenomenon have been controlled. Only by eliminating all possible alternative explanations can we arrive at a definite conclusion about cause and effect. In previous chapters, we saw that various uncontrolled factors that threaten the internal validity of an experiment are called *confounding* factors (they are also called confounds). In Table 9.2 are eight types of confounds, using the terminology of Campbell and Stanley (1966; see also Cook & Campbell, 1979). These potential confoundings are called **threats to internal validity.** Researchers commonly refer to these threats to evaluate the internal validity of research.

Researchers use true experiments to control all these threats to internal validity. Sometimes, however, researchers must compromise between their general aim of gaining valid knowledge regarding the effectiveness of a treatment and the realization that controlling threats to internal validity is not always possible. In these circumstances, quasi-experiments are used because "we must do the best we can with what is available to us" (Campbell, 1969, p. 411). As we review quasi-experimental research designs, we will see that a researcher's primary challenge is to rule out these threats to internal validity as alternative explanations for research findings.

Before considering specific quasi-experimental research designs, however, we should examine some threats to internal validity that even true experiments do not control. These threats may be especially problematic in natural settings.

Table 9.2 Threats to Internal Validity

Threat	Description
History	When an event occurs at the same time as treatment and produces changes in participants' behavior, this event becomes an alternative explanation for participants' behavior (rather than treatment); thus, participants' "history" includes events, other than treatment, which affect their behavior.
Maturation	Participants naturally change over time; these maturational changes, not treatment, may explain any changes in participants during the experiment.
Testing	Taking a test generally affects subsequent testing; thus, participants' performance on a measure at the end of the study may differ from an initial testing, not because of treatment but because they are familiar with the measure.
Instrumentation	Instruments used to measure participants' performance may change over time (e.g., observers may become bored or tired); thus, changes in participants may not be due to treatment but to changes in the instruments used to measure performance.
Regression	Participants sometimes perform very well or very poorly on a measure because of chance factors (e.g., luck). These chance factors are not likely to be present in a second testing, so their scores will not be so extreme—the scores *regress to the mean.* These regression effects, not the effect of treatment, may account for changes in participants' performance over time.
Subject mortality	When participants are lost from the study (attrition), the group equivalence formed at the start of the study may be destroyed; thus, differences between treatment and control groups at the end of the study may be due to differences in who remained in each group, rather than to the effects of treatment.
Selection	When differences exist between individuals in treatment and control groups at the start of the study, these differences become alternative explanations for any differences observed at the end of the study (rather than treatment).
Interactions with selection	When one group of participants responds differently to an external event (history), matures differently, or is measured more sensitively by a test (instrumentation), these threats (rather than treatment) may account for any group differences at the end of a study.

Source: Campbell & Stanley (1966)

The first threat, *contamination,* comes in several forms (Cook & Campbell, 1979). Contamination occurs when there is communication about the experimental intervention between groups of participants. For example, members of a treatment group may discuss the intervention with individuals in the control group. When this happens, control participants' performance in the experiment may worsen if they resent being "controls" or may improve if they want to show they can be just as good as experimental group participants. Contamination can also lead to "diffusion of treatment," in which control participants apply treatments to themselves (a kind of experimental self-help program). Thus, the members of the control group are no longer "control" participants but, instead, are also receiving "second-hand" treatment. Diffusion of treatment may reduce the likelihood that researchers will see a difference between treatment and control groups, even if the intervention is effective.

A second threat all researchers face is the *Hawthorne effect*, named after the electric plant where the following events took place. Researchers were interested in examining how workplace conditions, such as lighting, affected productivity in the Hawthorne electric plant in Cicero, Illinois, between 1924 and 1932 (Roethlisberger, 1977). These researchers observed that *both* the experimental and the control groups increased their productivity in the study. This "Hawthorne effect" describes changes in people's performance when they know "significant others" (e.g., researchers, company bosses) are interested in them or care about their living or work conditions. You may see that the Hawthorne effect represents a special type of reactivity, which we've learned can occur when people change their behavior when they know they're being observed. When the Hawthorne effect occurs, it may be impossible to observe differences between treatment and control groups, even if the intervention is effective.

THE EFFECTS OF ALCOHOL WARNING LABELS: A QUASI-EXPERIMENT

The natural setting of Greenfield and colleagues' (1999) research placed limits on the extent to which they could *control* relevant variables and *randomly assign* individuals to treatment (alcohol warning labels) and control conditions (no warning labels). They couldn't randomly assign individuals to live in the United States or Canada. Thus, we characterize their research as a *quasi-experiment.*

In order to evaluate the effectiveness of warning labels, Greenfield and colleagues (1999) surveyed national samples of U.S. residents and a comparable sample of Ontario, Canada, residents. If you know your geography, you might raise the concern of whether *contamination* effects occurred. Ontario borders several U.S. states: Minnesota, Michigan, and New York. It's possible that Ontario residents were exposed to alcohol warning labels on containers purchased in the United States or through the media (e.g., billboards, magazines, newspapers); this would represent *diffusion of treatment.* In fact, Greenfield and colleagues observed that over the years of their survey (1990–1994), contamination was a problem, ranging from 12% (1994) to 19% (1991) of Ontario residents who had seen the label during the study. Thus, any effects of the warning label may be obscured because both the treatment and control groups had at least some exposure to the warning label.

THE RESEARCHERS' POINT OF VIEW

Question to Dr. Greenfield: Can you explain how contamination influenced your interpretation of your results?

Good question. Early on, when exposure rates to the U.S. warning label were low in Ontario, we tended not to make much of the issue. In a way, the exposure in Ontario provided an opportunity. It can be argued that

reporting seeing the label there means something qualitatively different—
certainly not repeated exposure (on virtually every container in the United
States, one can assume an opportunity to see the label existed). In Ontario,
we hypothesized, seeing the label might have less impact.

QUASI-EXPERIMENTS

Generally speaking, quasi-experiments include an intervention or treatment
and provide a comparison, but they lack the degree of control found in true experiments (review Table 9.1). Quasi-experimental researchers must be prepared
to look for additional kinds of evidence that might allow them to rule out confoundings not controlled by their experimental procedure. For example, selection threats occur when differences exist between treatment and control groups
at the start of the study. To deal with this threat, researchers can look at
"pretest" measures administered to all participants at the beginning of a study
(prior to the intervention). If the groups are equivalent on pretest measures, the
researcher can be more confident that selection is not an alternative explanation
for any group differences following the intervention.

In addition to supplementary data such as pretest measures, researchers can
logically analyze the experimental situation to rule out threats to internal validity. For example, the researcher can check to make sure that instruments worked
consistently throughout the study or can examine whether attrition differed
among groups of participants. By examining additional sources of evidence and
analyzing the experimental situation, researchers often can make a strong argument for the internal validity of the research design, even though a true experiment was not performed. However, it's important for researchers to recognize
the specific shortcomings of quasi-experimental procedures and be prepared to
address these shortcomings through whatever evidence or logic is available.

Perhaps the most serious limitation to experimentation in natural settings is
that experimenters frequently are unable to assign participants randomly to
conditions. Just as randomization is the hallmark of true experiments, *lack of
randomization* is the hallmark of quasi-experiments. This occurs, for instance,
when an intact group is singled out for treatment and when administrative
decisions or practical considerations prevent the random assignment of
participants.

Nonequivalent Control Group Design

Even when random assignment is not possible or practical, researchers can create a quasi-experimental design with considerable internal validity if two conditions are met: (1) a group *like* the treatment group serves as a comparison
group and (2) researchers obtain pretest and posttest measures from individuals in *both* the treatment and comparison groups. In this research design, because researchers select a comparison group using methods other than random

assignment, they cannot assume that individuals in the treatment and control groups are equivalent on all important characteristics (i.e., a selection threat exists). Therefore, it is essential that researchers administer a pretest to both groups to assess their similarity on the dependent measure. Campbell and Stanley (1966) call this quasi-experimental procedure a **nonequivalent control group design.** It can be outlined as follows:

$$\frac{O_1 \times O_2}{O_1 \quad O_2}$$

The dashed line indicates that the treatment and comparison groups were not formed by assigning participants randomly to conditions. We see that the group above the dashed line receives the treatment ($\times$), but the comparison group (below the dashed line) completes pretest (O_1) and posttest (O_2) measures ("observations") but does not receive the treatment.

By adding a comparison group, threats to internal validity due to history, maturation, testing, instrumentation, and regression may be ruled out. A brief look at the logic of experimental design will help show why this occurs. We wish to begin a study with two similar groups; then one group receives the intervention and the other does not. If the two groups' posttest scores differ following treatment, we first must rule out alternative explanations for why the groups differ before we can claim that treatment caused the difference.

If the groups have similar pretest measures, on average, *and* both groups have similar experiences (except for the treatment), then we *assume* that history, maturation, testing, instrumentation, and regression effects occur to *both* groups equally. Thus, we can assume that both groups change naturally at the same rate (maturation), experience the same effect of multiple testing, or are exposed to the same external events (history). If both groups experience these effects in the *same* way, we cannot use these possible alternative explanations to account for group *differences* on posttest measures. Therefore, they no longer are threats to internal validity.

Thus, *researchers gain a tremendous advantage in their ability to make causal claims simply by adding a comparison group.* However, these causal claims also depend on forming similar groups at the start of the study. Even when *pretest* scores are the same, on average, for the treatment and control groups in a nonequivalent control group design, we cannot conclude the groups are equivalent on *all possible* dimensions. Researchers may assess participants on only one pretest measure, or at best on a few measures. Just because individuals do not differ on one measure does not mean they wouldn't differ on other measures that are relevant to their behavior in the situation.

More important, these groups must have comparable experiences, except for the treatment, during the duration of the study. Because this is difficult to realize in the real world, threats to internal validity due to *interactions with selection* typically are not eliminated in this design. That is, the two groups might experience different events (selection $\times$ history), or may mature at different rates (selection $\times$ maturation). These threats become alternative explanations for any differences between treatment and comparison groups at the conclusion of the study. Thus, although the nonequivalent control group design is a powerful tool for conducting research in natural settings, we must always be sensitive to alternative explanations due to selection and interactions with selection.

As you are approaching the end of a course on research methods in psychology, you might appreciate learning about the results of a quasi-experimental study that examined the effect of taking a research methods course on reasoning about real-life events (VanderStoep & Shaughnessy, 1997). The researchers used a nonequivalent control group design to compare students enrolled in two sections of a research methods course with students in two sections of a developmental psychology course. Researchers examined students' performance on a test emphasizing methodological reasoning about everyday events. Students in both kinds of classes completed reasoning tests at the beginning and at the end of the semester. Results revealed that research methods students showed greater improvement than did the developmental students in the control group. Taking a research methods course improved students' ability to think critically about real-life events. This quasi-experiment is described in the sample APA manuscript that appears in Appendix B of this textbook.

THE EFFECTS OF ALCOHOL WARNING LABELS: ESTABLISHING A NONEQUIVALENT CONTROL GROUP

We discussed earlier that Greenfield and his colleagues (1999) compared drinking-related behaviors in the United States and Ontario, Canada. Ontario was selected because it is demographically similar to the United States, and Ontario does not have a Canadian or Provincial warning label on alcohol containers (Greenfield et al., 1999). However, we cannot assume that the citizens surveyed in each country were similar. Thus, selection may threaten the internal validity of Greenfield and colleagues' quasi-experiment. Any group differences in alcohol-related behaviors may be due to differences in the groups at the start of the study.

Because of the timing of the legislation and subsequent evaluation, Greenfield et al. (1999) were not able to assess U.S. and Canadian residents' alcohol-related attitudes and behaviors *prior to* the intervention (i.e., a *pretest*). Instead, they used various known demographic characteristics about the United States and Ontario to establish the comparability of their groups. Although Ontario is demographically similar to the United States, Greenfield and colleagues noted several differences: Ontario has a lower minimum drinking age, more restricted access to alcohol, higher alcohol taxes, fewer people who abstain from alcohol, and more heavy drinkers. Thus, any differences in alcohol-related behaviors in the United States and Canada after the warning label is introduced may be caused by these pre-existing differences, not the warning label. This is the *selection threat to internal validity*.

THE RESEARCHERS' POINT OF VIEW

Question to Dr. Greenfield: How did you decide to select citizens of Ontario, Canada for your comparison group?

The decision was actually made by my predecessor, but the rationales were several: (1) we wanted a demographically similar, close-by site in which the [warning label] policy did not exist (was not implemented); (2) we wanted a site large enough to look for broad population impact or its lack, but not unwieldy in size like another whole country; (3) we wanted a place with good telephone coverage since this research used a telephone survey design; and (4) we wanted a place where we had good collegial contacts, and the Addiction Research Foundation (ARF) of Toronto provided that, with Dr. Norman Giesbrecht of ARF serving as a consultant to the project.

Interrupted Time-series Design

In some situations we can observe changes in a dependent variable for some time before and after a treatment is introduced. When used in research, this is called a **simple interrupted time-series design** (Cook & Campbell, 1979). The essential ingredient of this design is that researchers obtain periodic measures before and after a treatment has been introduced. It can be outlined in the following way:

$$O_1 \ O_2 \ O_3 \ O_4 \ O_5 \times O_6 \ O_7 \ O_8 \ O_9 \ O_{10}$$

The Os refer to the repeated observations made before and after the intervention ($\times$). These situations may arise when a new product is introduced, a new social reform instituted, or a special advertising campaign begun. For example, Campbell (1969) used an interrupted time-series design to analyze whether a police crackdown on speeding ordered by the Connecticut governor decreased the number of traffic fatalities in the state. Researchers often use archival data, rather than direct observation, for time-series designs. Because statistics related to traffic accidents are regularly kept by state agencies, Campbell had available a wealth of archival data for pretreatment and posttreatment measures. Besides number of fatalities, Campbell looked at the number of speeding violations, number of drivers having their licenses suspended, and other measures related to driving behavior. Figure 9.1 shows the percentage of suspensions of licenses for speeding (as a percentage of all license suspensions) before and after the crackdown. The clear *discontinuity* in the time graph provides evidence that the treatment (the police crackdown) increased the number of suspended licenses for speeding.

As Campbell points out, only abrupt changes—discontinuities—in the time graph can be interpreted as evidence for treatment effectiveness. In general, gradual changes are indistinguishable from normal fluctuations over time. The

Figure 9.1   Suspensions of licenses for speeding, as a percentage of all suspensions. (From Campbell, 1969.)

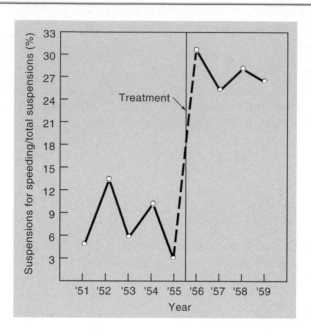

main problem facing researchers using the simple interrupted time-series design is ruling out alternative explanations for the shift in the time series. Thus, history threats, in which another event occurs at the same time as the intervention, represent the most troublesome threats to internal validity in the simple interrupted time-series design (Cook & Campbell, 1979).

Researchers must also consider the instrumentation threat to internal validity in the simple interrupted time-series design (Cook & Campbell, 1979). When agencies and governments start new programs or new social policies, they often also change the way records are kept or the procedures used to collect information. This threat suggests that, rather than the intervention changing people's behavior, behavior only *appears* to be different because record keeping has changed. For an instrumentation threat to be plausible, researchers must show how changes in instrumentation occurred at exactly the same time as the intervention (Campbell & Stanley, 1966).

Most other threats to internal validity are controlled in the simple interrupted time-series design. Problems of maturation, testing, and regression are mostly eliminated by examining the multiple observations both before and after treatment. For example, logically we can expect maturation effects to be gradual rather than discontinuous. Thus, when researchers observe a sharp discontinuity they can generally assume that the discontinuity is not due to maturation effects. The presence of multiple observations offers researchers a distinct advantage over situations in which only one pretest and one posttest observation are available.

Time Series with Nonequivalent Control Group Design

Researchers can enhance the interrupted time-series design greatly by including a control group. This procedure is identical to what we examined when constructing a nonequivalent control group design. In this case, the researcher must find a group that is similar to the treatment group and that allows opportunity for multiple observations before and after the time that the treatment is administered to the experimental group. We can outline this **time series with nonequivalent control group design** as follows:

$$\frac{O_1 \, O_2 \, O_3 \, O_4 \, O_5 \times O_6 \, O_7 \, O_8 \, O_9 \, O_{10}}{O_1 \, O_2 \, O_3 \, O_4 \, O_5 \quad O_6 \, O_7 \, O_8 \, O_9 \, O_{10}}$$

As before, a dashed line is used to indicate that the control group and the experimental group were not randomly assigned. In addition to the threats controlled in the simple interrupted time-series design, this design permits researchers to control threats due to history. For history to threaten the validity of this design, an external event must influence one group and not the other at precisely the same time as the intervention. For example, in his study of Connecticut's crackdown on speeding, Campbell (1969) compared traffic fatality data in Connecticut with similar data from neighboring states. Although traffic fatalities in Connecticut showed a decline immediately following the crackdown, data from comparable states did not exhibit any such decline. The difference between observations for Connecticut and those for neighboring states (which we can assume are similar to Connecticut in weather conditions, automobile use, etc.) allowed Campbell to rule out alternative explanations for the decrease in traffic fatalities.

THE EFFECTS OF ALCOHOL WARNING LABELS: A (MODIFIED) TIME-SERIES WITH NONEQUIVALENT CONTROL GROUP DESIGN

Greenfield et al. (1999) described the results of telephone surveys of U.S. and Ontario residents during the years 1990, 1991, 1993, and 1994; thus, we can characterize this study as a *time-series design*. As we've discussed, U.S. residents served as the treatment (alcohol warning label) group, and Ontario residents served as the *nonequivalent control group*.

We can note one important difference between their research design and the *time-series with nonequivalent control group design*. Greenfield and his colleagues were not able to gain information about U.S. and Ontario residents' alcohol-related attitudes and behaviors prior to the 1989 intervention because of the timing and implementation of the U.S. law. Thus, their design can be diagrammed as follows:

United States: $\dfrac{\times \, O_1 \, O_2 \, O_3 \, O_4}{}$

Ontario, Canada: $O_1 \, O_2 \, O_3 \, O_4$

In time-series designs, we look for *discontinuities* in the time-series data when comparing observations before and after the intervention. Because Greenfield and colleagues did not have pre-intervention observations (baseline), it's impossible to identify any discontinuity that coincides with the intervention. To deal with this problem, Greenfield et al. assumed that exposure to the warning label would increase over time in the United States, but not in Ontario. Therefore, they predicted that, if the warning label were effective, alcohol-related attitudes and behaviors would change in the United States during the 1990–1994 time period, but would not change in Ontario.

Greenfield and colleagues' (1999) first analyses compared U.S. and Ontario drinkers (those who reported drinking alcohol at least once in their lifetime) to see if there were differences in how many saw the warning label in the previous 12 months, and whether they remembered what the message said. Consistent with their prediction, awareness of the warning label rose for U.S. residents (from 30% of the sample in 1990 to 43% of the sample in 1993 and 1994), but did not rise for Ontario residents (from 16% of the sample in 1990 to 12% of the sample in 1994). The U.S. residents who were most likely to be aware of the label were heavy drinkers (consuming alcohol at least weekly and on occasion drinking five or more drinks) and respondents between 18 and 29 years old (Greenfield et al., 1999). In addition, among individuals who were aware of the label, U.S. residents tended to recall the warning label message more accurately across the years of the study than Ontario residents.

Greenfield et al.'s (1999) next step was to examine U.S. and Ontario residents' alcohol-related attitudes and behaviors. One behavior they investigated concerned whether respondents talked with others about the effects of drinking in three areas: driving, pregnancy, and health. We'll examine their results for conversations about drinking and driving to illustrate the effects of the warning label. In both the United States and Ontario, the proportion of respondents who conversed with others about drinking and driving decreased over time. Greenfield et al. interpreted this and related findings as indicating an overall decreasing trend in public concern about the risks of alcohol. However, U.S. respondents who saw the label were more likely to talk with others about drinking and driving than were those who were not aware of the label. You may recall from Chapter 8 that reversing a downward trend indicates an effective treatment.

Talking is one thing; whether people actually change their behavior is another. Greenfield and colleagues (1999) also described findings for U.S. and Ontario residents' reports of whether they drink and drive. Here the findings were more mixed. Across all years of the study in the United States, those who had seen the label were more likely to report they deliberately chose not to drive after drinking at least once in the previous year. That's the good news. The bad news is that U.S. respondents who reported seeing the label also were more likely to report drinking and driving than were respondents who didn't see the label. These data are problematic, however, because those who are most likely to see the label and drive after drinking are the heaviest drinkers. These individuals may be less affected by a warning message.

Greenfield et al. (1999) cautioned that many challenges in conducting this study limit our ability to establish cause-and-effect relationships between alcohol warning labels and alcohol-related attitudes and behaviors. In particular, selection threats and contamination limit our ability to form definite conclusions. We can also ask whether threats due to interactions with selection limit the interpretation of these findings. For example, a selection × history threat would become an alternative explanation for differences between U.S. and Ontario residents if alcohol-related messages from other sources (e.g., media) were more likely in one country. To rule out this alternative explanation, Greenfield and his colleagues also have conducted extensive studies of alcohol-related messages during the 1990–94 time period (e.g., Kaskutas et al., 1998; Lemmens et al., 1999).

Greenfield and colleagues (1999) noted that they observed modest effects of the warning label, even though the intervention—the warning label—was literally and figuratively small. They concluded that small benefits, when applied to the entire population, can have major impact, particularly in light of the large costs of alcohol-related problems in the United States. Regarding reminding people of the risks of alcohol use (the purpose of the warning labels), Greenfield and colleagues concluded, "Although results are mixed, we believe the pattern of evidence, taken as a whole, suggests that Congressional intent to remind is being met to a modest extent" (pp. 279–280).

THE RESEARCHERS' POINT OF VIEW

Questions to Dr. Greenfield: The data collection effort must have been massive. Can you describe any particular problems or issues due to the large sample size or survey methods?

Of course, such a large-scale survey (2,000 cases per year in the United States for three years, initially, and 1,000 each in Ontario for the last two of these, then an extension with a further 1,000 cases in each site for two more years) is expensive, although much less so than our national in-person household interview surveys. In general, we had few problems, although response rates were a problem in 1994, the last year, dropping from 64% in 1990 to 53% in 1994. We weighted results according to Census estimates for gender and age, and corrected for multiple phones in the household [which increases the likelihood of being included in the sample in a telephone survey that uses "random digit dialing"]. Our fieldwork subcontractor [Survey Design and Analysis, Inc., Ann Arbor, MI] did an excellent job, and we feel the data came to us very clean.

Your findings about alcohol-related behaviors (e.g., drinking and driving) are mixed. Were you surprised by any of your findings?

Of course if one is a believer, one would have liked to see more of this effect—less drunk driving among those recalling the message on the label. This is the classic self-selection problem, however, since the heavier drinkers are more exposed to the label and are also more likely to report drunk driving, and possibly those least likely to be influenced by health messages. This is why public health people take heart that *some* effect on precautionary behaviors that might reduce risks ARE observed.

What would you have gained with baseline information and why couldn't you get these data?

Like many policies that come through legislative action, there was only a brief time between enactment and policy implementation. Funding from NIH sources via peer review can take at least one or two years between proposal and award start date. Our sponsor, the National Institute on Alcohol Abuse and Alcoholism, awarded us supplemental funding to jump-start the process, allowing U.S. data to be collected prior to the November 1989 implementation. In addition, the evaluation design would have been stronger if we had had several years of prior data—an extended baseline. This might have clarified whether the U.S. prebaseline exposure rates (6 to 8%) were from true early exposure as labels began to phase in before the required date or due to false positives [respondents falsely reporting they'd seen the label, perhaps confusing it with media reports].

PROGRAM EVALUATION

Organizations that produce goods and products have a ready-made index of success. If a company is set up to make beach balls, its success is ultimately determined by its profits from the sale of beach balls. At least theoretically, we can assess the efficiency and effectiveness of an organization by examining its financial ledgers. Increasingly, however, a different type of organization has a critical role in our society. Because these organizations typically provide services rather than goods or products, Posavac and Carey (1997) refer to them as *human service organizations.* For example, hospitals, schools, police departments, and government agencies provide a variety of services ranging from emergency room care to fire prevention inspections. Because making a profit is not the goal of these organizations, we need another method to distinguish between effective and ineffective agencies. This is precisely the role of program evaluation: to assess the effectiveness of human service organizations.

The Goals of Program Evaluation

The basic goal of **program evaluation** is to provide feedback to administrators of human service organizations in order to help them decide what services to provide to whom and how to provide them most effectively and efficiently (Posavac & Carey, 1997). Program evaluation is *interdisciplinary* because it draws on principles of political science, sociology, economics, education, and psychology. We discuss program evaluation at the end of this chapter on research in natural settings because it represents the most large-scale application of the principles and methods we examined in this book. We've seen an application of program evaluation in Greenfield et al.'s evaluation of the U.S. government's program to increase our awareness of the health consequences of alcohol use.

According to Posavac and Carey (1997), program evaluators examine four main questions about programs and services: needs, process, outcome, and efficiency (see Table 9.3).

When program evaluators assess *needs*, they seek to determine whether the needs of the people for whom the agency might provide service are being met. For example, if a city government were to consider instituting a program of recreational activities for senior citizens in the community, the city would first want to determine whether senior citizens actually need or want such a program and, if they do, what kind of program would be most attractive to them. Program evaluators often use survey research methods to assess needs.

Table 9.3   Four Questions of Program Evaluation (Posavac & Carey, 1997)

Needs	Is an agency or organization meeting the needs of the people it serves?
Process	How is a program being implemented (is it going as planned)?
Outcome	Has a program been effective in meeting its stated goals?
Efficiency	Is a program cost-efficient relative to alternative programs?

Once a program has been set up, program evaluators may ask about the *process* that has been established. Programs are not always implemented the way they were planned, and it is essential to know what actually *is* being done when a program is implemented. For example, if senior citizens are not using a recreational program designed specifically for them, it's possible the program was inadequately implemented. A process evaluation answers questions about how a program is actually being carried out, and permits administrators to make adjustments in how services are delivered to strengthen the existing program (Posavac & Carey, 1997). Program evaluators may use observational methods to investigate process questions.

An evaluation of *outcome* is just that; researchers ask whether the program has been effective in meeting its stated goals. For example, do senior citizens now have access to more recreational activities, and are they pleased with these activities? Are these particular activities preferred over other activities? Researchers evaluating the outcome of a community watch program designed to curb neighborhood crime might assess whether there were decreases in burglaries and assaults following the implementation of the program.

Evaluators might also ask about the *efficiency* of the program—that is, about its cost. Government agencies and organizations often have to make choices among alternative services they are capable of delivering. Administrators need information about how successful a program is (outcome evaluation) and about the program's cost (efficiency evaluation) to make informed decisions about whether to continue the program, to improve it, to try an alternative program, or to cut back on the program's services. These evaluations may use both experimental and quasi-experimental methods for research in natural settings. An evaluator may, for example, use a nonequivalent control group design to assess the effectiveness of a school reform program by comparing students' performance in two school districts, one with the reform program and one without. Program evaluators also use archival data to evaluate outcome and efficiency. For example, police records document the frequency of various crimes and can be used to assess the effectiveness of a community-watch program.

The Social Realities of Applied Research

The purpose of program evaluation is practical, not theoretical. Program evaluation is perhaps the most extreme case of applied research. Perhaps the greatest difference between theoretical, basic research and program evaluation lies in the political and social realities surrounding program evaluation. Governments at both local and national levels regularly propose, plan, and execute various types of social reforms, such as work incentive programs, educational or police reforms, and medical care for senior citizens. Unfortunately, the outcome of social reforms often cannot be meaningfully evaluated. Did a change in police techniques lead to reduced crime? Are more elderly people gaining access to public transportation after fares are lowered? We often cannot learn the answers to these questions because the political climate often is not ready for hard-headed evaluation. What public official, for instance, wants to be associated with a program that failed? Furthermore, many social reforms are implemented with the assumption they will be successful. Otherwise, why spend all that tax money? For many public administrators, it is advantageous to leave that assumption in people's minds rather than face the truth about what happened.

Social scientists need to convince administrators to use true experiments or quasi-experiments when instituting new social programs. For example, a randomization procedure, perhaps based on public lottery, could be used to decide which group receives a pilot program or gains access to scarce resources. Groups not receiving the program or the available resources would become comparison groups. The effect of a social "treatment" could then be meaningfully evaluated. At present, decisions regarding who gets what are often influenced by special interest groups—as the result of intense lobbying, for example—or are made on the basis of political favoritism.

Program evaluation based on sound experimental methodology offers policy makers at all levels (institution, community, city, state, federal) the information that can help them make more informed choices among possible treatments for social problems. Because resources inevitably are in short supply, it is critical that resources are put to the best possible use to improve society.

DISCUSSION OF THE RESEARCH EXAMPLE: THE EFFECTS OF ALCOHOL WARNING LABELS

Greenfield and colleagues' (1999) quasi-experiment represents *program evaluation* because they investigated the federal government's program to remind people of the risks of alcohol consumption. The program consisted of mandating warning labels on all alcohol containers. Greenfield and his colleagues examined the *outcome* of this law by seeking to determine if the law was effective in meeting its stated goals. They asked respondents whether they were aware of the alcohol warning label, and sought to determine whether it influenced individuals' alcohol-related attitudes and behaviors. As we've seen, U.S. residents who had purchased or consumed alcohol tended to be aware of the warning label, but the effects of the label on their behavior appeared to be mixed.

Several features of the quasi-experimental design limited Greenfield et al.'s conclusions. Although legislators recognized the need to evaluate the effects of the warning label, the way the law was implemented influenced these researchers' ability to determine whether the law is effective. Thus, although research on congressional legislation has made an important first step in this instance, future efforts will be maximized by allowing researchers greater control over the implementation and design of program evaluation.

THE RESEARCHERS' POINT OF VIEW

Questions to Dr. Greenfield: What would you like people to learn from your research?

I'd like government policy makers (legislators) to design evaluable policies, not only (as in this legislation) mandating studies, but also designing the implementation of interventions so that they could be better evaluated (e.g., by introducing them in a randomized fashion, etc.). I'd like researchers to appreciate both the difficulties and the opportunities for useful policy-relevant social science. I'd like the public to appreciate that science has a role to play and needs support and, in this case, to cherish the fact that a unique window of opportunity in the alcohol policy process opened briefly, assuring their right to better consumer information on a product which can be wonderful or horrendous, depending on how it is used.

You work at the Alcohol Research Group (ARG). Can you explain what this is and the work that you do? What projects are you working on now?

I am now director of the National Alcohol Research Center at ARG, one of 15 sponsored by the National Institute on Alcohol Abuse and Alcoholism. We conduct state-of-the-art social epidemiological studies of alcohol problems in the nation, bringing together multidisciplinary perspectives on these studies with direct policy implications, and training new scholars through two pre- and postdoctoral research traineeships. Our current interests include alcohol policy formation and analysis, alcohol mortality, prevention and health services research, and research methodology. We are working on improving measures of drinking patterns, problems, and risk factors.

READ MORE ABOUT IT

To read more about Greenfield and colleagues' research on alcohol warning labels, consult their article:

Greenfield, T. K., Graves, K. L., & Kaskutas, L. A. (1999). Long-term effects of alcohol warning labels: Findings from a comparison of the United States and Ontario, Canada. *Psychology and Marketing, 16,* 261–282.

You will find information about the effects of media messages on alcohol-related attitudes and behaviors in the following journal articles:

Kaskutas, L. A., Greenfield, T. K., Lee, M. E., & Cote, J. (1998). Reach and effect of health messages on drinking during pregnancy. *Journal of Health Education, 29,* 11–17.

Lemmens, P. H., Vaeth, P. A. C., & Greenfield, T. K. (1999). Coverage of beverage alcohol issues in the print media in the United States, 1985–1991. *American Journal of Public Health, 89,* 1555–1560.

If you are interested in learning more about program evaluation, consider the following book:
Posavac, E. J., & Carey, R. G. (1997). *Program evaluation* (5th ed.). Englewood Cliffs, NJ: Prentice-Hall.

KEY CONCEPTS

true experiments	simple interrupted time-series
threats to internal validity	design
quasi-experiments	time series with nonequivalent
nonequivalent control group	control group design
design	program evaluation

KEY POINTS TO LEARN

Quasi-experiments vs. True Experiments

- In true experiments, researchers manipulate an independent variable with treatment and comparison condition(s) and exercise a high degree of control (especially through random assignment to conditions).
- Researchers may experience difficulty gaining access to participants and permission to conduct true experiments in natural settings.
- Although random assignment is viewed by some as unfair because it may deprive individuals of a new treatment, it is still the best way to determine if a new treatment is effective.
- When evaluating the effect of a treatment, one way to establish a comparison group is to place individuals in a waiting list control group.
- Threats to internal validity are confoundings that serve as plausible alternative explanations for a research finding.
- The major classes of threats to internal validity include history, maturation, testing, instrumentation, regression, subject mortality, selection, and interactions with selection.

Quasi-experiments

- Quasi-experiments lack the degree of control found in true experiments; most notably, quasi-experiments typically lack random assignment.
- Quasi-experiments provide an important alternative when true experiments are not possible; researchers seek to eliminate threats to internal validity with supplementary data and logical analysis of the experimental situation.
- Threats to internal validity due to history, maturation, testing, instrumentation, and regression can be eliminated by adding a comparison group to form a nonequivalent control group design.
- Although groups may be comparable on a pretest measure in a nonequivalent control group design, this does not ensure that the groups are similar in all possible ways that are relevant to the study outcome.
- In a simple interrupted time-series design, researchers examine a series of observations both before and after a treatment; evidence for treatment effects

occurs when there are abrupt shifts (discontinuities) in the time-series data at the time the treatment was implemented.

- The major threats to internal validity in the simple interrupted time-series design are history effects and changes in measurement (instrumentation) that occur at the same time as the treatment.
- In a time-series with nonequivalent control group design, researchers make a series of observations before and after treatment for both a treatment group and a comparable comparison group; many threats to internal validity can be shown to be improbable when this design is used.

Program Evaluation

- Program evaluation is used to assess the effectiveness of human service organizations and provide feedback to administrators about their services.
- Program evaluators assess needs, process, outcome, and efficiency of social services.
- Despite the fact that persons in authority frequently show a reluctance to do experimentation, true experiments and quasi-experiments provide excellent approaches for evaluating social and institutional reforms.

CHECKING THE ESSENTIALS

1. Identify the three characteristics of a true experiment.
2. Describe briefly two obstacles that researchers face when they try to do experiments in natural settings.
3. Identify one threat to internal validity and explain how this threat is controlled in a true experiment.
4. Briefly outline the procedures and the logic of a nonequivalent control group design.
5. What is the primary evidence for the effectiveness of a treatment that is tested using a simple interrupted time-series design?
6. What threats to internal validity can researchers often eliminate in time-series with nonequivalent control group designs?
7. What is the basic goal of program evaluation?
8. Describe briefly the following issues that are addressed in program evaluation: needs, process, outcome, and efficiency.
9. What is the greatest difference between basic research and program evaluation (perhaps the most extreme case of applied research)?

APPLYING YOUR KNOWLEDGE

1. A quasi-experiment was used to determine whether multimedia instruction is effective. The same instructor taught two sections of introductory psychology. In one section (the treatment group), the instructor used multimedia instruction. In the other section the instructor covered the same material but did not use multimedia instruction. Students did not know when they registered for the course whether multimedia instruction would be used. The students were not randomly assigned to sections. Students' knowledge of the course material was assessed using two forms of a comprehensive introductory psychology test. The students in both sections were

tested on the second day of class (the pretest) and at the final exam (the posttest) on different forms of the test. The comprehensive test can be considered a reliable and valid test that can be used to compare the effectiveness of the instruction in the two sections.

A. What quasi-experimental design was used in the study?

B. Identify and briefly describe one threat to the internal validity of this study if it had tested only the students who had received multimedia instruction.

C. Draw a graph of results of this quasi-experiment. The pattern of results in your graph should support the conclusion that multimedia instruction was effective.

2. At a recent meeting of the Academic Affairs Board of your school, a proposal was submitted for a program to implement a new interdisciplinary approach to the teaching of Spanish and the cultural history component of required courses. The program will be modeled after existing programs in Greek and German. The Spanish program will begin in the fall of next year. Because of your extensive expertise, you have been asked to serve as a consultant to the Academic Affairs Board. Your task is to develop a procedure whereby the effectiveness of this new program can be evaluated. The board will obviously make the final decision, so what it needs from you is some alternative approaches and the pros and cons of each approach.

A. The first plan you are to develop should use a true experimental approach, so you should outline what a random groups design experiment of the new program would look like.

B. Explain why the board is likely to reject this first plan. Then develop what you think would be the best quasi-experimental design to test the program.

3. A small undergraduate college with a new physical fitness center has decided to introduce a health-enhancement program for faculty and staff. The program will be designed to take one semester to complete, with three 1-hour sessions per week. Comment critically on each of the following questions regarding ways in which program evaluation could be used in the development of this program.

A. The researcher doing the program evaluation for the college suggests doing an assessment of needs. How would this be helpful in planning the program?

B. The researcher next recommends that a process evaluation be done of the program. What information will this step provide?

C. What obstacles that generally exist in real-world settings, and probably apply in this situation, prevent the conduct of a true experiment to evaluate the outcome of the program? What quasi-experimental design could be used?

D. The researcher includes an assessment of the efficiency of the program in the recommendations. What costs do you think should be considered in determining the efficiency of the program?

EPILOGUE: HOW TO BE AN INTELLIGENT CONSUMER OF PSYCHOLOGICAL RESEARCH

INTRODUCTION

Our goal in this book has been to explore the ways in which psychologists use the scientific method to learn about mental processes and behavior. We hope you have come to appreciate the exciting but challenging task of conducting original research in psychology. Perhaps one day someone will interview you for a research methods book, wanting to know more about what you discovered regarding the way we think and behave, and asking you to share your thoughts with students about doing research in psychology.

No matter what the future holds, we can safely make one prediction. You will continue to learn about psychological research from reports on the Internet, in newspapers, magazines, and on radio and television. The public has an almost insatiable appetite for information related to psychology. And why not? Psychology is about us, who we are, what makes us tick, and many of us think we are about as interesting as things get. We are continually bombarded with "research news." Much of this research has direct application to our own lives. We may learn about a way to communicate with a relative who has Alzheimer's, have safe (or more enjoyable) sex, avoid arguments, alleviate depression, make better decisions, curb aggression, learn how to forgive, and so on. But (and this is a big *but*) how can we sort out the good research from the bad—what is really true from what is not yet confirmed, the research finding worth applying from the one that warrants a wait-and-see attitude?

Not everything published in the popular press represents "good" research. (In fact, if we consider all the available media outlets, probably most is not very good.) And even the best research has limitations, as you have learned again and again in this book. This issue is even more critical given the increased availability of good and bad research on the Internet. Questions of external validity, for instance, are extremely important when we talk about applying the results of laboratory research to our lives. On one hand, you are well ahead of most people when it comes to deciding what is good research. Your knowledge of research methods gives you an advantage over most consumers of psychological research. Nevertheless, you will frequently still be at a disadvantage when evaluating the value of research reported in the popular media. We conclude this book by offering some guidelines to help you apply your knowledge of the scientific method to understand research findings reported in the media and elsewhere. Following these recommendations should help you decide what to make of a research finding. Knowing the difference between good and bad research may save you money, help you deal with stress, allow you to solve personal problems, and possibly help you and your loved ones lead a more productive and healthy life.

GUIDELINES FOR EVALUATING RESEARCH FINDINGS

The following guidelines will prove useful when evaluating research reported in the popular media and in the many self-help books found in bookstores. These recommendations are based on what you have already learned about

Table 10.1   Guidelines for Evaluating Reports of Psychological Research

- Don't confuse pseudoscience or nonscience with science.
- Be skeptical.
- Be aware that scientists may disagree.
- Keep in mind that research is generally about averages.
- Whenever possible, go to the original source.

research methods and the scientific process. We will refer to some of these lessons as we discuss the guidelines (see Table 10.1).

Don't Confuse Pseudoscience or Nonscience with Science

How many times has the headline of a supermarket tabloid caught your eye as you prepared to check out with your groceries?

Mother Gives Birth to Two-Headed Baby!
Aliens Kidnap Traveling Salesman!
Apricot Pits Cure Cancer!
Scientists Discover Intelligence Pill!

Sometimes these reports are a bizarre twist on an otherwise true story. A two-headed baby turns out to be conjoined (Siamese) twins. At other times the writers of headlines "forget" to mention a critical detail in a story—for example, that an alien abduction was a dream. Occasionally the results of a single case are generalized to everyone: Apricot pits (according to a cancer survivor in Pasadena) cure cancer. Or the writers simply stretch the facts to grab people's attention: A drug that scientists indeed found to enhance maze learning in rats becomes scientists' discovery of an intelligence pill. Of course, at other times the information is simply nonsense. Whatever you want to call it, it isn't science. Yet hundreds of thousands of people read such tabloids and walk away amazed at what scientists have found.

What explains this gullibility? You may remember from Chapter 1 that Singer and Benassi (1981) suggest that an uncritical attitude has several sources. For example, they point to the many distortions in the media. The sheer pervasiveness of such reports may lend credibility to them. Singer and Benassi also point to possible deficiencies in human reasoning. Our everyday inferences are susceptible to many biases, including the tendency to seek only confirmatory evidence, to jump to conclusions, and to perceive causality in events when none is actually present (Zechmeister & Johnson, 1992).

Unfortunately, it isn't only the supermarket tabloids that give people a wrong impression of psychological research. We find evidence of silly science on talk shows and in many otherwise reasonable outlets. Walk into any large bookstore, seek out the psychology section, and you will find dozens of book titles related to dream analysis, the latest fads in psychotherapy, depression, self-esteem, aggression, and numerous other psychology-related topics. How do you know that what these authors are telling you is worth your time and money? Not all that is labeled "psychology" is based on the scientific method. Not all that is published as fact is based on good scientific research. Not all that is offered you in the way of "psychological" treatments, therapies, and solutions to personal problems has been investigated scientifically. And, unfortunately, purveyors of new treatments sometimes reject the negative results of rigorously controlled studies (see, for example, Jacobson, Mulick, & Schwartz, 1995). Who should you believe? What questions should you ask?

At this point, you should be able to take advantage of your knowledge of research methods in psychology. Some defining principles of the scientific method were outlined in Chapter 1. What is science and what is pseudoscience or nonscience?

Millions of people seem unable to recognize pseudoscience. Dreams and hopes blur their vision and disturb their reason. And we are all susceptible to cognitive biases. A confirmation bias, for example, leads us to seek evidence that confirms *our* view of the world (and not look for conflicting results). Some of the more obvious characteristics of pseudoscience are listed in Table 10.2. Take a close look so you can recognize them when they appear in research reports.

And what makes for "real" science? You know that the presence of fancy machines, with all their lights and whistles, doesn't make it science. Neither does the word of someone with an advanced degree (e.g., Ph.D., Psy.D., M.D.) or with "celebrity" status (i.e., a "prominent personality") make it good science. You have learned that science is something abstract. It is an approach to knowledge that differs from everyday approaches to knowledge. If knowledge is scientifically based, then we want to ask to what extent the ideas presented are based on empirical, systematic, and controlled observation. What was the nature of the research? What type of research design, for instance, was used?

Table 10.2   How To Recognize Pseudoscience

- Evidence is based largely on testimonials (that is, personal accounts).
- Results take advantage of unusual but real coincidences (that is, chance events).
- Those advocating more rigorously controlled investigation are dismissed or ridiculed.
- Defenders of a phenomenon reject explanations based on plausible natural causes.
- Evidence comes from a few, highly selected (positive) studies.
- Negative findings or failures to replicate are ignored or dismissed for various reasons.
- Claims are supported by prominent personalities whose views are not to be questioned.
- Conflicting versions or details of an event are minimized or ignored.
- Phenomena are said to be weakened or disappear if there are too many controls.
- Suggestions that trickery or deception produced the results are not permitted.
- Results are obtained under conditions that can't be verified by independent observers.
- Appeals are made to forces outside the realm of real science.

Source: Based in large part on Jacobson et al. (1995), as well as James Randi's comments in his book *Flim-Flam!* (1982; especially pages 37–41, "paranormal chicanery).

Was a true experiment done? Were participants randomly assigned to conditions? What were the operational definitions? Were the measures valid and reliable? The answers to these and other questions will help you sort out the scientific from the pseudoscientific and nonscientific.

Be Skeptical

As you also saw in Chapter 1, an important characteristic of a scientist is a skeptical attitude. You, too, need to be skeptical (at least initially) about reports of scientific findings.

Nature is complex; finding simple answers to life's problems is not easy. In fact, we must realize that most of the answers will not be simple ones. When answers are found, they frequently are only part of the total answer or are tentative, awaiting more research. Not only is nature complicated, but scientists are human; they make mistakes. You have seen the many ways in which a research study may go wrong: biased samples, confoundings, inadequate statistical conclusions, insensitive design, low external validity. Bad things can happen to good researchers. Or to say it another way, even good researchers may be in error (of course, bad researchers are in error more often). It is usually a good idea to wait until more evidence about a new research finding is forthcoming and other scientists become aware of the details of the published research. What do other experts say? Initial research findings typically are not conclusive. They are just that: initial findings on a long path of discovery. Novel findings must also pass the scientist's test of replication. Can other, independent researchers show the same thing? Until they do, it may be wise to withhold judgment.

A skeptical attitude is particularly important when a causal relationship is claimed. You know that correlation is not causality, but many people do not. You are aware that research results involving a natural groups variable (e.g., gender, age) may show statistical significance, but that these results are merely correlational and a causal claim is not warranted. Others are not so aware, including many who should be. When hearing that X "caused" Y, you should ask, have the researchers met the three conditions for establishing causal relationship: covariation, time-order relationship, and the all-important elimination of alternative explanations?

Be Aware That Scientists May Disagree

Disagreement doesn't make it bad research; in fact it may be very good research. Frequently, disagreement occurs at a theoretical level. When this happens, the facts may not necessarily be disputed; rather, what is often disputed is what the facts mean. Many people are upset, however, when they hear that scientists disagree. These people are looking for immediate answers, and disagreements among scientists suggest that the answers are not yet at hand or, worse, that science can't produce the answers. This may cause them to lose faith in the scientific process and to look elsewhere, perhaps to soothsayers, fortune tellers, and astrologers, or to trust their "gut" (intuitive) reaction. Intuition, as you know, plays an important role in our decision making, but, as a psychology student, you also know intuition should not always be trusted.

Individuals who quickly give up on science often are not knowledgeable about how science works. You have seen that scientists develop theories, their best guesses, about human behavior. A theory is then put to the test, and the results may or may not support the theory. Frequently the results are ambiguous (inappropriate research design? small effect size? inconclusive statistical result? possible confounding discovered?). Some scientists may argue that the results support another theory, whereas others may suggest that more research is needed.

When reputable scientists disagree we can be pretty sure that the evidence offered is not yet conclusive. Again, this doesn't mean that scientists don't know what they are doing or that answers won't ever be forthcoming. But it does demand our patience, based on an understanding of the often slow pace of research, as we wait for more research to be done.

A disagreement among scientists made headline news in 1998. *Newsweek* (9/7/98) ran a cover story entitled "Do Parents Matter?" The feature article detailed the developmental theory of Judith Harris, which is found in her book *The Nurture Assumption: Why Children Turn Out the Way They Do; Parents Matter Less Than You Think and Peers Matter More* (Free Press, 1998). Perhaps you have heard about this feisty author and her controversial theory. The title of her book says it all: Parents may not have the effect on children that we (and intuition) would suggest they do. Rather, she argues, peers (and genes) are much more important in shaping a child's future. Harris, although she does not have a Ph.D. in psychology, does a respectable job of summarizing the scientific evidence (*good* scientific evidence) to support her theory. She cites many scientific studies from various disciplines (psychology, sociology, anthropology). In fact, she did such an impressive job that her theoretical paper describing these ideas in more rigorous scientific fashion was published in *Psychological Review* (1995), one of the premier scientific journals in psychology. The experts who reviewed her manuscript when it was submitted to the journal clearly judged it to be of significant scientific value. Other experts have commented favorably, and the American Psychological Association bestowed an award on her at its annual meeting in 1999.

But Harris' ideas are far from accepted by all psychologists. According to the *Newsweek* article, a recent president of the APA said, "She's all wrong." One of the foremost developmental psychologists in the field was quoted as saying he was "embarrassed for psychology." Many psychologists believe her position is too extreme. Some have suggested that she ignored evidence against her position and relied mainly on evidence supporting her view (the confirmation bias described earlier). Other experts believe she has misinterpreted some of the evidence.

Whom do we believe? Do parents matter? The answer is a bit unsettling: The exact role played by parents in shaping a child is not clear. Obviously, the experts disagree, but neither the scientists nor the field of psychological science is to blame. Trying to unravel the interaction of nature (genes) and nurture (environment) and their effects on our development is a complex task. In general, the more complex the question, the greater is the likelihood that researchers will disagree (see, for example, Azar, 1999).

More research is needed. And until we see the fruits of more research it is best to take a wait-and-see attitude. That doesn't mean that we shouldn't try to find out more about what Harris and her supporters, as well as nonsupporters, have to say. The question is a critical one, and we may be ready to argue one way or the other. Science, nevertheless, has a way to go before it can tell us exactly how we develop. But those who believe in the scientific method as a way of knowing trust that one day we will have better answers to these questions.

Keep in Mind That Research Is Generally About Averages

Scientific psychology is most typically a nomothetic discipline. This means that research psychologists are interested in average, or typical, behavior. What might be said about people in general? You have seen this approach applied repeatedly as we discussed research based on group methodology. Individuals are selected or assigned to different conditions of a research study. The researcher is generally concerned with the differences among the average (mean) performance of the various conditions. Consider, for instance, the interesting research by James Pennebaker and Martha Francis (1996), discussed in Chapter 6, who looked at the effect of revealing very personal emotional stories on people's physical health. *In general,* the people who wrote about emotional life events were healthier than those who wrote about superficial life events. But everyone didn't necessarily behave the same. Not everyone who wrote about personal emotional experiences responded the same way. As a student of psychology, you are well aware of individual differences.

What lesson does this hold for individuals who are looking at the results of a research study and wondering whether the findings apply to them? The answer is simple, if a bit disconcerting: It isn't easy to determine whether a research finding will apply to you. How do you know whether you are like those people who, shall we say, scored high as opposed to those scored low? Are you more similar to those who responded favorably to a treatment or more like those for whom the treatment did not work? You can't always tell. As we noted, there is individual variation in the way similar people respond to a treatment. All the participants in Pennebaker and Francis' (1996) study were college students, all were about the same age, and all were attending the same school, yet not all reacted the same to the experimental treatment. Therefore, even if we judge ourselves (superficially) to be "like" those in a research study, we usually can't say for sure how we would respond. Remember, researchers typically report differences among means (averages). Of course, things are even trickier when research participants *as a group* differ from us in important ways. If the research sample is a different gender or younger, for instance, or perhaps even a different animal species (for example, rats or chimps), we know we will have to address questions of external validity before we can judge whether group differences apply to our situation.

Knowing that research is usually based on averages, and obtained from participants who often are not like us, may be frustrating as we seek to find out whether "this applies to me." But such knowledge may also keep us from running here and there in the false hope of finding a quick solution to some of our problems or those of friends and relatives. Only by carefully examining the nature of the research participants, the research design, the specific procedures used, and the data obtained, can we get the information necessary to help determine if "we" should be included in the result. Until such information is in hand, we should be cautious about accepting a research finding as one applying to "me."

Whenever Possible, Go to the Original Source

When possible, try to get past the condensed version and the inevitable distortions that accompany a brief news article. If your source is a brief newspaper article, a few spoken lines on a radio news show, or a few minutes of TV time, you simply will not have enough information to judge whether a research study is good or not. Brevity of news reports is one reason why we noted earlier that, even armed with your knowledge of research methods, you often will be at a disadvantage when learning about research from the media.

Even lengthier articles appearing in news magazines, or perhaps popular science magazines, frequently do not include enough detail to allow you to make a reasonable judgment about the validity of the findings. And, on many occasions, the topics discussed are beyond our expertise; no one is expected to know everything about everything. This also puts us at a disadvantage when seeking to find out if a research finding is trustworthy.

When you want to evaluate a research finding for yourself, the fifth principle comes into play: Go to the original source whenever possible. There are several important things you can find out by looking up the original source. One thing you will want to determine is whether the research was published in a "peer-reviewed" journal. Only when researchers subject their results to public review by knowledgeable experts can you begin to trust their findings. Even if you don't have the expertise to adequately comprehend the specifics of the research, knowing that it was published in a reputable scientific journal is at least circumstantial evidence in favor of trusting the finding (but, of course, it is not a guarantee). When the original source is not a peer-reviewed journal but is perhaps a "technical report" or a "presentation" at a scientific convention, you need to be even more cautious about accepting the findings as conclusive. Technical reports and most convention presentations are given only minimal peer review. "Testimonials" and "advertisements" are, of course, even more problematic.

You will also want to check out who sponsored the research. Is there any reason to suspect that the research and reporting of results may be less than objective? Who has a stake in this research? Crossen (1994) noted that a national survey sponsored by the zinc industry showed that 62 percent of respondents wanted to keep the penny (which is zinc-based) in circulation, and a survey sponsored by a manufacturer of cellular phones showed that 70% of respondents (all of whom used cellular phones) agreed that people who use cellular telephones are more successful in business. Knowing that the sponsor of the research has a stake in its outcome does not automatically discredit the research, though. High-quality research may be done even when the sponsor can be shown to gain from a particular outcome, but such relationships may cause some concern until the results are replicated by an independent group of researchers (which is what we assume an ethical business or corporation sponsor of scientific research also would want).

Finally, with the original source in hand, if you feel unprepared to critically evaluate it, at least you are in a position to take the article to someone more knowledgeable and get an expert opinion. This should not embarrass you. Many research psychologists find they are often unable to evaluate critically a published research article that is outside their particular area of expertise. Such is the unfortunate price of scientific specialization. Even experienced researchers frequently ask colleagues for their opinions about research published in a relatively unfamiliar area. Consulting an expert for advice about a published research article will simply make you a member of the club—that is, the club of people concerned about good research and its potential application in our lives.

TIPS ON READING A NEWSPAPER (OR MAGAZINE) REPORT OF A RESEARCH FINDING

As previously mentioned, the latest scientific news may bring hope for a chance to improve our lives. But how should we approach our reading of newspapers and news magazines, particularly when the stories relate to recent "scientific" findings?

The principles we outlined above should help. For example, sorting out the pseudoscientific from the scientific and maintaining a skeptical attitude are necessary goals when reading media accounts. And we want, when possible, to find and read the original source. As one newspaper editor was quoted as saying, "You have to take everything with a grain of salt until the last word comes in. I hate to tell people I don't believe everything I read, but the fact is anybody who believes everything they read is nuts" (Schmitz, 1991, p. 42).

Headlines, those few words that seek to grab our attention and to motivate us to read the article, frequently are written by people who know little about the contents of the article. The headline writer's job is to capture the meaning of an article in a few interesting words. Often a headline is written as fact or an absolute: "Cure for Depression Found," "Schizophrenia Linked to Diet," "Intelligence Test Invalid." Such statements often seem less factual and absolute when we read the article, but the headline writer did his or her job if we bought the newspaper (and read the article). Unfortunately, the headline "fact" is often what stays with us (especially if we haven't read the entire article).

We followed our own recommendations recently when looking into a phenomenon called the "Mozart effect." Perhaps you have heard about this widely

Don't confuse bad science with good science.

"Ulrich, that's bad science and you know it!"

publicized effect. In fact, as we write this, we have on our desk a newspaper clipping with a large banner headline: "Classical Music Good for Babies' Brains" (*The New Mexican*, June 27, 1999, p. E–5). Exactly what does Mozart effect refer to? We knew what newspapers and magazine articles had been saying, but we had no idea what was the nature of the research behind the many claims. A typical statement comes from the newspaper clipping. The newspaper reporter says that the Mozart effect "refers to a body of research that suggests certain types of music can heighten brainpower" (p. E–5). The newspaper article describes how mothers are rushing to play classical music to infants in the hope of raising their children's intelligence. In fact, the feature writer reports that more than 1 million new mothers around the country will be given a CD called "Smart Symphonies." The program is being sponsored by the NARAS Foundation, a nonprofit group associated with the National Academy of Recording Arts & Sciences, as well as a company making infant formula (which also will be distributed free to new mothers in the same bag).

That listening to music might raise the intelligence scores of newborns is certainly an interesting proposition. And the idea had a certain salience for one of the authors of your book as his daughter was about to have a child, his first grandchild. Should he start shipping classical music to his daughter in preparation for the birth of her child? If more than a million women are playing CDs to their newborn children, would his grandchild be left out of the explosion in intelligence that will come from this experience?

The newspaper article told us nothing worthwhile about the original research, at least nothing we could use to determine whether it was good research.

Although as psychologists we had heard about the Mozart effect, our information came second-hand and with few details, so we went to the original source. The article that got things rolling was published in 1993 in *Nature,* a respectable journal of general science published in England (so far so good). When we looked at the original article (Rauscher, Shaw, & Ky, 1993), however, we saw that it was not a full-blown article but a short report describing a study with college students. In the experiment a single group of students listened to a 10-minute Mozart piece, sat in silence for 10 minutes, or listened to relaxation instructions for 10 minutes before being asked to perform a spatial reasoning test (that is, it was a repeated measures design). Performance was found to be better after listening to Mozart than after listening to relaxation instructions or sitting in silence. But the researchers also reported that the effect disappeared after a 10- to 15-minute period. We hardly could believe it. More than a million women are being given CDs with the hope of increasing the intelligence of their children based on an effect produced on one specific type of reasoning test with college students and which lasted 15 minutes at most.

To find out more we looked at other research studies investigating the Mozart effect published since this seminal finding (see, for example, Rauscher & Shaw, 1998). We also used the Internet to chase down related stories. Some unsettling facts emerged. First, other investigators have failed to replicate the basic finding with college students using a variety of tasks (e.g., Rauscher & Shaw, 1998; Steele, Bass, & Crook, 1999). Second, the amount of published research done with children has been slight; most has concentrated on college students. Third, major funding for one of the principal investigators comes from grants from the National Association of Music Merchants as well as NARAS (yep, the umbrella group giving away CDs to mothers), and other musical foundations. As previously mentioned, just because sponsors of the research have a reason to gain from a positive outcome of research findings does not mean the sponsored research is biased. But we do see how scientific findings of limited generality might, in the hands of nonscientists (for example, marketing agents and publicists), appear more applicable than they really are, especially when corporations may benefit from these findings.

To the researchers' credit, they caution that "more work is needed before substantial practical applications can be derived" (Rauscher & Shaw, 1998, p. 840). And more research is underway, some of it with children. But who is going to tell the millions of women who are playing Mozart to their children that the practical implications of this small and less than reliable effect produced (when it is found) mainly with college students has yet to be worked out? And, as regards the potential effects on that grandchild of ours, we believe that much more needs to be discovered about the Mozart effect before we spend money on CDs and raise a mother's expectation that intelligence will increase soon after her child listens to classical composers. How about getting a colorful mobile to stimulate visual activity and eye-hand coordination?

By the way, it was a boy!

A STATISTICS

The primary goal of data analysis is to determine whether our observations support a claim about behavior (Abelson, 1995). We have discussed several such claims in this book. For example, researchers could claim that writing about traumatic events in our lives improves our physical health, or that people accused of an act they didn't do will nevertheless falsely confess to it. Whatever the claim, we must examine the data carefully to find out if our claim is supported by the evidence. Data analysis follows three distinct stages: checking the data, summarizing the data, and confirming what the data reveal (see Chapter 6). The goal of this appendix is to explain the rationale for some of the basic statistical techniques that we can use to support a claim about behavior. Specifically, we discuss statistical methods associated with summarizing data (the second stage of data analysis) and with confirming what our data reveal (the third stage). (Thus, we will assume the data have been carefully inspected and "cleaned." See Chapter 6.) Most of these statistical procedures are now done using a computer. Your understanding of the more basic techniques, however, will be enhanced if you are familiar with the actual computational procedures.

SUMMARIZE THE DATA: MEASURES OF CENTRAL TENDENCY, VARIABILITY, AND EFFECT SIZE

Researchers first describe data by asking what values the data tend to "center around"; that is, they calculate measures of **central tendency.** When data are measured on an interval or ratio scale, two common descriptive statistics are the *mean* and *standard deviation.*

The *mean* is the most commonly reported measure of central tendency and is determined by dividing the sum of the scores by the number of scores contributing to that sum. The formula for the mean is

$$\bar{X} = \Sigma X / n \qquad \text{where} \quad X = \text{individual score}$$
$$n = \text{sample size}$$
$$\Sigma = \text{"sum of"}$$

The mean represents the average, or typical, score. The mean of a population is symbolized as μ (Greek letter mu); the mean of a sample is indicated by $\underline{M}$ when reported in text—for example, in a Results section. [The symbol $\bar{X}$ (read "X bar") is typically used in statistical formulas.] The mean should always be reported as a measure of central tendency. If there are extreme scores in the distribution, or the data are skewed, then the median should also be reported as a measure of central tendency. The *median* is the middle point in a distribution; half the scores in a distribution fall above the median and half fall below. The median is calculated by ranking all the scores from lowest to highest and identifying the value that splits the distribution into two halves, each half having the same number of values. In a normal (symmetrical) distribution, the mean and median have the same value. The median is the best measure of central tendency when the distribution includes extreme scores because it is less influenced than is the mean by the extreme scores.

Whenever you report a measure of central tendency, it should always be accompanied by an appropriate measure of dispersion, or **variability.** Measures of central tendency indicate the center of a frequency distribution; measures of variability indicate the breadth, or degree of dispersion of the distribution. The crudest measure of variability is the range. The *range* is determined by subtracting the lowest score in the distribution from the highest score. For example, in a small distribution made up of the scores 1, 3, 5, 7, the range is equal to $7 - 1$, or 6.

The most commonly used measure of dispersion that is reported along with the mean is the standard deviation. The *standard deviation* tells you approximately how far on the average a score is from the mean. It is equal to the square root of the average squared deviation of scores in the distribution about the mean. The standard deviation of a sample is defined as

$$s = \sqrt{\frac{\Sigma (X - \bar{X})^2}{n - 1}} \qquad \text{where} \quad X = \text{individual score}$$
$$\bar{X} = \text{sample mean}$$
$$n = \text{sample size}$$
$$\Sigma = \text{"sum of"}$$

For reasons that need not concern us here, the average of the squared deviations about the sample mean must involve division by $n - 1$ (rather than n) to provide an unbiased estimate of the population standard deviation. The standard deviation of a population is symbolized as σ (Greek letter sigma); the standard deviation of a sample of scores is indicated as SD when appearing in text, but it is often symbolized as s in statistical formulas. (The *variance*, a measure of dispersion used in various inferential statistics, is the square of the standard deviation—that is, s^2.)

Measures of **effect size** indicate the strength of the relationship between the independent and the dependent variables. There are several measures of effect size (Kirk, 1996). We will illustrate one of these measures and how to interpret an effect size for a difference between two means.

One commonly used measure of effect size in experimental research is called Cohen's d, after statistician Jacob Cohen (see Cohen, 1988, for more information about d). It is a ratio that measures the difference between two group means divided by a measure of the variability of scores in the two groups.

$$\text{Cohen's } d = \frac{\overline{X}_1 - \overline{X}_2}{\sigma}$$

The population standard deviation (σ) is obtained by pooling the within-group variability and dividing by the total number (N) of scores in both groups. A formula for the common *population* standard deviation using sample variances is:

$$\sigma = \sqrt{\frac{(n_1 - 1)s_1^2 + (n_2 - 1)s_2^2}{N}}$$

where n_1 = sample size of Group 1
n_2 = sample size of Group 2
$N = n_1 + n_2$
s_1^2 = variance of Group 1
s_2^2 = variance of Group 2

The "size" of the effect of the independent variable (the difference between the two group means) is always expressed in terms of how different the scores are relative to the average variability. If there is a lot of variability in participants' scores, the denominator for d is large. To be able to observe the effect of the independent variable, given this large variability, the difference between two group means must be especially large. When the variability is small (the denominator for d is small), the same difference between means will result in a larger effect size (see Chapter 6).

What can we say about effect sizes? When are they big? little? Fortunately, Cohen (1988) provides some guidelines to help us interpret d ratios. In general, effect sizes for independent variables are classified as small, medium, or large. A medium effect for a two-group experiment is a d of .50, whereas a small and large effect are ds of .20 and .80, respectively.

CONFIRM WHAT THE DATA REVEAL: COMPARING TWO MEANS

When comparing two means, we generally want to know if the difference between the means matters. Is the difference large enough for us to want to pay attention to it? One approach to this question is to consider the effect size for the difference. As you saw, we can use measures of *effect size* to describe whether mean differences can be regarded as small, medium, or large. Another approach, however, makes use of inferential statistics to determine whether group differences are *statistically significant.* Null hypothesis testing is the most common form of inferential statistics used to make these decisions. A third alternative is to use confidence intervals (see Chapter 6) to determine if a difference matters. We will first examine the procedures for null hypothesis testing, then we will outline the steps required for using confidence intervals.

Null Hypothesis Testing

The statistical technique known as **null hypothesis testing** focuses on the nature of the control provided by balancing through random assignment. Remember that random assignment does not *eliminate* the differences among subjects. Random assignment simply *distributes* individual differences across the groups in the experiment. As a consequence, group means may differ just by chance, or due to what statisticians call "error variation." Recall that we assess the effect of our independent variable by looking for differences among the means for the different conditions. However, if the means can differ because of error variation, and not necessarily because of the independent variable, we cannot be sure if the independent variable has had an effect. The general rationale for null hypothesis testing was discussed in Chapter 6, and you will want to review that discussion before continuing.

Two independent groups.   The most common inferential statistic for null hypothesis testing involving two groups is the *t*-test. We can define t for independent groups as the difference between sample means divided by the standard error of the difference between means ($s_{\bar{X}_1 - \bar{X}_2}$):

$$t = \frac{\bar{X}_1 - \bar{X}_2}{s_{\bar{X}_1 - \bar{X}_2}} \quad \text{where } s_{X_1-X_2} = \sqrt{\left[\frac{(n_1 - 1)s_1^2 + (n_2 - 1)s_2^2}{n_1 + n_2 - 2}\right]\left[\frac{1}{n_1} + \frac{1}{n_2}\right]}$$

As you saw in Chapter 6, we begin with the assumption that there is no real difference between the population means (i.e., the null hypothesis); thus, we have only two possible conclusions when we examine the results of our statistical test: We either reject the null hypothesis or we fail to reject the null hypothesis. Outcomes (i.e., observed differences between means) that lead us to reject the null hypothesis are said to be *statistically significant.* A statistically significant outcome indicates that the difference between means we observed in our experiment (assuming the null hypothesis is true) is larger than would be expected if error variation alone (i.e., chance) were responsible for group differences. The probability we choose to indicate an outcome is statistically significant is called the *level of significance*. The level of significance is indicated by the Greek letter alpha (α). Thus, we speak of the .05 level of significance, which we report as $\alpha = .05$.

To determine whether an outcome is statistically significant, we compare the obtained probability value with our level of significance, $\alpha = .05$. If the probability value is less than .05, we reject the null hypothesis. This allows us to state that the observed mean difference is probably not due to error variation—that is, that the independent variable had a reliable effect on the dependent variable. If our obtained probability value is greater than .05, we fail to reject the null hypothesis. This would indicate that the observed difference between means could be likely if we assume error variation is responsible, and we would withhold judgment about the effect of the independent variable (i.e., the results would be inconclusive). Statistical software programs typically provide the actual probability of an obtained t as part of the output, thus circumventing the need to consult a table of t values. In fact, the *Publication Manual of the American Psychological Association* (1994) advises that the exact probability be reported.

Unfortunately, as you saw in Chapter 6, no matter what decision we reach and no matter how carefully we reach it, there is always some chance we are making an error. A *Type I error* occurs when we reject the null hypothesis when it is true. When we make a Type I error, we claim that the independent variable has a reliable effect on behavior, when the "true state of the world" is that the variable does not affect behavior. A *Type II error* is failing to reject the null hypothesis when it is false. When we make a Type II error, we claim that the independent variable does not affect behavior, when the "true state of the world" is that the variable does affect behavior.

A Type II error is apt to result if our experiment was not sensitive or if the statistical test was of low power. The **sensitivity** of an experiment is the likelihood that it will detect an effect of the independent variable if the independent variable does, in fact, have an effect. An experiment is said to have sensitivity; a statistical test is said to have power. The **power** of a statistical test is the probability of correctly rejecting the null hypothesis—that is, detecting the effect of the independent variable when there truly is one. The most important factor affecting the power of a statistical test is the sample size. In general, larger sample sizes make a statistical test more powerful. Using power tables (e.g., Cohen, 1988), researchers can identify the sample size they need to detect an expected effect size (based on previous research) with a certain level of significance (usually $\alpha = .05$) with a desired level of power.

Two Dependent Groups (Repeated Measures).   Thus far we have considered experiments involving two independent groups of subjects. As you are aware, experiments can also be carried out by having each subject participate in each condition of the experiment or by "matching" subjects on a measure related to the dependent variable (e.g., IQ scores, weight, etc.). Such experiments are called dependent groups, matched pairs, within-subjects designs, or repeated measures designs (see Chapter 6). The logic of *null-hypothesis significance testing* (NHST) is the same in a repeated measures design as it is in an independent groups design. However, the *t* test comparing two means takes on a different form in a repeated measures design. The *t* test in this situation is typically called a dependent *t*, direct-difference *t*, or repeated measures (within-subjects) *t*. When each subject is in both conditions of the experiment, *t* is defined as:

$$t = \frac{\overline{D}}{s_{\overline{D}}} \quad \text{where} \quad \overline{D} = \text{mean of difference scores, and}$$
$$s_{\overline{D}} = \text{standard error of difference scores, where}$$

$$s_{\overline{D}} = \frac{s_D}{\sqrt{n}}$$

The numerator of the repeated measures *t* is the mean of the difference scores (called "D bar") and is algebraically equivalent to the difference between the sample means (i.e., $\overline{X}_1 - \overline{X}_2$). Statistical significance is determined by comparing the *p* value for the obtained *t* with the level of significance (e.g., .05). If you do not have the exact *p* value, you can consult a table of critical values of *t* with $df = n - 1$ (see Table A.3). In this case, *n* refers to the number of participants or pairs of scores in the experiment.

Confidence Intervals

A **confidence interval** gives us information about the probable range of values we can expect for a population characteristic, such as the population mean (see also "margin of error" in Chapter 5). We cannot estimate the population value exactly because of sampling error; the best we can do is to estimate a range of probable values. The smaller the range of values expressed in the confidence interval, the better is the estimate of the population value.

In computing a confidence interval, we specify a range of values within which we can have a certain degree of confidence that the population mean is included within the interval. As you may suspect, the larger the interval we specify, the greater our confidence that the mean will be included, but larger intervals give us less specific information about the exact value of the population mean. As a compromise, researchers have agreed that the 95% confidence interval and the 99% confidence interval will be used when an interval estimate of the population mean is desired. The confidence interval is centered around our point estimate of the mean ($\overline{X}$), and the boundaries of the 95% confidence interval can be calculated using the following formulas:

$$\text{Upper limit of 95\% confidence interval} = \overline{X} + [t_{crit})]_{\alpha=.05} [s_{\overline{X}}]$$

$$\text{Lower limit of 95\% confidence interval} = \overline{X} - [t_{crit})]_{\alpha=.05} [s_{\overline{X}}]$$

We have already examined the procedures for computing the sample mean ($\overline{X}$). We turn now to a description of the standard error of the mean ($s_{\overline{X}}$).

In doing inferential statistics, we use the sample mean as a point estimate of the population mean. That is, we use a single value ($\overline{X}$) to estimate (infer) the population mean (μ). It is often helpful to be able to determine how much error there is in estimating μ on the basis of $\overline{X}$. The central limit theorem in mathematics tells us that, if we draw an infinite number of samples of the same size and we compute $\overline{X}$ for each of these samples, the mean of these sample means ($\mu_{\overline{X}}$) will be equal to the population mean (μ), and the standard deviation of the sample means ($\sigma_{\overline{X}}$) will be equal to the population standard deviation (σ) divided by the square root of the sample size ($\sqrt{n}$). The standard deviation of this theoretical sampling distribution of the mean is called the *standard error of the mean*. Typically, we do not know the standard deviation of the population, so we estimate it on the basis of a sample using the formula

$$s_{\overline{X}} = \frac{s}{\sqrt{n}}$$

Small values of $s_{\overline{X}}$ suggest that we have a good estimate of the population mean, and large values of $s_{\overline{X}}$ suggest that we have only a rough estimate of the population mean. The formula for the standard error of the mean indicates that our ability to estimate the population mean on the basis of a sample depends on the size of the sample (large samples lead to better estimates) and on the variability in the population from which the sample was drawn, as estimated by the sample standard deviation (the less variable the scores in a population, the better our estimate of the population mean will be).

The level of significance, alpha (.05), is based on the procedures for inferential statistics tests previously described. In the case of confidence intervals, $\alpha =$ (1 − level of confidence), expressed as a proportion. Thus, for the 95% confidence interval, $\alpha = 1 - .95 = .05$ and, for the 99% confidence interval, $\alpha = 1 - .99 = .01$. The t statistic included in the equation (t_{crit}) is defined by the number of degrees of freedom ($n - 1$), and the t is determined by looking it up in Table A.3.

How do we interpret confidence intervals for a single mean? A 95% confidence interval allows us to say with .95 confidence that this interval has "captured" the population mean.

The procedure and logic for constructing *confidence intervals for a difference between means* is similar to that for setting confidence intervals for a single mean. Because our interest is now in the difference between the population means (i.e., "the effect" of our independent variable), we substitute $\overline{X}_1 - \overline{X}_2$ for $\overline{X}$ and use the standard error of the mean difference rather than the standard error of the mean. The formula for the standard error of the mean difference is

$$s_{\overline{X}_1 - \overline{X}_2} = \sqrt{\left[\frac{(n_1 - 1)s_1^2 + (n_2 - 1)s_2^2}{n_1 + n_2 - 2}\right]\left[\frac{1}{n_1} + \frac{1}{n_2}\right]}$$

The .95 confidence interval for the difference between two population means is defined as

$$CI(.95) = (\bar{X}_1 - \bar{X}_2) \pm (t_{crit})(s_{\bar{X}_1 - \bar{X}_2})$$

where t_{crit} is found in Table A.3
with $df = (n_1 + n_2 - 2)$ at alpha $= .05$

How do we interpret a 95% confidence interval for the difference between two means? We can say that the odds are 95/100 that the obtained confidence interval contains the true population mean difference or effect size. When establishing confidence intervals for a mean difference (as in this example), if the interval includes zero then we cannot say if an effect is present. When a "zero" mean difference is a probable value for our effect, we must accept the possibility that an effect is not present. Confidence intervals give us a probable range for our effect. If zero is among the probable values, then we should admit our uncertainty regarding the presence of an effect (e.g., Abelson, 1997).

Confidence intervals, too, can be constructed for the population mean difference in a repeated measures design involving two conditions. As with the t test, however, the underlying calculations change for this situation. The .95 confidence interval for the difference between two means in a repeated measures design can be defined as

$$CI(.95) = (\bar{X}_1 - \bar{X}_2) + (t_{crit})(s_{\bar{D}})$$

where t_{crit} is found in Table A.3
with $df = n - 1$ at alpha $= .05$

Recommendations for Comparing Two Means

You can use the following recommendations when evaluating the data from a study looking at the difference between two means. First, keep in mind the final goal of data analysis: to make a case based on observations for a claim about behavior. In order to make the best case possible, you will want to explore various alternatives for data analysis. Don't fall into the trap of thinking that there is only one way to provide evidence for a claim about behavior. When there is a choice (and there almost always is), as recommended by the APA's Task Force on Statistical Inference (Wilkinson et al., 1999), *use the simplest possible analysis.* Second, when using null hypothesis testing, be sure to understand its limitations and what the outcome of such tests allows you to say. In many research situations, and in nearly all applied situations, effect size information is an important, even necessary, complement to null hypothesis testing. Finally, consider reporting confidence intervals for effect sizes.

DATA ANALYSIS INVOLVING MORE THAN TWO GROUPS

Thus far we have discussed the stages of data analysis in the context of a two-group experiment. We can think of a two-group experiment as representing two levels of one independent variable. What happens when we have more than two levels (groups) or, as is often the case in psychology, more than two independent variables? The most frequently used statistical procedure for analyzing results of psychology experiments involving more than two groups is the analysis of variance (ANOVA).

ANOVA is a special case of confirmatory data analysis examining statistical significance under the null hypothesis. In the remainder of this appendix, we will examine data analysis and interpretation of experiments using ANOVA. It is assumed that these analyses will be done using a computer; thus, emphasis will be on interpreting the output obtained from a typical statistical computer package. It should be noted that we consider only cases when all groups (or cells) in the experiment are the same size. We will also assume that the data in our illustrations have already passed through the first, exploratory stage of data analysis when data are inspected carefully, any anomalies are noted, and editing and cleaning have taken place as necessary. Prior to examining the ANOVA results, we summarize the results using major descriptive statistics. *Appropriate summaries of the data should be performed first before doing any further analyses.*

We will consider two research designs: single-factor analysis of independent groups designs and two-factor analysis for independent groups designs (complex designs).

Single-Factor Analysis of Variance for Independent Groups Designs

The single-factor analysis of variance for independent groups designs is used to analyze the results of random groups and natural groups designs involving one independent variable with two or more levels. (The assumptions underlying the test strictly apply only to the random groups design.)

The data in the following table represent the number of words correctly recalled (out of a possible 20) on a retention test in an experiment investigating memory-training techniques. Five participants were randomly assigned to each of four groups (defined by the method of study that individuals were instructed to use to learn the words in preparation for the memory test). The control method involved no specific instructions, but in the three experimental groups the participants were instructed to study by making up a story using the to-be-remembered words (story method), to use rhymes to remember the words (rhyme method), or to use visual imagery (imagery method). The independent variable being manipulated was instruction, symbolized by the letter A. The levels of this independent variable can be differentiated by using the symbols, a_1, a_2, a_3, and a_4 for the four respective groups. The number of participants within each group is referred to as n—in this case, $n = 5$. The total number of individuals in the experiment is symbolized as N; in this case, $N = 20$. Finally, the number of groups is referred to as a—in this case, $a = 4$.

An important step in the analysis of any experiment is to set up a data matrix like the table on the next page. The number of correct responses is listed for each person in each of the four groups, with each participant identified with a unique subject number. In order to understand the results of an experiment, it is essential to summarize the data prior to examining the outcome of the ANOVA. Below the data matrix, the mean, standard deviation, and range (minimum and maximum scores) are provided for each group.

Before examining the statistical significance of an F ratio, try to get an impression of what the summary statistics are telling you. Look to see if there is a

	Instruction (A)						
Control		Story		Imagery		Rhymes	
Subject	(a_1)	Subject	(a_2)	Subject	(a_3)	Subject	(a_4)
1	12	6	15	11	16	16	14
2	10	7	14	12	16	17	14
3	9	8	13	13	13	18	15
4	11	9	12	14	12	19	12
5	8	10	12	15	15	20	12
Mean	10.0		13.2		14.4		13.4
Standard deviation	1.6		1.3		1.8		1.3
Range	8–12		12–15		12–16		12–15

visible effect of the independent variable; that is, see if there is substantial variation among the means. (Later, we will examine how to calculate an effect size in this situation.) The range, or difference between the minimum and maximum values, is useful in identifying floor and ceiling effects.

Our examination of the summary statistics reveals that there appears to be systematic variation among the means; the largest difference is seen between the control group (10.0) and the imagery group (14.4). All the experimental means are larger than the control mean. You will want to refer to the means as you "read" the ANOVA summary table. Note that the range is similar for all the groups; the standard deviations, too, are fairly similar. This indicates the variation within each group is about the same. Moreover, an inspection of the highest scores in each group shows that ceiling effects are not a problem in this data set (as total possible was 20). With these facts in mind, we can proceed to an examination of the results of our F test.

The ANOVA Summary Table. The ANOVA summary table for the omnibus F test for the independent groups design previously described is reported in the following table (see next page). Remember that there were four groups of size $n = 5$ and, thus, overall $N = 20$.

The probability for the F ratio in this experiment of .002 appears in the far right column of the summary table. Because this probability is less than the conventional level of significance (.05), we can conclude that this F ratio is statistically significant. The results of null hypothesis testing using ANOVA would be summarized in a research report as follows:

$$\underline{F}(3, 16) = 7.82, \underline{p} = .002$$

At this point, we know that the omnibus F test was statistically significant. In other words, these results, assuming the null hypothesis is true, are unlikely in

Analysis of Variance Summary Table

Source	Sum-of-Squares	df	Mean-Square	F ratio	p
Group (between)	54.550	3	18.183	7.821	0.002
Error	37.220	16	2.325		

this situation. Thus, we conclude that there was an overall effect of the independent variable of type of memory training in the experiment. This tells us that something happened in the experiment, but it does not specify exactly what happened. It does not, for instance, tell us the degree of relationship between the independent and dependent variable; thus, we should consider calculating an effect size for our independent variable.

Calculating Effect Size for Independent Groups Designs.   The psychology literature contains many different measures of effect size, which depend on the particular research design, test statistic, and other peculiarities of the research situation (e.g., Cohen, 1992; Cooper & Hedges, 1994; Kirk, 1996; Rosenthal & Rosnow, 1991). Actually, knowing one measure of effect size, we usually can translate it to another, comparable measure without too much difficulty (see, for example, Rosenthal & Rosnow, 1991).

An important class of effect size measures that applies to experiments with more than two groups is based on measures of "strength of association" (Kirk, 1996). What these measures have in common is that they allow estimates of the proportion of total variance in the dependent variable scores accounted for by the effect of the independent variable. A popular strength of association measure is "eta squared." It is easily calculated based on information found in the ANOVA summary table for the omnibus F test (although many computer programs automatically provide eta squared as a measure of effect size). In this case, eta squared is defined as the Sum of Squares between-groups divided by the total Sum of Squares (SS between + SS error). In our example,

$$\text{eta squared} = \frac{\text{SS between}}{\text{SS total}} = \frac{54.55}{54.55 + 37.22} = .594$$

We can thus conclude that memory training accounted for .594 of the total variance in the dependent variable. Although eta squared as a measure of effect size is the proportion of variance accounted for by the independent variable, it is much more meaningful when there are only two conditions. When calculated with more than two conditions, its meaning is rather nonspecific (see Rosenthal & Rosnow, 1991). Like the omnibus F test, it does not tell us exactly what we want to know. Whenever possible, we will want to specify more clearly the source of an overall effect.

Eta, or the square root of eta squared, may be interpreted similarly to the correlation coefficient r, and effect sizes may be assessed using the guidelines for r. A small, medium, and large effect size based on r corresponds to .10, .30, and .50 (Cohen, 1988).

Two-Factor Analysis of Variance for Independent Groups Designs

The two-factor analysis of variance for independent groups designs is used for the analysis of experiments in which each of two independent variables was manipulated at two or more levels. The logic of complex designs with two independent variables and the conceptual basis for the analysis of these experiments were discussed in some detail in Chapter 7 (see the example research study by Bazzini & Shaffer, 1999). Also in Chapter 7, we discussed how to "read" an ANOVA summary table for a complex design involving independent groups. It may be helpful to review this discussion in Chapter 7 before moving ahead. We will move directly to the calculation of effect sizes using information in an ANOVA table obtained from a sample computer output.

An analysis of variance summary table for an experiment with two independent variables (hand and delay) is shown below. The hand variable had two levels, and the delay variable had three levels (i.e., a 2 × 3 design). There were five participants randomly assigned to the six conditions of the experiment represented by the factorial combination of the two variables (i.e., $N = 30$).

As you can see, each of the variables was statistically significant as a main effect; the interaction between the two variables was also statistically significant. The obtained probabilities (.001) were all less than the conventional level of significance of .05. Again, refer to Chapter 7 for information about the interpretation of both main effects and interactions in a complex design.

A common measure of effect size for a complex design using ANOVA is eta squared, or proportion of variance accounted for, which was discussed in the context of single-factor designs. In calculating eta squared, it is recommended that we focus only on the effect of interest (see Rosenthal & Rosnow, 1991). Specifically, eta squared can be defined as

$$\text{eta squared} = \frac{SS_{\text{effect of interest}}}{SS_{\text{effect of interest}} + SS_{\text{error}}}$$

(see Rosenthal & Rosnow, 1991, p. 352).

Analysis of Variance Summary Table

Source	Sum-of-Squares	df	Mean-Square	F Ratio	p
Hand	149.633	1	149.633	61.075	0.001
Delay	93.800	2	46.900	19.143	0.001
Hand × Delay	60.467	2	30.233	12.340	0.001
Error	58.800	24	2.450		

Thus, eta squared is obtained for each of the three effects in our sample experiment by the following:

Factor A (hand):

$$\text{eta squared} = \frac{149.633}{149.633 + 58.80} = .718$$

Factor B (delay):

$$\text{eta squared} = \frac{93.80}{93.80 + 58.80} = .615$$

Interaction (A × B):

$$\text{eta squared} = \frac{60.467}{60.467 + 58.80} = .507$$

STATISTICAL TABLES

On the following pages are statistical tables to assist you in your research:

Table A.1 Table of Random Numbers: Use this table to randomly assign participants to conditions or to randomize orders of conditions in a repeated measures design (e.g., block randomization).

For Tables A.2 - A.4, first choose your level of significance (alpha = .05 or alpha = .01). Then calculate the appropriate statistic for your data set. Using the *df* for your statistic and your chosen level of significance, identify the critical value of your statistic in the corresponding table. If your observed value (the one you calculated), is greater than the critical value, your result is statistically significant (i.e., reject the null hypothesis).

Table A.2 Values of *r* at the .05 and .01 Levels of Significance: Use this table to identify whether an observed correlation coefficient in your data set is statistically significant (*df* = N - 2).

Table A.3 Selected Values from the *t* Distribution: Use this table to identify whether an observed value of *t* in your data set is statistically significant, and for computing confidence intervals. For an independent groups *t* test, *df* = n1 + n2 - 2.

Table A.4 Critical Values of the *F* Distribution: Use this table to identify whether an observed value for *F* in your data set is statistically significant.

Table A.1 Table of Random Numbers*

Col. Line	(1)	(2)	(3)	(4)	(5)	(6)	(7)	(8)	(9)	(10)	(11)	(12)	(13)	(14)
1	10480	15011	01536	02011	81647	91646	69179	14194	62590	36207	20969	99570	91291	90700
2	22368	46573	25595	85393	30995	89198	27982	53402	93965	34095	52666	19174	39615	99505
3	24130	48360	22527	97265	76393	64809	15179	24830	49340	32081	30680	19655	63348	58629
4	42167	93093	06243	61680	07856	16376	39440	53537	71341	57004	00849	74917	97758	16379
5	37570	39975	81837	16656	06121	91782	60468	81305	49684	60672	14110	06927	01263	54613
6	77921	06907	11008	42751	27756	53498	18602	70659	90655	15053	21916	81825	44394	42880
7	99562	72905	56420	69994	98872	31016	71194	18738	44013	48840	63213	21069	10634	12952
8	96301	91977	65463	07972	18876	20922	94595	56869	69014	60045	18425	84903	42508	32307
9	89579	14342	63661	10281	17453	18103	57740	84378	25331	12566	58678	44947	05585	56941
10	85475	36857	53342	53988	53060	59533	38867	62300	08158	17983	16439	11458	18593	64952
11	28918	68578	88231	33276	70997	79936	56865	05859	90106	31595	01547	85590	91610	78188
12	63553	40961	48235	03427	49626	69445	18663	72695	52180	20847	12234	90511	33703	90322
13	09429	93969	52636	92737	88974	33488	36320	17617	30015	08272	84115	27156	30613	74952
14	10365	61129	87529	85689	48237	52267	67689	93394	01511	26358	85104	20285	29975	89868
15	07119	97336	71048	08178	77233	13916	47564	81506	97735	85977	29372	74461	28551	90707
16	51085	12765	51821	51259	77452	16308	60756	92144	49442	53900	70960	63990	75601	40719
17	02368	21382	52404	60268	89368	19885	55322	44819	01188	65255	64835	44919	05944	55157
18	01011	54092	33362	94904	31273	04146	18594	29852	71585	85030	51132	01915	92747	64951
19	52162	53916	46369	58586	23216	14513	83149	98736	23495	64350	94738	17752	35156	35749
20	07056	97628	33787	09998	42698	06691	76988	13602	51851	46104	88916	19509	25625	58104
21	48663	91245	85828	14346	09172	30168	90229	04734	59193	22178	30421	61666	99904	32812
22	54164	58492	22421	74103	47070	25306	76468	26384	58151	06646	21524	15227	96909	44592
23	32639	32363	05597	24200	13363	38005	94342	28728	35806	06912	17012	64161	18296	22851
24	29334	27001	87637	87308	58731	00256	45834	15298	46557	41135	10367	07684	36188	18510
25	02488	33062	28834	07351	19731	92420	60952	61280	50001	67658	32586	86679	50720	94953
26	81525	72295	04839	96423	24878	82651	66566	14778	76797	14780	13300	87074	79666	95725
27	29676	20591	68086	26432	46901	20849	89768	81536	86645	12659	92259	57102	80428	25280
28	00742	57392	39064	66432	84673	40027	32832	61362	98947	96067	64760	64584	96096	98253
29	05366	04213	25669	26422	44407	44048	37937	63904	45766	66134	75470	66520	34693	90449
30	91921	26418	64117	94305	26766	25940	39972	22209	71500	64568	91402	42416	07844	69618

continued

Table A.1 Table of Random Numbers* (concluded)

Col. Line	(1)	(2)	(3)	(4)	(5)	(6)	(7)	(8)	(9)	(10)	(11)	(12)	(13)	(14)
31	00582	04711	87917	77341	42206	35126	74087	99547	81817	42607	43808	76655	62028	76630
32	00725	69884	62797	56170	86324	88072	76222	36086	84637	93161	76038	65855	77919	88006
33	69011	65795	95876	55293	18988	27354	26575	08625	40801	59920	29841	80150	12777	48501
34	25976	57948	29888	88604	67917	48708	18912	82271	65424	69774	33611	54262	85963	03547
35	09763	83473	93577	12908	30883	18317	28290	35797	05998	41688	34952	37888	38917	88050
36	91567	42595	27958	30134	04024	86385	29880	99730	55536	84855	29080	09250	79656	73211
37	17955	56349	90999	49127	20044	59931	06115	20542	18059	02008	73708	83517	36103	42791
38	46503	18584	18845	49618	02304	51038	20655	58727	28168	15475	56942	53389	20562	87338
39	92157	89634	94824	78171	84610	82834	09922	25417	44137	48413	25555	21246	35509	20468
40	14577	62765	35605	81263	39667	47358	56873	56307	61607	49518	89696	20103	77490	18062
41	98427	07523	33362	64270	01638	92477	66969	98420	04880	45585	46565	04102	46880	45709
42	34914	63976	88720	82765	34476	17032	87589	40836	32427	70002	70663	88863	77775	69348
43	70060	28277	39475	46473	23219	53416	94970	25832	69975	94884	19661	72828	00102	66794
44	53976	54914	06990	67245	68350	82948	11398	42878	80287	88267	47363	46634	06541	97809
45	76072	29515	40980	07391	58745	25774	22987	80059	39911	96189	41151	14222	60697	58583
46	90725	52210	83974	29992	65831	38857	50490	83765	55657	14361	31720	57375	56228	41546
47	64364	67412	33339	31926	14883	24413	59744	92351	97473	89286	35931	04110	23726	51900
48	08962	00358	31662	25388	61642	34072	81249	35648	56891	69352	48373	45578	78547	81788
49	95012	68379	93526	70765	10592	04542	76463	54328	02349	17247	28865	14777	62730	92277
50	15664	10493	20492	38391	91132	21999	59516	81652	27195	48223	46751	22923	32261	85653

*Source: *Table of 105,000 Random Decimal Digits*, Statement no. 4914, File no. 261-A-1, Interstate Commerce Commission, Washington, D.C. May 1949.

Table A.2 Values of *r* at the .05 and .01 Levels of Significance*

df	.05	.01	df	.05	.01	df	.05	.01
1	.997	1.000	16	.468	.590	35	.325	.418
2	.950	.990	17	.456	.575	40	.304	.393
3	.878	.959	18	.444	.561	45	.288	.372
4	.811	.917	19	.433	.549	50	.273	.354
5	.754	.874	20	.423	.537	60	.250	.325
6	.707	.834	21	.413	.526	70	.232	.302
7	.666	.798	22	.404	.515	80	.217	.283
8	.632	.765	23	.396	.505	90	.205	.267
9	.602	.735	24	.388	.496	100	.195	.254
10	.576	.708	25	.381	.487			
11	.553	.684	26	.374	.478			
12	.532	.661	27	.367	.470			
13	.514	.641	28	.361	.463			
14	.497	.623	29	.355	.456			
15	.482	.606	30	.349	.449			

*Adapted from Table VII of Fisher and Yates, *Statistical Tables for Biological, Agricultural, and Medical Research,* 6th ed., 1974. Published by Oliver and Boyd, Limited, Publishers, Edinburgh, by permission of the authors and publishers. Published by Longman Group Ltd., London.

Table A.3 Selected Values from the *t* Distribution*

Instructions for use: To find a value of *t*, locate the row in the left-hand column of the table corresponding to the number of degrees of freedom (*df*) associated with the standard error of the mean, and select the value of *t* listed for your choice of α. The value given in the column labeled $\alpha = .05$ is used in the calculation of the 95% confidence interval, and the value given in the column labeled $\alpha = .01$ is used to calculate the 99% confidence interval.

df	$\alpha = .05$	$\alpha = .01$	*df*	$\alpha = .05$	$\alpha = .01$
1	12.71	63.66	18	2.10	2.88
2	4.30	9.92	19	2.09	2.86
3	3.18	5.84	20	2.09	2.84
4	2.78	4.60	21	2.08	2.83
5	2.57	4.03	22	2.07	2.82
6	2.45	3.71	23	2.07	2.81
7	2.36	3.50	24	2.06	2.80
8	2.31	3.36	25	2.06	2.79
9	2.26	3.25	26	2.06	2.78
10	2.23	3.17	27	2.05	2.77
11	2.20	3.11	28	2.05	2.76
12	2.18	3.06	29	2.04	2.76
13	2.16	3.01	30	2.04	2.75
14	2.14	2.98	40	2.02	2.70
15	2.13	2.95	60	2.00	2.66
16	2.12	2.92	120	1.98	2.62
17	2.11	2.90	Infinity	1.96	2.58

*This table is adapted from Table 12 in *Biometrika tables for statisticians*, vol. 1 (3d ed.), New York: Cambridge University Press, 1970, edited by E. S. Pearson and H. O. Hartley, by permission of the *Biometrika* Trustees.

Table A.4 Critical Values of the F Distribution*

Instructions for use: To find a value of F, locate the cell in the table formed by the intersection of the row containing the degrees of freedom associated with the denominator of the F-ratio and the column containing the degrees of freedom associated with the numerator of the F-ratio. The numbers listed in boldface type are the critical values of F at $\alpha = .05$; the numbers listed in Roman type are the critical values of F at $\alpha = .01$. As an example, suppose we have adopted the 5% level of significance and wish to evaluate the significance of an F with $df_{num} = 2$ and $df_{denom} = 12$. From the table we find that the critical value of $F(2, 12) = 3.89$ at $\alpha = .05$. If the obtained value of F equals or exceeds this critical value, we will reject the null hypothesis; if the obtained value of F is smaller than this critical value, we will not reject the null hypothesis.

df denom	|	Degrees of freedom for numerator																
	1	2	3	4	5	6	7	8	9	10	12	15	20	24	30	40	60	Infinity
1	**161**	**200**	**216**	**225**	**230**	**234**	**237**	**239**	**241**	**242**	**244**	**246**	**248**	**249**	**250**	**251**	**252**	**254**
	4052	4999	5403	5624	5764	5859	5923	5981	6022	6056	6106	6157	6209	6325	6261	6287	6313	6366
2	**18.5**	**19.0**	**19.2**	**19.2**	**19.3**	**19.3**	**19.4**	**19.4**	**19.4**	**19.4**	**19.4**	**19.4**	**19.4**	**19.4**	**19.5**	**19.5**	**19.5**	**19.5**
	98.5	99.0	99.2	99.2	99.3	99.3	99.4	99.4	99.4	99.4	99.4	99.4	99.4	99.5	99.5	99.5	99.5	99.5
3	**10.1**	**9.55**	**9.28**	**9.12**	**9.01**	**8.94**	**8.89**	**8.85**	**8.81**	**8.79**	**8.74**	**8.70**	**8.66**	**8.64**	**8.62**	**8.59**	**8.57**	**8.53**
	34.1	30.8	29.5	28.7	28.2	27.9	27.7	27.5	27.4	27.2	27.0	26.9	26.7	26.6	26.5	26.4	26.3	26.1
4	**7.71**	**6.94**	**6.59**	**6.39**	**6.26**	**6.16**	**6.09**	**6.04**	**6.00**	**5.96**	**5.91**	**5.86**	**5.80**	**5.77**	**5.75**	**5.72**	**5.69**	**5.63**
	21.2	18.0	16.7	16.0	15.5	15.2	15.0	14.8	14.7	14.6	14.4	14.2	14.0	13.9	13.8	13.8	13.6	13.5
5	**6.61**	**5.79**	**5.41**	**5.19**	**5.05**	**4.95**	**4.88**	**4.82**	**4.77**	**4.74**	**4.68**	**4.62**	**4.56**	**4.53**	**4.50**	**4.46**	**4.43**	**4.26**
	16.3	13.3	12.1	11.4	11.0	10.7	10.5	10.3	10.2	10.0	9.89	9.72	9.55	9.47	9.38	9.29	9.20	9.02
6	**5.99**	**5.14**	**4.76**	**4.53**	**4.39**	**4.28**	**4.21**	**4.15**	**4.10**	**4.06**	**4.00**	**3.94**	**3.87**	**3.84**	**3.81**	**3.77**	**3.74**	**3.67**
	13.8	10.9	9.78	9.15	8.75	8.47	8.26	8.10	7.98	7.87	7.72	7.56	7.40	7.31	7.23	7.14	7.06	6.88
7	**5.59**	**4.74**	**4.35**	**4.12**	**3.97**	**3.87**	**3.79**	**3.73**	**3.68**	**3.64**	**3.57**	**3.51**	**3.44**	**3.41**	**3.38**	**3.34**	**3.30**	**3.23**
	12.2	9.55	8.45	7.85	7.46	7.19	6.99	6.84	6.72	6.62	6.47	6.31	6.16	6.07	5.99	5.91	5.82	5.65
8	**5.32**	**4.46**	**4.07**	**3.84**	**3.69**	**3.58**	**3.50**	**3.44**	**3.39**	**3.35**	**3.28**	**3.22**	**3.15**	**3.12**	**3.08**	**3.04**	**3.01**	**2.93**
	11.3	8.65	7.59	7.01	6.63	6.37	6.18	6.03	5.91	5.81	5.67	5.52	5.36	5.28	5.20	5.12	5.03	4.86
9	**5.12**	**4.26**	**3.86**	**3.63**	**3.48**	**3.37**	**3.29**	**3.23**	**3.18**	**3.14**	**3.07**	**3.01**	**2.94**	**2.90**	**2.86**	**2.83**	**2.79**	**2.71**
	10.6	8.02	6.99	6.42	6.06	5.80	5.61	5.47	5.35	5.26	5.11	4.96	4.81	4.73	4.65	4.57	4.48	4.31
10	**4.96**	**4.10**	**3.71**	**3.48**	**3.33**	**3.22**	**3.14**	**3.07**	**3.02**	**2.98**	**2.91**	**2.85**	**2.77**	**2.74**	**2.70**	**2.66**	**2.62**	**2.54**
	10.0	7.56	6.55	5.99	5.64	5.39	5.20	5.06	4.94	4.85	4.71	4.56	4.41	4.33	4.25	4.17	4.08	3.91
11	**4.84**	**3.98**	**3.59**	**3.36**	**3.20**	**3.09**	**3.01**	**2.95**	**2.90**	**2.85**	**2.79**	**2.72**	**2.65**	**2.61**	**2.57**	**2.53**	**2.49**	**2.40**
	9.65	7.21	6.22	5.67	5.32	5.07	4.89	4.74	4.63	4.54	4.40	4.25	4.10	4.02	3.94	3.86	3.78	3.60
12	**4.75**	**3.89**	**3.49**	**3.26**	**3.11**	**3.00**	**2.91**	**2.85**	**2.80**	**2.75**	**2.69**	**2.62**	**2.54**	**2.51**	**2.47**	**2.43**	**2.38**	**2.30**
	9.33	6.93	5.95	5.41	5.06	4.82	4.64	4.50	4.39	4.30	4.16	4.01	3.86	3.78	3.70	3.62	3.54	3.36
13	**4.67**	**3.81**	**3.41**	**3.18**	**3.03**	**2.92**	**2.83**	**2.77**	**2.71**	**2.67**	**2.60**	**2.53**	**2.46**	**2.42**	**2.38**	**2.34**	**2.30**	**2.21**
	9.07	6.70	5.74	5.21	4.86	4.62	4.44	4.30	4.19	4.10	3.96	3.82	3.66	3.59	3.51	3.43	3.34	3.17

Degrees of freedom for denominator

continued

Table A.4   Critical Values of the F Distribution* (concluded)

Degrees of freedom for numerator

Denominator df	1	2	3	4	5	6	7	8	9	10	12	15	20	24	30	40	60	Infinity
14	**4.60**	**3.74**	**3.34**	**3.11**	**2.96**	**2.85**	**2.76**	**2.70**	**2.65**	**2.60**	**2.53**	**2.46**	**2.39**	**2.35**	**2.31**	**2.27**	**2.22**	**2.13**
	8.86	6.51	5.56	5.04	4.69	4.46	4.28	4.14	4.03	3.94	3.80	3.66	3.51	3.43	3.35	3.27	3.18	3.00
15	**4.54**	**3.68**	**3.29**	**3.06**	**2.90**	**2.79**	**2.71**	**2.64**	**2.59**	**2.54**	**2.48**	**2.40**	**2.33**	**2.29**	**2.25**	**2.20**	**2.16**	**2.07**
	8.68	6.36	5.42	4.89	4.56	4.32	4.14	4.00	3.89	3.80	3.67	3.52	3.37	3.29	3.21	3.13	3.05	2.87
16	**4.49**	**3.63**	**3.24**	**3.01**	**2.85**	**2.74**	**2.66**	**2.59**	**2.54**	**2.49**	**2.42**	**2.35**	**2.28**	**2.24**	**2.19**	**2.15**	**2.11**	**2.01**
	8.53	6.23	5.29	4.77	4.44	4.20	4.03	3.89	3.78	3.69	3.55	3.41	3.26	3.18	3.10	3.02	2.93	2.75
17	**4.45**	**3.59**	**3.20**	**2.96**	**2.81**	**2.70**	**2.61**	**2.55**	**2.49**	**2.45**	**2.38**	**2.31**	**2.23**	**2.19**	**2.15**	**2.10**	**2.06**	**1.96**
	8.40	6.11	5.18	4.67	4.34	4.10	3.93	3.79	3.68	3.59	3.46	3.31	3.16	3.08	3.00	2.92	2.83	2.65
18	**4.41**	**3.55**	**3.16**	**2.93**	**2.77**	**2.66**	**2.58**	**2.51**	**2.46**	**2.41**	**2.34**	**2.27**	**2.19**	**2.15**	**2.11**	**2.06**	**2.02**	**1.92**
	8.29	6.01	5.09	4.58	4.25	4.01	3.84	3.71	3.60	3.51	3.37	3.23	3.08	3.00	2.92	2.84	2.75	2.57
19	**4.38**	**3.52**	**3.13**	**2.90**	**2.74**	**2.63**	**2.54**	**2.48**	**2.42**	**2.38**	**2.31**	**2.23**	**2.16**	**2.11**	**2.07**	**2.03**	**1.98**	**1.88**
	8.18	5.93	5.01	4.50	4.17	3.94	3.77	3.63	3.52	3.43	3.30	3.15	3.00	2.92	2.84	2.76	2.67	2.49
20	**4.35**	**3.49**	**3.10**	**2.87**	**2.71**	**2.60**	**2.51**	**2.45**	**2.39**	**2.35**	**2.28**	**2.20**	**2.12**	**2.08**	**2.04**	**1.99**	**1.95**	**1.84**
	8.10	5.85	4.94	4.43	4.10	3.87	3.70	3.56	3.46	3.37	3.23	3.09	2.94	2.86	2.78	2.69	2.61	2.42
22	**4.30**	**3.44**	**3.05**	**2.82**	**2.66**	**2.55**	**2.46**	**2.40**	**2.34**	**2.30**	**2.23**	**2.15**	**2.07**	**2.03**	**1.98**	**1.94**	**1.89**	**1.78**
	7.95	5.72	4.82	4.31	3.99	3.76	3.59	3.45	3.35	3.26	3.12	2.98	2.83	2.75	2.67	2.58	2.50	2.31
24	**4.26**	**3.40**	**3.01**	**2.78**	**2.62**	**2.51**	**2.42**	**2.36**	**2.30**	**2.25**	**2.18**	**2.11**	**2.03**	**1.98**	**1.94**	**1.89**	**1.84**	**1.73**
	7.82	5.61	4.72	4.22	3.90	3.67	3.50	3.36	3.26	3.17	3.03	2.89	2.74	2.66	2.58	2.49	2.40	2.21
26	**4.23**	**3.37**	**2.98**	**2.74**	**2.59**	**2.47**	**2.39**	**2.32**	**2.27**	**2.22**	**2.15**	**2.07**	**1.99**	**1.95**	**1.90**	**1.85**	**1.80**	**1.69**
	7.72	5.53	4.64	4.14	3.82	3.59	3.42	3.29	3.18	3.09	2.96	2.81	2.66	2.58	2.50	2.42	2.33	2.13
28	**4.20**	**3.34**	**2.95**	**2.71**	**2.56**	**2.45**	**2.36**	**2.29**	**2.24**	**2.19**	**2.12**	**2.04**	**1.96**	**1.91**	**1.87**	**1.82**	**1.77**	**1.65**
	7.64	5.45	4.57	4.07	3.75	3.53	3.36	3.23	3.12	3.03	2.90	2.75	2.60	2.52	2.44	2.35	2.26	2.06
30	**4.17**	**3.32**	**2.92**	**2.69**	**2.53**	**2.42**	**2.33**	**2.27**	**2.21**	**2.16**	**2.09**	**2.01**	**1.93**	**1.89**	**1.84**	**1.79**	**1.74**	**1.62**
	7.56	5.39	4.51	4.02	3.70	3.47	3.30	3.17	3.07	2.98	2.84	2.70	2.55	2.47	2.39	2.30	2.21	2.01
40	**4.08**	**3.23**	**2.84**	**2.61**	**2.45**	**2.34**	**2.25**	**2.18**	**2.12**	**2.08**	**2.00**	**1.92**	**1.84**	**1.79**	**1.74**	**1.69**	**1.64**	**1.51**
	7.31	5.18	4.31	3.83	3.51	3.29	3.12	2.99	2.89	2.80	2.66	2.52	2.37	2.29	2.20	2.11	2.02	1.80
60	**4.00**	**3.15**	**2.76**	**2.53**	**2.37**	**2.25**	**2.17**	**2.10**	**2.04**	**1.99**	**1.92**	**1.84**	**1.75**	**1.7**	**1.65**	**1.59**	**1.53**	**1.39**
	7.06	4.98	4.13	3.65	3.34	3.12	2.95	2.82	2.72	2.63	2.50	2.35	2.20	2.12	2.03	1.94	1.84	1.60
120	**3.92**	**3.07**	**2.68**	**2.45**	**2.29**	**2.17**	**2.09**	**2.02**	**1.96**	**1.91**	**1.83**	**1.75**	**1.66**	**1.61**	**1.55**	**1.50**	**1.43**	**1.25**
	6.85	4.79	3.95	3.48	3.17	2.96	2.79	2.66	2.56	2.47	2.34	2.19	2.03	1.95	1.86	1.76	1.66	1.38
Infinity	**3.84**	**3.00**	**2.60**	**2.37**	**2.21**	**2.10**	**2.01**	**1.94**	**1.88**	**1.83**	**1.75**	**1.67**	**1.57**	**1.52**	**1.46**	**1.39**	**1.32**	**1.00**
	6.83	4.61	3.78	3.32	3.02	2.80	2.64	2.51	2.41	2.32	2.18	2.04	1.88	1.79	1.70	1.59	1.47	1.00

Degrees of freedom for denominator

*This table is abridged from Table 18 in *Biometrika tables for statisticians*, vol. 1 (3d ed.), New York: Cambridge University Press, 1970, edited by E. S. Pearson and H. O. Hartley, by permission of the *Biometrika* Trustees.

B COMMUNICATION IN PSYCHOLOGY

Scientific research is a public activity. A clever hypothesis, an elegant research design, meticulous data-collection procedures, reliable results, and an insightful theoretical interpretation of the findings are not useful to the scientific community unless they are made public. As one writer suggests emphatically, "Until its results have gone through the painful process of publication, preferably in a refereed journal of high standards, scientific research is just play. Publication is an indispensable part of science" (Bartholemew, 1982, p. 233).

What does publishing journal articles have to do with you? If you attend graduate school in psychology, you will likely be involved in publishing your research and writing research proposals. Even if you do not pursue a professional career in psychology, the principles involved in writing a good research report are applicable to a wide variety of employment situations. For example, a memo to your department manager describing the outcome of a recent sale may have much the same content and format as a short journal article. Of more immediate concern, you may have to write a research report in your research methods course. This appendix will help you write it well.

The primary source for scientific writing in psychology is the fourth edition of the *Publication Manual* of the American Psychological Association (1994). Editors and authors use this manual to ensure a consistent style across the many journals in psychology. It includes chapters on the content and organization of a manuscript; the expression of ideas; APA editorial style; manuscript preparation; and manuscript acceptance and production. The publication manual also includes information about ethical issues in scientific writing (see our discussion of this in Chapter 3) and instructions for submitting manuscripts in electronic form.

This appendix draws heavily on the *Publication Manual* (1994),[1] but it is not intended as a substitute for the *Publication Manual*. If advanced study in psychology is in your future, you should add the *Publication Manual* to your personal library. Another resource available from APA that you might find helpful is Gelfand, H., & Walker, C. J. (1994). *Mastering APA style: Student's workbook and training guide.* (You can order both from the American Psychological Association, 750 First Street, N.E., Washington, DC 20002-4242.) If you have reached that exciting point in the research process when you are preparing a manuscript for submission to a scientific journal, you should read a brief article written by Robert J. Sternberg (1992). Sternberg's article was published in the monthly newsletter of the American Psychological Society, the *APS Observer.* Its title says it all: "How to Win Acceptances by Psychology Journals: 21 Tips for Better Writing."

TIPS FOR WRITING EFFECTIVELY

- *Know your audience.* If you assume that your readers know more than they actually do, you will leave them confused. If you underestimate your readers, you risk boring them with unnecessary details. Either risk increases the likelihood that what you have written will not be read. But if you must err, it is better to underestimate your readers. This might result in your including more detail than necessary, but it will be easier for your instructor to help you learn to "edit out" the nonessential material than to "edit in" essential material that you have omitted. Whatever audience you choose, make the selection before you begin to write, and keep that audience in mind every step of the way.
- *Identify your purpose.* The principal purposes of a research report are to describe and to convince. You want first to describe what you have done and what you have found and, second, to convince the reader that your interpretation of these results is an appropriate one.
- *Write clearly.* The *Publication Manual* (1994) outlines the road to clarity:

  > You can achieve clear communication, which is the prime objective of scientific reporting, by presenting ideas in an orderly manner and by expressing yourself smoothly and precisely. By developing ideas clearly and logically and leading readers smoothly from thought to thought, you make the task of reading an agreeable one. (p. 23)

- *Be concise.* Writing concisely can best be achieved by saying only what needs to be said. Short words and short sentences are easier for readers to understand. Wordiness can best be eliminated by editing your own writing across successive drafts and asking others to edit drafts of your paper.

- *Be precise.* Precision in using language means choosing the right word for what you want to say. The *Publication Manual* (1994) contains sage advice regarding precision of expression:

  > Make certain that every word means exactly what you intend it to mean. Sooner or later most authors discover a discrepancy between their accepted meaning of a term and its dictionary definition. In informal style, for example, *feel* broadly substitutes for *think* or *believe,* but in scientific style such latitude is not acceptable. (p. 28)

- *Follow grammatical rules.* Adherence to grammatical rules is absolutely necessary for good writing because failure to do so distracts the reader and can introduce ambiguity. It also makes you, the writer, look bad and, as a consequence, can weaken your credibility with your reader (and your argument).

- *Write fairly:* You should strive to choose words and use constructions that acknowledge people fairly and objectively. The American Psychological Association has developed guidelines (*Publication Manual,* 1994) regarding bias in the language authors use:

  > As a publisher, APA accepts authors' word choices unless those choices are inaccurate, unclear, or ungrammatical. As an organization, APA is committed both to science and to the fair treatment of individuals and groups, and policy requires authors of APA publications to avoid perpetuating demeaning attitudes and biased assumptions about people in their writing. Constructions that might imply bias against persons on the basis of gender, sexual orientation, racial or ethnic group, disability, or age should be avoided. Scientific writing should be free of implied or irrelevant evaluation of the group or groups being studied. (p. 46)

- *Write an interesting report.* The *Publication Manual* provides useful advice about the overall tone of scientific writing:

  > Although scientific writing differs in form from literary writing, it need not and should not lack style or be dull. In describing your research, present the ideas and findings directly, but aim for an interesting and compelling manner that reflects your involvement with the problem. (p. 6)

One way to try to achieve an appropriate tone in writing your research reports is to strive to tell a good story about your research. Good research makes for good stories, and well-told stories are good for advancing research.

TIPS FOR WRITING THE SECTIONS OF A RESEARCH REPORT

A research report consists of the following sections:

Title page	Results	Author Note
Abstract	Discussion	Footnotes
Introduction	References	Tables
Method	Appendixes	Figures

In this appendix we will briefly discuss each of the sections; more complete descriptions are provided in the *Publication Manual* (1994). We will focus on the content of the four major sections of a research report: Introduction, Method, Results, and Discussion. Along with the brief descriptions of each section we include tips to help you write each major section. We have also included a sample paper at the end of the appendix that illustrates the APA format of a research report. The sample paper includes notes to highlight important aspects of the final typed draft of a research report.

Title Page

The first page of a research report is the title page. It indicates what the research is about (i.e., the title), who did the research (i.e., the authors), where the research was done (i.e., authors' affiliation), and a brief heading to indicate to readers what the article is about (the "running head"). The APA *Publication Manual* describes what an effective title should be: "A title should summarize the main idea of the paper simply and, if possible, with style. It should be a concise statement of the main topic and should identify the actual variables or theoretical issues under investigation and the relation between them" (p. 7).

TIPS FOR WRITING A TITLE: A common format for the title of a research report is "[The Dependent Variable(s)] as a Function of [the Independent Variable(s)]." For example, "Anagram Solution Time as a Function of Problem Difficulty" is a good title. The title must not only be informative but also brief; the recommended length is 10 to 12 words. Most important of all, be sure your title describes as specifically as possible the content of your research.

Abstract

The second page of the report, the Abstract, appears under that single word, which is typed as a centered heading (see sample paper). The abstract is a one-paragraph summary of the content and purpose of the research report. The abstract should be 100 to 120 words long (about 10 double-spaced typewritten lines). Abstracts are used by information services to index and retrieve articles. The abstract should identify four elements of your research: (a) the problem under investigation; (b) the experimental method, including the tests and apparatus that were used, data-gathering procedures, and pertinent characteristics of participants; (c) the findings; and (d) the conclusions and implications of the findings. The abstract, in other words, should highlight the critical points made in the introduction, method, results, and discussion sections of the research report. A well-written abstract can have a big influence on whether the rest of a journal article will be read.

TIPS FOR WRITING AN ABSTRACT: Writing a good abstract is challenging. The best way to meet this challenge is to write it last. By writing the abstract after you have written the rest of the report, you will be able to *abstract*, or paraphrase, your own words more easily.

Introduction

The title of your report appears at the top of the third page as a centered heading, and then the first paragraph of the introduction section begins immediately (see sample paper). The introduction serves three primary objectives: (1) to introduce the problem being studied; (2) to summarize the relevant background literature that led you to the present research problem and approach; and (3) to state the purpose and rationale of the present study with a logical development of the predictions or hypotheses guiding the research. The order in which these objectives are met in any given report may vary, but the order in which they are described here is the most common one. All three of these objectives share a purpose: to give the reader a firm sense of what you are doing and why you are doing it.

The second objective, that of summarizing related research studies, is not to provide an exhaustive literature review. Instead, care should be taken to select the most pertinent studies to develop the rationale of your experiment. In summarizing these selected studies, you should emphasize whatever details of the earlier work will best help the reader understand what you have done and why. You must acknowledge the contributions of other researchers to your understanding of the problem. Of course, if you quote directly from another person's work, you must use quotation marks (see Chapter 3 for advice about citing others' work).

TIPS FOR WRITING THE INTRODUCTION: In order to write an effective introduction, be sure you can answer the following four questions *before* beginning to write:

"• What is the point of the study?
• How do the hypothesis and the experimental design relate to the problem?
• What are the theoretical implications of the study, and how does the study relate to previous work in the area?
• What are the theoretical propositions tested, and how were they derived?" (American Psychological Association, 1994, p. 11)

Method

The Method section follows right after the introduction. The Method section is usually identified by a centered heading ("Method"), with a double space separating it from the preceding and following text (see sample paper). The introduction provides a broad outline of the research you have done; the Method fills in the details. The three most common subsections of the Method section are "Participants," "Materials" (Apparatus), and "Procedure." Each of these subsections is introduced by an underlined subheading that usually begins at the left margin (see sample paper). The *Publication Manual* presents a straightforward description of the goals of the Method section:

> The Method section describes in detail how the study was conducted. Such a description enables the reader to evaluate the appropriateness of your methods and the reliability and the validity of your results. It also permits experienced investigators to replicate the study if they so desire. (p. 12)

TIPS FOR WRITING THE METHOD SECTION: The key to writing a good Method section is organization. Fortunately, the structure of this section is so consistent across research reports that a few basic subsections provide the pattern of organization you need for most research reports. Before describing the content of these subsections, however, we must address the question that students writing their first research report ask most frequently: "How much detail should I include?" The quality of your paper will be adversely affected if you include either too much or too little detail. The rule stated in the *Publication Manual* seems simple enough: "Include in these subsections only the information essential to comprehend and replicate the study" (p. 13). As previously mentioned, the best way to learn how to follow this rule is to read the Method sections of journal articles and to write your own research reports. Be sure to get feedback from your instructor concerning the appropriate level of detail for your research reports.

In the first subsection of the Method section, *Participants,* you should report the total number of participants, as well as major demographic characteristics such as sex and age. You should identify the number of participants assigned to experimental conditions or natural groups. If individuals dropped out of the experiment, you should identify the number and explain why they left the experiment.

In the *Materials* subsection you should describe any instruments, questionnaires, or measures that played a central role in the research. Your description should include the general characteristics of the materials, as well as any specific features that will help the reader understand participants' responses in your study. If you use materials developed by another investigator, be sure to cite the work of that investigator.

The *Procedure* subsection allows you to describe participants' experiences in your study from the beginning to the end of the session. Before writing the *Procedure,* you should prepare a checklist that identifies all the important features of your procedure. The *Publication Manual* recommends that the Method section, particularly the procedure subsection, "should tell the reader what you did and how you did it in sufficient detail so that a reader could reasonably replicate your study" (pp. 14–15).

Results

The centered heading "Results" introduces this third major section of the body of a research report (see sample paper). You should use your Results section to answer the questions you raised in your introduction. However, the guiding principle in the Results section is to "stick to the facts." The *Publication Manual* provides an excellent overview of the objectives of a Results section:

> The Results section summarizes the data collected and the statistical treatment of them. First, briefly state the main results or findings. Discussing the implications of the results is not appropriate here. Mention all relevant results, including those that run counter to the hypothesis. Do not include individual raw scores or raw data, with the exception, for example, of single-case designs or illustrative samples. (p. 15)

We have provided more detailed tips for writing the Results section because students frequently have less experience with writing about quantitative information.

TIPS FOR WRITING A RESULTS SECTION: We suggest you follow these steps when writing your Results section:

- *Step 1.* A Results section paragraph begins by stating the purpose of the analysis. The reason(s) for doing an analysis should be stated succinctly; often, no more than a phrase is necessary. There are two reasons for making the purpose for each analysis explicit. It helps your reader follow the logic of your analysis plan. And, perhaps more important, it ensures that you will never try to report an analysis whose purpose you do not understand.
- *Step 2.* The second step in writing a paragraph in the Results section is to identify the descriptive statistic used to summarize the results for a given dependent variable. For example, you could use the mean number of words recalled to summarize the results in each condition of a memory experiment.
- *Step 3.* The third step is to present a summary of your descriptive statistic across conditions. Whenever possible, measures of central tendency should be accompanied by corresponding measures of variability. If there are only two or three conditions in your experiment, this summary can be presented in the text itself. For instance, you could summarize the results of a two-group study by saying, "The mean number of correct responses for the experimental group was 10.5 ($\underline{SD}$ = 2.1), whereas that for the control group was 5.2 ($\underline{SD}$ = 1.8)." More commonly, however, you will have more data to summarize, and you will need to present your findings in either a table or a figure (graph).
- *Step 4.* You should not expect a table or figure to be self-sufficient. You can help direct your readers' attention to the highlights of the data in the table or figure, focusing especially on the aspects of the results that are consistent with (or discrepant from) the hypotheses you proposed in

the introduction. Usually, the same data are not reported in both a table and a figure. Tables provide a more precise description of the results, but figures make it easier to see trends or patterns in the data.

- *Step 5.* The fifth step in writing a paragraph of the Results section is to present the results that confirm what the data reveal. In this step, you report confidence intervals, tests of statistical significance, and measures of effect size. For instance, you might write "The overall effect of the drug variable was statistically significant, $\underline{F}(3, 64) = 7.15$, $\underline{p} = .005$. The effect size (eta) was .45."

- *Step 6.* The final step in writing a paragraph in the Results section is to state a brief conclusion. For example, if the mean number correct in the experimental group is 10, that in the control group is 5, and this difference is statistically significant, an appropriate concluding statement is "The control group did worse than the experimental group." In this simple example the conclusion may seem obvious, but appropriate concluding statements are essential in more complex analyses.

Discussion

The fourth major section of your report, the discussion, begins with a centered heading (see sample paper). The Discussion section, unlike the Results section, contains more than just the facts. In the words of the *Publication Manual,*

> After presenting the results, you are in a position to evaluate and interpret their implications, especially with respect to your original hypothesis. You are free to examine, interpret, and qualify the results, as well as to draw inferences from them. (p. 18)

The discussion is written in a tone and style consistent with the introduction. Be careful, however, to keep the statements you make in the discussion consistent with the data reported in the results. For instance, you should not report that one group did better than another if the comparison between these groups was not statistically significant—at least not without some qualification of what you mean by "better."

The discussion includes a description of how your findings relate to the relevant literature, most of which you cited in the introduction. If your results are not consistent with your original hypotheses, you should suggest an explanation for these discrepancies. If the reasons for your results are unclear, you should not hesitate to say so. It sometimes is necessary and helpful to include a paragraph describing limitations or problems in the research. As noted in the *Publication Manual,* however, "do not dwell compulsively on every flaw" (p. 19). If appropriate, conclude the discussion by proposing additional research that should be done on the problem you are investigating. The reader will not learn much if you say, "It would be interesting to do this experiment with younger participants." The reader can learn much more if you explain how you would expect the results to differ with younger participants and what you would conclude if the results of the proposed experiment were to turn out as expected. Remember, the watchword in proposing new research is to be *specific.*

TIPS FOR WRITING THE DISCUSSION SECTION: Again, the *Publication Manual* gives good advice for authors beginning to write their Discussion section:

"In general, be guided by the following questions:

- What have I contributed here?
- How has my study helped to resolve the original problem?
- What conclusions and theoretical implications can I draw from my study?

The responses to these questions are the core of your contribution, and readers have a right to clear, unambiguous, and direct answers" (p. 19).

References

The References section, which appears with a centered heading on a separate page after the discussion (see sample paper), includes the complete citation for each reference. "Just as data in the paper support interpretations and conclusions, so reference citations document statements made about the literature" (American Psychological Association, 1994, p. 20).

You can save your readers much aggravation if you follow the reference formats closely and proofread your reference list carefully. The references are listed in alphabetical order by the last name of the first author of each article. If there are two articles by the same author(s), they are arranged in ascending order by year of publication.

Appendixes

Appendixes are rare in published research articles, but they are a bit more common in students' research reports. (Instructors may require you to submit an appendix including your raw data, the worksheets for a statistical analysis, or the computer printout of the analyses.) The appendix can also be used to provide a verbatim copy of the instructions to participants or a list of the specific materials used in the experiment. An appendix is identified with a letter; reference to the appendix in the text is made using this letter. For instance, you might write, "The complete instructions can be found in Appendix A."

Author Note

The author note appears on a separate page under the centered heading "Author Note" immediately after the References section (or after the Appendixes, if there are any). The *Publication Manual* provides a concise description of the contents of an author note:

The author note (a) identifies the departmental affiliation of each author, (b) identifies sources of financial support, (c) provides a forum for authors to acknowledge colleagues' professional contributions to the study and personal assistance, and (d) tells whom the interested reader may contact for further information concerning the article. (p. 21)

Footnotes

Because they are not used for citing references, footnotes are rare in research reports. When footnotes appear in the text, they are of two types: content footnotes and copyright permission footnotes. Content footnotes supplement or expand on the text material. Copyright permission footnotes acknowledge the source of extensive quotations. In the typed manuscript, footnotes appear on a separate page following the References section under the centered heading "Footnotes."

Tables

Tables are an effective and efficient way to present data such as means and standard deviations. Each table appears on a separate page at the end of your paper (not within the text of the paper) after the References and Footnotes pages. You should refer to the table when you discuss the data (e.g., in the Results section). Each table should have a brief title that identifies the variables displayed in the table, and columns and rows should be labeled clearly. All of the data entries should be reported to the same number of decimal places, and the values should be aligned with the corresponding row and column headings. A table appears in the sample APA-format manuscript.

Figures

Figures, like tables, are a concise way to present data. Typically, the levels of the independent variable are plotted on the horizontal axis (x-axis) and the dependent variable is plotted on the vertical axis (y-axis). When there is a second independent variable in a complex design, the levels of the second independent variable are plotted within the figure as lines (in a line graph) or bars (in a bar graph), and are labeled in a figure legend (see Chapter 7 for an example). As with tables, you should refer your reader to the figure when you report the data it displays. Figures appear last in the paper, after any tables, each on a separate page. If figures are included, they should be preceded by a "Figure Captions" page ("Figure Caption" if there's one figure). The words "Figure Captions" appear centered at the top of the page and each figure title is identified in a list, for example:

Figure Captions

<u>Figure 1.</u> Mean recall as a function of drug dosage level (100, 200, 300 mg).
<u>Figure 2.</u> Mean number of intrusions following manipulation of neutral, surprise, or fear emotional responses.

*First few words of title
appear before page number.* ⟶ Taking a Research   1

Running head: RESEARCH METHODS AND REAL-LIFE EVENTS

*Number pages
consecutively,
beginning with
title page.*

Type at left margin.

Taking a Research Methods Course Improves Real-Life Reasoning

Scott W. VanderStoep and John J. Shaughnessy

Hope College

*Use upper and lower case for
title, name, and affiliation
(centered).*

*Note:
    Use one-inch margins at top,
bottom, right, and left of all pages.
Use left justification only.*

*No paragraph
indentation*

Center, do not underline

Taking a Research   2

Abstract

We examined the extent to which students who take a research methods course improve their reasoning about real-life events. If social science majors improve their methodological and statistical reasoning over four years of college, a logical source of this improvement in psychology would be the research methods course. We tested students in research methods and in developmental psychology courses on methodological and statistical reasoning at the beginning and the end of the term. As expected, reasoning scores of research methods students improved more than did scores of developmental psychology students. These results have implications for teaching because they support our intuitive notions that what we are teaching has real-life value.

Note:
    *Abstract should be a single paragraph of
about 120 words.*
    *Doublespace between all lines of the
manuscript. Do not use italic or bold fonts,
and use one font size throughout
manuscript.*

Title appears centered on page 3, with first
letter of major words in caps.

Taking a Research   3

Taking a Research Methods Course Improves Real-Life Reasoning

Teachers get excited when students recognize the relevance of
what they are taught to something outside the classroom. We are
pleased when students tell us that what they learned in our class
helped them with some other aspect of their lives or that our class
taught them to think like a psychologist. Likewise, we are
disappointed when students simply memorize factual information
without reflecting on its relevance or when they fail to see even the
most obvious examples of the applicability of course material to new
situations.

What students take away from psychology courses will depend
on the course. In a developmental psychology course, for example,
students may reflect on their own childhood and how it has made
them who they are, they may see how the course material can make
them better parents, or they may learn how to deal more effectively
with aging parents and grandparents. Each content course in
psychology has such real-life applications.

Leave one
space at
the end
of all
sentences.

Identify all
authors
(surnames
only) the
first time
you cite a
source.

What do students take away from a research methods course? We
hope they learn how to conduct psychological research, including the
mechanics of experimental design, survey sampling, and data analysis.
Beyond learning how to conduct research, however, learning about
research methods has the potential for teaching students real-life
thinking and reasoning skills that may be useful in a variety of settings.

The ability to reason methodologically and statistically is a
domain-general cognitive activity that students can transfer to a variety
of contexts (Nisbett, Fong, Lehman, & Cheng, 1987). Furthermore,
instruction has been shown to improve students' methodological and
statistical reasoning. Specifically, undergraduates who majored in social

Note: Use past tense to
describe the study.

science disciplines showed greater improvements in methodological and statistical reasoning than either natural science majors or humanities majors (Lehman & Nisbett, 1990). We expected, at least among psychology courses, that taking a research methods course would explain a large part of the change in methodological and statistical reasoning. Thus, we tested whether taking a research methods course would improve reasoning more than another undergraduate course such as developmental psychology.

Use ampersand to indicate "and" for references within parentheses.

Method

Center, no underline, only the first letter in caps.

Flush with left margin, underline, only first letter in caps.

Participants

Participants were students enrolled in two research methods sections and two developmental psychology sections at a four-year liberal arts college. The research methods sections were taught by different instructors; the developmental psychology sections were taught by a third instructor. The second author was the instructor for one of the research methods courses. Thirty-one students from the research methods classes and 32 students from the developmental psychology classes took both the pretest and the posttest. Most were traditional-age college students. A majority of students were female (78%), although no gender differences were found in reasoning scores (see Results). The mean ACT composite score of incoming students at this institution is 24, and the mean high school GPA is 3.4.

Use words to express numbers less than 10.

Always use words to express numbers that begin a sentence.

Materials

Use numbers to express values 10 and above.

Each form of the instrument for measuring methodological and statistical reasoning contained seven items. Three items involved statistical reasoning and four items involved methodological reasoning. Two forms were used and were counterbalanced across pretest and posttest. Some of the items were modified versions of those used previously by Lehman and Nisbett (1990); others were created for

Year of publication appears in parentheses after surname of authors.

Taking a Research   5

this study. The statistical reasoning questions tested whether students could recognize examples of regression to the mean and the law of large numbers when applied to everyday events. The methodological reasoning items tested whether students recognized concepts such as a spurious causal relationship and selection bias. All of the items were phrased in everyday language with no reference to methodological or statistical concepts. The scenarios were followed by four or five alternatives that might explain the event. Although all responses were plausible explanations, we agreed that one response best illustrated methodological and statistical reasoning. Participants' scores could range from 0 to 7 based on how many correct answers they selected. An example question illustrating a spurious causal relationship is:

Suppose it were discovered that those who majored in math, engineering, or computer science scored higher on tests measuring "problem-solving" ability at the end of four years of college than did those students who did not major in these fields. How would you interpret this information?

a. Physical science training has positive effects that improve complex reasoning ability.

b. Math, engineering, and computer science majors have more class assignments that require students to use complex reasoning.

c. It may be that the physical science majors differ on many other things besides problem-solving ability and they would have scored higher at the beginning of their freshman year as well.

d. It is likely that physical science students will score lower on tests of <u>verbal</u> ability.

Answer 'C' demonstrates that the relationship between selection of major and future problem-solving skill may not be causal, based only on the evidence provided (i.e., no pretest scores).

Note:
Method, Results, and Discussion sections do
not begin on new page (unless coincidentally).

Taking a Research   6

<u>Procedure</u>

     We administered the instrument to students in their classrooms on the second day of the semester and again near the end of the semester. Students were told that the stories were similar to events they might read about in a newspaper or encounter in everyday conversation.

Results ⟵ *Center, no underline.*

     Pretest and posttest means were calculated for the number of correct responses on the seven methodological and statistical reasoning items for the two courses. There were no gender differences, $\underline{t}(61) = 1.01$, $\underline{p} = .275$, and no between-instructor differences for the Research Methods professors, $\underline{t}(29) = 1.10$, $\underline{p} = .28$, in methodological and statistical reasoning.

Degrees of freedom for statistical tests are reported in parentheses (with no space after statistical term).

     The means and standard deviations for the number of correct responses on the seven methodological and statistical reasoning items for the two courses are presented in Table 1. The increase from pretest to posttest was greater for the research methods students than for the developmental psychology students, $\underline{F}(1, 61) = 13.10$, $\underline{p} = .002$. The effect size (eta) for this interaction was .45.

Underline all statistical terms.

Note use of spaces and punctuation when typing statistics.

     We also found that the number of psychology courses students had taken was a significant predictor of posttest methodological and statistical reasoning scores. Further analyses were done to assess the relative contribution of the research methods course while accounting for the contribution of the number of courses taken. The results of these analyses showed that there is an effect of taking a research methods course on students' reasoning beyond that accounted for by the number of psychology courses the students have taken.

Center, no underline. ⟶ Discussion

     Our study extends work by Lehman and Nisbett (1990) on the effects of undergraduate education on student reasoning. Whereas

Year of publication appears in parentheses even when reference has appeared previously in manuscript.

Taking a Research   7

Lehman and Nisbett found long-term effects of certain courses, we found more specifically that a course in methodology can be important in cultivating students' ability to think critically about real-life events.

General reasoning skills are important, especially when information is modified and updated very rapidly. For example, a student taking a social psychology course in 1996 will be learning very different material than a student who took the course in 1970. We do not know what tomorrow's domain-specific knowledge will be, or whether what we are teaching today will still be relevant in the future. However, if we can teach students to develop general thinking skills, then the importance and relevance of our courses will be greater (see also Nisbett et al., 1987). If psychology majors can be taught general skills that they can apply to novel domains, we can better ensure the relevance of what we teach. Students taking research methods classes may not remember the precise definition of a confounding variable, or how exactly to design a randomized blocks experiment. However, our results suggest that they may leave with some general skills that they can use while watching the evening news, shopping for automobiles, voting, or deciding whether or not to adopt a new weight-loss technique which they have seen advertised.

As psychology instructors, we have intuitive notions about the usefulness of the skills we teach our students. We talk confidently about the benefits of an undergraduate major in psychology and how "thinking like a psychologist" helps students in many areas of life. Our results suggest that there is value in learning to think like a psychologist. There is more to real-life thinking than is represented by our small set of items, but we are pleased that our intuitions held up to empirical scrutiny.

Use "et al." following surname of first author for work with three or more authors. Note: First citation to this work lists all authors (see p. 3).

Note:
References section begins on a new page immediately after the Discussion section.

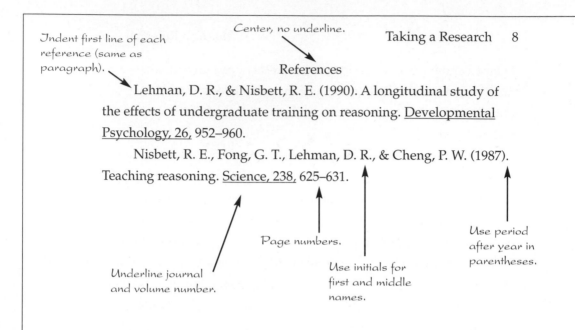

Indent first line of each reference (same as paragraph).

Center, no underline.

Taking a Research   8

References

Lehman, D. R., & Nisbett, R. E. (1990). A longitudinal study of the effects of undergraduate training on reasoning. <u>Developmental Psychology, 26,</u> 952–960.

Nisbett, R. E., Fong, G. T., Lehman, D. R., & Cheng, P. W. (1987). Teaching reasoning. <u>Science, 238,</u> 625–631.

Underline journal and volume number.

Page numbers.

Use initials for first and middle names.

Use period after year in parentheses.

Note:
    List references in alphabetical order using first author's surname. Double-space references, no extra space between references.

Center, no underline.

↓

Taking a Research   9

Author Note

Scott VanderStoep, Department of Psychology; John Shaughnessy, Department of Psychology.

We thank Jim Motiff and Jane Dickie for the use of their classroom time. This sample paper is a modified version of a published article of the same title by VanderStoep, S. W., & Shaughnessy, J. J. (1997). <u>Teaching of Psychology, 24,</u> 122–124.

Send correspondence concerning this article to Scott VanderStoep, Department of Psychology, Hope College, P.O. Box 9000, Holland, MI 49422-9000 (email: <u>vanderstoep@hope.edu</u>).

Note:
First paragraph provides authors' department affiliation. Second paragraph includes acknowledgment of people who assisted with the research. Last paragraph specifies author's address for correspondence.

Table 1

Mean Pretest and Posttest Reasoning Scores for Developmental
Psychology and Research Methods Students

	Course	
Time of Test	Developmental	Research Methods
Pretest	2.38 (1.29)	3.00 (1.69)
Posttest	2.84 (1.59)	4.97 (1.49)

Note. Standard deviations are in parentheses.

C

SELF-TESTS

Chapter 1
Introduction: The Science of Psychology

Matching
Identify which description best corresponds to each of the following terms.

Terms

1. _____ scientific method
2. _____ empirical approach
3. _____ basic research
4. _____ applied research
5. _____ multimethod approach

Descriptions

    A. A type of research that is conducted in order to change people's lives for the better

    B. An approach to gaining knowledge that relies on direct observation and experimentation to answer questions

    C. A method that has been emphasized for over 100 years as the basis of investigation in psychology

    D. An approach to research that searches for answers using various research methodologies

    E. A type of research that is conducted primarily to understand behavior and mental processes

Completion
Complete each statement by providing the appropriate term.

1. Scientists gain a clearer picture of the factors that produce a phenomenon by exercising _____ over the conditions under which they make observations.
2. A _____ measure is one that measures what it claims to measure; it is a "truthful" measure.
3. A _____ measure is one that provides consistent measurements.
4. A _____ exists when two measures of the same people, events, or things vary together.
5. A statement about the cause of an event or a behavior is referred to as a(n) _____ _____.

Multiple Choice
Choose the one best answer for each question.

1. When scientists report their findings they strive to describe
   a. only what they have observed.
   b. what they have observed along with their personal interpretations.
   c. only their personal interpretations.
   d. only the aspects of what they have observed that differ from what they expected to observe.
2. What characteristic distinguishes scientific hypotheses from casual, every-day hypotheses?
   a. intuitive appeal
   b. circularity
   c. testability
   d. certainty
3. Which of the following characterizes the majority of the research conducted in psychology?
   a. qualitative research using the idiographic approach
   b. qualitative research using the nomothetic approach
   c. quantitative research using the idiographic approach
   d. quantitative research using the nomothetic approach
4. Which of the following statements best describes the relationship between correlation and causation?
   a. Correlation is unrelated to causation.
   b. Correlation directly implies causation.
   c. Correlation does not imply causation.
   d. Correlation and causation are synonymous.
5. Which is the primary goal of research that psychologists strive to achieve when they conduct controlled experiments?
   a. prediction
   b. understanding
   c. description
   d. covariation

Chapter 2
The Research Process

Matching
Identify which description best corresponds to each of the following terms.

Terms

1. _____ PsycLIT/PsychInfo
2. _____ rule of parsimony
3. _____ observational/correlational research designs
4. _____ single-case designs
5. _____ American Psychological Association

Descriptions

A. Research designs used when the researchers seek to describe or predict an aspect of behavior
B. Research designs used when the researchers seek to describe, predict, understand, or treat the behavior and mental processes of one individual
C. An important criterion used by researchers in evaluating theories based on the simplicity of the explanation provided by the theory
D. CD-ROM and online versions of *Psychological Abstracts*, published summaries of research reports taken from more than 1,000 national and international periodicals
E. Researchers report their research at annual conferences and publish their research in journals sponsored by professional organizations such as this one.

Completion
Complete each statement by providing the appropriate term.

1. _____ is a potential source of bias that arises when we attempt to understand the behavior of individuals in a different culture through the framework or views of *our own* culture.
2. A logically organized set of statements that defines events (concepts), describes relationships among these events, and explains the occurrence of these events is called a scientific _____.
3. In order to test psychological theories, researchers must develop testable _____ that represent simpler and more tentative explanations for behavior.
4. A(n) _____ definition defines a concept solely in terms of the methods that are used to produce and measure it.

Multiple Choice

Choose the one best answer for each question.

1. Which of the following statements is *false* regarding searching the psychological literature before beginning a research project?
   a. The process of conducting a literature search should be discouraging for a researcher who finds that other researchers have investigated the same or similar ideas.
   b. The process of conducting a literature search can provide a wealth of ideas for research projects.
   c. The process of conducting a literature search is much less tedious than it was 10 years ago.
   d. The process of conducting a literature search reminds researchers that science is a cumulative endeavor, with current research building on previous research.

2. An experimental design should be used when the researcher seeks to answer a question that deals with
   a. describing or predicting an aspect of behavior.
   b. identifying the causes of a relationship between variables.
   c. examining the correlation between two or more individual differences variables.
   d. describing, predicting, understanding, or treating the behavior of one individual.

3. Which research design should researchers use if they are seeking to examine the causal effect of an independent variable on a dependent variable but they cannot control other important variables in the research?
   a. single-case design
   b. experimental design
   c. quasi-experimental design
   d. observational/correlational design

4. Which of the following does a researcher need to know in order to conduct statistical analyses using computer software?
   a. good knowledge of research design
   b. good knowledge of statistics
   c. familiarity with the requirements and capabilities of the statistical software package
   d. all of the above

5. The primary basis on which journal editors decide whether to publish reports they receive for possible publication in a professional journal is the
   a. amount of experience the author of the report has in the research area.
   b. complexity of the reported research.
   c. comments made by experts in the field (peer review).
   d. institution with which the author of the report is affiliated.

Chapter 3
Ethical Issues in Psychological Research

Matching
Identify which description best corresponds to each of the following terms.

Terms

1. _____ minimal risk
2. _____ informed consent
3. _____ privacy
4. _____ deception

Descriptions

    A. Researchers must obtain this in written form when participants are exposed to more than minimal risk.

    B. When the harm or discomfort participants may experience in the research *is not greater* than what they may experience in their daily life

    C. Refers to the rights of individuals to decide how information about them is communicated to others

    D. An ethical issue that arises when researchers withhold information from participants or when participants are intentionally misinformed about an aspect of the research

Completion
Complete each statement by providing the appropriate term.

1. Institutions such as colleges and hospitals are required by law to form committees to review research sponsored by the institution before the research can begin. The committees that protect the rights and welfare of human participants are called _____ _____ _____.

2. Researchers and members of ethical review committees rely on a subjective evaluation of the negative and positive consequences of conducting the proposed research for both individuals and society. The name given to this decision rule is the _____ _____.

3. Researchers use _____ at the end of a research session to educate participants about the research and to leave the participants with positive feelings about their participation.

4. Presenting substantial portions of another person's written work as your own is called _____.

Multiple Choice

Choose the one best answer for each question.

1. When should researchers consult with the proper authorities about the appropriate procedures for institutional review of their research project?
   a. before submitting the research for publication
   b. before beginning the research project
   c. before testing the last participant in the research project
   d. before analyzing the data from the research project

2. Researchers can avoid the potential of social injury or risk for the participants in their research project if the researchers
   a. ensure the internal validity of their study.
   b. obtain informed consent from each participant.
   c. protect the confidentiality of participants' responses.
   d. avoid using deception in their research.

3. Which of the following is *not* one of the major dimensions that researchers need to consider when deciding what information is private?
   a. the sensitivity of the information that the researcher is seeking
   b. the amount of information that the researcher is seeking
   c. the setting in which the researcher is seeking the information
   d. the manner in which the information will be disseminated to others

4. Under what condition is it always unethical to deceive research participants?
   a. when deceiving participants to get them to participate in research in which they would not normally take part or in research that involves serious risk
   b. when withholding information might lead participants to act according to the instructions provided by the experimenter
   c. when concealing the true nature of the experiment might lead participants to behave as they normally would
   d. when deceiving participants places them at minimal risk by participating in the experiment

5. Animal review boards (IACUCs) are responsible for ensuring the welfare and humane treatment of animals used in research. Which of the following is *not* one of the issues that animal review boards decide?
   a. adequacy of procedures for controlling pain
   b. adequacy of the training of personnel who will be doing the testing and care of the animals
   c. adequacy of the experimental design for gaining important new information
   d. adequacy of the budget for carrying out the proposed research

Chapter 4
Observational Research

Matching
Identify which description best corresponds to each of the following terms.

Terms

1. _____ situation sampling
2. _____ participant observation
3. _____ quantitative data analysis
4. _____ interobserver reliability
5. _____ demand characteristics

Descriptions

A. Research participants may try to use these cues in the research situation to guess what behaviors are expected or to guide their behavior.
B. A method of research that is frequently used by anthropologists who seek to understand the culture and behavior of groups by living and working with members of the group
C. The goal of this approach is to provide a numerical summary of research findings; frequently, descriptive statistics are calculated as a basis of the numerical summary.
D. Researchers use this technique when they make their observations in many different circumstances, locations, and conditions.
E. A measure of the degree to which two independent observers agree about their observations

Completion
Complete each statement by providing the appropriate term.

1. Direct observation of behavior in a natural setting *without* any attempt by the observer to intervene is called _____ _ _____.
2. The most extreme form of intervention in observational methods arises when the researcher manipulates one or more variables in a natural setting. This method is called a(n) _____ _____.
3. Researchers can observe behavior indirectly by studying the physical traces or records of people's behavior. These indirect methods are called _____ _____.
4. The presence of an observer can lead people to change their behavior because they know they are being observed. This potential problem in observational research is called _____.
5. Systematic errors in recording behavior can result from an observer's expectations. This problem in observational research is called _____ _____.

Multiple Choice
Choose the one best answer for each question.

1. Researchers who conduct observational studies typically use a combination of time sampling and situation sampling to achieve
   a. maximum interobserver reliability.
   b. nominal scales of measurement.
   c. internally valid samples of behavior.
   d. representative samples of behavior.
2. Which of the following observational methods represents a middle ground between passive nonintervention and the systematic control and manipulation of variables in laboratory methods?
   a. naturalistic observation
   b. structured observation
   c. a field experiment
   d. participant observation
3. Researchers who use archival records can face a potential problem when portions of the record are missing or incomplete. This potential problem can arise from either selective deposit or
   a. selective survival.
   b. selective bias.
   c. archival distortion.
   d. archival attrition.
4. Which one of the following scales of measurement is a researcher using when he or she measures whether or not an individual makes eye contact with another person?
   a. nominal scale
   b. ordinal scale
   c. interval scale
   d. ratio scale
5. Researchers who use narrative records seek to provide a verbal summary of observations and to develop a theory that explains behavior in the narrative records. This approach to data analysis represents
   a. quantitative data analysis with selective recording of behavior.
   b. quantitative data analysis with comprehensive recording of behavior.
   c. qualitative data analysis with comprehensive recording of behavior.
   d. qualitative data analysis with selective recording of behavior.

Chapter 5

Correlational Research: Surveys

Matching
Identify which description best corresponds to each of the following terms.

Terms

1. _____ correlational research
2. _____ population
3. _____ response bias
4. _____ longitudinal design
5. _____ social desirability

Descriptions

    A. The same sample of respondents is surveyed more than once such that the researcher can determine the direction and extent of change for *individual* respondents.

    B. One consequence of the reactive measurement involved in survey research whereby people may feel pressure to respond as they think they "should" rather than what they actually believe

    C. The set of all cases of interest, such as all the students on your campus for a survey done to determine students' attitudes toward the campus computing facilities

    D. The representativeness of a sample can be threatened when not all the sample respondents complete the survey, such as when people are too busy or not interested enough in the study to return a completed questionnaire.

    E. An approach to psychological research in which researchers assess relationships among naturally occurring variables, such as the relationship between hours spent watching television and students' test scores in school

Completion

Complete each statement by providing the appropriate term.

1. A measure has _____ when it is a measure that assesses the concept that it is intended to measure.
2. A sample that exhibits characteristics that are the same as those in the population from which the sample was drawn is a _____ sample.
3. _____ sampling is the approach that has been used when all members of the population have an equal chance of being included in a sample.
4. We can determine the direction and strength of a correlation by computing a _____ _____.
5. Rather than providing a precise estimate of a population value, we can determine a range of values with the idea that the true population value is likely to be within the range. This range of values is called the _____ ____ _____.

Multiple Choice
Choose the one best answer for each question.

1. Which of the following factors does *not* influence the size of a reliability coefficient for a measure of students' understanding of course material?
   a. number of items used to measure students' understanding of the material
   b. how much the individuals differ in their understanding of the material
   c. how much discriminant validity the measure of understanding has from other measures, such as intelligence
   d. the way in which the measure is administered (e.g., whether the instructions are clear and the testing situation is free of distractions)

2. A sample is considered to be biased when the characteristics of the sample
   a. differ randomly from those of the target population.
   b. correspond well to those of the target population.
   c. differ haphazardly from those of the target population.
   d. differ systematically from those of the target population.

3. When researchers use the successive independent samples design and mistakenly draw samples from different populations at the various times of the survey, the researchers are likely to face the problem of
   a. noncomparable samples.
   b. stratified samples.
   c. archival samples.
   d. response bias samples.

4. Which of the following problems in survey research is peculiar to longitudinal survey research design?
   a. selection bias
   b. respondent mortality (attrition)
   c. response bias
   d. reactive measurement

5. Which of the following statements could you make if you knew that the correlation between the time high school students spend watching TV and their scores on a school achievement test was −.64?
   a. The more time students spend watching TV, the lower their scores on a school achievement test will be.
   b. The more time students spend watching TV, the higher their scores on a school achievement test will be.
   c. Spending more time watching TV causes students to do more poorly on a school achievement test.
   d. The amount of time students spend watching TV and their scores on a school achievement test are entirely unrelated to each other.

Chapter 6
Experimental Research Designs

Matching
Identify which description best corresponds to each of the following terms.

Terms

1. _____ independent groups design
2. _____ repeated measures design
3. _____ external validity
4. _____ descriptive statistics
5. _____ effect size

Descriptions

   A. A measure that indicates the strength of the relationship between the in-dependent variable and the dependent variable
   B. Each individual in the experiment participates in each condition of the experiment.
   C. A characteristic of a study that refers to the extent to which findings from an experiment can be generalized to individuals, settings, and conditions beyond the scope of the specific experiment
   D. Individuals in the experiment participate in only one group of the exper-iment, with each group representing a different condition of the inde-pendent variable.
   E. The information that is used in the step of data analysis in which the data are summarized to begin to answer the question, what happened in the experiment?

Completion
Complete each statement by providing the appropriate term.

1. When the independent variable of interest and a different, potential inde-pendent variable are allowed to covary, a(n) _____ is present in the experiment.
2. The most common technique that is used to form comparable groups in an independent groups design is _____ _____.
3. Even though the same people participate in each condition of an experiment using the repeated measures design, each individual can change over time as he or she is repeatedly tested. The changes people undergo are called

   _____ _____.
4. _____ involves repeating the procedures used in an experiment to determine whether the same results are obtained a second time with dif-ferent participants.

5. When the outcome of an experiment indicates that the difference between the means observed in the experiment is larger than would be expected by chance if the null hypothesis were true, the outcome is _____ _____.

Multiple Choice
Choose the one best answer for each question.

1. Which of the following is the factor that researchers manipulate so that it is the only factor allowed to vary systematically in an experiment?
   a. independent variable
   b. internal validity
   c. external validity
   d. dependent variable

2. Which of the following is *not* one of the conditions that must be met in order to state confidently that the independent variable *caused* differences between groups in the dependent variable?
   a. establishing a covariation between the independent and dependent variables
   b. establishing a time-order relationship such that the change in the independent variable preceded the change in the dependent variable
   c. establishing that the independent variable is the *only* factor that could ever cause a change in the dependent variable
   d. eliminating plausible alternative explanations for the differences in the dependent variable

3. What is the general rule for balancing practice effects in repeated measures design experiments?
   a. Each condition of the experiment must appear in only one ordinal (first, second, third, etc.) position.
   b. Each condition of the experiment must appear in each ordinal position equally often.
   c. Each condition of the experiment must appear in each ordinal position exactly once.
   d. Each condition must appear only in the first ordinal position.

4. When a confidence interval for the difference between two means obtained in an experiment includes the value zero, the researcher can conclude that
   a. the results for the effect of the independent variable are inconclusive.
   b. the independent variable did have an effect.
   c. the independent variable did not have an effect.
   d. the results for the effect of the independent variable will likely be replicated.

5. One approach to the use of inferential statistics to decide whether an independent variable has had a reliable effect on the dependent variable begins by assuming that the independent variable had no effect. This approach is called
   a. alpha hypothesis testing.
   b. statistical error testing.
   c. significance level testing.
   d. null hypothesis testing.

Chapter 7

Complex Designs

Matching

Identify which description best corresponds to each of the following terms.

Terms

1. _____ factorial combination

2. _____ analysis of variance

3. _____ level of significance (alpha)

4. _____ simple main effect

Descriptions

A. The statistics test most commonly used with null hypothesis testing to analyze complex design experiments.
B. Researchers use this when doing complex designs to pair each level of one independent variable with each level of another independent variable.
C. When the probability associated with an *F* test for the main effect of an independent variable is less than this value, we say that the effect of the independent variable is statistically significant.
D. The effect of one independent variable *at one level* of a second independent variable in a complex design.

Completion

Complete each statement by providing the appropriate term.

1. Experiments in which two or more independent variables are studied simultaneously in one experiment are called _____ _____.
2. The overall effect of an independent variable in a complex design is called a(n) _____ effect.
3. A(n) _____ effect occurs when the effect of one independent variable differs depending upon the level of a second independent variable.
4. A(n) _____ effect is a potential problem that can arise in an experiment when participants' scores reach a maximum possible score on the dependent variable.

Multiple Choice
Choose the one best answer for each question.

1. Which of the following patterns indicates that there has been no interaction in a complex design experiment when the results are plotted in a line graph?
    a. when the lines intersect forming a crossing pattern
    b. when the lines start out apart and converge to the same point
    c. when the lines start out at the same point and diverge from each other
    d. when the lines are parallel

2. Which of the following is *not* one of the effects that can occur in a complex design experiment involving the two independent variables, dating status and type of scenario?
    a. main effect of dating status
    b. main effect of type of scenario
    c. moderator effect of dating status with type of scenario
    d. interaction effect of dating status and type of scenario

3. What follow-up analyses are researchers likely to use to identify the source of an omnibus interaction effect after an analysis of variance indicates that the interaction is statistically significant?
    a. main effects of each independent variable
    b. analytical comparisons involving each independent variable
    c. analysis of the medians for each condition of the experiment
    d. simple main effects

4. When no interaction occurs in a complex design experiment involving two independent variables, the
    a. effects of each independent variable can be generalized across the levels of the other independent variable.
    b. internal validity of each independent variable is increased.
    c. sensitivity of the overall experiment is decreased.
    d. effects of each independent variable must be interpreted differently because of the absence of an interaction.

5. Which of the following is one of the critical steps researchers should follow when they want to draw causal inferences based on the natural-groups design?
    a. identify a second individual differences variable that is correlated with the individual differences variable of interest to the researcher
    b. develop a theory explaining why a difference in performance should occur between groups differentiated using the individual differences variable of interest
    c. demonstrate in a complex design experiment an interaction involving the individual differences variable of interest and a second individual differences variable
    d. demonstrate in a complex design experiment a main effect of the individual differences variable of interest *and* a main effect of a manipulated independent variable

Chapter 8

Single-case Research Designs

Completion
Complete each statement by providing the appropriate term.

1. The single-case research design that involves an intensive description and analysis of a single individual is called a(n) _____ _____.
2. In a _____ _____ the researcher manipulates the independent variable of interest (usually a treatment) systematically for one individual whose behavior is being continually monitored.
3. The first stage of a single-case experiment is usually an observation stage in which researchers record the individual's behavior prior to any treatment. This first stage is called the _____ stage.
4. In one commonly used single-case experimental design researchers demonstrate that behavior changes systematically when they alternate "No Treatment" and "Treatment" conditions. This design is sometimes called a reversal design; more formally it is called the _____ design.
5. In the _____ _____ design researchers establish several baselines and then they repeatedly introduce the treatment across different situations, behaviors, or subjects one at a time to determine whether the results replicate.

Multiple Choice
Choose the one best answer for each question.

1. Which of the following is *not* an advantage of the case study method?
   a. Case studies provide a rich source of insights into possible causes of people's behavior.
   b. Case studies are especially useful for studying events that occur frequently.
   c. Case studies provide an opportunity to "try out" new therapeutic techniques.
   d. Case studies can provide useful evidence to support or challenge psychological theories.
2. Researchers are often unable to control extraneous variables when they use the case study method. This lesser degree of control makes it difficult to use to case study method to
   a. develop descriptions of behavior.
   b. draw cause-effect conclusions about behavior.
   c. develop predictions of behavior.
   d. consider alternative theoretical explanations of behavior.

3. The baseline stage of a single-case experimental design is useful to researchers because behavior during the baseline allows the researchers to
    a. get an initial idea of whether the treatment will be effective.
    b. determine whether an individual is likely to benefit from the treatment.
    c. describe behavior before administering the treatment and predict what behavior will be like in the future without treatment.
    d. determine the best way to administer the treatment in light of the individual's behavior during the baseline.

4. Which of the following patterns provides considerable evidence in an ABAB design that the treatment caused the behavior change?
    a. when the behavior changes both when the treatment is introduced and when the treatment is withdrawn
    b. when the behavior changes when the treatment is introduced and when the behavior stays constant when the treatment is withdrawn
    c. when the behavior remains constant when the treatment is introduced but changes when the treatment is withdrawn
    d. when the behavior remains the same across both of the baseline and treatment stages

5. Which of the following issues deserves special consideration when researchers consider using the ABAB design?
    a. limited external validity of single-case experimental designs
    b. excessive variability of the baseline in single-case experimental designs
    c. change in behavior prior to the end of the baseline stage
    d. justification for withdrawing a potentially beneficial treatment

6. What do each of the multiple baselines in the multiple-baseline single-case experimental design represent?
    a. individual case studies
    b. inevitable sources of confounding
    c. redundant sources of evidence
    d. replications built into the design

7. A baseline in a single-case experimental design will be most effective in detecting a change due to the treatment if the baseline has a(n)
    a. increasing trend.
    b. decreasing trend.
    c. stable pattern.
    d. highly variable pattern.

8. Which of the following statements concerning the external validity of single-case experiments is false?
   a. The external validity of single-case experiments can be established because the single-case design is well suited to the study of interactions among variables.
   b. The external validity of single-case experiments is likely enhanced because the types of interventions in these experiments frequently produce sizable changes in behavior.
   c. Evidence for the external validity of single-case experiments can be established from the use of multiple-baseline designs.
   d. Evidence for the external validity of single-case experiments can be established when researchers use the procedures of single-case designs with a small group of individuals.

Chapter 9

Quasi-experimental Designs and Program Evaluation

Matching
Identify which description best corresponds to each of the following terms.

Terms

1. _____ true experiments
2. _____ threats to internal validity
3. _____ nonequivalent control group design
4. _____ simple interrupted time-series design
5. _____ time series with nonequivalent control group

Descriptions

   A. Research that is characterized by some type of intervention, an appropriate comparison, and a high degree of control over the arrangement of experimental conditions
   B. A quasi-experimental design in which researchers make multiple observations of both a treatment group and a comparable comparison group before and after the treatment is administered
   C. Uncontrolled factors that can make it difficult to draw causal inferences when quasi-experiments are done
   D. A quasi-experimental design in which researchers observe changes in a dependent variable for some time before and after a treatment is introduced
   E. A quasi-experimental design in which a group *like* the treatment group serves as a comparison group and researchers obtain pretest and posttest measures from individuals in both groups

Completion
Complete each statement by providing the appropriate term.

1. When it is not feasible to do true experiments in the "real world" researchers use experimental procedures that only *approximate* the conditions of highly controlled laboratory experiments. These procedures that lack the high degree of control possible in true experiments are called _____ _____.

2. _____ is a threat to internal validity that can arise when an event occurs at the same time as the treatment and thus there are events other than the treatment that can affect participants' behavior.

3. _____ is a threat to internal validity that can arise when changes that the participants naturally undergo over time may explain any changes in the participants during the experiment.

4. There are threats to internal validity that even true experiments do not control. One such threat can arise when participants feel resentment or a sense of rivalry or when there is diffusion of treatments across groups. The general term used to describe this threat to internal validity is called _____.

5. _____ _____ is an interdisciplinary approach to applied research that provides feedback to administrators of human service organizations in order to help them decide what services to provide to whom and how to provide them most effectively and efficiently.

Multiple Choice
Choose the one best answer for each question.

1. Which of the following characteristics of true experiments is most often lacking in quasi-experiments?
   a. implementation of some type of intervention or treatment
   b. appropriate comparison or "control" condition
   c. potential for contamination due to diffusion of treatments
   d. high degree of control, especially the ability to assign participants randomly to conditions

2. Which of the following represents a threat to the internal validity of a study because differences exist between individuals in the treatment and control groups at the start of the study?
   a. maturation
   b. subject mortality
   c. selection
   d. regression

3. What is the primary evidence for the effectiveness of a treatment that is tested using an interrupted time series design?
   a. clear discontinuity in the time graph at the point of the intervention
   b. alternation of increasing and decreasing trends in the time graph around the point of the intervention
   c. strong decreasing trend in the time graph that continues through the point of the intervention
   d. highly variable responses in the time graph surrounding the point of the intervention
4. When researchers who are conducting a program evaluation try to determine whether a program is being implemented the way it was planned, they are addressing the program evaluation question of
   a. needs
   b. process
   c. outcome
   d. efficiency
5. What is the greatest difference between basic research and program evaluation (perhaps the most extreme case of applied research)?
   a. the internal validity of the findings obtained in these two approaches
   b. the importance of the goals that can be achieved with these two approaches
   c. the quality of the research that can be done using these two approaches
   d. the political and social realities surrounding these two approaches

SELF-TEST ANSWERS

Chapter 1   Introduction: The Science of Psychology
Matching 1. C; 2. B; 3. E; 4. A; 5. D
Completion 1. control; 2. valid; 3. reliable; 4. correlation; 5. causal inference
Multiple Choice 1. a; 2. c; 3. d; 4. c; 5. b

Chapter 2   The Research Process
Matching 1. D; 2. C; 3. A; 4. B; 5. E
Completion 1. Ethnocentrism; 2. theory; 3. hypotheses; 4. operational
Multiple Choice 1. a; 2. b; 3. c; 4. d; 5. c

Chapter 3   Ethical Issues in Psychological Research
Matching 1. B; 2. A; 3. C; 4. D
Completion 1. Institutional Review Boards (IRBs); 2. risk/benefit ratio; 3. debriefing; 4. plagiarism
Multiple Choice 1. b; 2. c; 3. b; 4. a; 5. d

Chapter 4   Observational Research
    Matching 1. D; 2. B; 3. C; 4. E; 5. A
    Completion 1. naturalistic observation; 2. field experiment;
    3. unobtrusive (indirect) measures; 4. reactivity; 5. observer bias
    Multiple Choice 1. d; 2. b; 3. a; 4. a; 5. c

Chapter 5   Correlational Research: Surveys
    Matching 1. E; 2. C; 3. D; 4. A; 5. B
    Completion 1. validity; 2. representative; 3. probability; 4. correlation
    coefficient; 5. margin of error
    Multiple Choice 1. c; 2. d; 3. a; 4. b; 5. a

Chapter 6   Experimental Research Designs
    Matching 1. D; 2. B; 3. C; 4. E; 5. A
    Completion 1. confounding; 2. random assignment; 3. practice effects;
    4. Replication; 5. statistically significant
    Multiple Choice 1. a; 2. c; 3. b; 4. a; 5. d

Chapter 7   Complex Designs
    Matching 1. B; 2. A; 3. C; 4. D
    Completion 1. complex designs; 2. main; 3. interaction; 4. ceiling
    Multiple Choice 1. d; 2. c; 3. d; 4. a; 5. b

Chapter 8   Single-case Research Designs
    Completion 1. case study; 2. single-case experiment; 3. baseline;
    4. ABAB; 5. multiple-baseline
    Multiple Choice 1. b; 2. b; 3. c; 4. a; 5. d; 6. d; 7. c; 8. a

Chapter 9   Quasi-experimental Designs and Program Evaluation
    Matching 1. A; 2. C; 3. E; 4. D; 5. B
    Completion 1. quasi-experiments; 2. History; 3. Maturation;
    4. contamination; 5. Program evaluation
    Multiple Choice 1. d; 2. c; 3. a; 4. b; 5. d

GLOSSARY

ABAB design (reversal design) A single-case experimental design in which an initial baseline stage (A) is followed by a treatment stage (B), a return to baseline (A), and then another treatment stage (B); the researcher observes whether behavior changes on introduction of the treatment, reverses when the treatment is withdrawn, and improves again when the treatment is reintroduced.

applied research See **basic versus applied research.**

archival data Source of evidence based on records or documents relating the activities of individuals, institutions, governments, and other groups; used as an alternative to or in conjunction with other research methods.

baseline stage The first stage of a single-case experiment, in which a record is made of an individual's behavior prior to any intervention.

basic versus applied research Whereas basic research mainly seeks knowledge about nature simply for the sake of understanding it better, applied research seeks knowledge that will modify or improve the present situation; however, basic and applied research are considered to have a reciprocal relationship—for example, when basic research is used to identify abstract principles that can be applied in real-world settings, and when applied research is used to reveal possible limitations or extensions of these principles.

biased sample A sample in which the distribution of characteristics is systematically different from that of the parent population.

case study An intensive description and analysis of an individual.

causal inference The identification of the cause or causes of a phenomenon, by establishing covariation of cause and effect, a time-order relationship with cause preceding effect, and the elimination of plausible alternative causes.

ceiling (or floor) effect A measurement problem whereby the researcher cannot measure the effects of an independent variable or a possible interaction because performance has reached a maximum (or minimum) in any condition of the experiment.

central tendency Statistical concept that refers to the typical score in a distribution; the most common statistic is the mean, or average.

complex design An experiment in which two or more independent variables are studied simultaneously.

confederate Someone in the service of a researcher who is instructed to behave in a certain way in order to help produce an experimental treatment.

confidence intervals Intervals that indicate the range of values in which we can expect a population value to fall with a specified degree of confidence (e.g., .95).

confounding Occurs when the independent variable of interest systematically covaries with a second, unintended independent variable.

control Key component of the scientific method whereby the effect of various factors possibly responsible for a phenomenon are isolated; three basic types of control are manipulation, holding conditions constant, and balancing.

correlation Exists when two measures of the same people, events, or things vary together; the presence of a correlation makes it possible to predict values on one variable by knowing the values on the second variable.

correlation coefficient   A statistic that indicates how well two measures vary together; absolute size ranges from 0.0 (no correlation) to 1.00 (perfect correlation); direction of covariation is indicated by the sign of the coefficient, a plus (+) indicating that both measures covary in the same direction or a minus (−) indicating that the variables vary in opposite directions.

correlational research   Research in which the goal is to identify predictive relationships among naturally occurring variables.

counterbalancing   A control technique for distributing (balancing) practice effects across the conditions of a repeated measures design.

cross-sectional design   A survey research design in which one or more samples of the population are selected and information is collected from the samples at one time.

debriefing   The process following a research session through which participants are informed about the rationale for the research in which they participated, about the need for any deception, and about their specific contribution to the research. Important goals of debriefing are to clear up any misconceptions and to leave participants with a positive feeling toward psychological research.

deception   Intentionally withholding information about significant aspects of a research project from a participant or presenting misinformation about the research to participants.

demand characteristics   Cues and other information used by participants to guide their behavior in a psychological study, often leading participants to do what they believe the observer (experimenter) expects them to do.

dependent variable   A measure of behavior used by a researcher to assess the effect (if any) of the independent variables.

descriptive statistics   Numerical measures of sample characteristics, such as the mean (average score) and standard deviation (degree of dispersion around the mean).

effect size   An index of the strength of the relationship between the independent variable and dependent variable.

empirical approach   An approach to acquiring knowledge that emphasizes direct observation and experimentation as a way of answering questions.

ethnocentrism   An attempt to understand the behavior of individuals in different cultures based solely on experiences in one's own culture.

experimenter effects   Experimenters' expectations which may lead them to treat subjects differently in different groups or to record data in a biased manner.

external validity   The extent to which the results of a research study can be generalized to different populations, settings, and conditions.

field experiment   A procedure in which one or more independent variables is manipulated by an observer in a natural setting to determine the effect on behavior.

floor effect   See **ceiling (or floor) effect.**

hypothesis   A tentative explanation for a phenomenon.

independent variable   A factor for which a researcher either selects or manipulates at least two levels in order to determine its effect on behavior.

inferential statistics   Means of testing whether the differences in a dependent variable that are associated with various conditions of an experiment are reliable—that is, larger than would be expected on the basis of chance alone.

informed consent   The explicitly expressed willingness to participate in a research project, based on a clear understanding of the nature of the research, of the consequences of not participating, and of all the factors that might be expected to influence willingness to participate.

interaction   Occurs when the effect of one independent variable differs depending on the level of a second independent variable.

internal validity   The degree to which differences in performance can be attributed unambiguously to an effect of an independent variable, as opposed to an effect of another (uncontrolled) variable; an internally valid study is free of confoundings.

interobserver reliability   The degree to which two independent observers agree.

interrupted time-series design   See **simple interrupted time-series design** and **time-series with nonequivalent control group design.**

longitudinal design   A research design in which the same sample of respondents is interviewed (tested) more than once.

main effect   The overall effect of an independent variable in a complex design.

margin of error   In survey research, an estimate of the difference between a result obtained from a sample (e.g., the sample mean) and the corresponding true population value (e.g., population mean).

matched groups design   A type of independent groups design in which the researcher forms comparable groups by matching subjects on a pretest task and then randomly assigning the members of these matched sets of subjects to the conditions of the experiment.

measurement scale   One of four levels of physical and psychological measurement: nominal (categorizing), ordinal (ranking), interval (specifying distance between stimuli), and ratio (having an absolute zero point).

minimal risk   A research participant is said to experience minimal risk when probability and magnitude of harm or discomfort anticipated in the research are not greater than that ordinarily encountered in daily life or during the performance of routine tests.

multimethod approach   An approach to hypothesis testing that seeks evidence by collecting data using several measures of behavior; a recognition of the fact that any single measure of behavior can result from some artifact of the measuring process.

multiple-baseline design   A single-case experimental design in which the effect of a treatment is demonstrated by showing that behaviors in more than one baseline change as a consequence of the introduction of a treatment; multiple baselines are established for different individuals, for different behaviors in the same individual, or for the same individual in different situations.

$N = 1$ designs   See **single-case experiment.**

narrative record   A record intended to provide a more or less faithful reproduction of behavior as it originally occurred.

natural groups design   A type of independent groups design in which the conditions represent the selected levels of a naturally occurring independent variable—for example, the individual differences variable of age.

naturalistic observation   Observation of behavior in a more or less natural setting without any attempt by the observer to intervene.

nomothetic approach   An approach to research that seeks to establish broad generalizations or laws that apply to large groups (populations) of individuals; the average, or typical, performance of a group is emphasized.

nonequivalent control group design   A quasi-experimental method in which a comparison is made between control and treatment groups that have been established on a basis other than through random assignment of participants to groups.

null hypothesis testing   A statistical procedure in which, as the first step in statistical inference, the independent variable is assumed to have had no effect.

observer bias   Systematic errors in observation, often resulting from the observer's expectancies regarding the outcome of a study (i.e., expectancy effects).

operational definition   A procedure whereby a concept is defined solely in terms of the operations used to produce and measure it.

participant observation   Observation of behavior by someone who also has an active and significant role in the situation or context in which behavior is recorded.

physical traces   A source of evidence that is based on the remnants, fragments, and products of past behavior; used as an alternative to or in conjunction with other research methods.

plagiarism   The presentation of another's ideas or work without clearly identifying the source.

population   A set of all the cases of interest.

power   Probability in a statistical test that a false null hypothesis will be rejected (i.e., correct decision).

practice effects   Changes that individuals undergo with repeated testing. These include the summation of both positive (e.g., familiarity with the task) and negative (e.g., boredom) factors associated with repeated measurement.

privacy   The right of individuals to decide how information about them is to be communicated to others.

program evaluation   Research that seeks to determine whether a change proposed by an institution, a government agency, or another unit of society is needed and likely to have an effect as planned or, when implemented, to actually have an effect.

qualitative data analysis   Obtaining verbal summaries and theoretical explanations of behavior.

quantitative data analysis   Obtaining numerical summaries of behavior in statistical terms—for example, based on measures of central tendency (mean) and variability (standard deviation).

quasi-experiments   Procedures that resemble the characteristics of true experiments—for example, an intervention or a treatment is used and a comparison is provided—but procedures lack the degree of control found in true experiments.

random assignment   The most common technique for forming groups as part of an independent groups design; the goal is to establish equivalent groups by balancing individual differences.

random groups design   The most common type of independent groups design in which subjects are randomly assigned to each group such that groups are considered comparable at the start of the experiment.

random sampling   See **simple random sampling (random selection).**

reactivity   The influence that an observer has on the behavior under observation; behavior influenced by an observer may not be representative of usual behavior.

reliability   A measurement is reliable when it is consistent.

repeated measures design   Research design in which each subject participates in all conditions of the experiment (i.e., measurement is repeated on the same subject).

replication   Repetition of the exact procedures used in an experiment to determine whether the same results are obtained.

representativeness   A sample is representative to the extent that it has the same distribution of characteristics as the population from which it was selected; the ability to generalize from sample to population is critically dependent on representativeness.

response bias   A threat to the representativeness of a sample that occurs when some participants selected to respond to a survey systematically fail to complete the survey (e.g., due to failure to complete a lengthy questionnaire or to reply with a request to participate in a phone survey).

risk/benefit ratio   The subjective evaluation of the risk of the proposed research relative to the benefit, both to the individual and to society.

sample   Something less than all the cases of interest; in survey research, a subset of the population used to represent the population.

scientific method   An approach to knowledge that emphasizes empirical rather than intuitive processes, testable hypotheses, systematic and controlled observation of operationally defined phenomena, data collection using accurate and precise instrumentation, valid and reliable measures, and objective reporting of results; scientists tend to be critical and, most important, skeptical.

selection bias   A threat to the representativeness of a sample that occurs when the procedures used to select a sample result in the over- or underrepresentation of a significant segment of the population.

sensitivity   Refers to the likelihood that the effect of the independent variable will be detected when that variable does, indeed, have an effect.

simple interrupted time-series design   A quasi-experimental procedure in which changes in a dependent variable are observed for a period of time both before and after a treatment is introduced.

simple random sampling (random selection)   A type of probability sampling in which each possible sample of a specified size in the population has an equal chance of being selected.

single-case experiment   A procedure that focuses on behavior change in one individual ($N = 1$) by systematically contrasting conditions within that individual while continuously monitoring behavior.

situation sampling   The random or systematic selection of situations in which observations are to be made with the goal of representativeness across circumstances, locations, and conditions.

social desirability   Pressures on survey respondents to answer as they think they should respond in accordance with what is most socially acceptable, not in accordance with what they actually believe.

statistically significant   When the probability of an obtained difference in an experiment is smaller than would be expected if chance alone were assumed to be responsible for the difference, the difference is statistically significant.

stratified random sampling   A type of probability sampling in which the population is divided into subpopulations called strata and random samples are drawn from each of these strata.

structured observation   A variety of observational methods using intervention in which the degree of control is often less than in field experiments; frequently used by clinical and developmental psychologists when making behavioral assessments.

successive independent samples design   A survey research design in which a series of cross-sectional surveys is done and the same questions are asked of each succeeding sample of respondents.

theory   A logically organized set of propositions that defines events, describes relationships among events, and explains the occurrence of these events; scientific theories guide research and organize empirical knowledge.

threats to internal validity   Possible causes of a phenomenon that must be controlled so a clear cause-and-effect inference can be made.

time sampling   The selection of observation intervals, either systematically or randomly, with the goal of obtaining a representative sample of behavior.

time-series with nonequivalent control group design (See also **simple interrupted time-series design**.)   A quasi-experimental procedure that improves the validity of a simple time-series design by including a nonequivalent control group; both treatment and comparison groups are observed for a period of time both before and after the treatment.

true experiment   An experiment in which a treatment (intervention) is implemented with a high degree of control, permitting an appropriate comparison (e.g., between the treatment and control groups) such that an unambiguous decision can be made concerning the effect of the treatment.

unobtrusive (nonreactive) measures   Measures of behavior that eliminate the problem of reactivity because observations are made in such a way that the presence of the observer is not detected by those being observed.

validity   The "truthfulness" of a measure; a valid measure is one that measures what it claims to measure.

variability   Statistical concept that refers to the dispersion of scores in a distribution; the most common statistic is standard deviation (the average distance of scores from the mean of the distribution).

variable   A condition (factor) that can vary, either quantitatively or qualitatively, along an observable dimension. Researchers both measure and control variables.

REFERENCES

Abelson, R. P. (1995). *Statistics as principled argument.* Hillsdale, NJ: Erlbaum.

Abelson, R. P. (1997). On the surprising longevity of flogged horses: Why there is a case for the significance test. *Psychological Science, 8,* 12–15.

American Psychiatric Association. (1994). *Diagnostic and statistical manual of mental disorders* (4th ed.). Washington, DC: Author.

American Psychological Association. (1992). Ethical principles of psychologists and code of conduct. *American Psychologist, 47,* 1597–1611.

American Psychological Association. (1994). *Publication manual* (4th ed). Washington, DC: Author.

American Psychological Association. (1998). Summary report of journal operations, 1997. *American Psychologist, 53,* 983–984.

Anderson, C. A., & Bushman, B. J. (1997). External validity of "trivial" experiments: The case of laboratory aggression. *Review of General Psychology, 1,* 19–41.

Anderson, J. R. (1990). *The adaptive character of thought.* Hillsdale, NJ: Erlbaum.

Anderson, J. R. (1993). *Rules of the mind.* Hillsdale, NJ: Erlbaum.

Astin, A. W., Parrott, S. A., Korn, W. S., & Sax, L. J. (1997). *The American freshman: Thirty year trends.* Los Angeles: Higher Education Research Institute, UCLA.

Azar, B. (1999, May). Why experts often disagree. *APA Monitor,* 13.

Banaji, M. R., & Crowder, R. G. (1989). The bankruptcy of everyday memory. *American Psychologist, 44,* 1185–1193.

Bartholemew, G.A. (1982). Scientific innovation and creativity: A zoologist's point of view. *American Zoologist, 22,* 227–335.

Baumrind, D. (1985). Research using intentional deception: Ethical issues revisited. *American Psychologist, 40,* 165–174.

Bazzini, D. G., & Shaffer, D. R. (1999). Resisting temptation revisited: Devaluation versus enhancement of an attractive suitor by exclusive and nonexclusive daters. *Personality and Social Psychology Bulletin, 25,* 162–176.

Berk, R. A., Boruch, R. F., Chambers, D. L., Rossi, P. H., & Witte, A. D. (1987). Social policy experimentation: A position paper. In D. S. Cordray & M. W. Lipsey (Eds.), *Evaluation studies review annual,* vol. 11 (pp. 630–672). Newbury Park, CA: Sage.

Blanck, P. D., Bellack, A. S., Rosnow, R. L., Rotheram-Borus, M. J., & Schooler, N. R. (1992). Scientific rewards and conflicts of ethical choices in human subjects research. *American Psychologist, 47,* 959–965.

Bolgar, H. (1965). The case study method. In B. B. Wolman (Ed.), *Handbook of clinical psychology* (pp. 28–39). New York: McGraw-Hill.

Boring, E. G. (1954). The nature and history of experimental control. *American Journal of Psychology, 67,* 573–589.

Bridgewater, C. A., Bornstein, P. H., & Walkenbach, J. (1981). Ethical issues and the assignment of publication credit. *American Psychologist, 36,* 524–525.

Brown, R., & Kulik, J. (1977). Flashbulb memories. *Cognition, 5,* 73–99.

Campbell, D. T. (1969). Reforms as experiments. *American Psychologist, 24,* 409–429.

Campbell, D. T., & Stanley, J. C. (1966). *Experimental and quasi-experimental designs for research.* Chicago: Rand McNally.

Christensen, L. (1988). Deception in psychological research: When is its use justified? *Personality and Social Psychology Bulletin, 14,* 664–675.

Cohen, J. (1988). *Statistical power analysis for the behavioral sciences* (2nd ed.). Hillsdale, NJ: Erlbaum.

Cohen, J. (1992). A power primer. *Psychological Bulletin, 112,* 155–159.

Converse, P. E., & Traugott, M. W. (1986, November 28). Assessing the accuracy of polls and surveys. *Science, 234,* 1094–1097.

Cook, T. D., & Campbell, D. T. (1979). *Quasi-experimentation: Design and analysis issues for field settings.* Chicago: Rand McNally.

Cooper, H. M., & Hedges, L. V. (Eds.) (1994). *The handbook of research synthesis.* New York: Russel Sage Foundation.

Crossen, C. (1994). *Tainted truth: The manipulation of fact in America.* New York: Simon & Schuster.

Crowne, D. P., & Marlowe, D. (1964). *The approval motive: Studies in evaluative dependence.* New York: Wiley.

Dainton, M., & Stafford, L. (1993). Routine maintenance behaviors: A comparison of relationship type, partner similarity and sex differences. *Journal of Social and Personal Relationships, 10,* 225–271.

Diener, E., & Crandall, R. (1978). *Ethics in social and behavioral research.* Chicago: The University of Chicago Press.

Epley, N., & Huff, C. (1998). Suspicion, affective response, and educational benefit as a result of deception in psychology research. *Personality and Social Psychology Bulletin, 24,* 759–768.

Erber, R. (1991). Affective and semantic priming: Effects of mood on category accessibility and inference. *Journal of Experimental Social Psychology, 27,* 480–498.

Fine, M. A., & Kurdek, L. A. (1993). Reflections on determining authorship credit and authorship order on faculty-student collaborations. *American Psychologist, 48,* 1141–1147.

Frost, R. O., & Hartl, T. L. (1996). A cognitive-behavioral model of compulsive hoarding. *Behaviour Research and Therapy, 34,* 341–350.

Garcia, F., Zechmeister, J. S., & Vas, S. N. (2000, May). Forgiveness and retaliation following an interpersonal offense: A laboratory investigation of arousal, harm, and apology. Poster session presented at the meeting of the Midwestern Psychological Association, Chicago, IL.

Garner, D. M., Olmstead, M. P., & Polivy, J. (1983). Development and validation of a multidimensional eating disorder inventory for anorexia nervosa and bulimia. *International Journal of Eating Disorders, 2,* 15–34.

Gilligan, C. (1982). *In a different voice: Psychological theory and women's development.* Cambridge, MA: Harvard University Press.

Goodall, J. (1987). A plea for the chimpanzees. *American Scientist, 75,* 574–577.

Goodman, S. H., Lahey, B. B., Fielding, B., Dulcan, M., Narrow, W., & Regier, D. (1997). Representativeness of clinical samples of youths with mental disorders: A preliminary population-based study. *Journal of Abnormal Psychology, 106,* 3–14.

Greenfield, T. K., Graves, K. L., & Kaskutas, L. A. (1999). Long-term effects of alcohol warning labels: Findings from a comparison of the United States and Ontario, Canada. *Psychology & Marketing, 16,* 261–282.

Haden, C. A. (1998). Reminiscing with different children: Relating maternal stylistic consistency and sibling similarity in talk about the past. *Developmental Psychology, 34,* 99–114.

Haden, C. A., Haine, R. A., & Fivush, R. (1997). Developing narrative structure in parent-child reminiscing across the preschool years. *Developmental Psychology, 33*, 295–307.

Harris, J. R. (1995). Where is the child's environment? A group socialization theory of development. *Psychological Review, 102*, 458–489.

Harris, J. R. (1998). *The nurture assumption: Why children turn out the way they do.* New York: Free Press.

Hartl, T. L., & Frost, R. O. (1999). Cognitive-behavioral treatment of compulsive hoarding: A multiple baseline experimental case study. *Behaviour Research and Therapy, 37*, 451–461.

Hass, R. G., Katz, I., Rizzo, N., Bailey, J., & Eisenstadt, D. (1991). Cross-racial appraisal as related to attitude ambivalence and cognitive complexity. *Personality and Social Psychology Bulletin, 17*, 83–92.

Heatherton, T. F., Mahamedi, F., Striepe, M., Field, A. E., & Keel, P. (1997). A 10-year longitudinal study of body weight, dieting, and eating disorder symptoms. *Journal of Abnormal Psychology, 106*, 117–125.

Heatherton, T. F., Nichols, P., Mahamedi, F., & Keel, P. K. (1995). Body weight, dieting, and eating disorder symptoms among college students 1982 to 1992. *American Journal of Psychiatry, 152*, 1623–1629.

Heatherton, T. F., & Polivy, J. (1992). Chronic dieting and eating disorders: A spiral model. In J. H. Crowther, S. E. Hobfall, M. A. P. Stephens, & D. L. Tennenbaum (Eds.), *The etiology of bulimia nervosa: The individual and familial context* (pp. 133–155). Washington, DC: Hemisphere Publishers.

Hersen, M., & Barlow, D. H. (1976). *Single-case experimental designs: Strategies for studying behavior change.* New York: Pergamon Press.

Hoaglin, D. C., Mosteller, F., & Tukey, J. W. (Eds.). (1991). *Fundamentals of exploratory analysis of variance.* New York: Wiley.

Holden, C. (1987). Animal regulations: So far, so good. *Science, 238*, 880–882.

Horton, S. V. (1987). Reduction of disruptive mealtime behavior by facial screening. *Behavior Modification, 11*, 53–64.

Jacobson, J. W., Mulick, J. A., & Schwartz, A. A. (1995). A history of facilitated communication: Science, pseudoscience, and antiscience. *American Psychologist, 50*, 750–765.

Johnson, D. (1990). Animal rights and human lives: Time for scientists to right the balance. *Psychological Science, 1*, 213–214.

Joswick, K. E. (1994). Getting the most from PsycLIT: Recommendations for searching. *Teaching of Psychology, 21*, 49–53.

Judd, C. M., Smith, E. R., & Kidder, L. H. (1991). *Research methods in social relations* (6th ed.). Fort Worth, TX: Holt, Rinehart and Winston.

Kaskutas, L. A., Greenfield, T. K., Lee, M. E., & Cote, J. (1998). Reach and effect of health messages on drinking during pregnancy. *Journal of Health Education, 29*, 11–17.

Kassin, S. A. (1997). The psychology of confession evidence. *American Psychologist, 52*, 221–233.

Kassin, S. A., & Kiechel, K. L. (1996). The social psychology of false confessions: Compliance, internalization, and confabulation. *Psychological Science, 7*, 125–128.

Kazdin, A. E. (1978). Methodological and interpretive problems of single-case experimental designs. *Journal of Consulting and Clinical Psychology, 46*, 629–642.

Kazdin, A. E. (1980). *Behavior modification in applied settings* (rev. ed.). Homewood, IL: Dorsey Press.

Kazdin, A. E. (1998). *Research designs in clinical psychology.* Boston: Allyn and Bacon.

Kazdin, A. E. (1999). Overview of research design issues in clinical psychology. In P. C. Kendall, J. N. Butcher, & G. N. Holmbeck (Eds.), *Handbook of research methods in clinical psychology* (2nd ed.) (pp. 3–30). New York: Wiley.

Keith, T. Z., Reimers, T. M., Fehrmann, P. G., Pottebaum, S. M., & Aubrey, L. W. (1986). Parental involvement, homework, and TV time: Direct and indirect effects on high school achievement. *Journal of Educational Psychology, 78,* 373–380.

Kelman, H. C. (1967). Human use of human subjects: The problem of deception in social psychological experiments. *Psychological Bulletin, 67,* 1–11.

Kelman, H. C. (1972). The rights of the subject in social research: An analysis in terms of relative power and legitimacy. *American Psychologist, 27,* 989–1016.

Kenny, D. A. (1979). *Correlation and causality.* New York: Wiley.

Keppel, G. (1991). *Design and analysis: A researcher's handbook* (3rd ed.). Englewood Cliffs, NJ: Prentice-Hall.

Kimble, G. A. (1989). Psychology from the standpoint of a generalist. *American Psychologist, 44,* 491–499.

Kimmel, A. J. (1996). *Ethical issues in behavioral research: A survey.* Cambridge, MA: Blackwell.

Kimmel, A. J. (1998). In defense of deception. *American Psychologist, 53,* 803–805.

Kirk, R. E. (1996). Practical significance: A concept whose time has come. *Educational and Psychological Measurement, 56,* 746–759.

Kirsch, I. (1978). Teaching clients to be their own therapists: A case-study illustration. *Psychotherapy: Theory, Research and Practice, 15,* 302–305.

Kohlberg, L. (Ed.) (1981). *The philosophy of moral development: Essays on moral development* (Vol. I). San Francisco: Harper & Row.

Kohlberg, L. (Ed.) (1984). *The philosophy of moral development: Essays on moral development* (Vol. II). San Francisco: Harper & Row.

Kubany, E. S. (1997). Application of cognitive therapy for trauma-related guilt (CT-TRG) with a Vietnam veteran troubled by multiple sources of guilt. *Cognitive and Behavioral Practice, 4,* 213–244.

Kuczmarski, R. J., Flegal, K. M., Campbell, S. M., & Johnson, C. L. (1994). Increasing prevalence of overweight among U.S. adults: The national health and nutrition examination surveys, 1960 to 1991. *Journal of the American Medical Association, 272,* 205–211.

Labov, I. (1982). Speech actions and reactions in personal narrative. In D. Tannen (Ed.), *Analyzing discourse: Text and talk* (pp. 219–247). Washington, DC: Georgetown University Press.

LaFrance, M., & Mayo, C. (1976). Racial differences in gaze behavior during conversations: Two systematic observational studies. *Journal of Personality and Social Psychology, 33,* 547–552.

Landers, S. (1987a, September). CARE urges protection for animals and labs. . . *APA Monitor,* 28–29.

Landers, S. (1987b, December). Lab checks: Rigid or reciprocal? *APA Monitor,* 6–7.

Langer, E. J., & Rodin, J. (1976). The effects of choice and enhanced personal responsibility for the aged: A field experiment in an institutional setting. *Journal of Personality and Social Psychology, 34,* 191–198.

Latané, B., & Bidwell, L. D. (1977). Sex and affiliation in college cafeterias. *Personality and Social Psychology Bulletin, 3,* 571–574.

Latané, B., & Darley, J. M. (1970). *The unresponsive bystander: Why doesn't he help?* New York: Appleton-Century-Crofts.

Lemmens, P. H., Vaeth, P. A. C., & Greenfield, T. K. (1999). Coverage of beverage alcohol issues in the print media in the United States, 1985-1991. *American Journal of Public Health, 89,* 1555–1560.

Levin, D. T., & Simons, D. J. (1997). Failure to detect changes to attended objects in motion pictures. *Psychonomic Bulletin and Review, 4,* 501–506.

Loftus, E. F., & Burns, T. E. (1982). Mental shock can produce retrograde amnesia. *Memory & Cognition, 10,* 318–323.

Lovaas, O. I. (1993). The development of a treatment-research project for developmentally disabled and autistic children. *Journal of Applied Behavior Analysis, 26,* 617–630.

Lovaas, O. I., Schaeffer, B., & Simmons, J. Q. (1965). Building social behaviors in autistic children by use of electric shock. *Journal of Research in Personality, 1,* 99–109.

Marx, M. H. (1963). The general nature of theory construction. In M. H. Marx (Ed.), *Theories in contemporary psychology* (pp. 4–46). New York: Macmillan.

Matsumoto, D. (1994). *Cultural influences on research methods and statistics.* Pacific Grove, CA: Brooks/Cole.

McCormick, C. T. (1972). *Handbook of the law of evidence* (2nd ed.). St. Paul, MN: West.

McGuire, W. J. (1997). Creative hypothesis generating in psychology: Some useful heuristics. *Annual Review of Psychology, 48,* 1–30.

Meehl, P. E. (1978). Theoretical risks and tabular asterisks: Sir Karl, Sir Ronald, and the slow progress of soft psychology. *Journal of Consulting and Clinical Psychology, 46,* 806–834.

Meehl, P. E. (1990a). Appraising and amending theories: The strategy of Lakatosian defense and two principles that warrant it. *Psychological Inquiry, 1,* 108–141.

Meehl, P. E. (1990b). Why summaries of research on psychological theories are often uninterpretable. *Psychological Reports, 66,* 195–244 (Monograph Supplement 1-V66).

Miles, M. B., & Huberman, A. M. (1994). *Qualitative data analysis* (2nd ed.). Thousands Oaks, CA: Sage.

Mook, D. G. (1983). In defense of external invalidity. *American Psychologist, 38,* 379–387.

Mooney, L. A., & Brabant, S. (1987). Deviance, deference, and demeanor: Birthday cards as ceremonial tokens. *Deviant Behavior, 8,* 377–388.

Myers, D. G. (1998). *Psychology* (5th ed.). New York: Worth.

Myers, D. G., & Diener, E. (1995). Who is happy? *Psychological Science, 6,* 10–19.

Neisser, I., & Harsch, N. (1992). Phantom flashbulbs: False recollections of hearing the news about *Challenger.* In E. Winograd & I. Neisser (Eds.), *Affect and accuracy in recall: Studies of "flashbulb memories"* (pp. 9–31). New York: Cambridge University Press.

Novak, M. A. (1991, July). "Psychologists care deeply" about animals. *APA Monitor,* 4.

O'Donnell, L. O., Stueve, A., San Doval, A., Duran, R., Atnafou, R., Haber, D., Johnson, N., Murray, H., Grant, I., Juhn, G., Tang, J., Bass, J., & Piessens, P. (1998). Violence prevention and young adolescents' participation in community youth service. *Journal of Adolescent Health, 24,* 28–37.

Orne, M. T. (1962). On the social psychology of the psychological experiment: With particular reference to demand characteristics and their implications. *American Psychologist, 17,* 776–783.

Parsonson, B. S., & Baer, D. M. (1992). The visual analysis of data, and current research into the stimuli controlling it. In T. R. Kratochwill & J. R. Levin (Eds.), *Single-case research design and analysis* (pp. 15–40). Hillside, NJ: Erlbaum.

Pennebaker, J. W. (1989). Confession, inhibition, and disease. In L. Berkowitz (Ed.), *Advances in experimental social psychology* (Vol. 22, pp. 211–244). New York: Academic Press.

Pennebaker, J. W., & Francis, M. E. (1996). Cognitive, emotional, and language processes in disclosure. *Cognition and Emotion, 10,* 601–626.

Persons, J. B., Burns, D. D., Perloff, J. M., & Miranda, J. (1993). Relationships between symptoms of depression and anxiety and dysfunctional beliefs about achievement and attachment. *Journal of Abnormal Psychology, 102,* 518–524.

Popper, K. R. (1959). *The logic of scientific discovery.* New York: Basic Books.

Posavac, E. J., & Carey, R. G. (1997). *Program evaluation* (5th ed.). Englewood Cliffs, NJ: Prentice-Hall.

Randi, J. (1982). *Flim-flam!* Buffalo, NY: Prometheus Books.

Rauscher, F. H., & Shaw, G. L. (1998). Key components of the Mozart effect. *Perceptual and Motor Skills, 86,* 835–841.

Rauscher, F. H., Shaw, G. L., & Ky, K. N. (1993). Music and spatial task performance. *Nature, 365,* 611.

Reese, E., Haden, C. A., & Fivush, R. (1993). Mother-child conversations about the past: Relationships of style and memory over time. *Cognitive Development, 8,* 403–430.

Riddoch, M. J., & Humphreys, G. W. (1992). The smiling giraffe: An illustration of a visual memory disorder. In R. Campbell (Ed.), *Mental lives: Case studies in cognition* (pp. 161–177). Oxford, England: Blackwell.

Rimm, D. C., & Masters, J. C. (1979). *Behavior therapy: Techniques and empirical findings* (2nd ed.). New York: Academic Press.

Roethlisberger, F. J. (1977). *The elusive phenomena: An autobiographical account of my work in the field of organized behavior at the Harvard Business School.* Cambridge, MA: Division of Research, Graduate School of Business Administration (distributed by Harvard University Press).

Rogoff, B. (1990). *Apprenticeship in thinking: Cognitive development in social context.* New York: Oxford University Press.

Rollin, B. E. (1985). The moral status of research animals in psychology. *American Psychologist, 40,* 920–926.

Rosenberg, M. (1965). *Society and the adolescent self-image.* Princeton, NJ: Princeton University Press.

Rosenfeld, A. (1981). Animal rights vs. human health. *Science, 81,* 18, 22.

Rosenhan, D. L. (1973). On being sane in insane places. *Science, 179,* 250–258.

Rosenthal, R. (1963). On the social psychology of the psychological experiment: The experimenter's hypothesis as unintended determinant of experimental results. *American Scientist, 51,* 268–283.

Rosenthal, R. (1966). *Experimenter effects in behavioral research.* New York: Appleton-Century-Crofts.

Rosenthal, R. (1976). *Experimenter effects in behavioral research* (Enlarged ed.). New York: Irvington.

Rosenthal, R. (1994). Science and ethics in conducting, analyzing, and reporting psychological research. *Psychological Science, 5,* 127–134.

Rosenthal, R., & Rosnow, R. L. (1991). *Essentials of behavioral research: Methods and data analysis* (2nd ed.). New York: McGraw-Hill.

Rusbult, C. E., & Buunk, B. P. (1993). Commitment processes in close relationships: A test of the investment model. *Journal of Social and Personal Relationships, 10,* 175–204.

Sacks, O. (1985). *The man who mistook his wife for a hat and other clinical tales.* New York: Harper & Row.

Sacks, O. (1995). *An anthropologist on Mars.* New York: Knopf.

Scheier, M. F., & Carver, C. S. (1985). Optimism, coping, and health: Assessment and implications of generalized outcome expectancies. *Health Psychology, 4,* 219–247.

Schmitz, A. (1991, November). Food news blues. *In Health,* 41–45.

Seligman, M. E. P., & Csikszentmihalyi, M. (2000). Positive psychology: An introduction. *American Psychologist, 55,* 5–14.

Shapiro, K. J. (1998). *Animal models of human psychology: Critique of science, ethics, and policy.* Seattle, WA: Hogrefe & Huber.

Sharpe, D., Adair, J. G., & Roese, N. J. (1992). Twenty years of deception research: A decline in subjects' trust? *Personality and Social Psychology Bulletin, 18*, 585–590.

Shaughnessy, J. J., Zechmeister, E. B., & Zechmeister, J. S. (2000). *Research methods in psychology* (5th ed.). Boston: McGraw-Hill.

Simons, D. J., & Levin, D. T. (1998). Failure to detect changes to people during a real-world interaction. *Psychonomic Bulletin and Review, 5*, 644–649.

Singer, B., & Benassi, V. A. (1981). Occult beliefs. *American Scientist, 69*, 49–55.

Smith, R. J. (1977). Electroshock experiment at Albany violates ethics guidelines. *Science, 198*, 383–386.

Steele, K. M., Bass, K. E., & Crook, M. D. (1999). The mystery of the Mozart effect: Failure to replicate. *Psychological Science, 10*, 366–369.

Sternberg, R. J. (1986). A triangular theory of love. *Psychological Review, 93*, 119–135.

Sternberg, R.J. (1992, September). How to win acceptances by psychology journals: 21 tips for better writing. *APS Observer, 14*, 19.

Strauss, A., & Corbin, J. (1990). *Basics of qualitative research.* Newbury Park, CA: Sage.

Sun, M. (1981). Laetrile brush fire is out, scientists hope. *Science, 212*, 758–759.

Thelen, M. H., Mann, L. M., Pruitt, J., & Smith, M. (1987). Bulimia: Prevalence and component factors in college women. *Journal of Psychosomatic Research, 31*, 73–78.

Thompson, T. L. (1982). Gaze toward and avoidance of the handicapped: A field experiment. *Journal of Nonverbal Behavior, 6*, 188–196.

Ulrich, R. E. (1991). Animal rights, animal wrongs and the question of balance. *Psychological Science, 2*, 197–201.

Underwood, B. J., & Shaughnessy, J. J. (1975). *Experimentation in psychology.* New York: Wiley: Robert E. Krieger, 1983.

VanderStoep, S. W., & Shaughnessy, J. J. (1997). Taking a course in research methods improves reasoning about real-life events. *Teaching of Psychology, 24*, 122–124.

Vygotsky, L. S. (1978). *Mind in society: The development of higher psychological processes.* (M. Cole, V. John-Steiner, S. Scribner, & E. Souberman, Trans.). Cambridge, MA: Harvard University Press.

Watson, J. B. [1914] (1967). *Behavior: An introduction to comparative psychology.* New York: Holt, Rinehart and Winston.

Webb, E. J., Campbell, D. T., Schwartz, R. D., Sechrest, L., & Grove, J. B. (1981). *Nonreactive measures in the social sciences* (2nd ed.). Boston: HoughtonMifflin.

Wilkinson, L. and the Task Force on Statistical Inference. (1999). Statistical methods in psychology journals: Guidelines and explanations. *American Psychologist, 54*, 594–604.

Zechmeister, E. B., & Johnson, J. E. (1992). *Critical thinking: A functional approach.* Pacific Grove, CA: Brooks/Cole.

CREDITS

PHOTOGRAPHS

Chapter 1

Page 6: Courtesy of the Research Center for Language and Semiotic Studies, Indiana University, Bloomington

Chapter 2

Page 24: (a) © Kim Steele/PhotoDisc (b) © Will Hart/Photo Edit (c) © Spencer Grant/Photo Edit
Page 28: © AP/Wide World Photos

Chapter 4

Page 92: From Daniel J. Simons and Daniel T. Levin, "Failure to Detect Changes to People During a Real-World Interaction" in *Psychonomic Bulletin and Review,* 1998, Vol. 5, Issue 4, pp. 644–648. Reprinted by permission of Psychonomic Society, Inc.
Page 93: From Daniel J. Simons and Daniel T. Levin, "Failure to Detect Changes to People During a Real-World Interaction" in *Psychonomic Bulletin and Review,* 1998, Vol. 5, Issue 4, pp. 644–648. Reprinted by permission of Psychonomic Society, Inc.

Chapter 5

Page 116: Photo by Joseph Mehling.

OTHER

Chapter 3

Box 3.1. Minimal Risk: What do you think? Reprinted with permission from J. J. Shaughnessy, E. B. Zechmeister, & J. S. Zechmeister (2000, 5/e), *Research Methods in Psychology* (pages 51–52). Boston: McGraw-Hill.
Box 3.2. Sample Informed Consent Form. Reprinted with permission from J. J. Shaughnessy, E. B. Zechmeister, & J. S. Zechmeister (2000, 5/e), *Research Methods in Psychology* (page 57). Boston: McGraw-Hill.
Box 3.3. Informed Consent: What do you think? Reprinted with permission from J. J. Shaughnessy, E. B. Zechmeister, & J. S. Zechmeister (2000, 5/e), *Research Methods in Psychology* (page 59). Boston: McGraw-Hill.

Chapter 5

Figure 5.3. Scatterplots. Reprinted with permission from J. J. Shaughnessy, E. B. Zechmeister, & J. S. Zechmeister (2000, 5/e), *Research Methods in Psychology* (page 131). Boston: McGraw-Hill.

Figure 5.4. Error bars. Reprinted with permission from J. J. Shaughnessy, E. B. Zechmeister, & J. S. Zechmeister (2000, 5/e), *Research Methods in Psychology* (page 140). Boston: McGraw-Hill.

Chapter 7

Figure 7.1 Adapted from Figure 1, page 167, D. G. Bazzini & D. R. Shaffer (1999), "Resisting temptation revisited: Devaluation versus enhancement of an attractive suitor by exclusive and nonexclusive daters," *Personality and Social Psychology Bulletin*, 25, 162–176. Reprinted with permission from Sage Publications, Inc.

Box 7.1, Figures 7.2, 7.3, 7.4: Interactions. Reprinted with permission from J. J. Shaughnessy, E. B. Zechmeister, & J. S. Zechmeister (2000, 5/e), *Research Methods in Psychology* (pages 306–307). Boston: McGraw-Hill.

Table 7.3 ANOVA Summary Table. Data provided by Doris G. Bazzini.

Chapter 8

Illustration of case study: Kirsch, I. Teaching clients to be their own therapists: A case study illustration. *Psychotherapy: Theory/Research/Practice/Training, 15,* 302–305. Copyright (1978) by Division of Psychotherapy (29) of the American Psychological Association. Reprinted with permission of editor, Wade H. Silverman.

Figure 8.1: Adapted from Figure 9.1, page 209, of A. E. Kazdin, *Research design in clinical psychology* (3rd ed.) Copyright © 1998 by Allyn & Bacon. Adapted with permission of author and publisher.

Figure 8.5. Multiple-baseline design. Reprinted from *Behaviour Research and Therapy, 37,* in T. L. Hart & R. O. Frost, "Cognitive-behavioral treatment of compulsive hoarding: A multiple baseline experimental case study," Figure 1, page 457, Copyright © 1999. Reprinted with permission of Elsevier Science and author.

Figure 8.6. Examples of Behavioral Records. Reprinted with permission from J. J. Shaughnessy, E. B. Zechmeister, & J. S. Zechmeister (2000, 5/e), *Research Methods in Psychology* (page 359). Boston: McGraw-Hill.

Chapter 9

Figure 9.1. Suspensions of licenses for speeding. From Figures 5 and 6, page 416, of D. T. Campbell (1969), "Reforms as experiments." *American Psychologist 24,* 409–429. Copyright © 1969 by the American Psychological Association. Reprinted with permission of publisher.

Appendix A

Table A.2. Values of r at the .05 and .01 levels of significance. Adapted from Table VII of Fisher and Yates, *Statistical Tables for Biological, Agricultural, and*

Medical Research 6th ed., 1974. Published by Oliver and Boyd, Limited, Publishers, Edinburgh, by permission of the publishers. Published by Longman Group Ltd., London.

Table A.3. Selected values from the *t* distribution. Adapted from Table 12 in *Biometrika tables for statisticians*, Vol. 1 (3rd ed.), New York Cambridge University Press, 1970, edited by E. S. Pearson and H. O. Hartley, by permission of the *Biometrika* Trustees.

Table A.4. Critical values of the *F* distribution. Abridged from Table 18 in *Biometrika tables for statisticians*, Vol. 1 (3rd ed.), New York, Cambridge University Press, 1970, edited by E. S. Pearson and H. O. Hartley, by permission of the *Biometrika* Trustees.

Appendix B

Extensive quotations from *Publication Manual of the American Psychological Association*, 4th ed. (1994). Washington, DC. Copyright © 1994 by the American Psychological Association. Reprinted by permission of the publisher. Neither the original nor this reproduction can be republished, photocopied, or distributed in any form, without the prior written permission of the APA.

NAME INDEX

SUBJECT INDEX